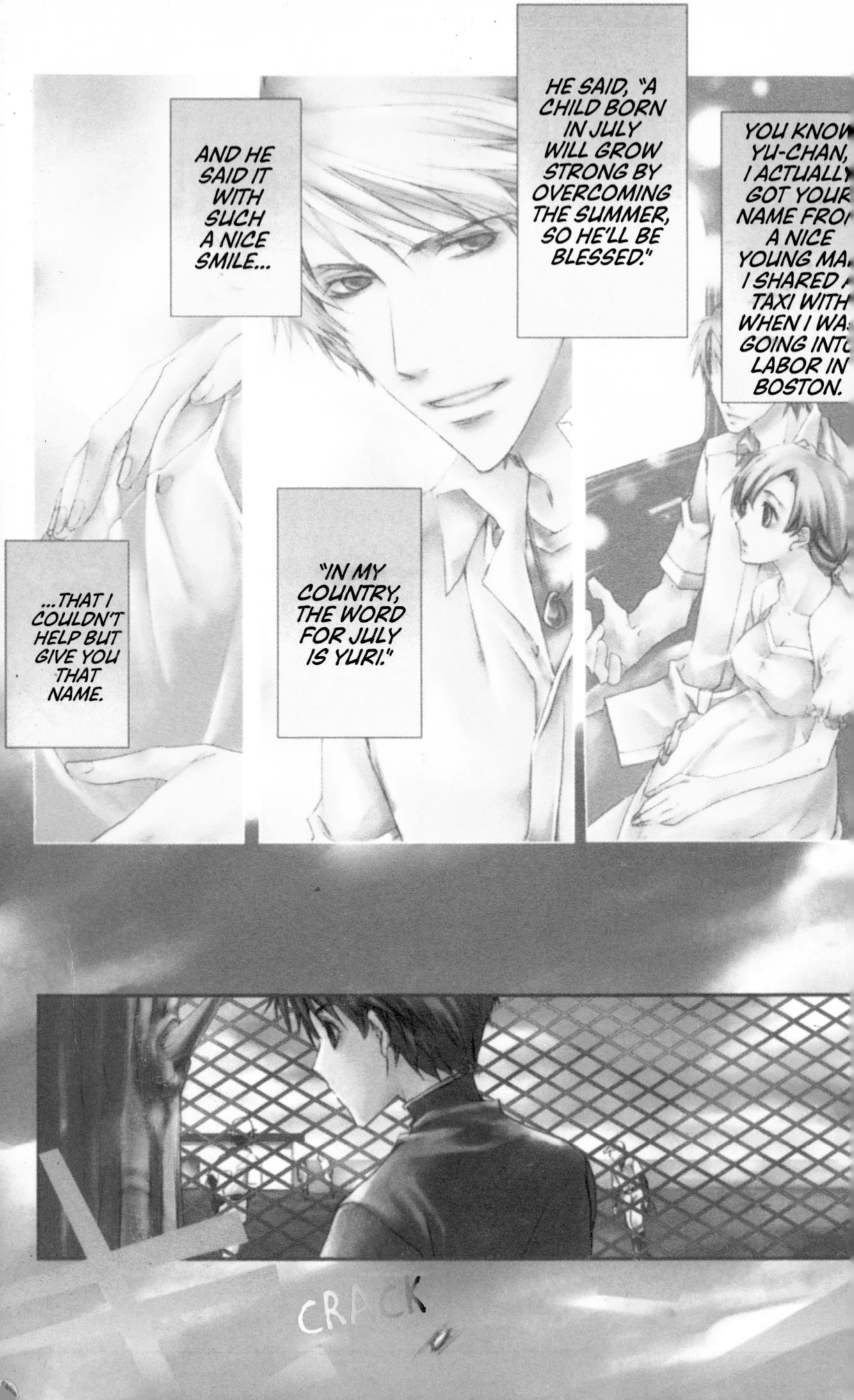
YOU KNOW YU-CHAN, I ACTUALLY GOT YOUR NAME FRO A NICE YOUNG MA I SHARED A TAXI WITH WHEN I WA GOING INT LABOR IN BOSTON.
HE SAID, "A CHILD BORN IN JULY WILL GROW STRONG BY OVERCOMING THE SUMMER, SO HE'LL BE BLESSED."
"IN MY COUNTRY, THE WORD FOR JULY IS YURI."
AND HE SAID IT WITH SUCH A NICE SMILE...
...THAT I COULDN'T HELP BUT GIVE YOU THAT NAME.
CRACK

by Temari Matsumoto

Original Story by
Tomo Takabayashi

WOW ...

THAT REALLY FLEW.

SAY, YU-CHAN...

YOU WERE BORN IN JULY, SO YOU'RE YURI. DON'T YOU THINK THAT'S WONDERFUL?

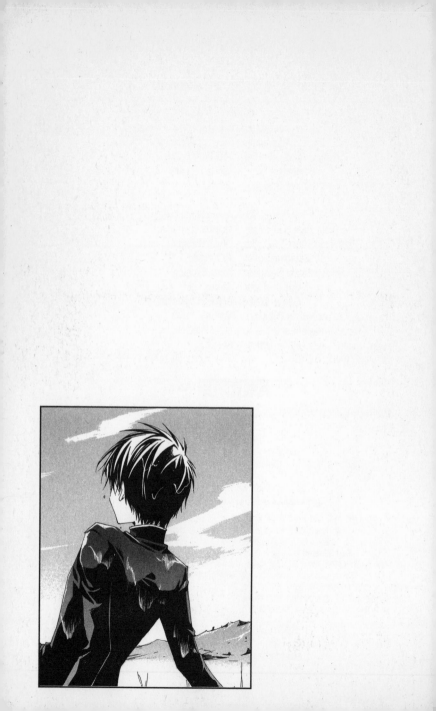

Kyo Kara MAOH! Volume 1
created by Temari Matsumoto
original story by Tomo Takabayashi

YA
GN
KYO
KARA
v.1

Translation - Jennifer Pan
English Adaptation - Karen S. Ahlstrom
Retouch and Lettering - Star Print Brokers
Production Artist - Michael Paolilli
Graphic Designer - John Lo

Senior Editor - Jenna Winterberg
Pre-Production Supervisor - Vicente Rivera, Jr.
Print-Production Specialist - Lucas Rivera
Managing Editor - Vy Nguyen
Senior Designer - Louis Csontos
Senior Designer - James Lee
Senior Editor - Bryce P. Coleman
Associate Publisher - Marco F. Pavia
President and C.O.O. - John Parker
C.E.O. and Chief Creative Officer - Stu Levy

A **TOKYOPOP** Manga

TOKYOPOP and are trademarks or registered trademarks of TOKYOPOP Inc.

TOKYOPOP Inc.
5900 Wilshire Blvd. Suite 2000
Los Angeles, CA 90036

E-mail: info@TOKYOPOP.com
Come visit us online at www.TOKYOPOP.com

KYOKARA MA NO TSUKU JIYUGYO! Volume 1
© Temari MATSUMOTO 2005
© Tomo TAKABAYASHI 2005
First published in Japan in 2005
by KADOKAWA SHOTEN PUBLISHING CO., LTD., Tokyo.
English translation rights arranged
with KADOKAWA SHOTEN PUBLISHING CO., LTD., Tokyo
through TUTTLE–MORI AGENCY, INC., Tokyo.
English text copyright © 2008 TOKYOPOP Inc.

ISBN: 978-1-4278-1099-1

First TOKYOPOP printing: October 2008
10 9 8 7 6 5 4 3 2 1
Printed in the USA

Kyo Kara MAOH™

Volume 1

Created by
Temari Matsumoto

HAMBURG // LONDON // LOS ANGELES // TOKYO

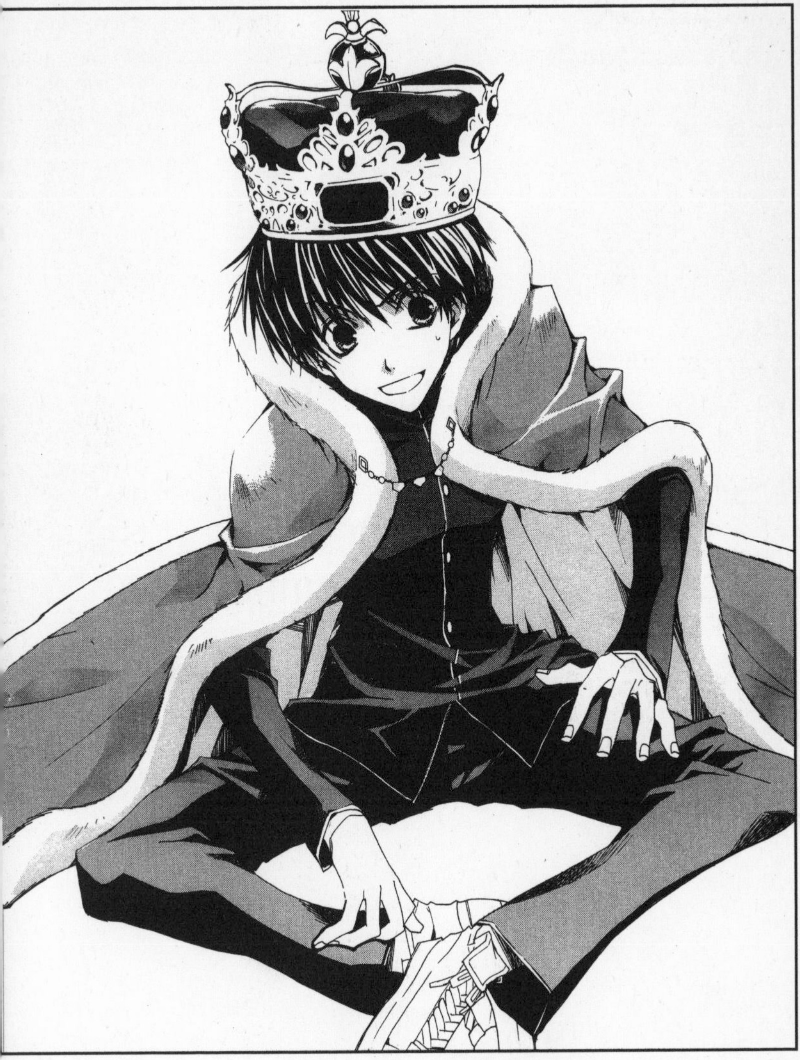

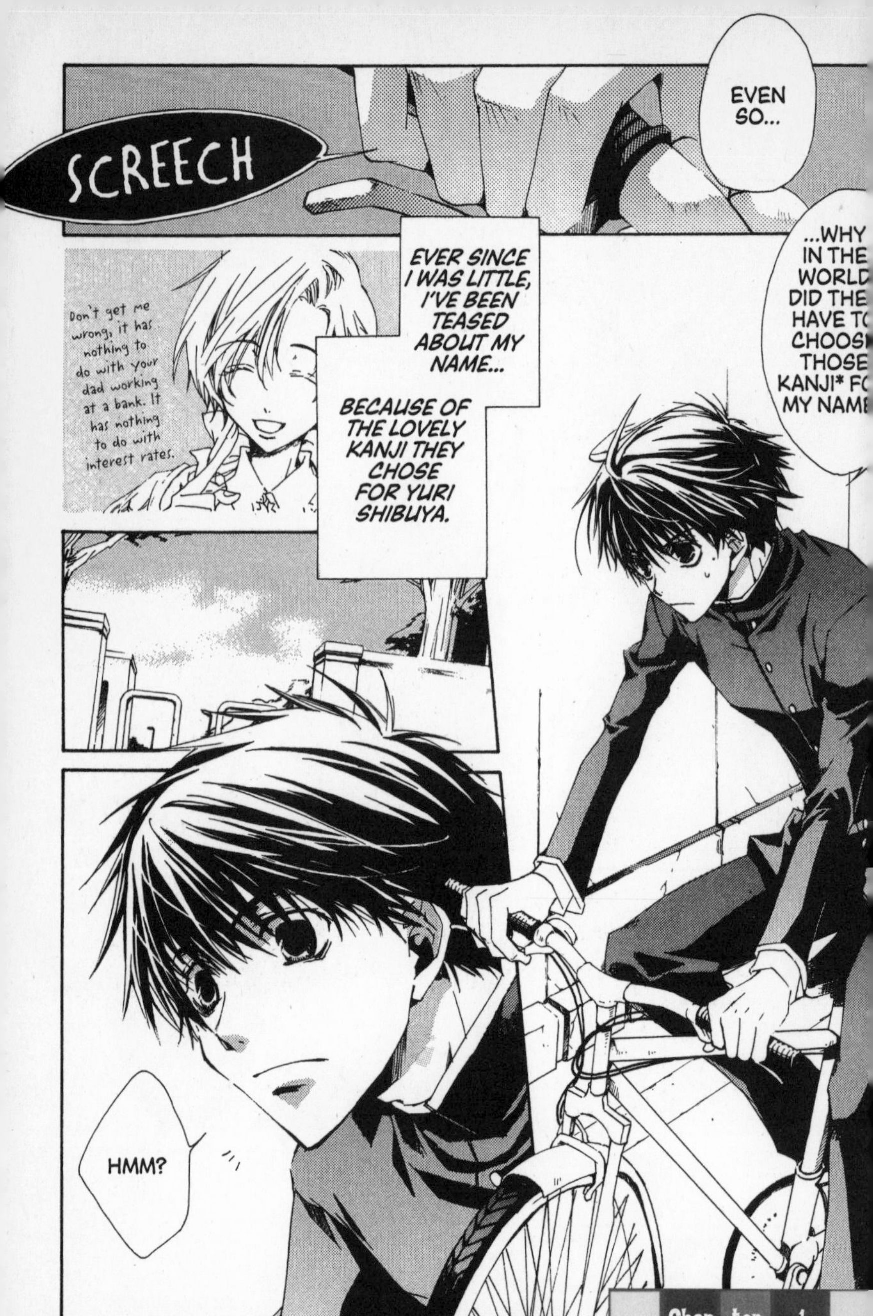
EVEN SO...
SCREECH
...WHY IN THE WORLD DID THE HAVE TO CHOOS THOSE KANJI* FO MY NAM
EVER SINCE I WAS LITTLE, I'VE BEEN TEASED ABOUT MY NAME...
BECAUSE OF THE LOVELY KANJI THEY CHOSE FOR YURI SHIBUYA.
Don't get me wrong, it has nothing to do with your dad working at a bank. It has nothing to do with interest rates.
HMM?
Chap ter 1
To the Other World-Go

*Yuri's *kanji* mean "advantageous" or "good rates" (as in bank interest rates).

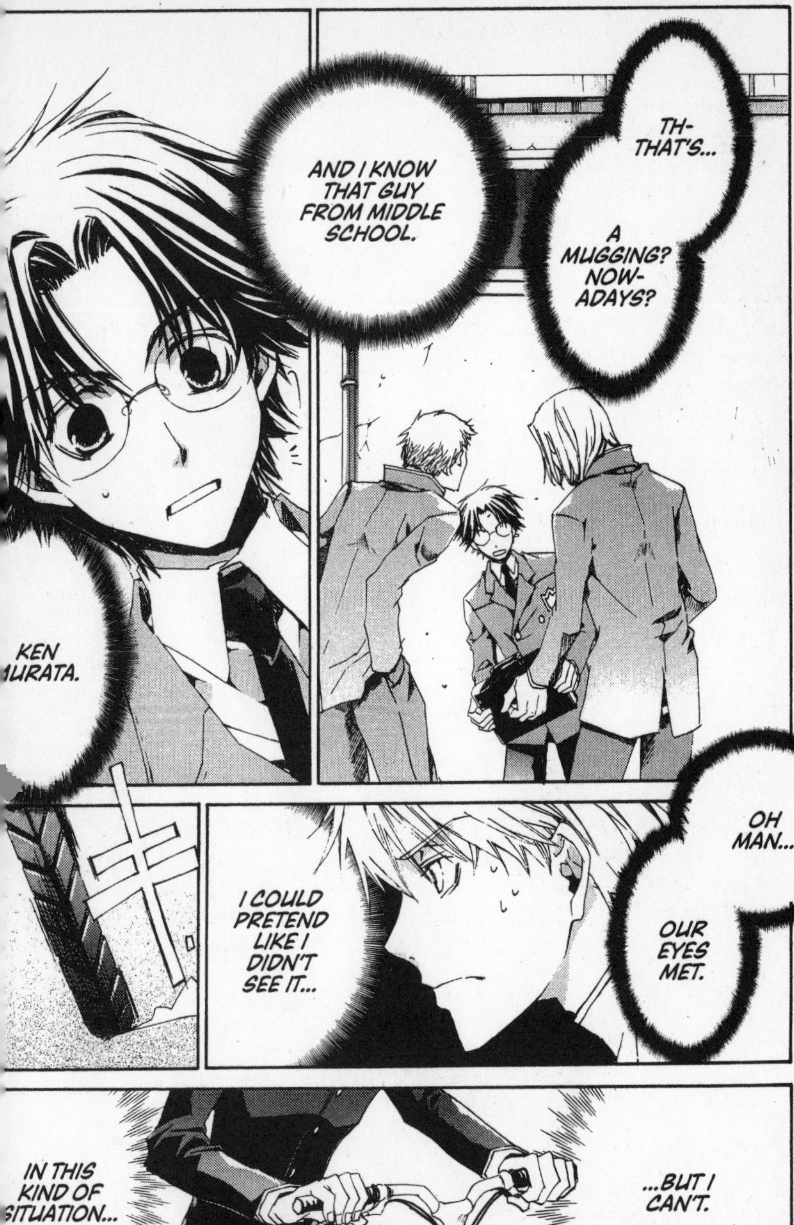
TH-THAT'S...
A MUGGING? NOW-ADAYS?
AND I KNOW THAT GUY FROM MIDDLE SCHOOL.
KEN MURATA.
OH MAN...
OUR EYES MET.
I COULD PRETEND LIKE I DIDN'T SEE IT...
...BUT I CAN'T.
IN THIS KIND OF SITUATION...

...I JUST CAN'T LET IT GO!

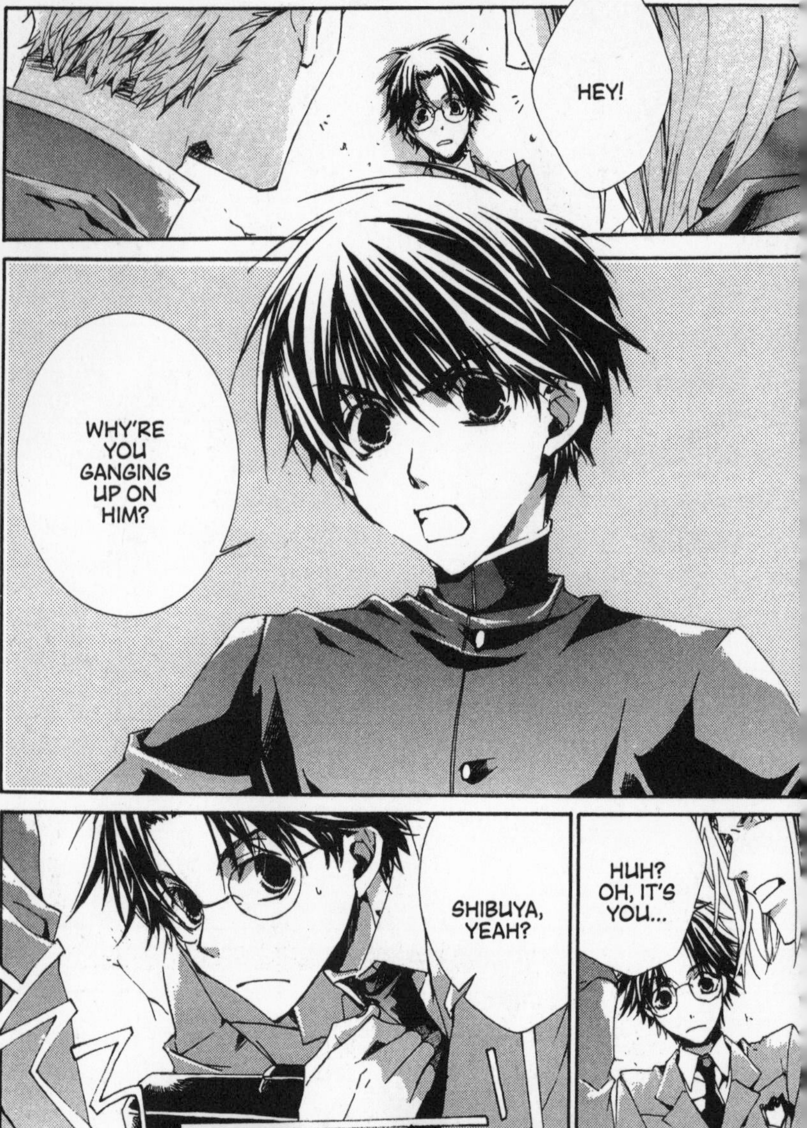
HEY!
WHY'RE YOU GANGING UP ON HIM?
HUH? OH, IT'S YOU...
SHIBUYA, YEAH?

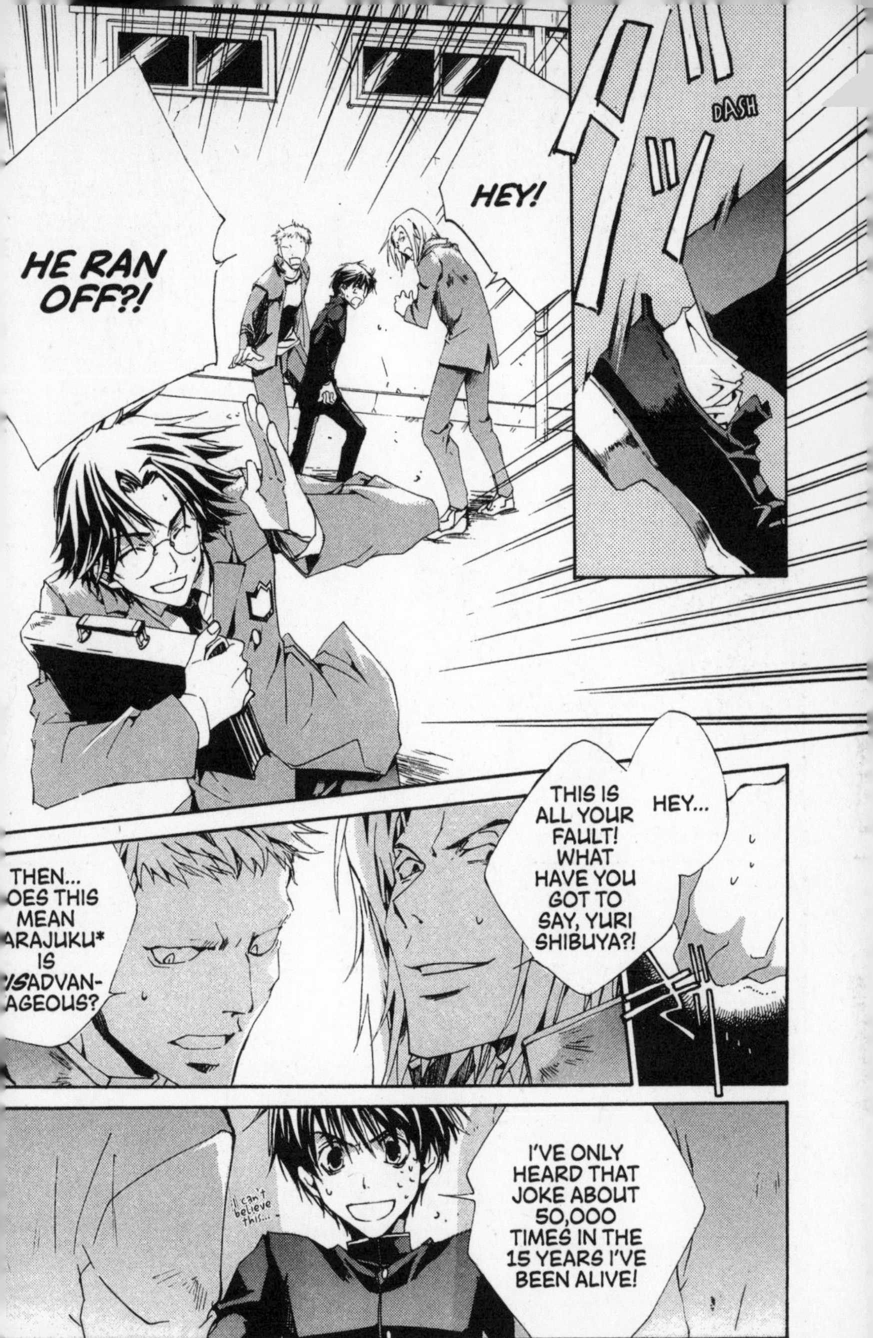
DASH
HEY!
HE RAN OFF?!
HEY...
THIS IS ALL YOUR FAULT! WHAT HAVE YOU GOT TO SAY, YURI SHIBUYA?!
THEN... OES THIS MEAN ARAJUKU* IS ISADVAN-AGEOUS?
I'VE ONLY HEARD THAT JOKE ABOUT 50,000 TIMES IN THE 15 YEARS I'VE BEEN ALIVE!
I can't believe this...

'Shibuya Yuuri, Harajuku Fuuri," a play on Yuri's name, means "advantage Shibuya, disadvantage Harajuku," eferring to adjacent wards of Tokyo.

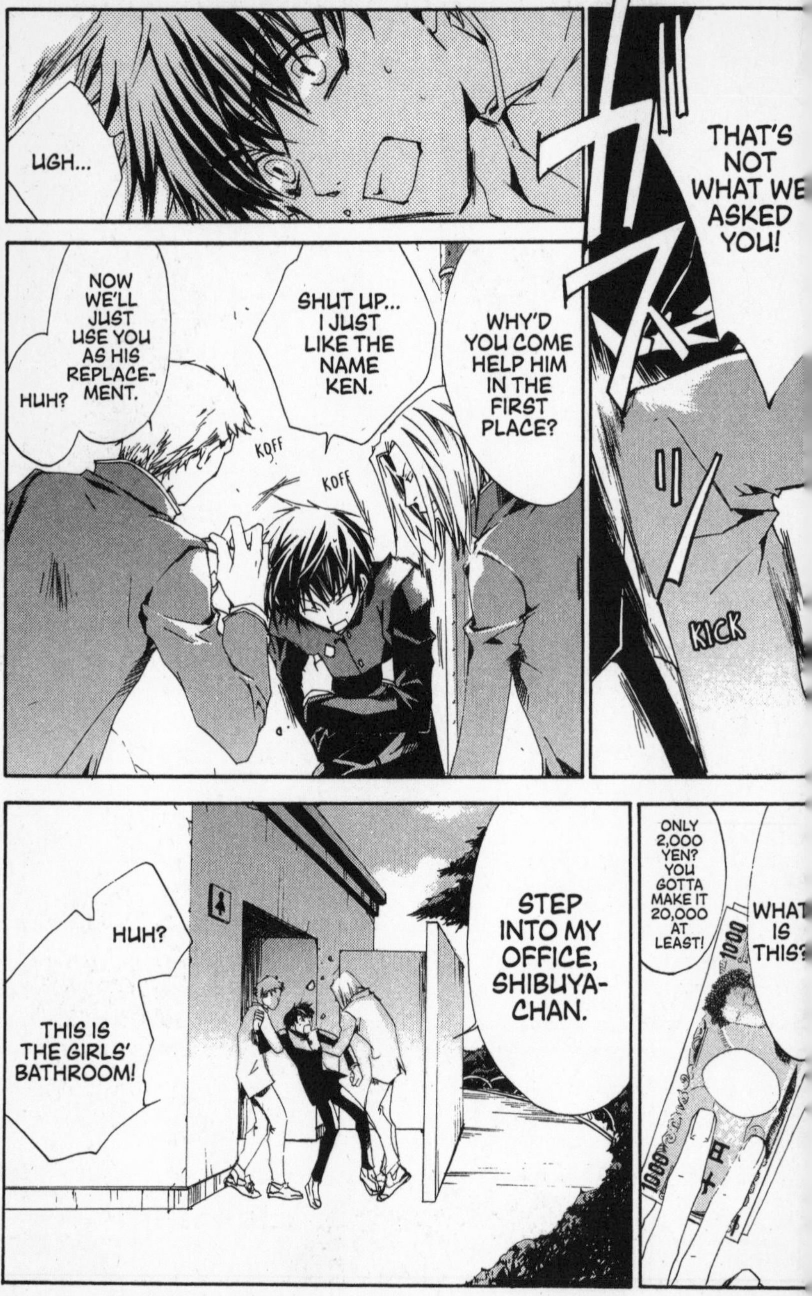
THAT'S NOT WHAT WE ASKED YOU!
KICK
UGH...
WHY'D YOU COME HELP HIM IN THE FIRST PLACE?
SHUT UP... I JUST LIKE THE NAME KEN.
KOFF
KOFF
NOW WE'LL JUST USE YOU AS HIS REPLACEMENT.
HUH?
WHAT IS THIS?
ONLY 2,000 YEN? YOU GOTTA MAKE IT 20,000 AT LEAST!
STEP INTO MY OFFICE, SHIBUYA-CHAN.
HUH?
THIS IS THE GIRLS' BATHROOM!

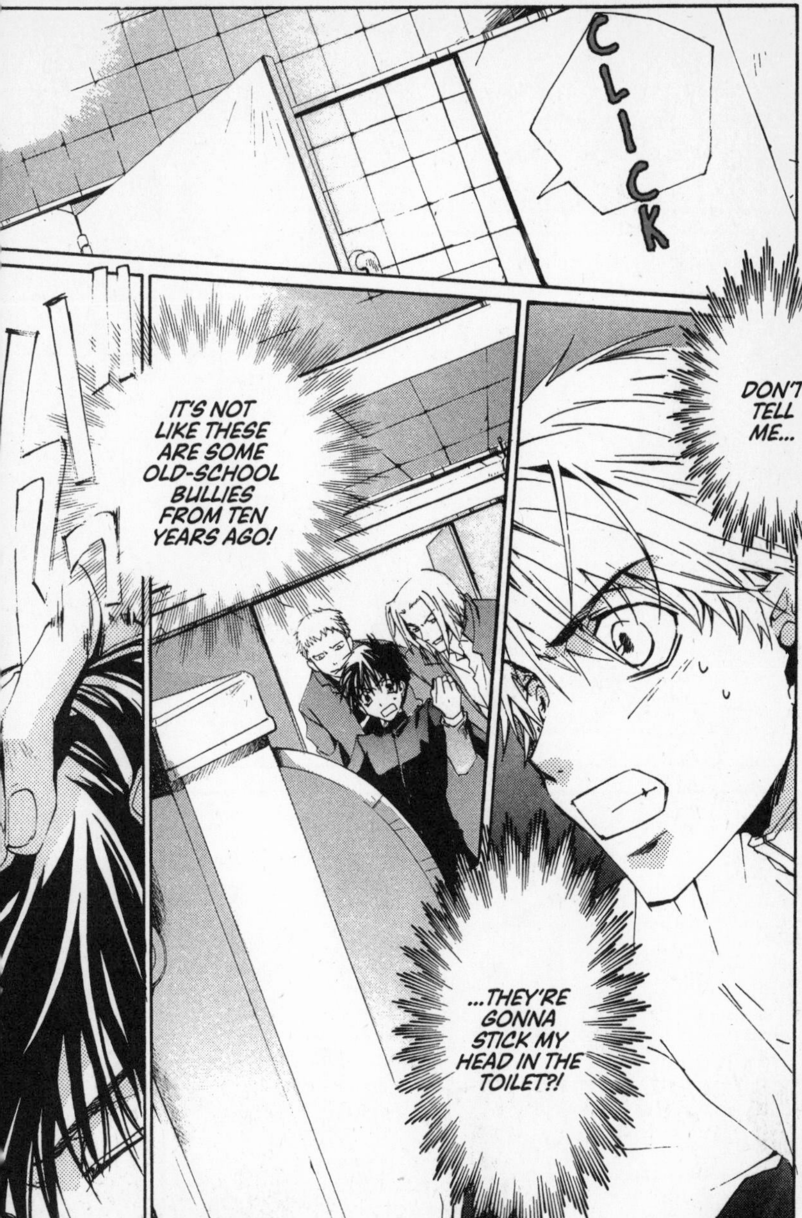
CLICK
DON'T TELL ME...
...THEY'RE GONNA STICK MY HEAD IN THE TOILET?!
IT'S NOT LIKE THESE ARE SOME OLD-SCHOOL BULLIES FROM TEN YEARS AGO!

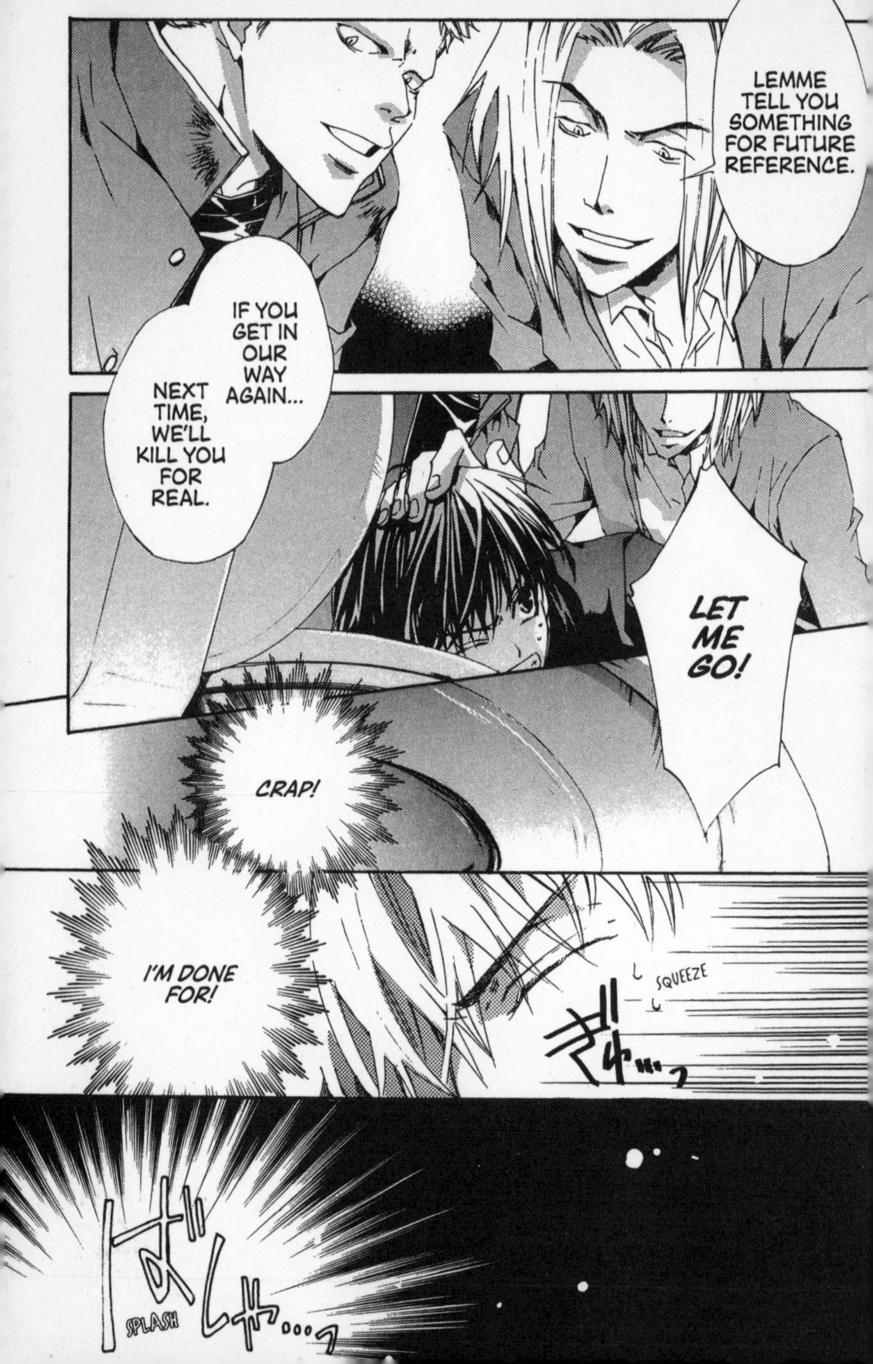
LEMME TELL YOU SOMETHING FOR FUTURE REFERENCE.
IF YOU GET IN OUR WAY AGAIN...
NEXT TIME, WE'LL KILL YOU FOR REAL.
LET ME GO!
CRAP!
SQUEEZE
I'M DONE FOR!
SPLASH

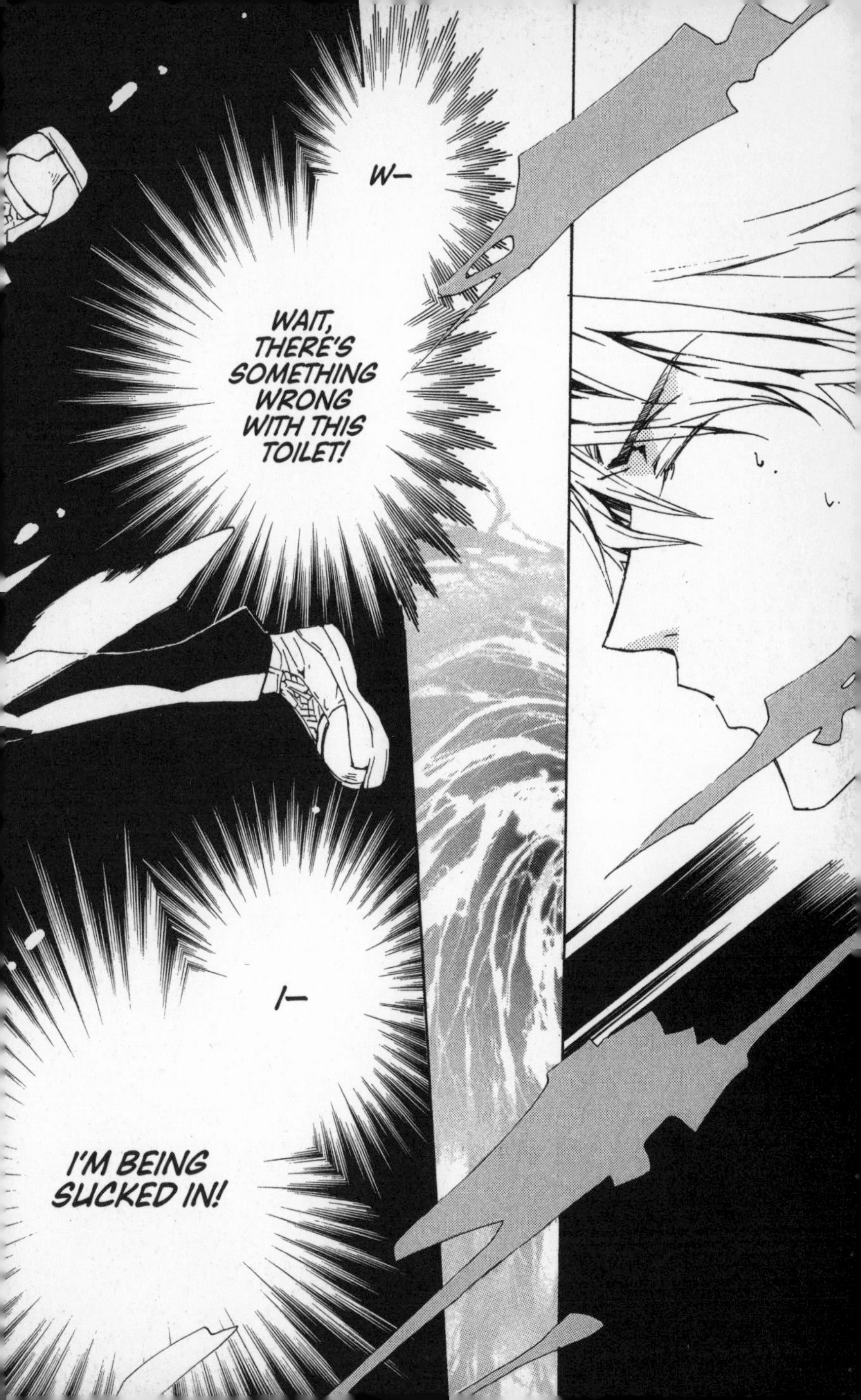
W–
WAIT, THERE'S SOMETHING WRONG WITH THIS TOILET!
I–
I'M BEING SUCKED IN!

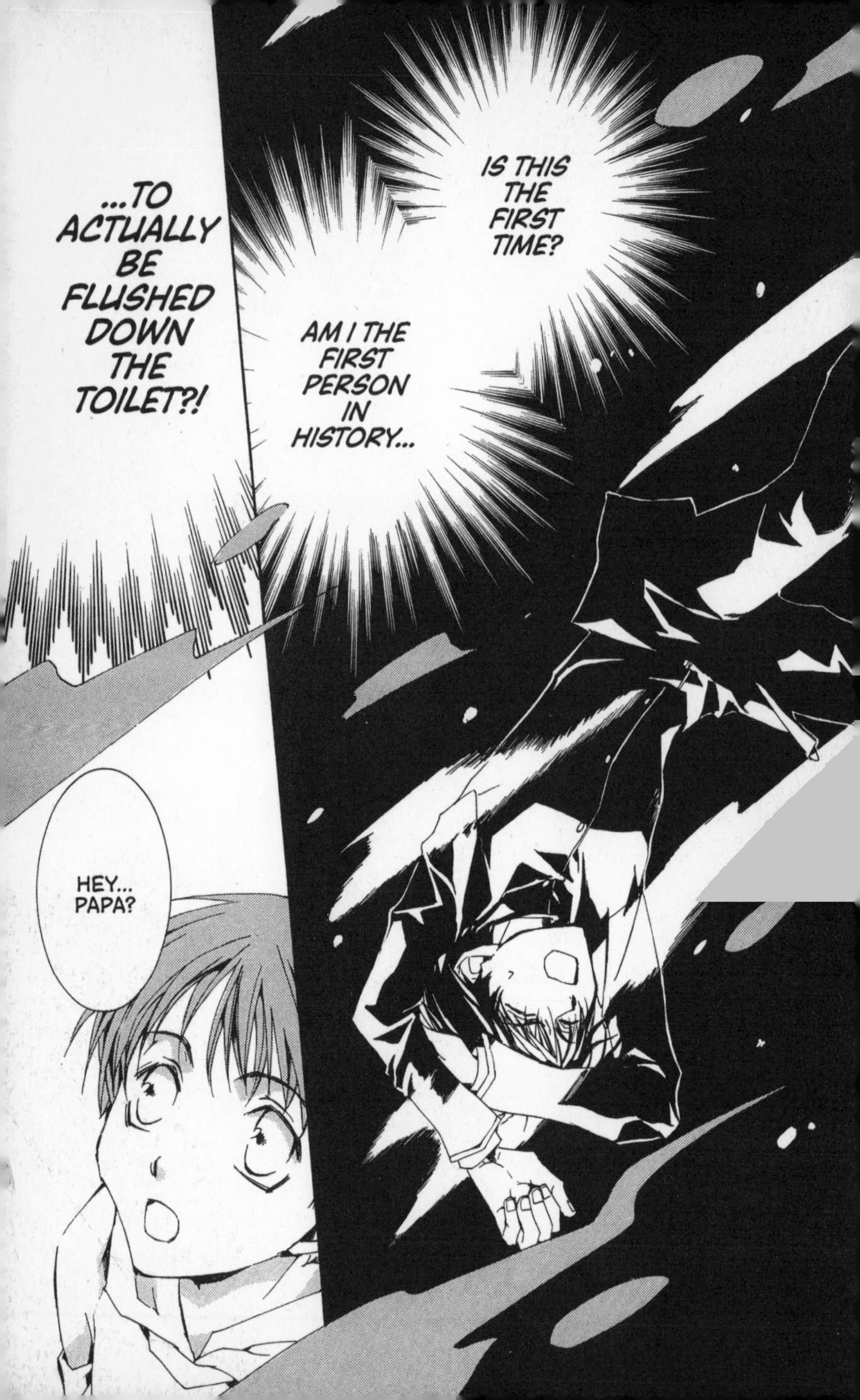
IS THIS THE FIRST TIME?
AM I THE FIRST PERSON IN HISTORY...
...TO ACTUALLY BE FLUSHED DOWN THE TOILET?!
HEY... PAPA?

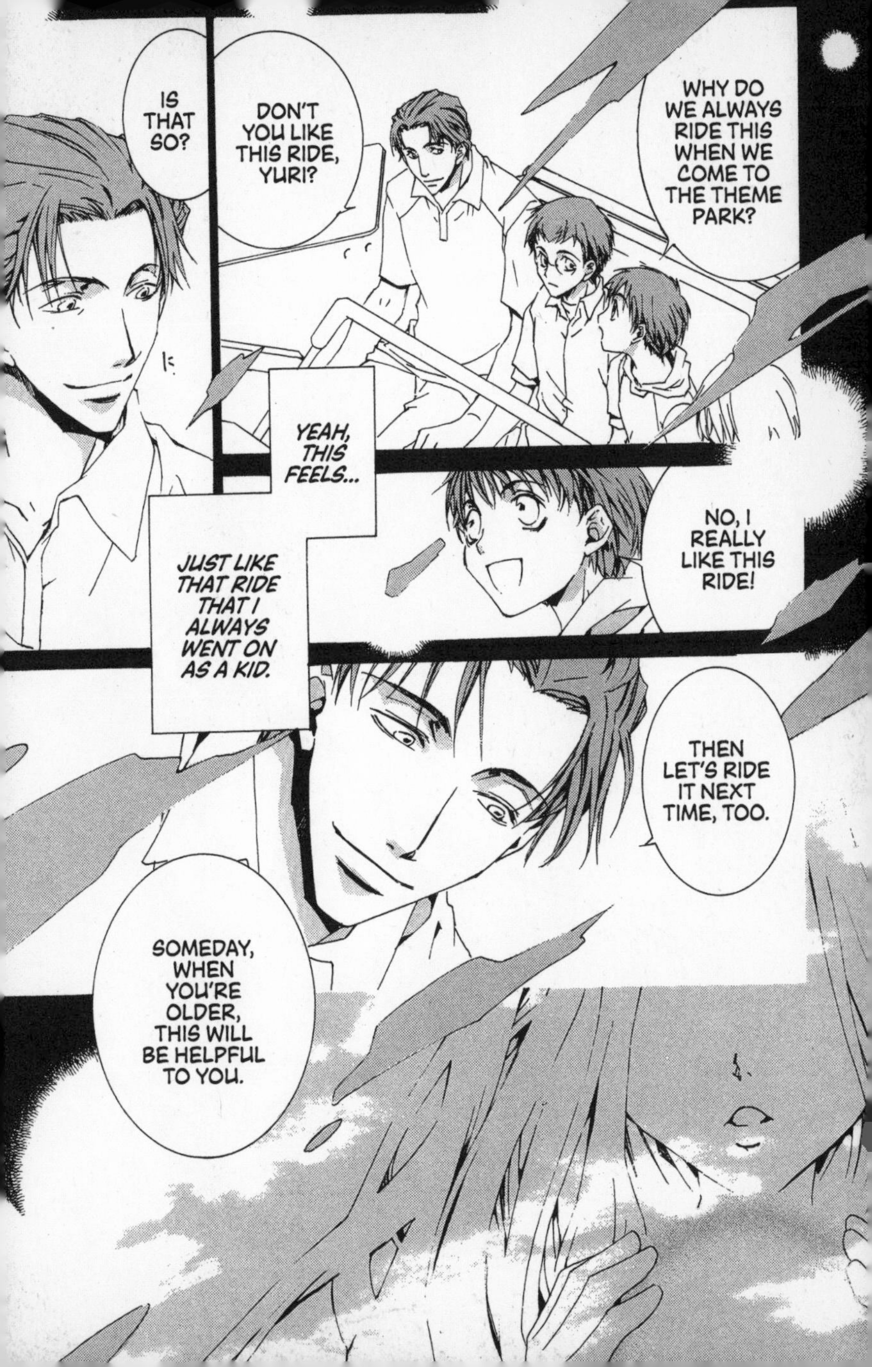
WHY DO WE ALWAYS RIDE THIS WHEN WE COME TO THE THEME PARK?
DON'T YOU LIKE THIS RIDE, YURI?
NO, I REALLY LIKE THIS RIDE!
IS THAT SO?
YEAH, THIS FEELS...
JUST LIKE THAT RIDE THAT I ALWAYS WENT ON AS A KID.
THEN LET'S RIDE IT NEXT TIME, TOO.
SOMEDAY, WHEN YOU'RE OLDER, THIS WILL BE HELPFUL TO YOU.

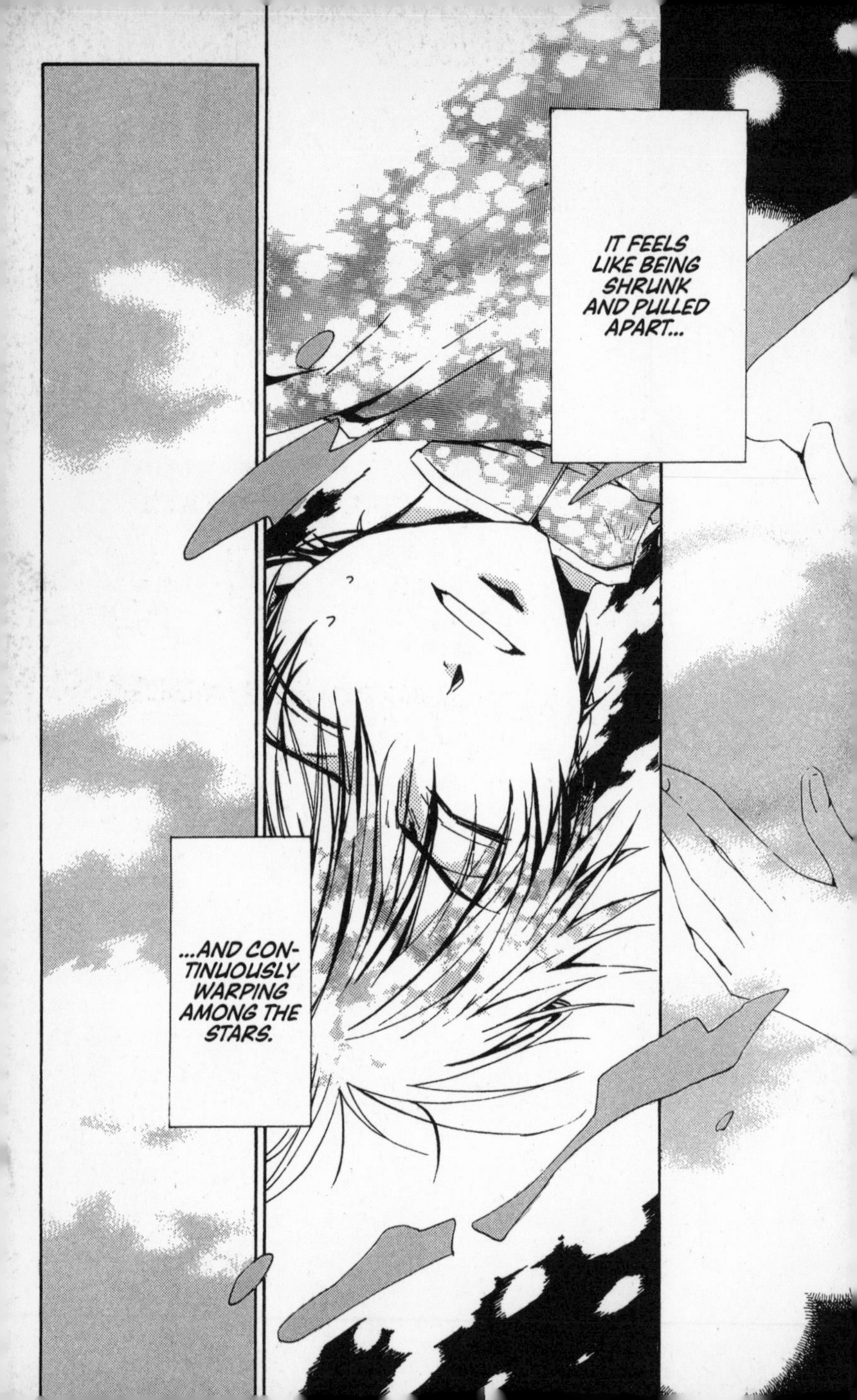
IT FEELS LIKE BEING SHRUNK AND PULLED APART...
...AND CON-TINUOUSLY WARPING AMONG THE STARS.

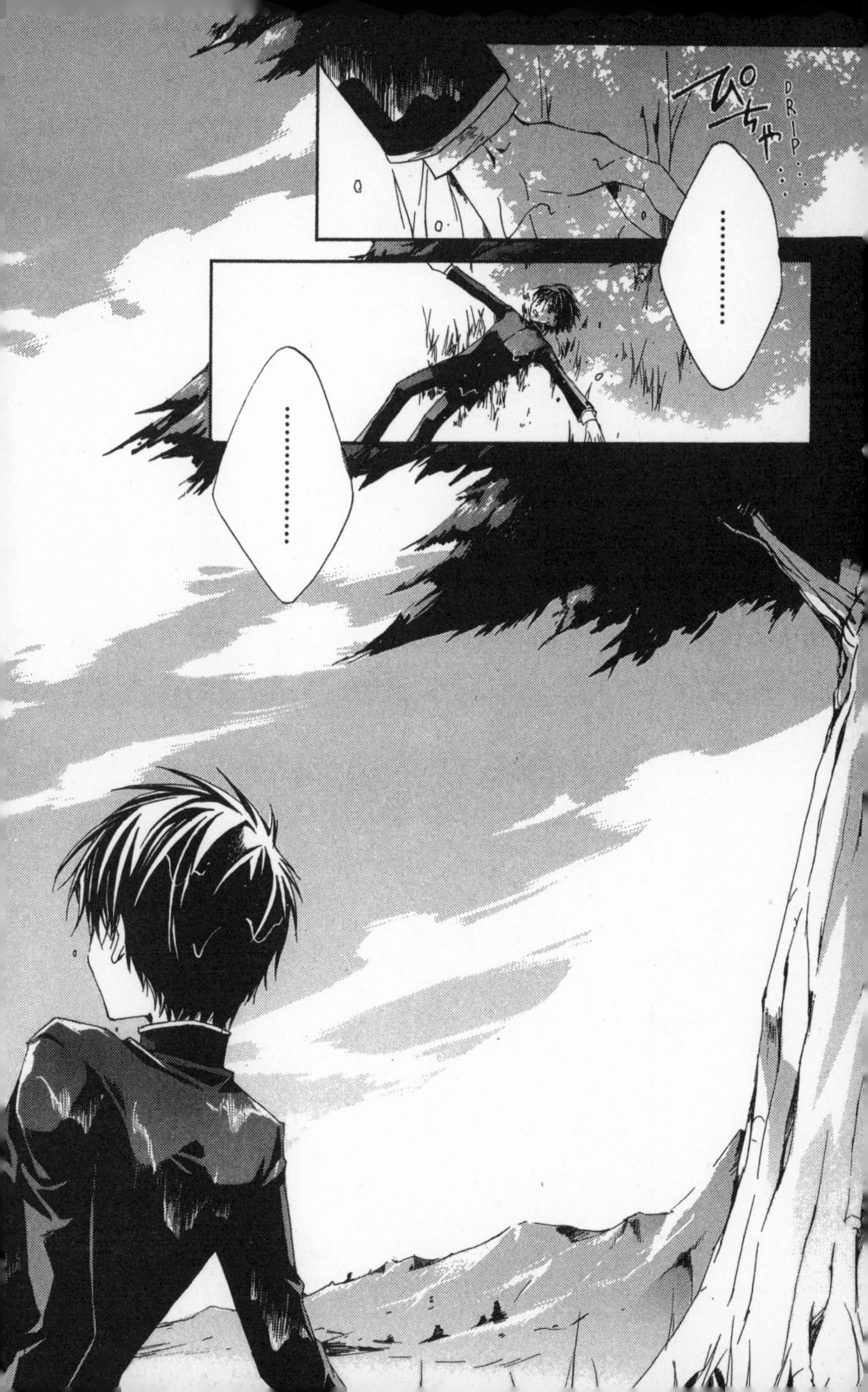
ぴちゃ
DRIP...
....
....

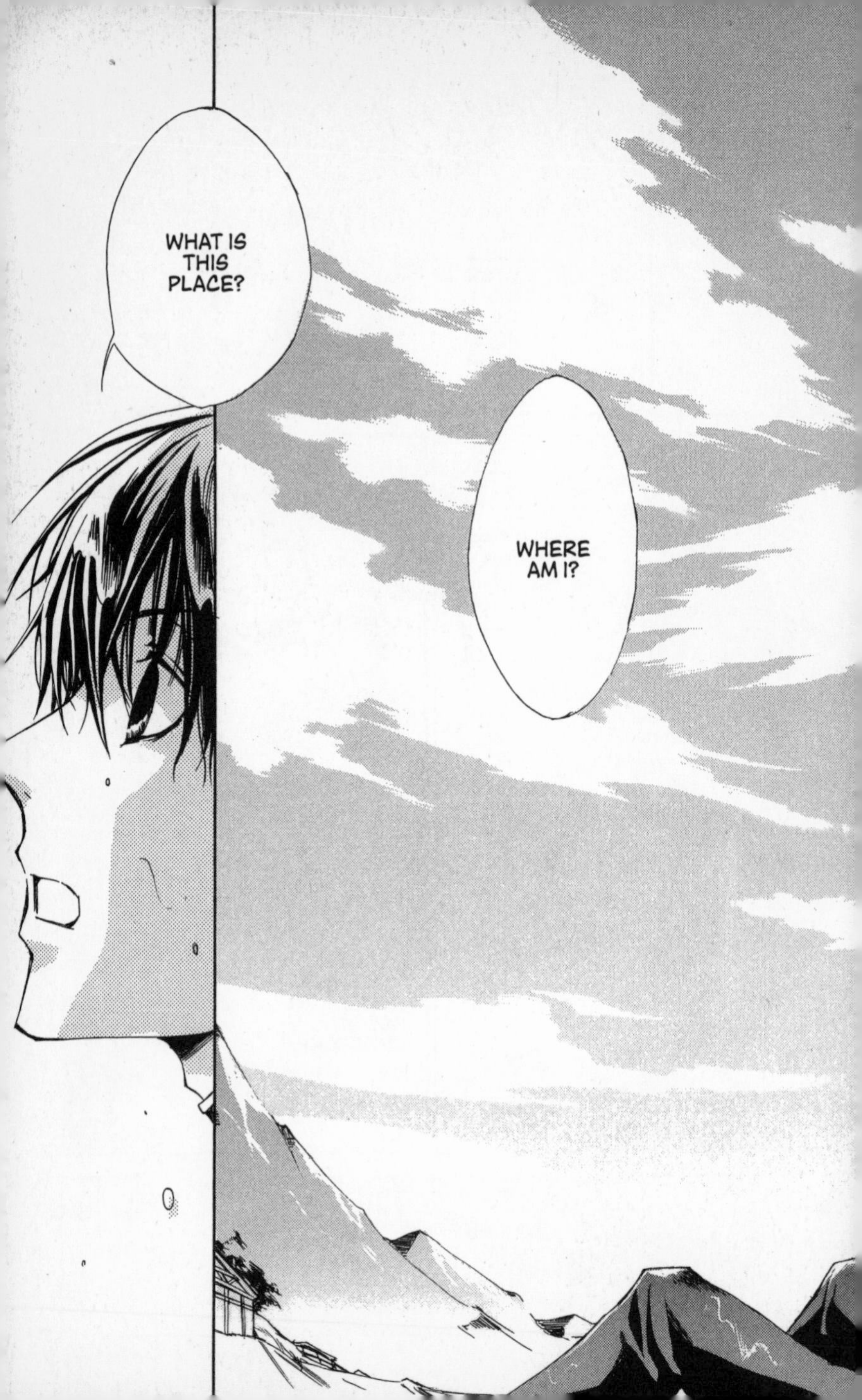
WHERE AM I?
WHAT IS THIS PLACE?

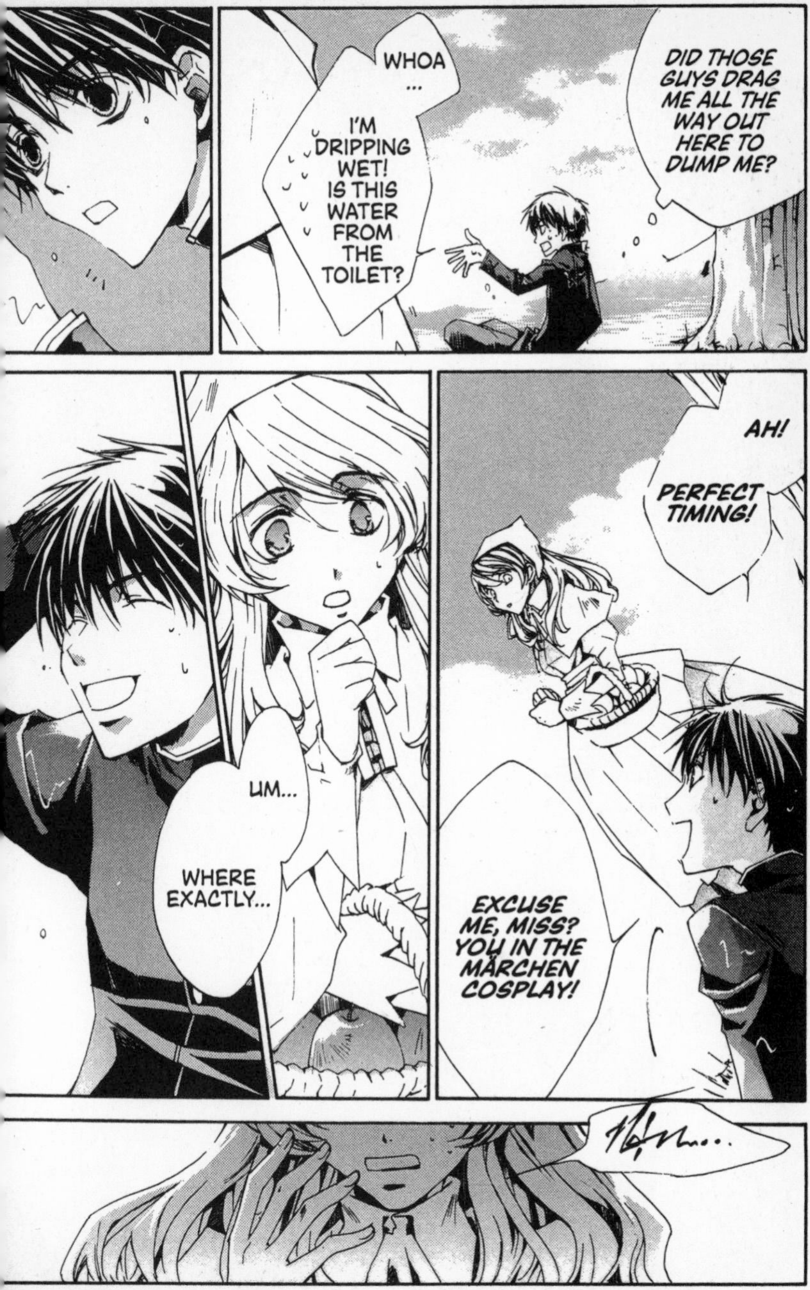
DID THOSE GUYS DRAG ME ALL THE WAY OUT HERE TO DUMP ME?
WHOA ...
I'M DRIPPING WET! IS THIS WATER FROM THE TOILET?
AH!
PERFECT TIMING!
EXCUSE ME, MISS? YOU IN THE MÄRCHEN COSPLAY!
UM...
WHERE EXACTLY...

*Märchen=German Fairy Tales

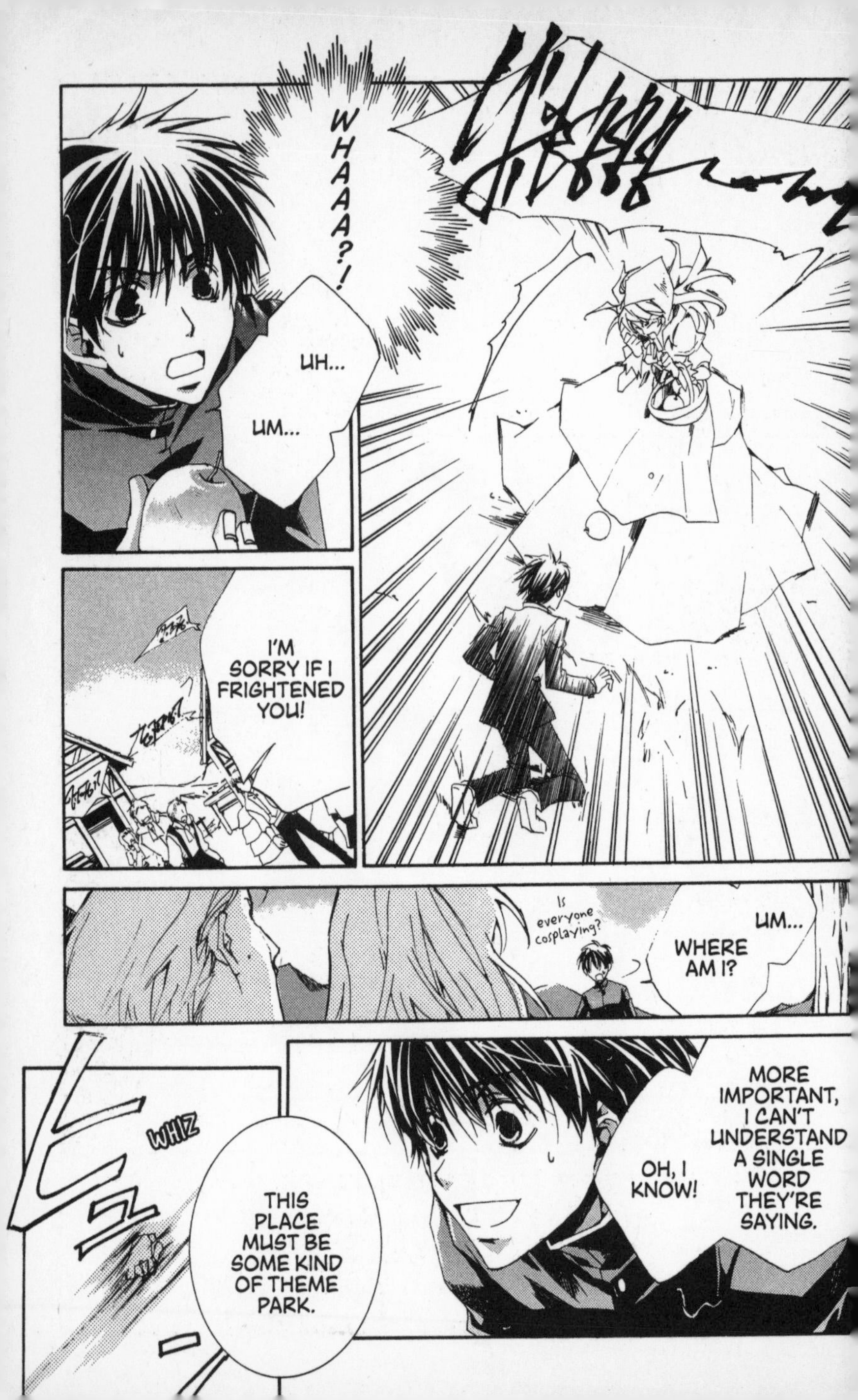
WHAAAA?!
UH...
UM...
I'M SORRY IF I FRIGHTENED YOU!
UM... WHERE AM I?
Is everyone cosplaying?
MORE IMPORTANT, I CAN'T UNDERSTAND A SINGLE WORD THEY'RE SAYING.
OH, I KNOW!
THIS PLACE MUST BE SOME KIND OF THEME PARK.
WHIZ

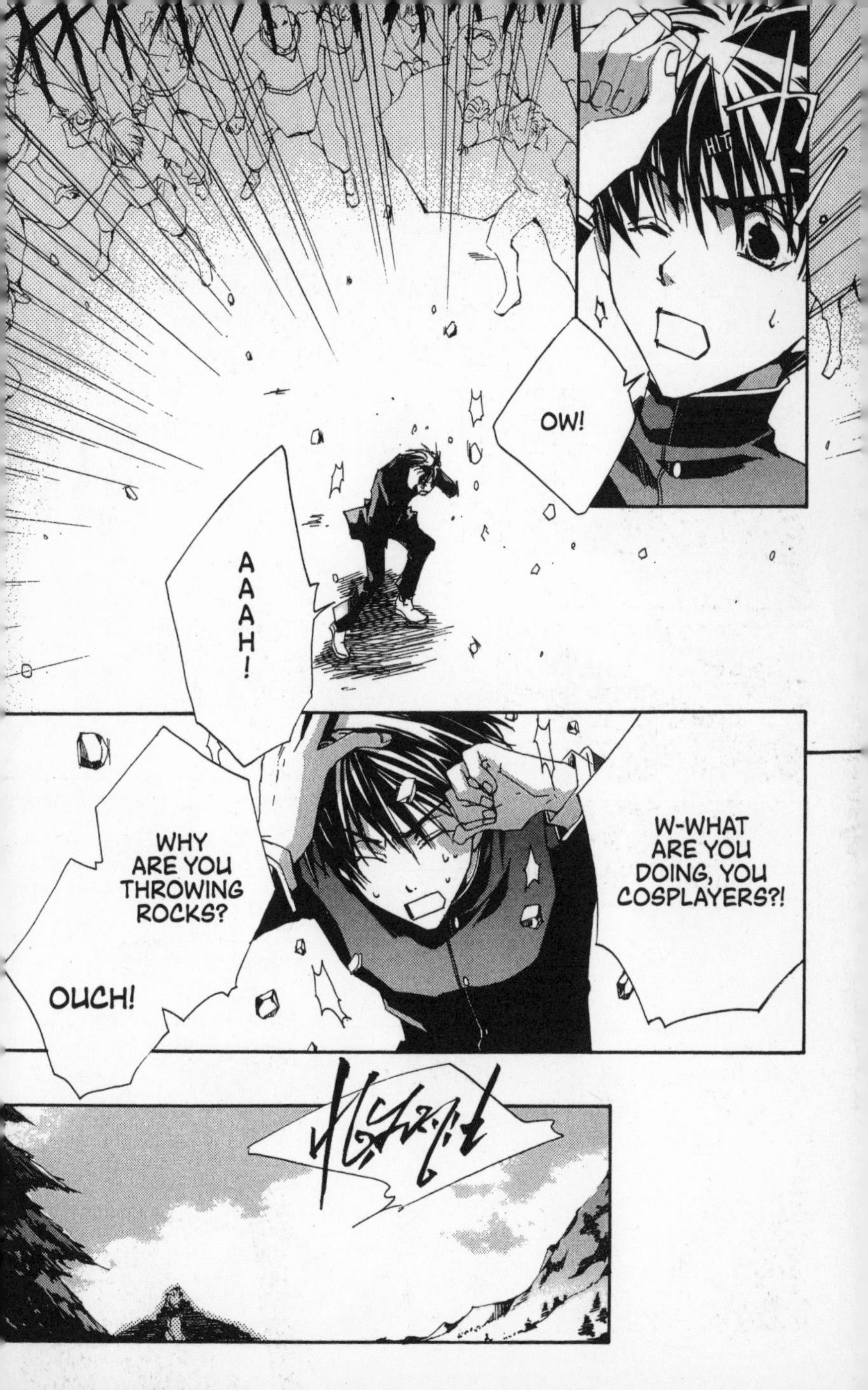
HIT
OW!
AAAH!
W-WHAT ARE YOU DOING, YOU COSPLAYERS?!
WHY ARE YOU THROWING ROCKS?
OUCH!

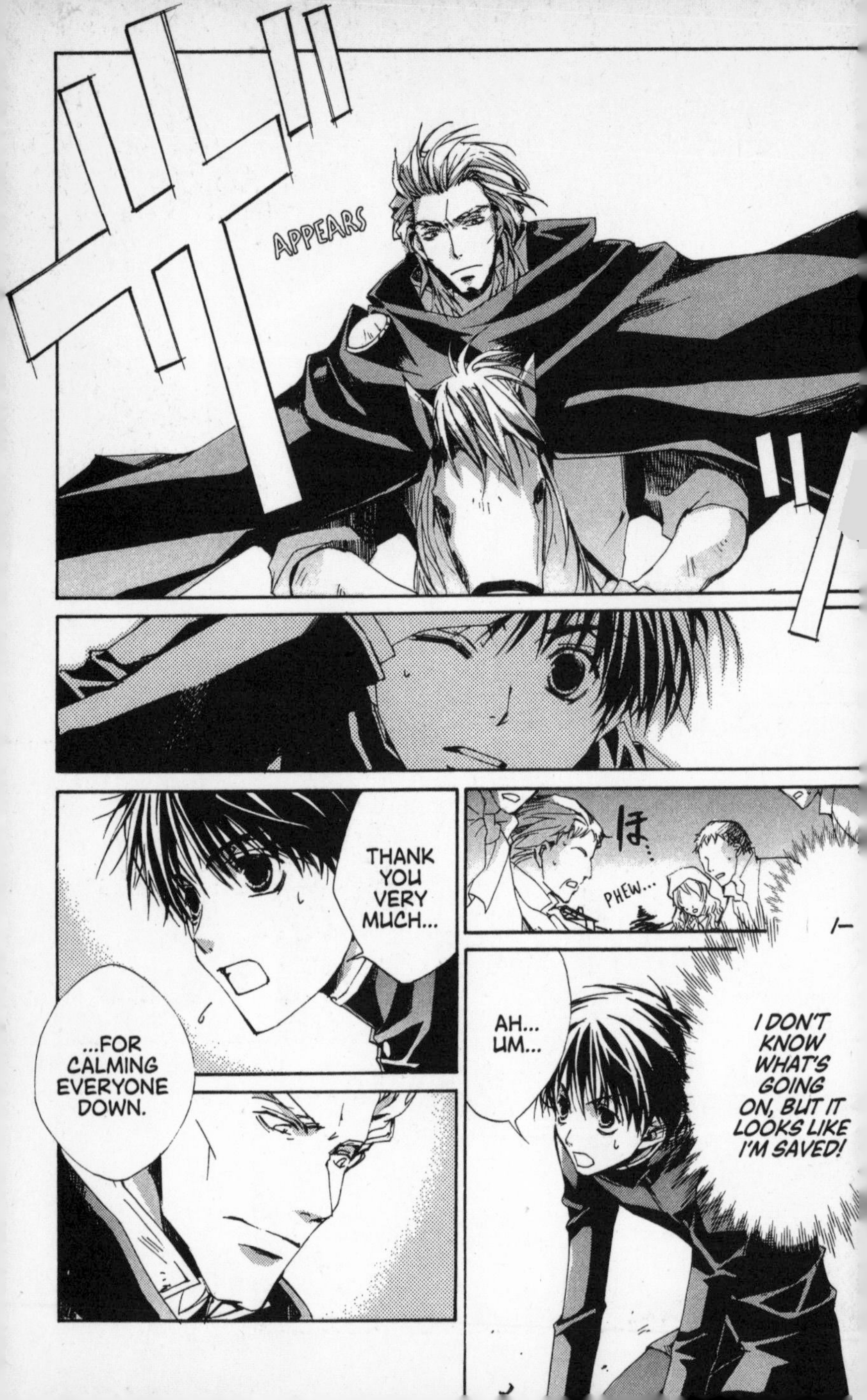
APPEARS
ほ...
PHEW...
AH... UM...
I DON'T KNOW WHAT'S GOING ON, BUT IT LOOKS LIKE I'M SAVED!
THANK YOU VERY MUCH...
...FOR CALMING EVERYONE DOWN.

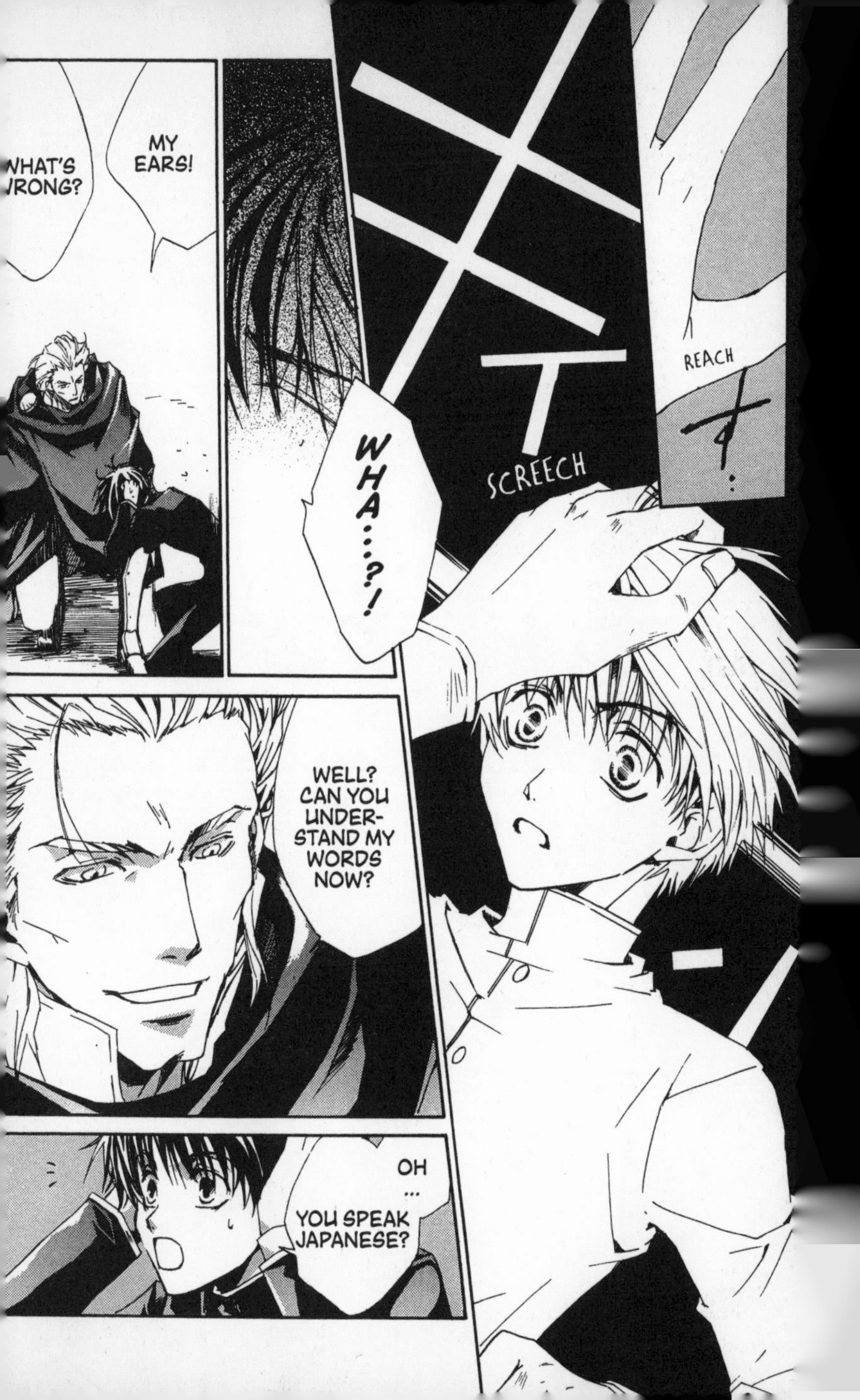

REACH
SCREECH
WHA...?!
MY EARS!
WHAT'S WRONG?
WELL? CAN YOU UNDER-STAND MY WORDS NOW?
OH ... YOU SPEAK JAPANESE?

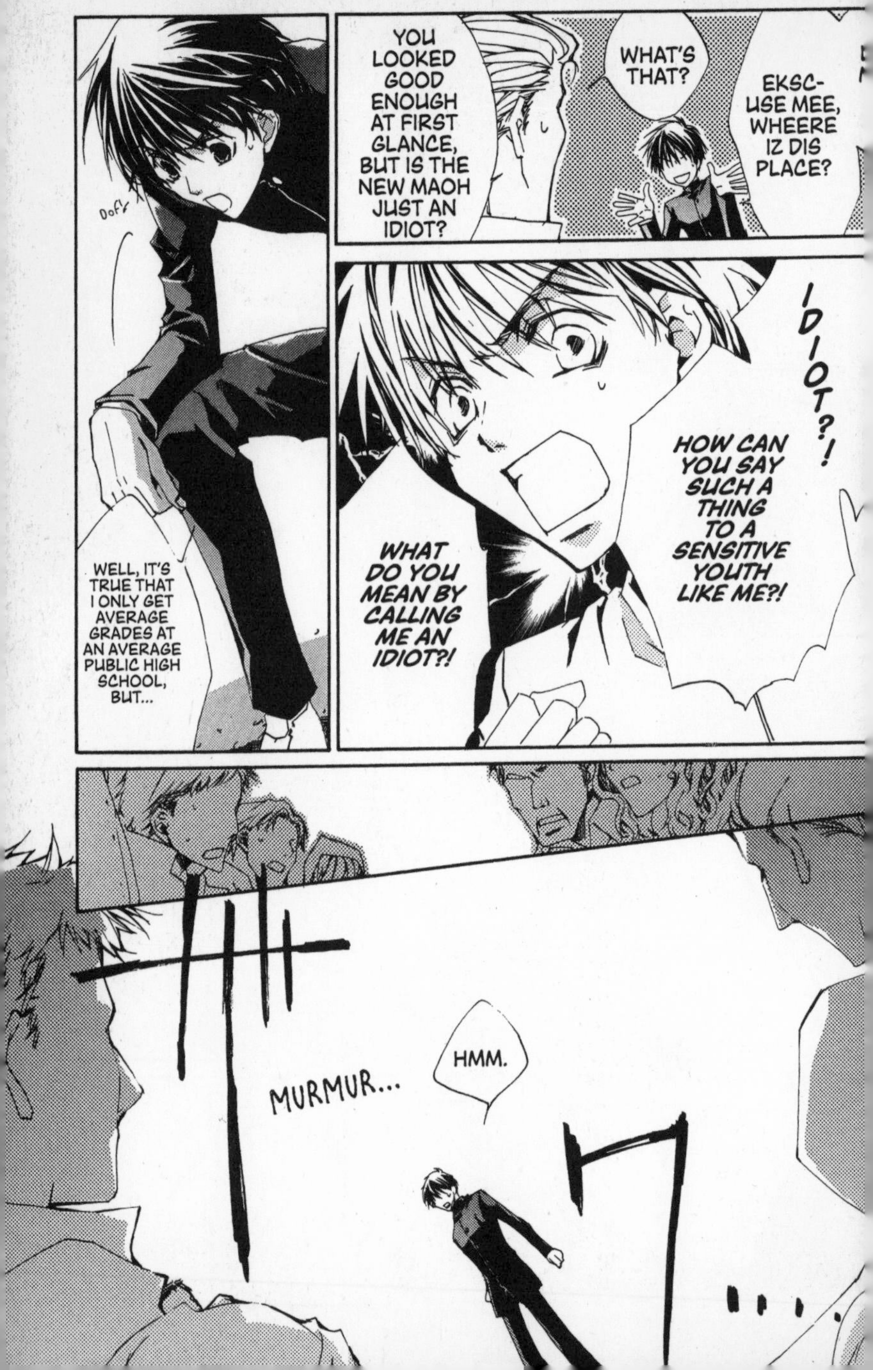
EKSC-USE MEE, WHEERE IZ DIS PLACE?
WHAT'S THAT?
YOU LOOKED GOOD ENOUGH AT FIRST GLANCE, BUT IS THE NEW MAOH JUST AN IDIOT?
IDIOT?!
HOW CAN YOU SAY SUCH A THING TO A SENSITIVE YOUTH LIKE ME?!
WHAT DO YOU MEAN BY CALLING ME AN IDIOT?!
WELL, IT'S TRUE THAT I ONLY GET AVERAGE GRADES AT AN AVERAGE PUBLIC HIGH SCHOOL, BUT...
HMM.
MURMUR...
...

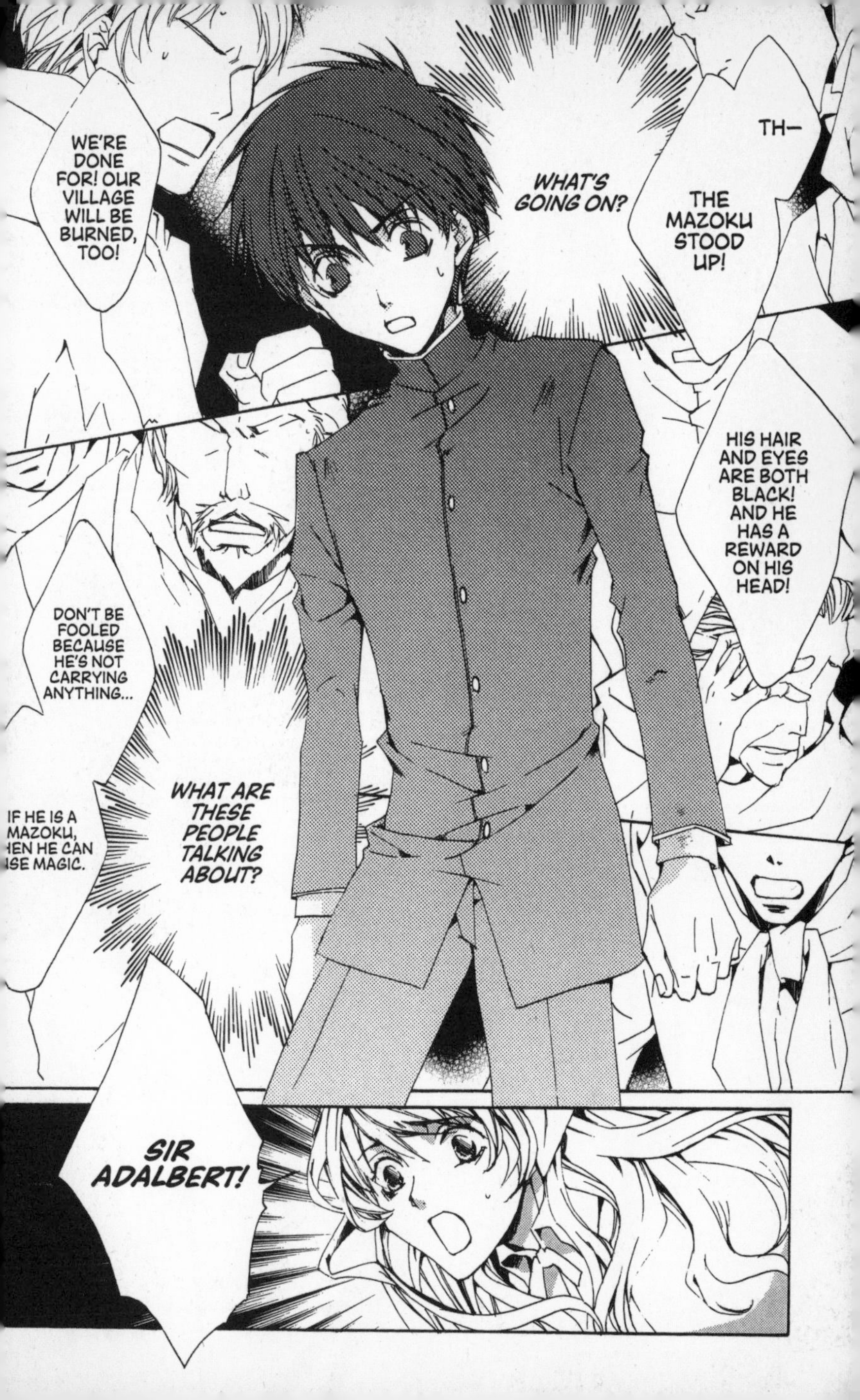
TH—
THE MAZOKU STOOD UP!
WHAT'S GOING ON?
WE'RE DONE FOR! OUR VILLAGE WILL BE BURNED, TOO!
HIS HAIR AND EYES ARE BOTH BLACK! AND HE HAS A REWARD ON HIS HEAD!
DON'T BE FOOLED BECAUSE HE'S NOT CARRYING ANYTHING...
WHAT ARE THESE PEOPLE TALKING ABOUT?
IF HE IS A MAZOKU, HEN HE CAN SE MAGIC.
SIR ADALBERT!

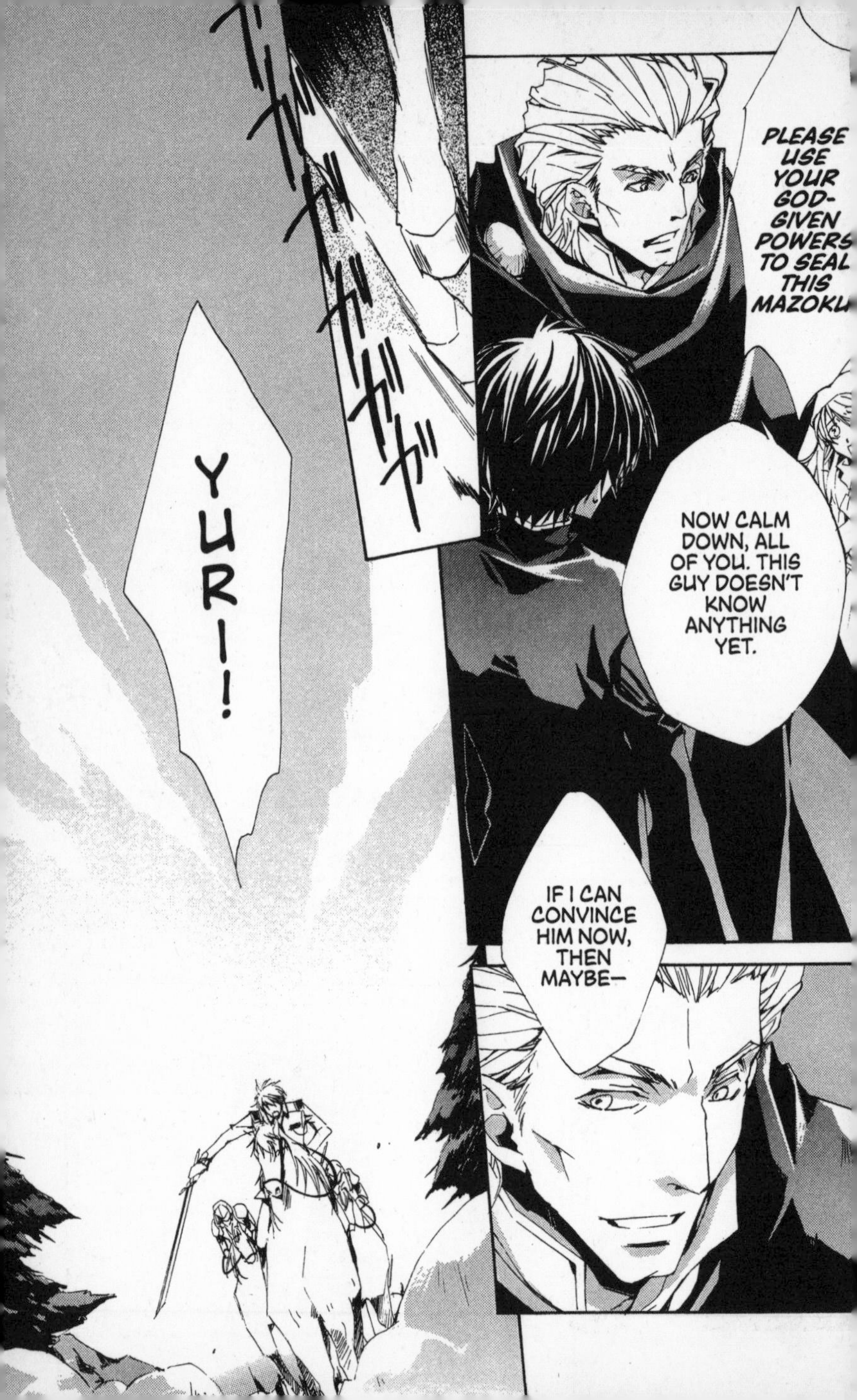
PLEASE USE YOUR GOD-GIVEN POWERS TO SEAL THIS MAZOKU
NOW CALM DOWN, ALL OF YOU. THIS GUY DOESN'T KNOW ANYTHING YET.
IF I CAN CONVINCE HIM NOW, THEN MAYBE—
YURI!!

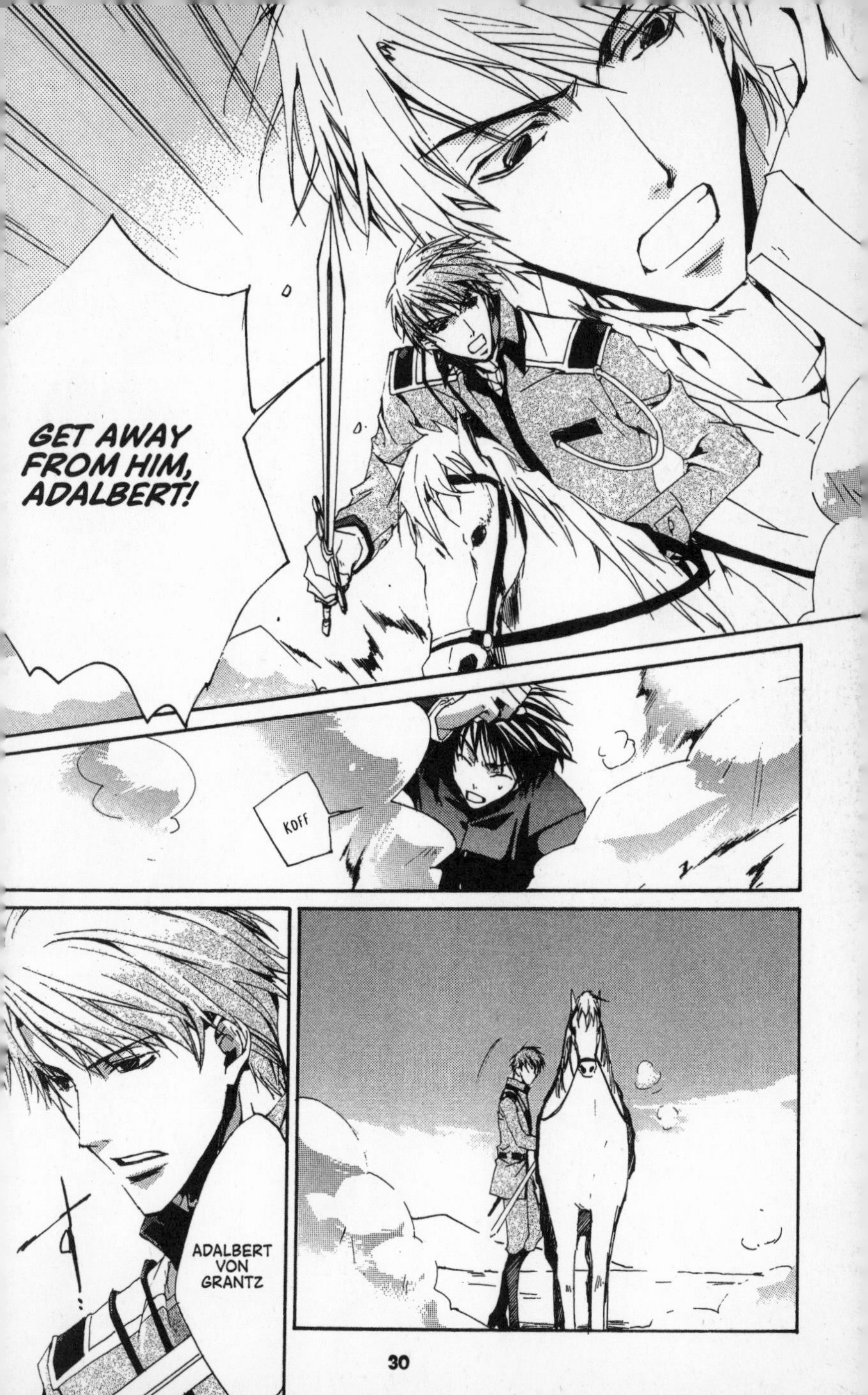
GET AWAY FROM HIM, ADALBERT!
KOFF
ADALBERT VON GRANTZ

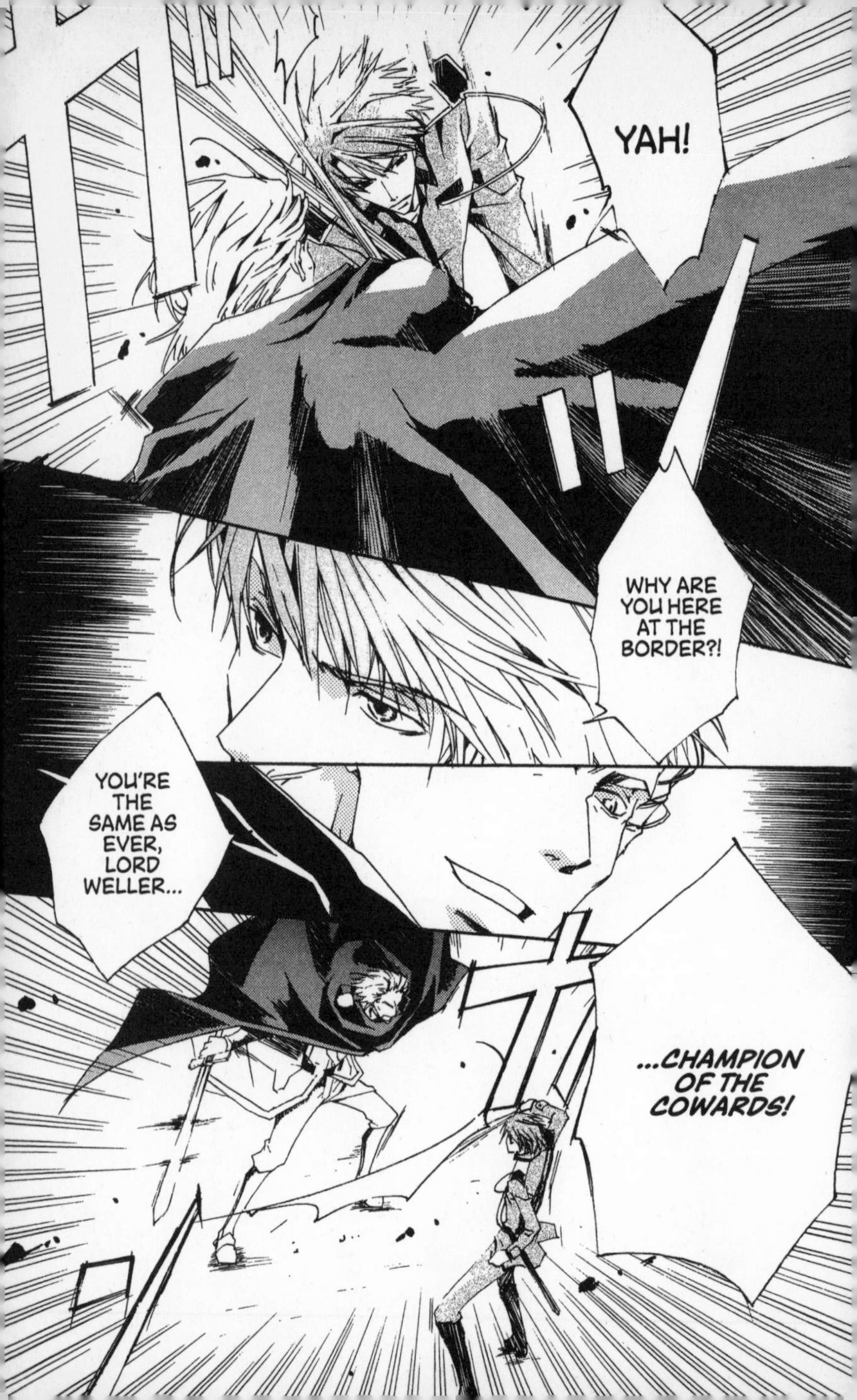
YAH!
WHY ARE YOU HERE AT THE BORDER?!
YOU'RE THE SAME AS EVER, LORD WELLER...
...CHAMPION OF THE COWARDS!

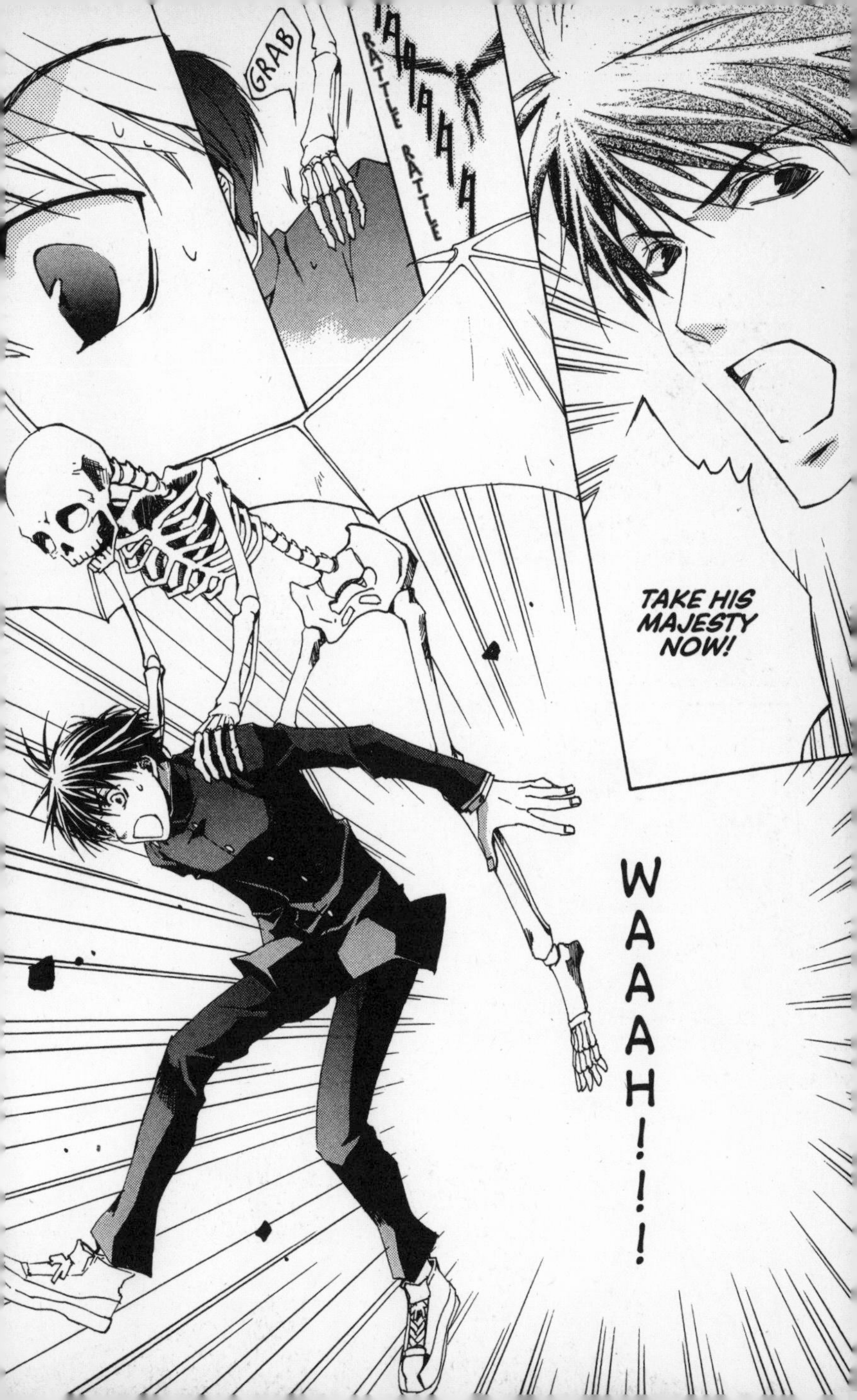
TAKE HIS MAJESTY NOW!
RATTLE
RATTLE
GRAB
WAAAH!!!

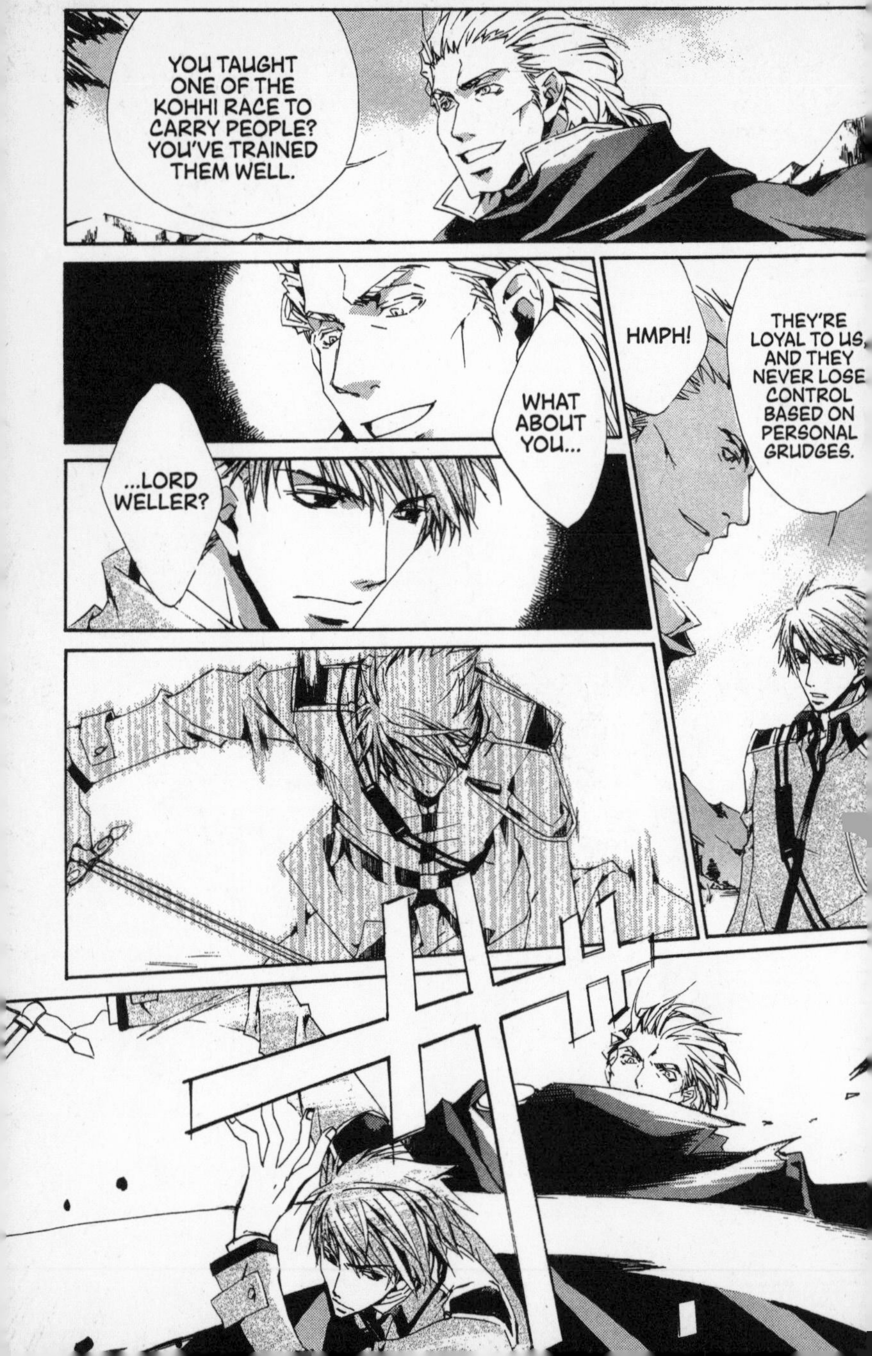

YOU TAUGHT ONE OF THE KOHHI RACE TO CARRY PEOPLE? YOU'VE TRAINED THEM WELL.
THEY'RE LOYAL TO US, AND THEY NEVER LOSE CONTROL BASED ON PERSONAL GRUDGES.
HMPH!
WHAT ABOUT YOU...
...LORD WELLER?

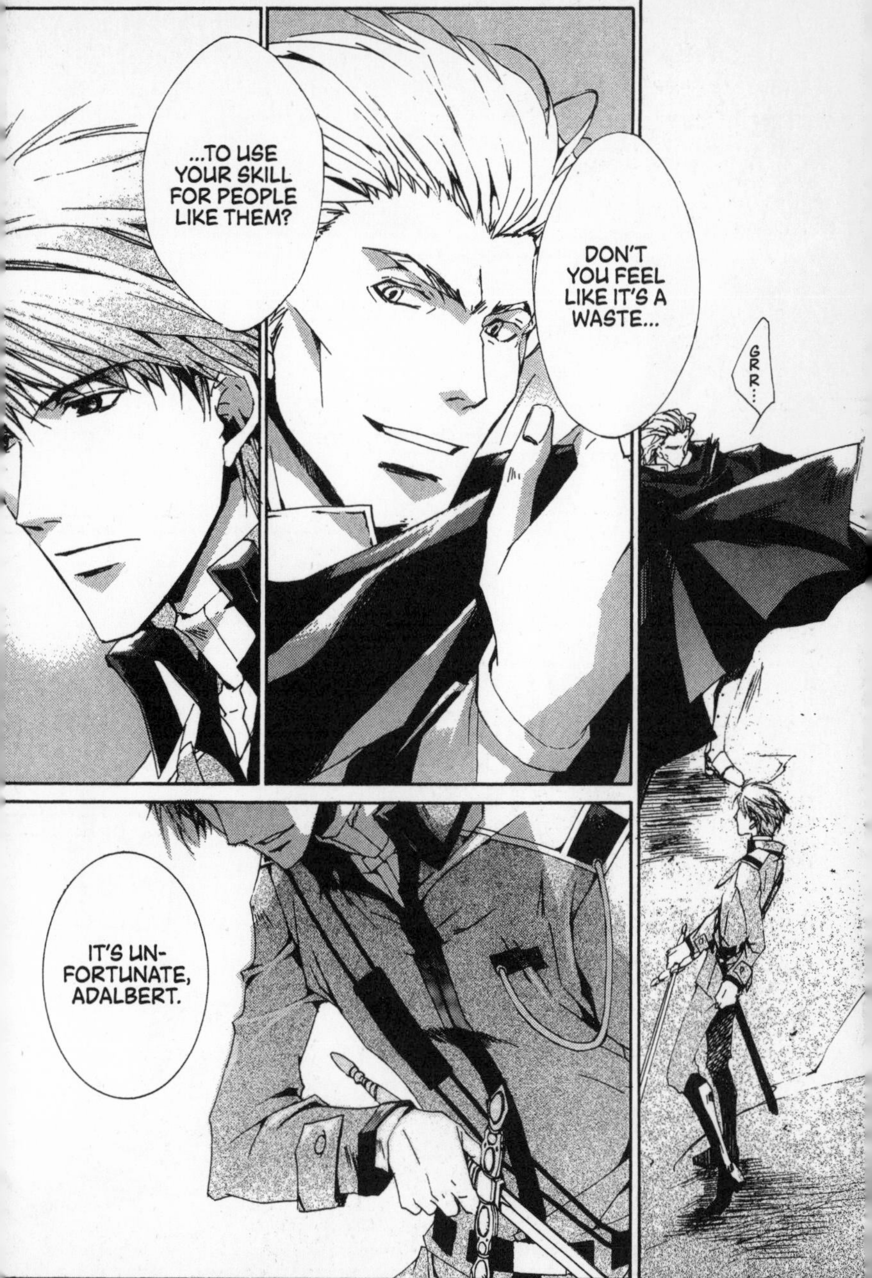
GRR...
DON'T YOU FEEL LIKE IT'S A WASTE...
...TO USE YOUR SKILL FOR PEOPLE LIKE THEM?
IT'S UN-FORTUNATE, ADALBERT.

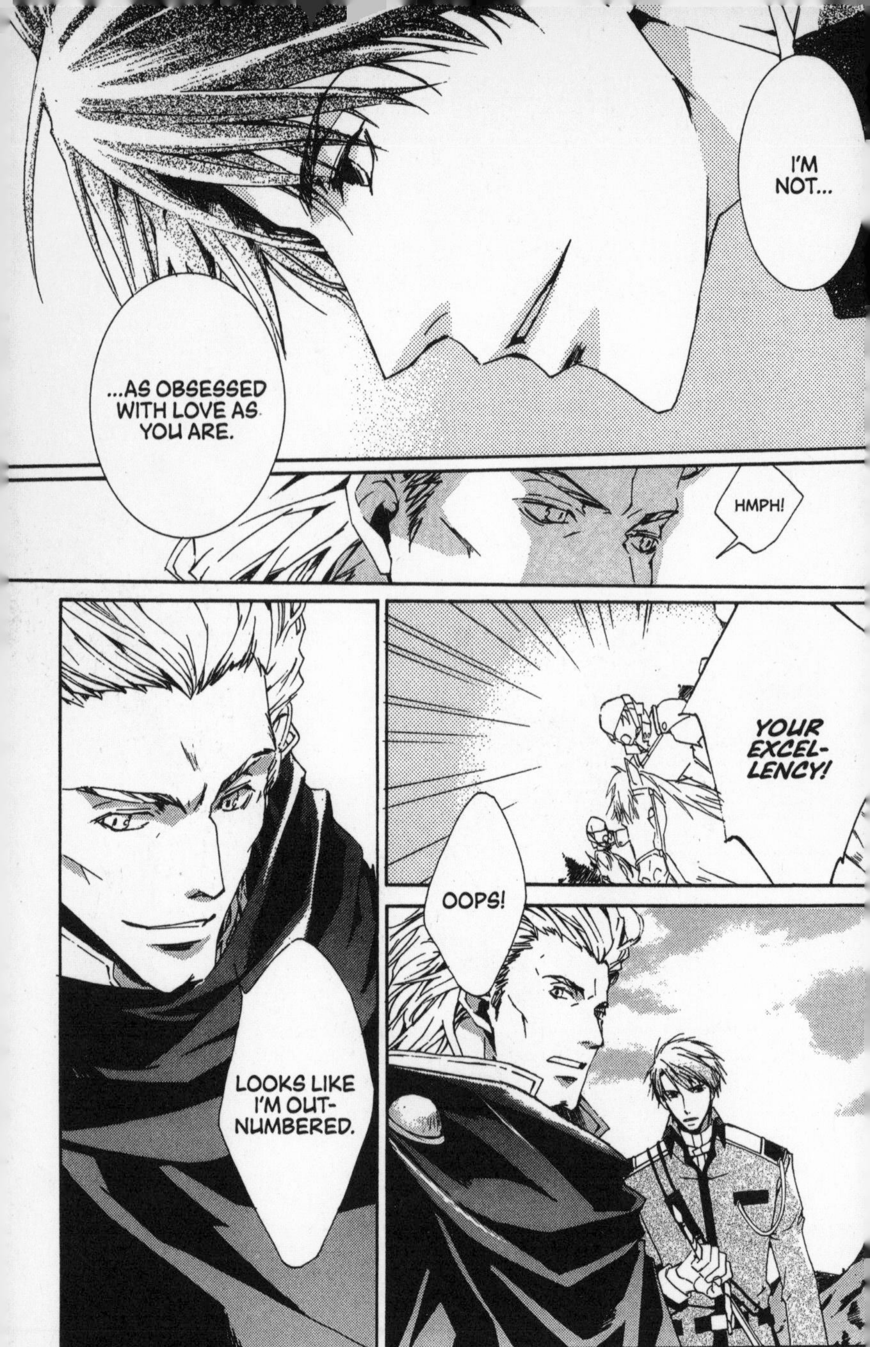
I'M NOT...
...AS OBSESSED WITH LOVE AS YOU ARE.
HMPH!
YOUR EXCEL-LENCY!
OOPS!
LOOKS LIKE I'M OUT-NUMBERED.

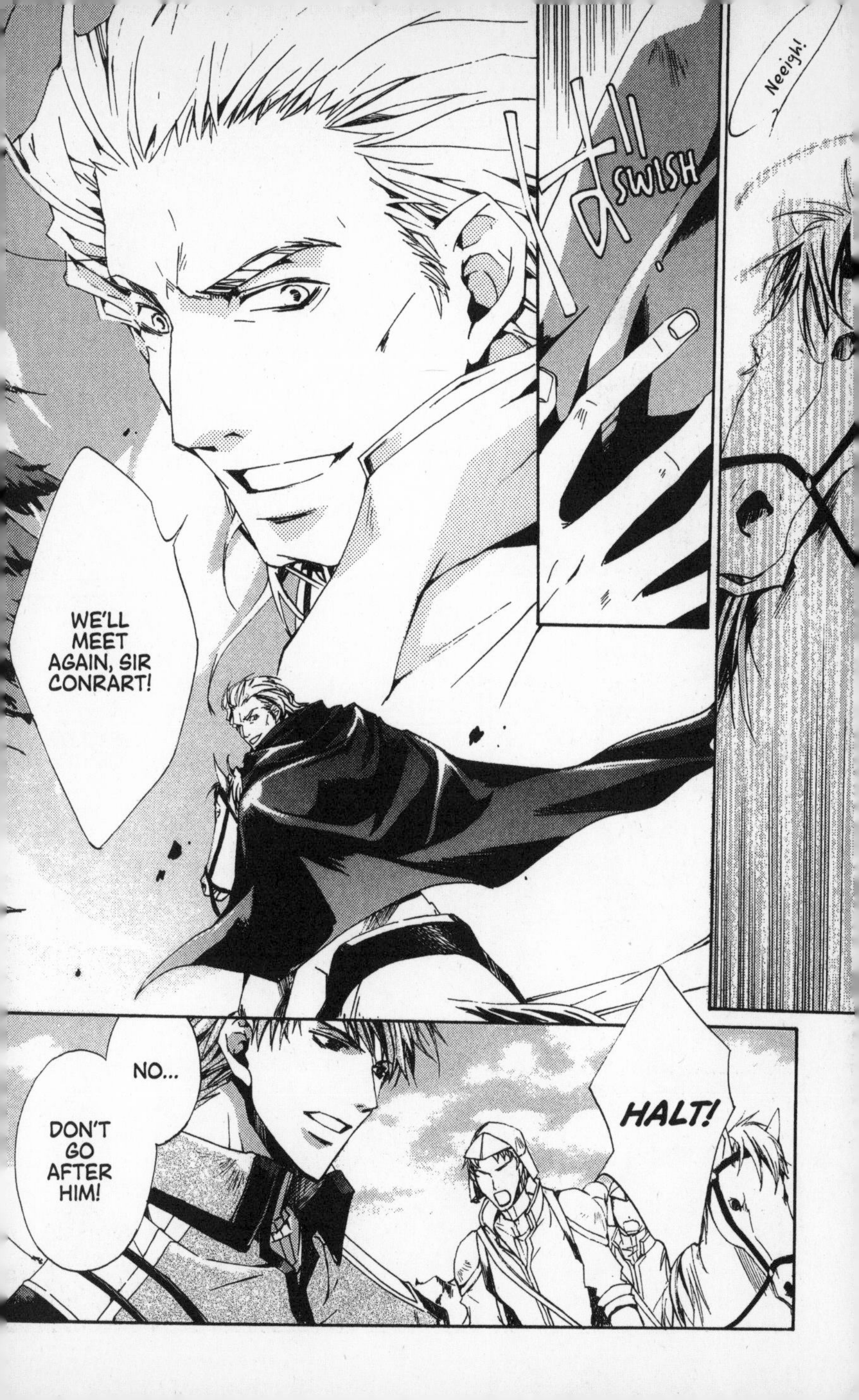
Neeigh!
SWISH
WE'LL MEET AGAIN, SIR CONRART!
HALT!
NO...
DON'T GO AFTER HIM!

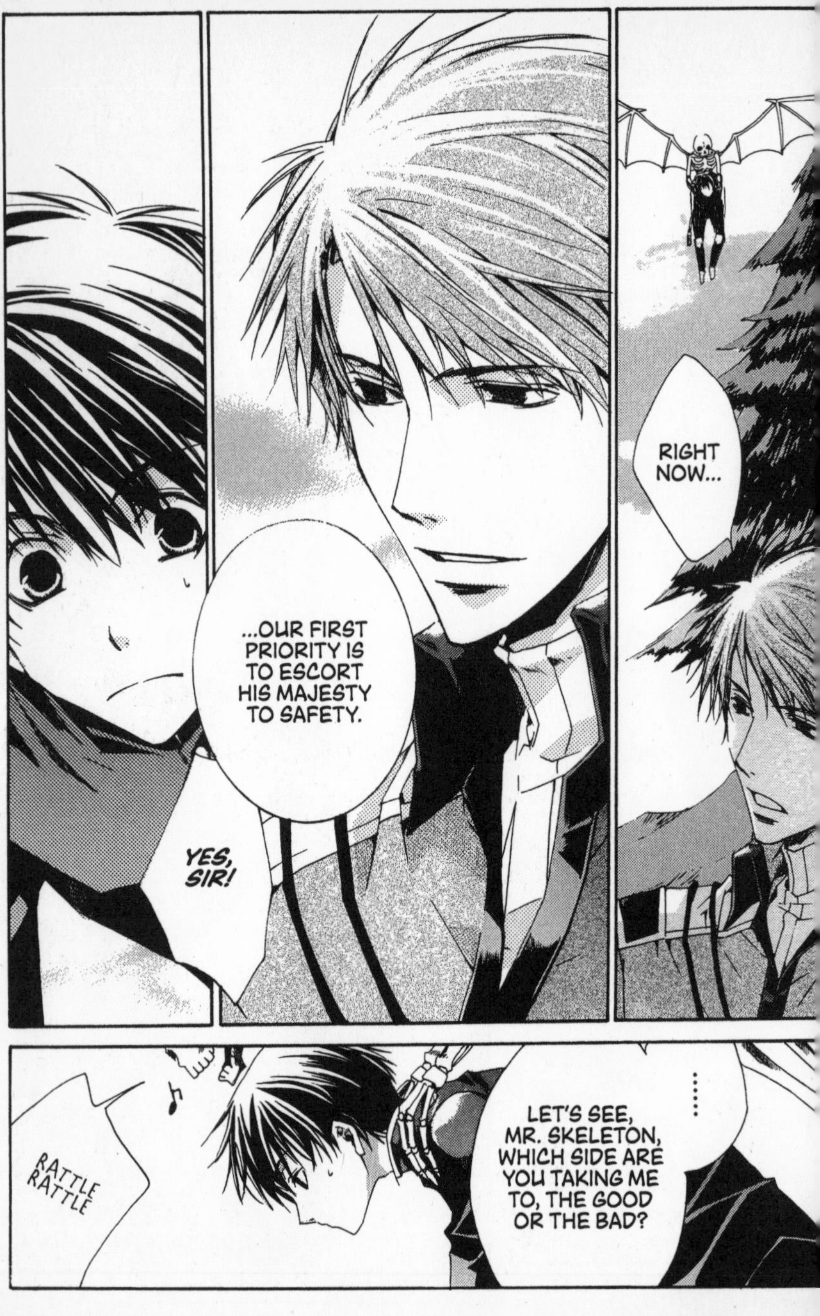
RIGHT NOW...
...OUR FIRST PRIORITY IS TO ESCORT HIS MAJESTY TO SAFETY.
YES, SIR!
......
LET'S SEE, MR. SKELETON, WHICH SIDE ARE YOU TAKING ME TO, THE GOOD OR THE BAD?
RATTLE RATTLE

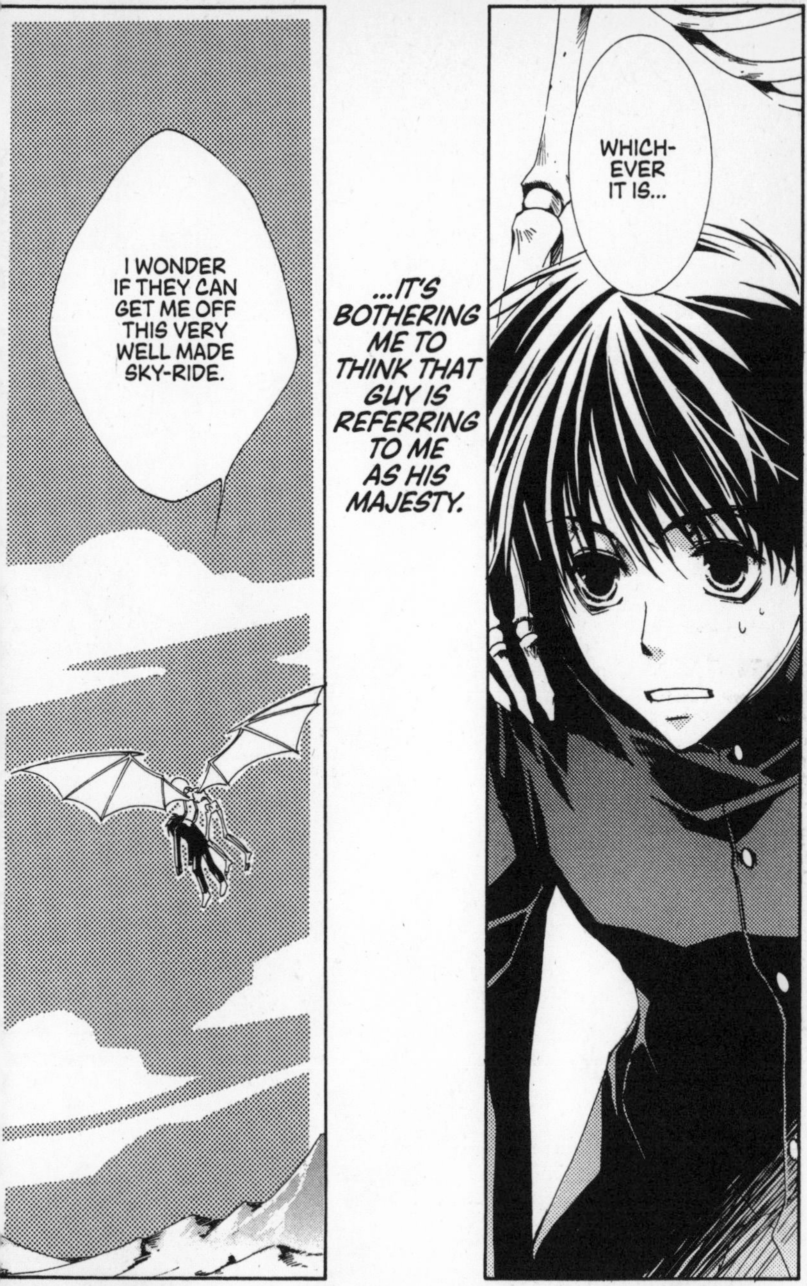
WHICH-EVER IT IS...
...IT'S BOTHERING ME TO THINK THAT GUY IS REFERRING TO ME AS HIS MAJESTY.
I WONDER IF THEY CAN GET ME OFF THIS VERY WELL MADE SKY-RIDE.

hapter 1 * End *

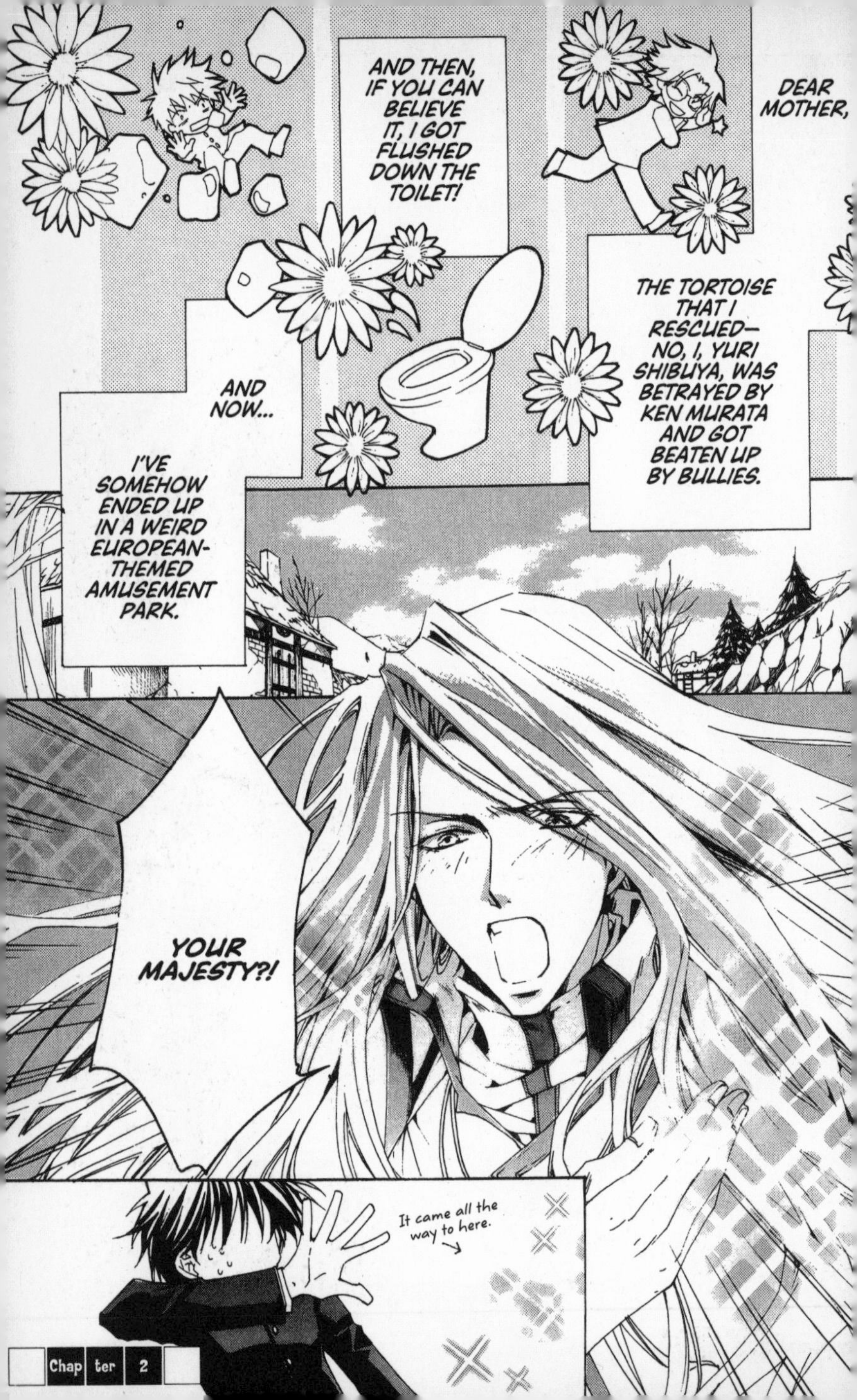
DEAR MOTHER,
THE TORTOISE THAT I RESCUED— NO, I, YURI SHIBUYA, WAS BETRAYED BY KEN MURATA AND GOT BEATEN UP BY BULLIES.
AND THEN, IF YOU CAN BELIEVE IT, I GOT FLUSHED DOWN THE TOILET!
AND NOW...
I'VE SOMEHOW ENDED UP IN A WEIRD EUROPEAN-THEMED AMUSEMENT PARK.
YOUR MAJESTY?!
It came all the way to here.
Chap ter 2

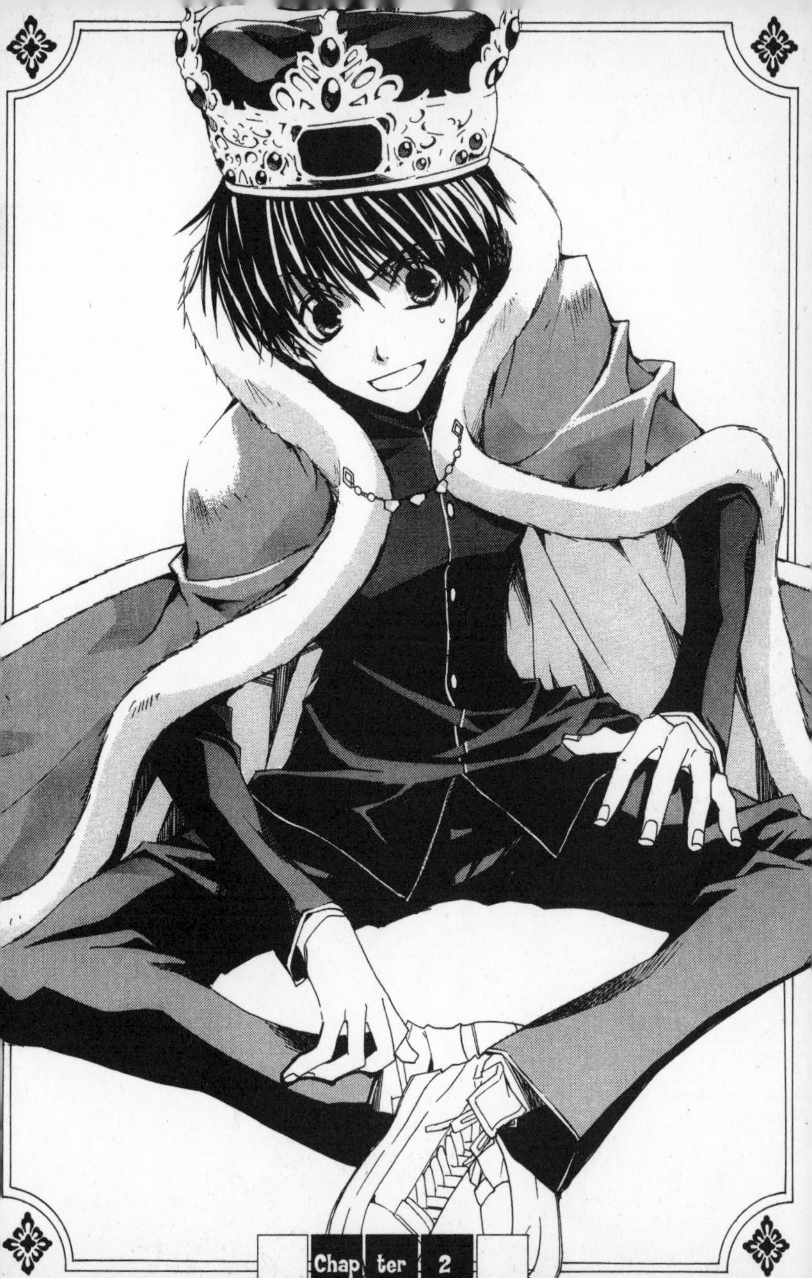

Chapter 2

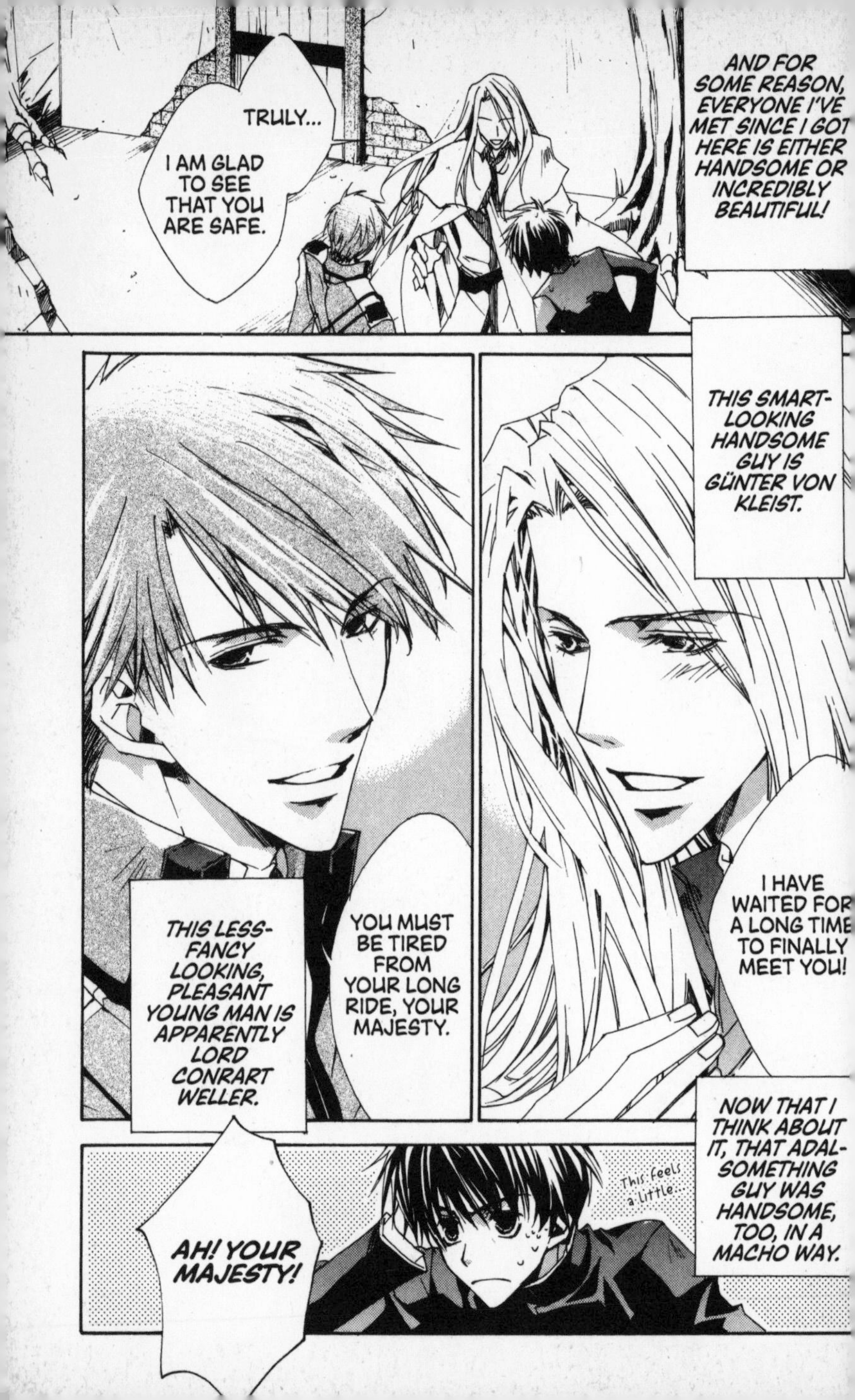
AND FOR SOME REASON, EVERYONE I'VE MET SINCE I GOT HERE IS EITHER HANDSOME OR INCREDIBLY BEAUTIFUL!
TRULY... I AM GLAD TO SEE THAT YOU ARE SAFE.
THIS SMART-LOOKING HANDSOME GUY IS GÜNTER VON KLEIST.
I HAVE WAITED FOR A LONG TIME TO FINALLY MEET YOU!
YOU MUST BE TIRED FROM YOUR LONG RIDE, YOUR MAJESTY.
THIS LESS-FANCY LOOKING, PLEASANT YOUNG MAN IS APPARENTLY LORD CONRART WELLER.
NOW THAT I THINK ABOUT IT, THAT ADAL-SOMETHING GUY WAS HANDSOME, TOO, IN A MACHO WAY.
This feels a little...
AH! YOUR MAJESTY!

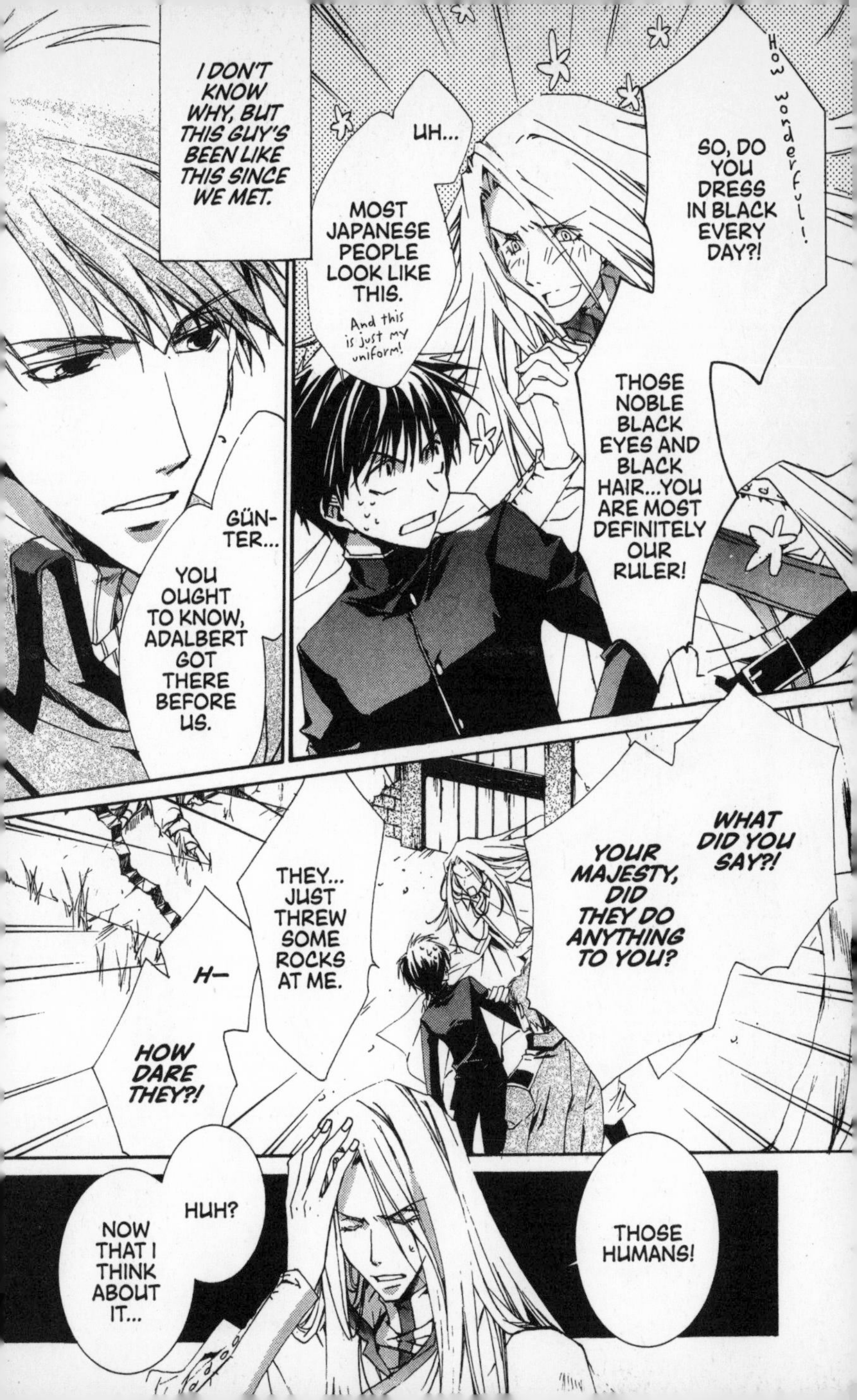
How wonderful!
SO, DO YOU DRESS IN BLACK EVERY DAY?!
THOSE NOBLE BLACK EYES AND BLACK HAIR...YOU ARE MOST DEFINITELY OUR RULER!
UH...
MOST JAPANESE PEOPLE LOOK LIKE THIS.
And this is just my uniform!
I DON'T KNOW WHY, BUT THIS GUY'S BEEN LIKE THIS SINCE WE MET.
GÜNTER...
YOU OUGHT TO KNOW, ADALBERT GOT THERE BEFORE US.
WHAT DID YOU SAY?!
YOUR MAJESTY, DID THEY DO ANYTHING TO YOU?
THEY... JUST THREW SOME ROCKS AT ME.
H—
HOW DARE THEY?!
THOSE HUMANS!
HUH?
NOW THAT I THINK ABOUT IT...

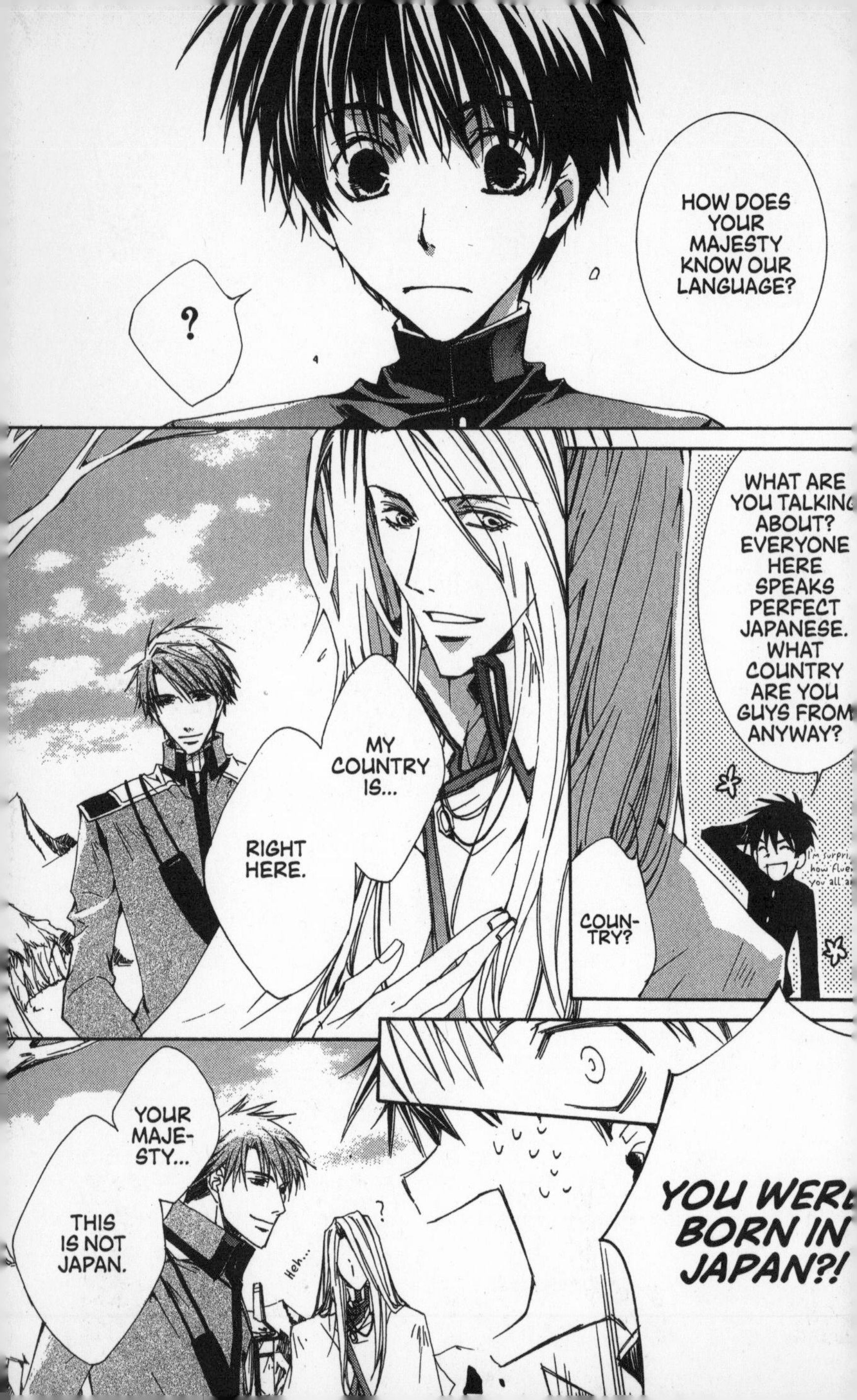
HOW DOES YOUR MAJESTY KNOW OUR LANGUAGE?
?
WHAT ARE YOU TALKING ABOUT? EVERYONE HERE SPEAKS PERFECT JAPANESE. WHAT COUNTRY ARE YOU GUYS FROM ANYWAY?
COUN-TRY?
MY COUNTRY IS...
RIGHT HERE.
YOU WERE BORN IN JAPAN?!
YOUR MAJE-STY...
THIS IS NOT JAPAN.
?
Heh...

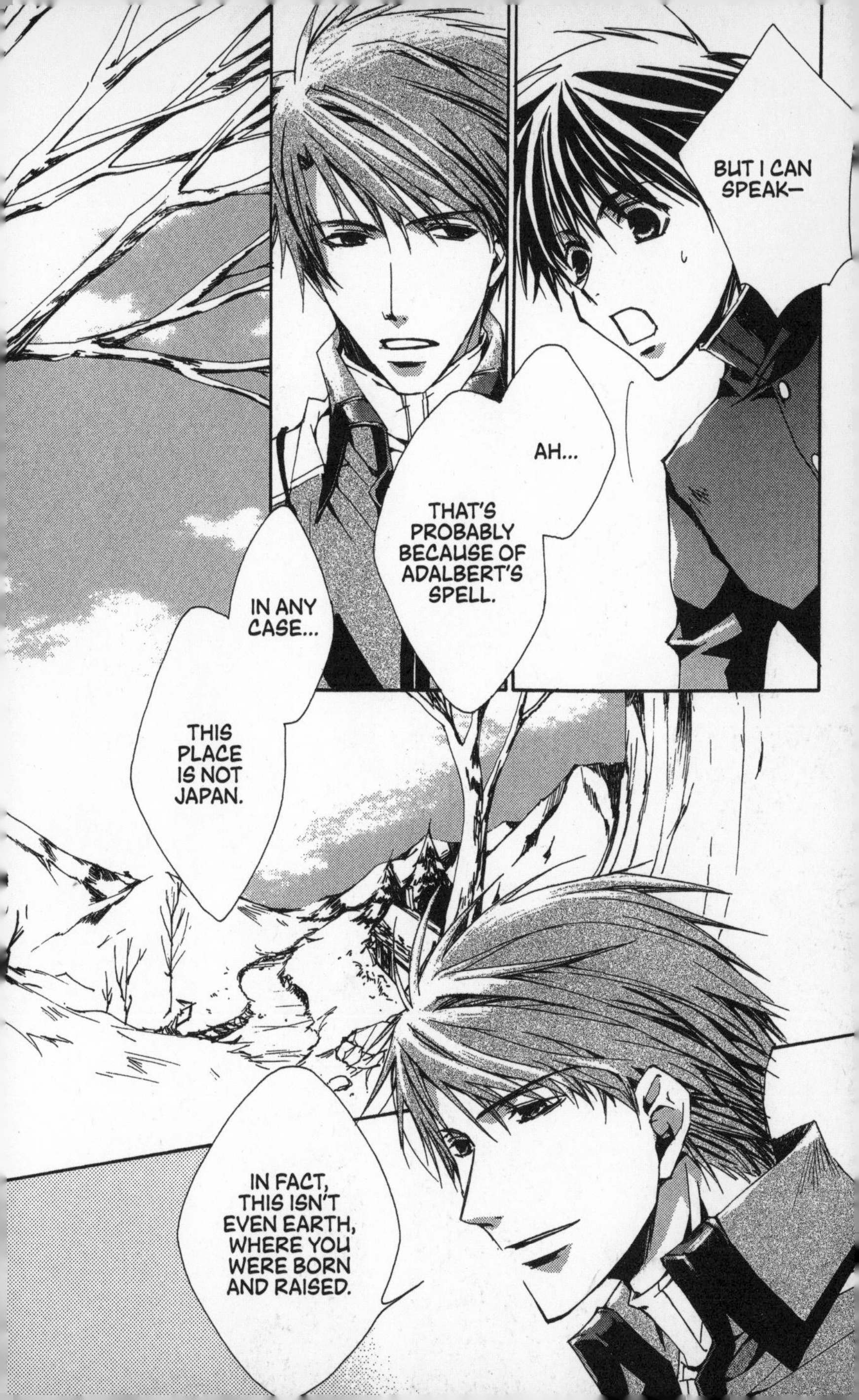
BUT I CAN SPEAK—
AH...
THAT'S PROBABLY BECAUSE OF ADALBERT'S SPELL.
IN ANY CASE...
THIS PLACE IS NOT JAPAN.
IN FACT, THIS ISN'T EVEN EARTH, WHERE YOU WERE BORN AND RAISED.

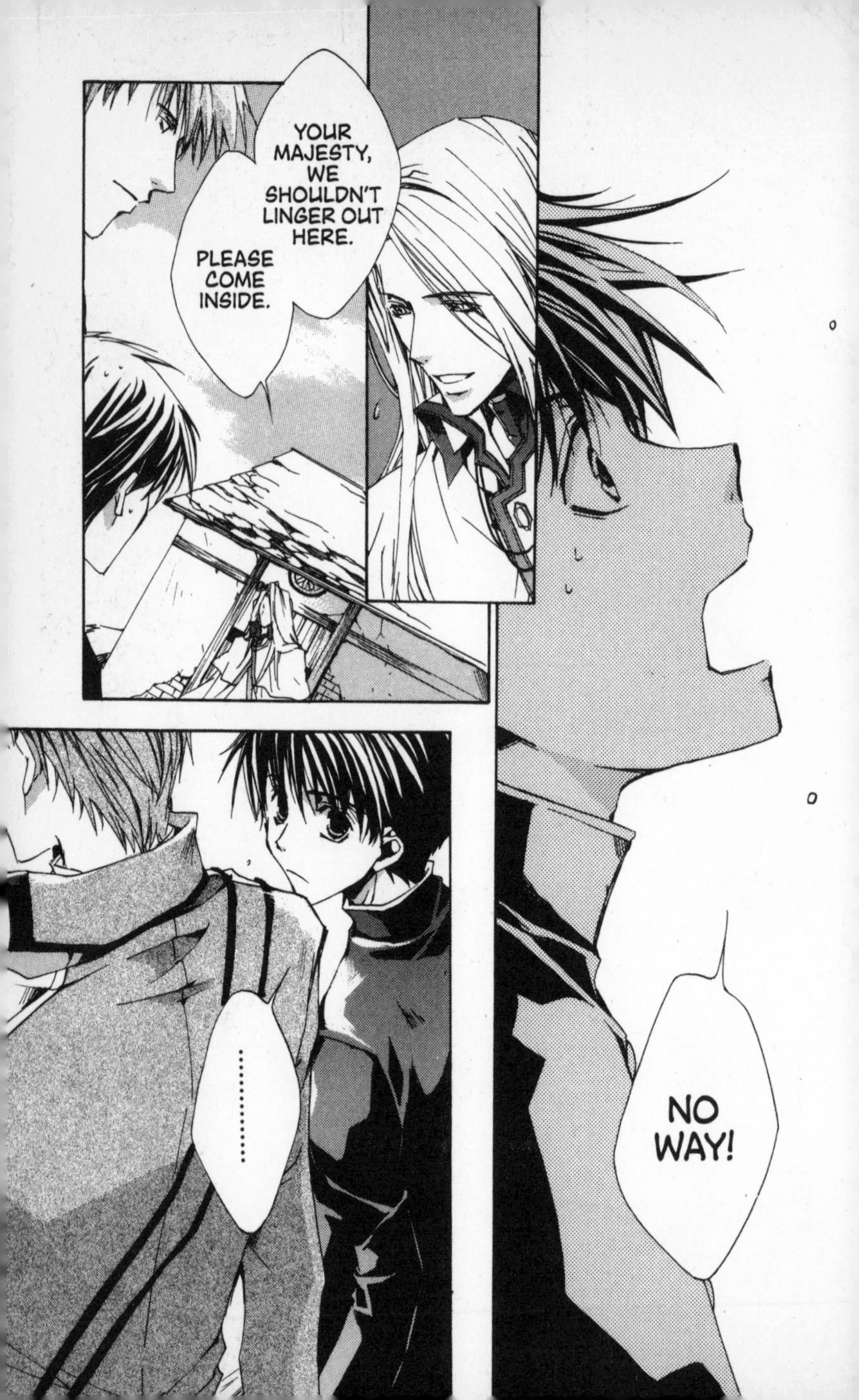
NO WAY!
YOUR MAJESTY, WE SHOULDN'T LINGER OUT HERE.
PLEASE COME INSIDE.
......

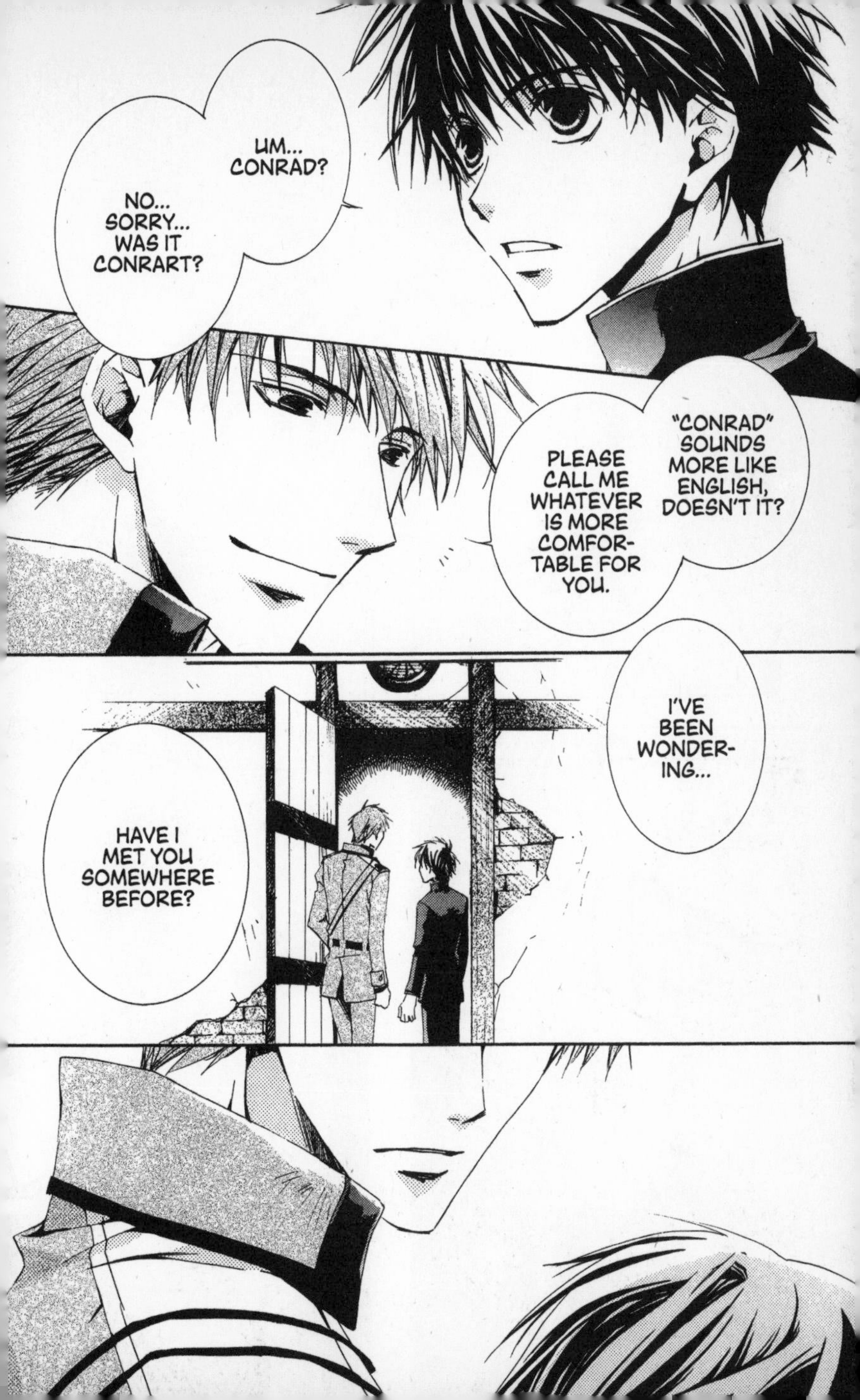
UM... CONRAD?
NO... SORRY... WAS IT CONRART?
"CONRAD" SOUNDS MORE LIKE ENGLISH, DOESN'T IT?
PLEASE CALL ME WHATEVER IS MORE COMFORTABLE FOR YOU.
I'VE BEEN WONDERING...
HAVE I MET YOU SOMEWHERE BEFORE?

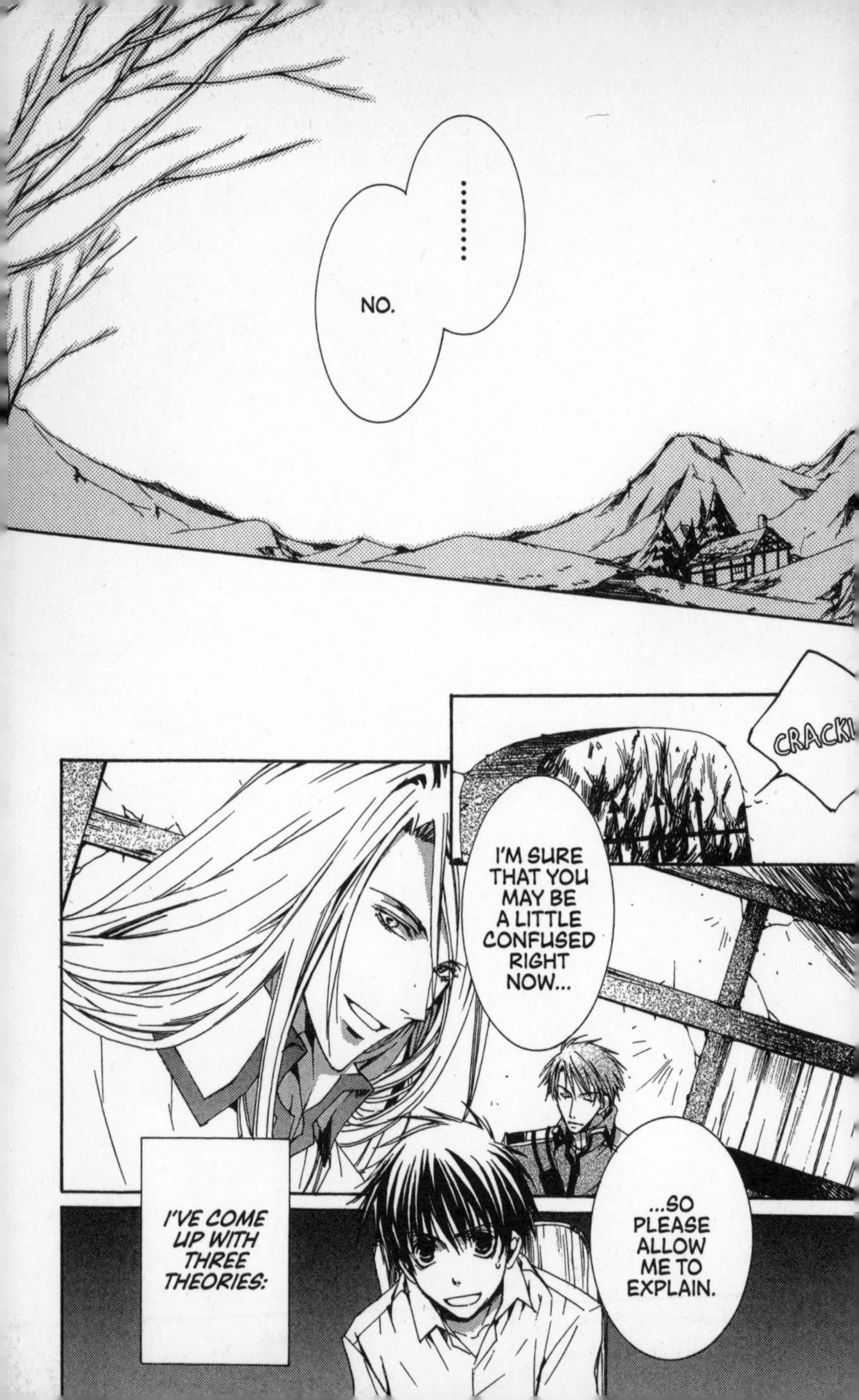
....
NO.
CRACKL
I'M SURE THAT YOU MAY BE A LITTLE CONFUSED RIGHT NOW...
...SO PLEASE ALLOW ME TO EXPLAIN.
I'VE COME UP WITH THREE THEORIES:

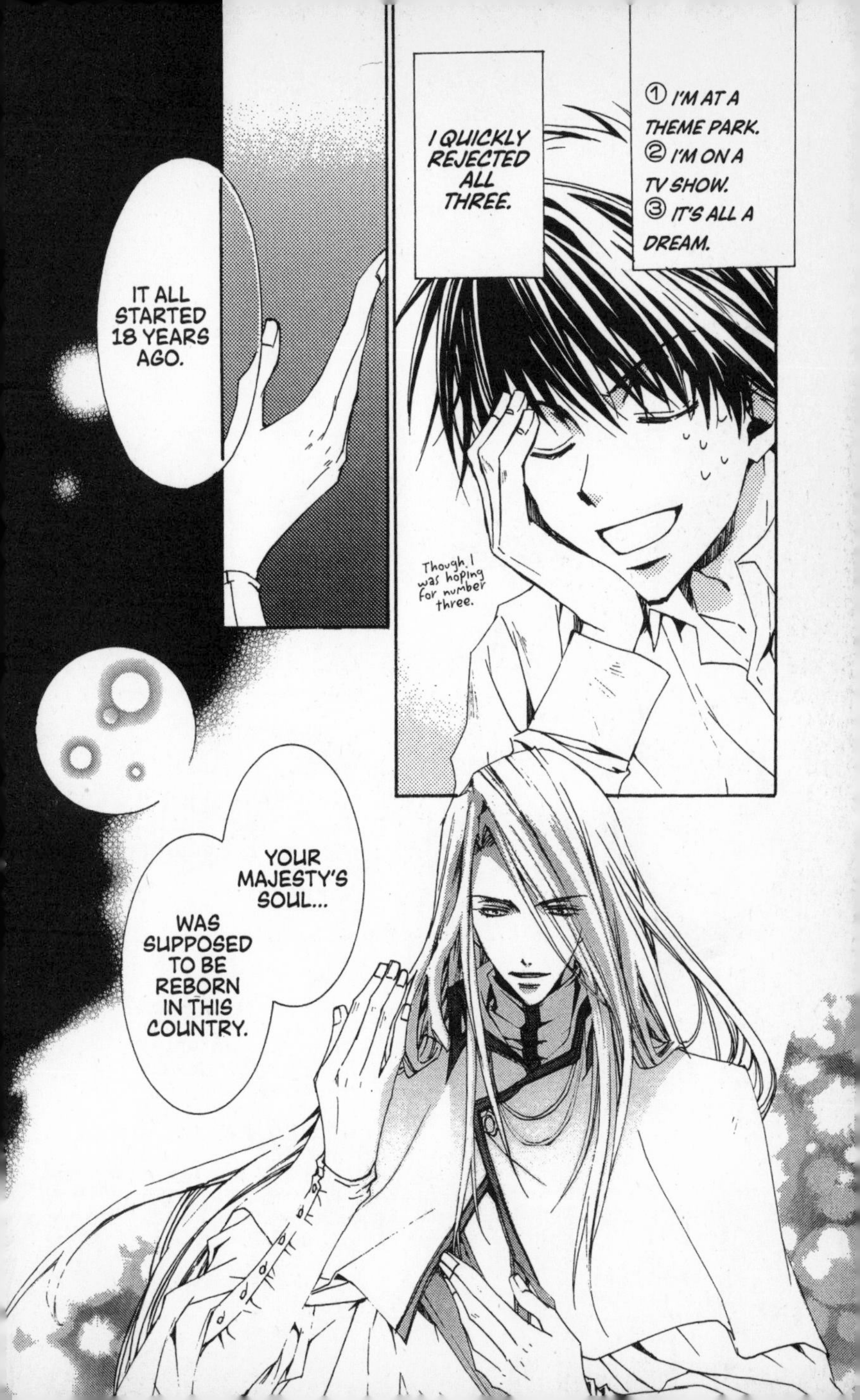

① I'M AT A THEME PARK. ② I'M ON A TV SHOW. ③ IT'S ALL A DREAM.
I QUICKLY REJECTED ALL THREE.
Though I was hoping for number three.
IT ALL STARTED 18 YEARS AGO.
YOUR MAJESTY'S SOUL...
WAS SUPPOSED TO BE REBORN IN THIS COUNTRY.

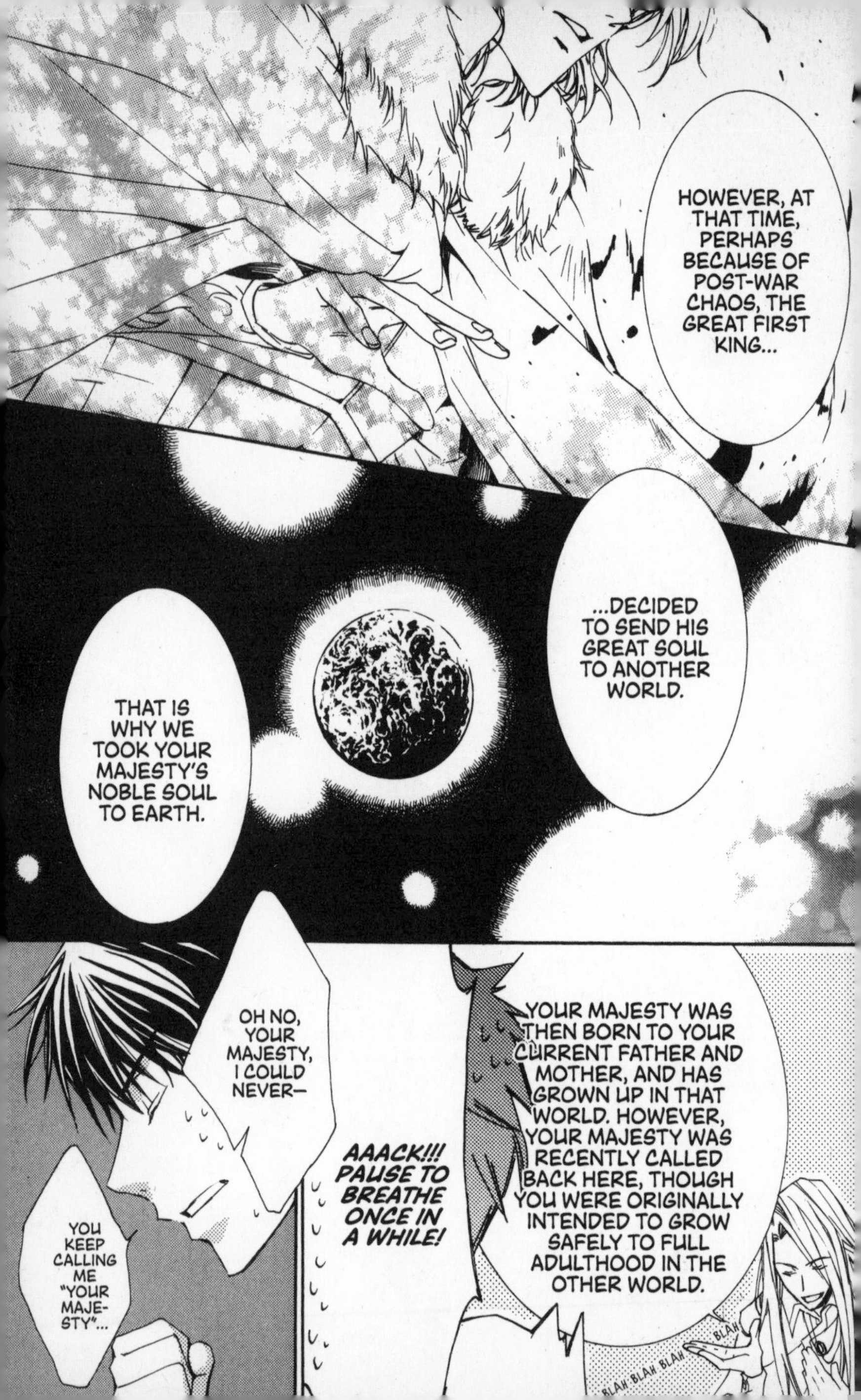
HOWEVER, AT THAT TIME, PERHAPS BECAUSE OF POST-WAR CHAOS, THE GREAT FIRST KING...
...DECIDED TO SEND HIS GREAT SOUL TO ANOTHER WORLD.
THAT IS WHY WE TOOK YOUR MAJESTY'S NOBLE SOUL TO EARTH.
YOUR MAJESTY WAS THEN BORN TO YOUR CURRENT FATHER AND MOTHER, AND HAS GROWN UP IN THAT WORLD. HOWEVER, YOUR MAJESTY WAS RECENTLY CALLED BACK HERE, THOUGH YOU WERE ORIGINALLY INTENDED TO GROW SAFELY TO FULL ADULTHOOD IN THE OTHER WORLD.
BLAH BLAH BLAH BLAH
AAACK!!! PAUSE TO BREATHE ONCE IN A WHILE!
OH NO, YOUR MAJESTY, I COULD NEVER—
YOU KEEP CALLING ME "YOUR MAJE-STY"...

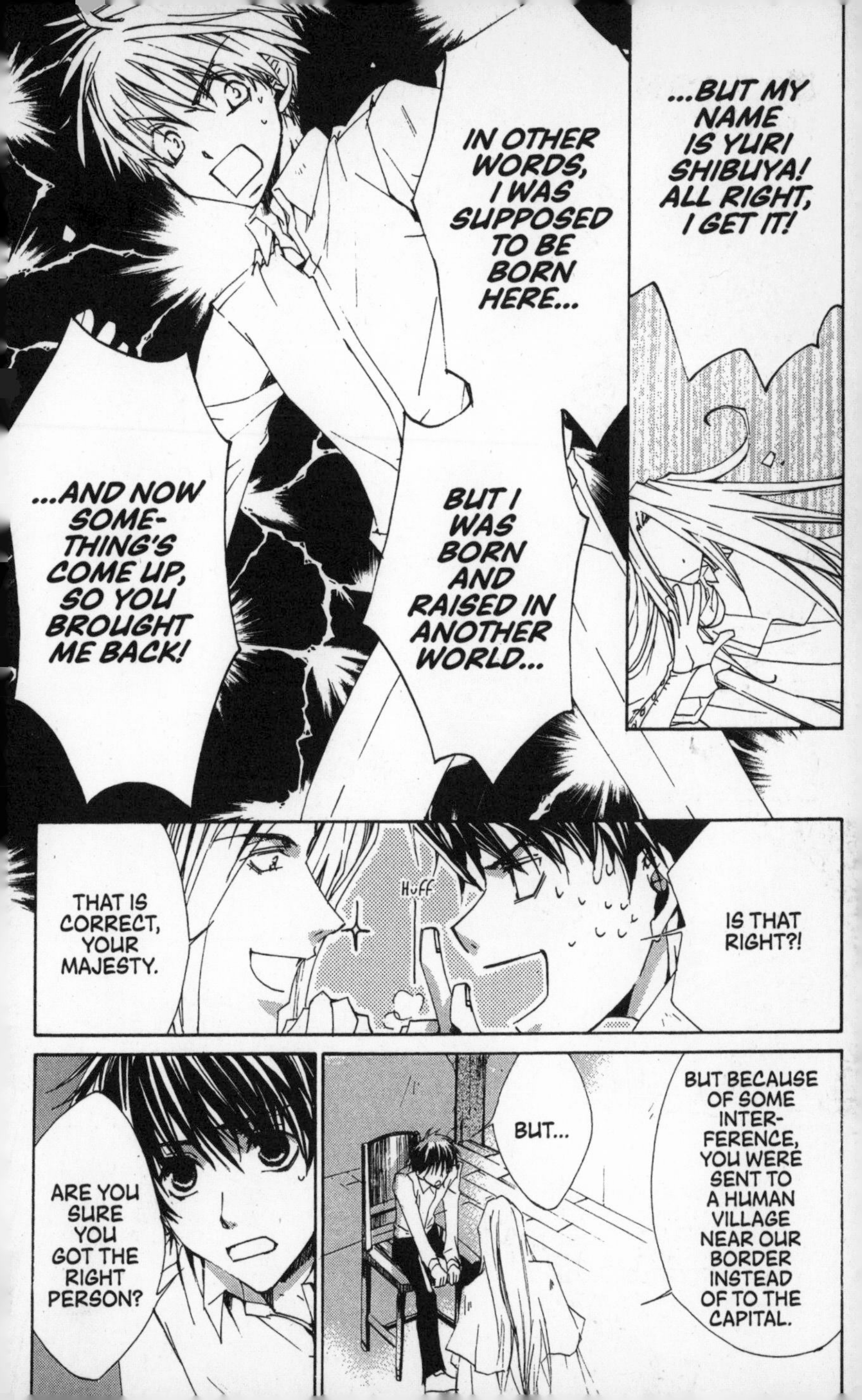
...BUT MY NAME IS YURI SHIBUYA! ALL RIGHT, I GET IT!
IN OTHER WORDS, I WAS SUPPOSED TO BE BORN HERE...
BUT I WAS BORN AND RAISED IN ANOTHER WORLD...
...AND NOW SOMETHING'S COME UP, SO YOU BROUGHT ME BACK!
IS THAT RIGHT?!
HUFF
THAT IS CORRECT, YOUR MAJESTY.
BUT BECAUSE OF SOME INTERFERENCE, YOU WERE SENT TO A HUMAN VILLAGE NEAR OUR BORDER INSTEAD OF TO THE CAPITAL.
BUT...
ARE YOU SURE YOU GOT THE RIGHT PERSON?

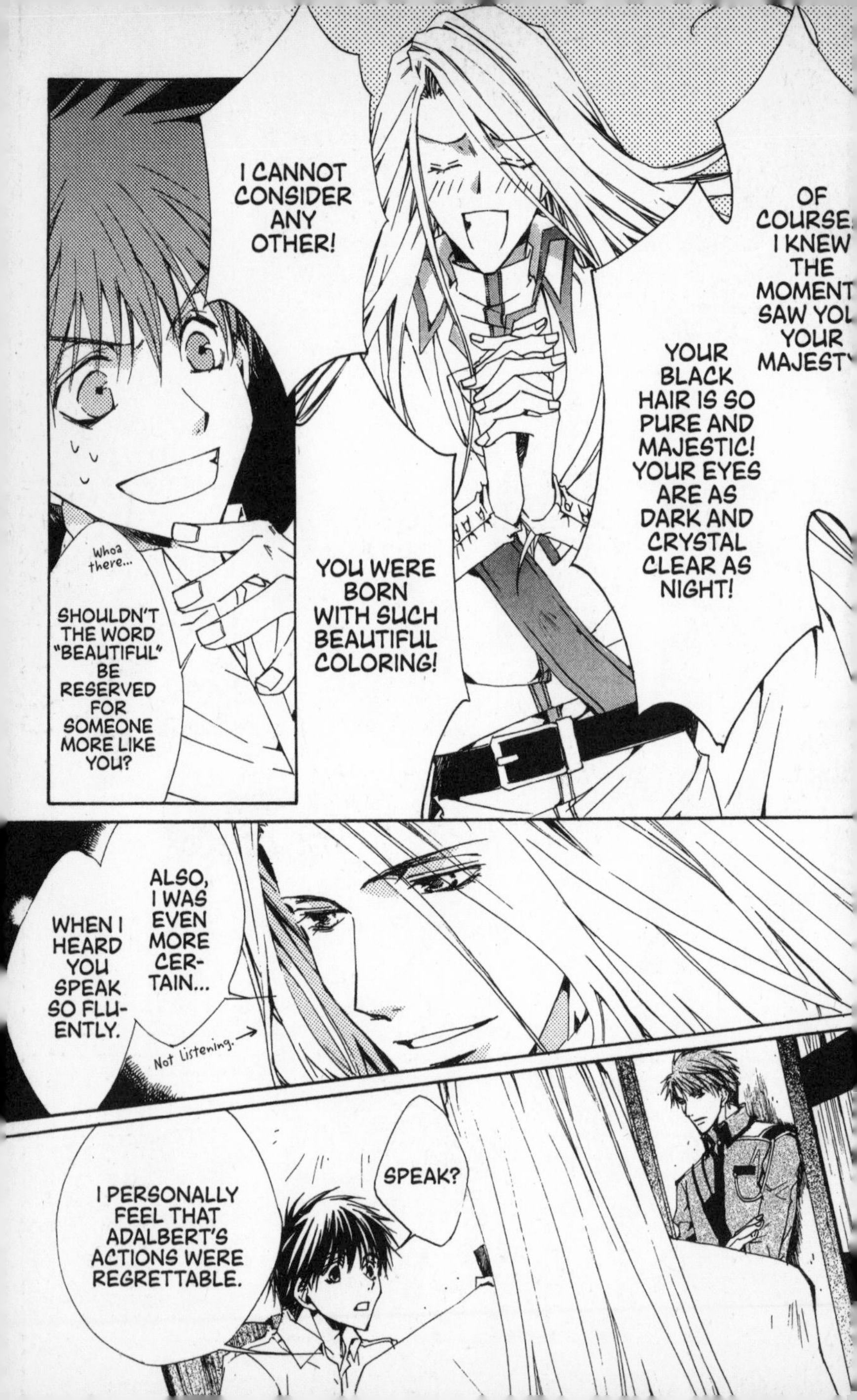
OF COURSE. I KNEW THE MOMENT SAW YOU YOUR MAJESTY
YOUR BLACK HAIR IS SO PURE AND MAJESTIC! YOUR EYES ARE AS DARK AND CRYSTAL CLEAR AS NIGHT!
I CANNOT CONSIDER ANY OTHER!
YOU WERE BORN WITH SUCH BEAUTIFUL COLORING!
Whoa there...
SHOULDN'T THE WORD "BEAUTIFUL" BE RESERVED FOR SOMEONE MORE LIKE YOU?
ALSO, I WAS EVEN MORE CER-TAIN...
WHEN I HEARD YOU SPEAK SO FLU-ENTLY.
Not listening.
SPEAK?
I PERSONALLY FEEL THAT ADALBERT'S ACTIONS WERE REGRETTABLE.

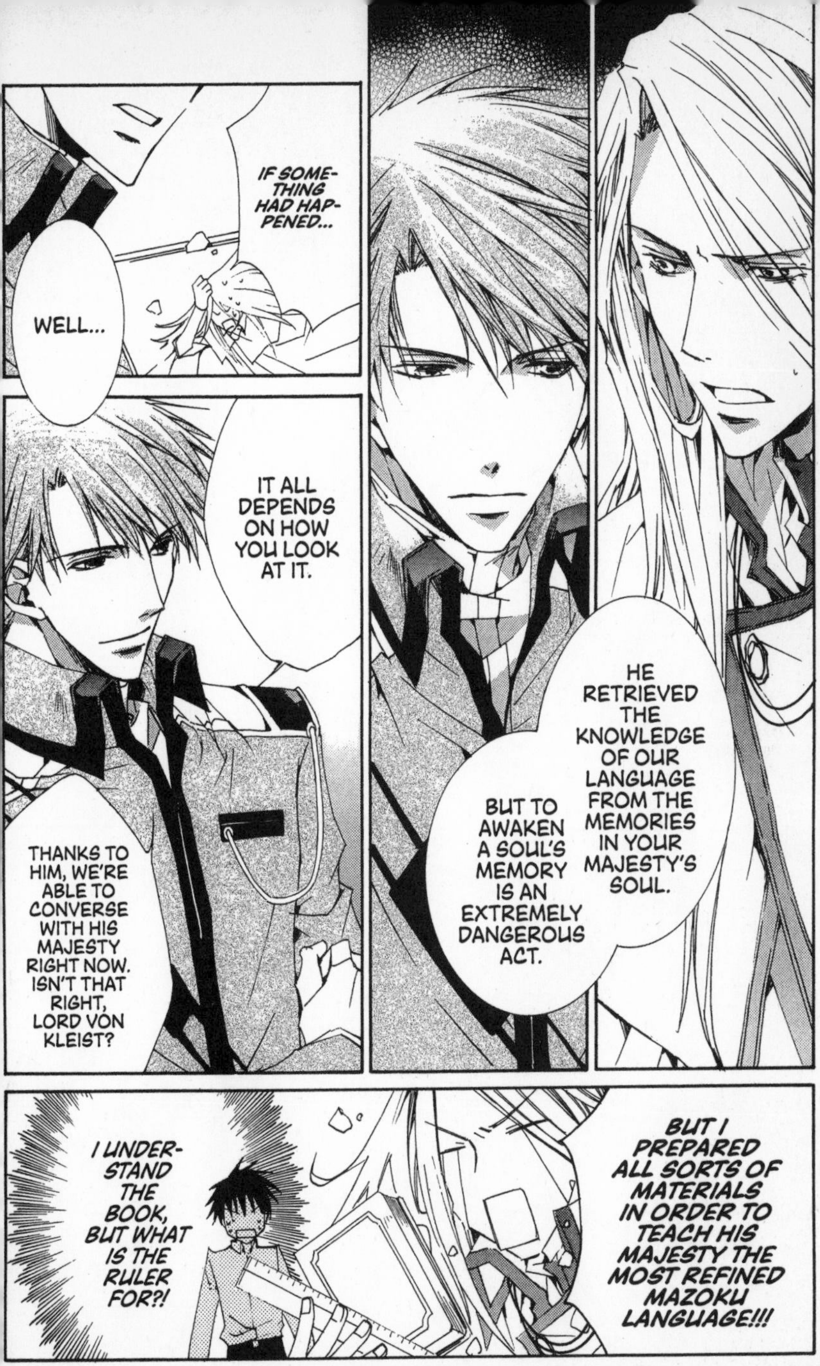
HE RETRIEVED THE KNOWLEDGE OF OUR LANGUAGE FROM THE MEMORIES IN YOUR MAJESTY'S SOUL.
BUT TO AWAKEN A SOUL'S MEMORY IS AN EXTREMELY DANGEROUS ACT.
IF SOME-THING HAD HAP-PENED...
WELL...
IT ALL DEPENDS ON HOW YOU LOOK AT IT.
THANKS TO HIM, WE'RE ABLE TO CONVERSE WITH HIS MAJESTY RIGHT NOW. ISN'T THAT RIGHT, LORD VON KLEIST?
BUT I PREPARED ALL SORTS OF MATERIALS IN ORDER TO TEACH HIS MAJESTY THE MOST REFINED MAZOKU LANGUAGE!!!
I UNDER-STAND THE BOOK, BUT WHAT IS THE RULER FOR?!

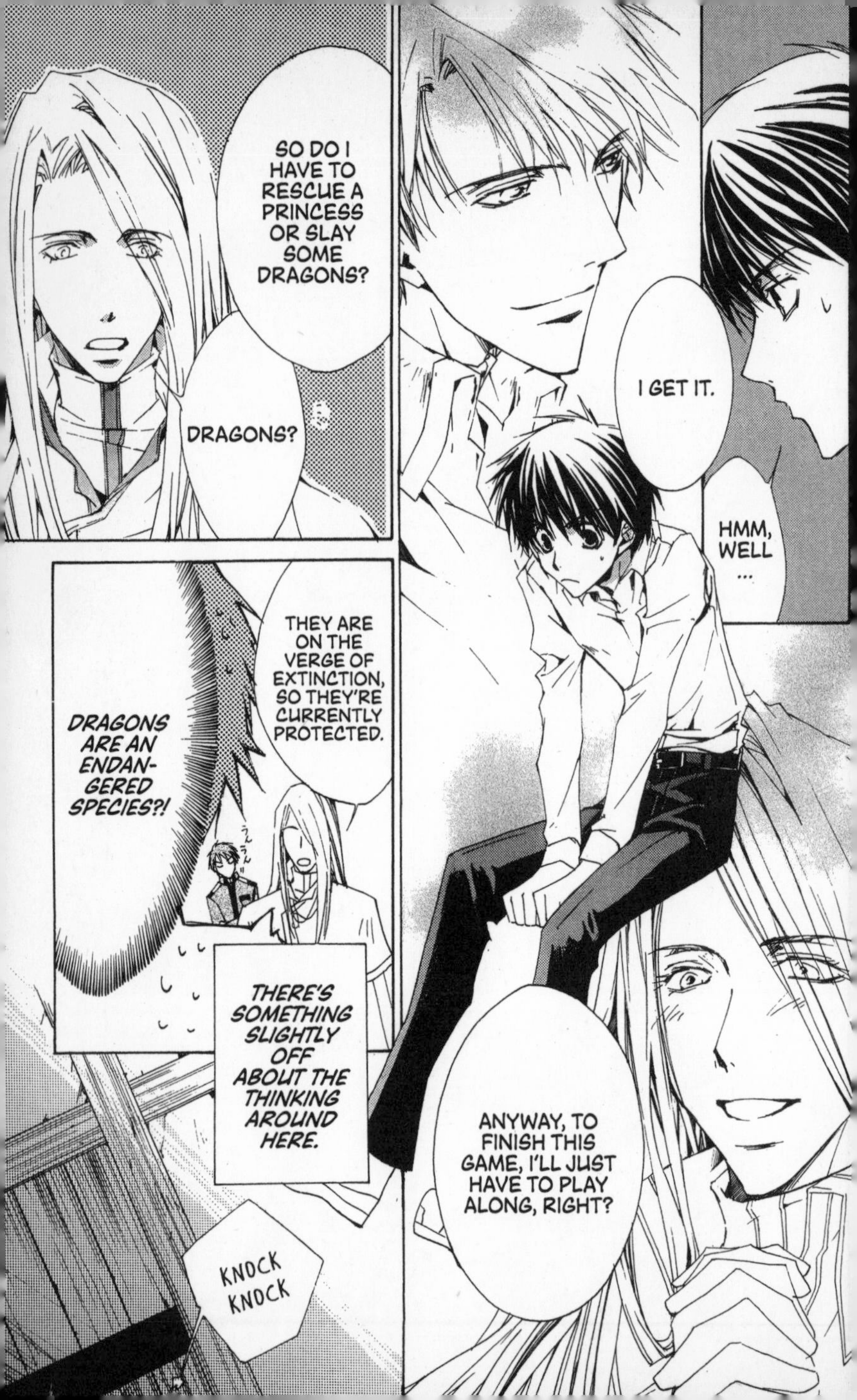
SO DO I HAVE TO RESCUE A PRINCESS OR SLAY SOME DRAGONS?
DRAGONS?
THEY ARE ON THE VERGE OF EXTINCTION, SO THEY'RE CURRENTLY PROTECTED.
DRAGONS ARE AN ENDAN-GERED SPECIES?!
THERE'S SOMETHING SLIGHTLY OFF ABOUT THE THINKING AROUND HERE.
I GET IT.
HMM, WELL ...
ANYWAY, TO FINISH THIS GAME, I'LL JUST HAVE TO PLAY ALONG, RIGHT?
KNOCK KNOCK

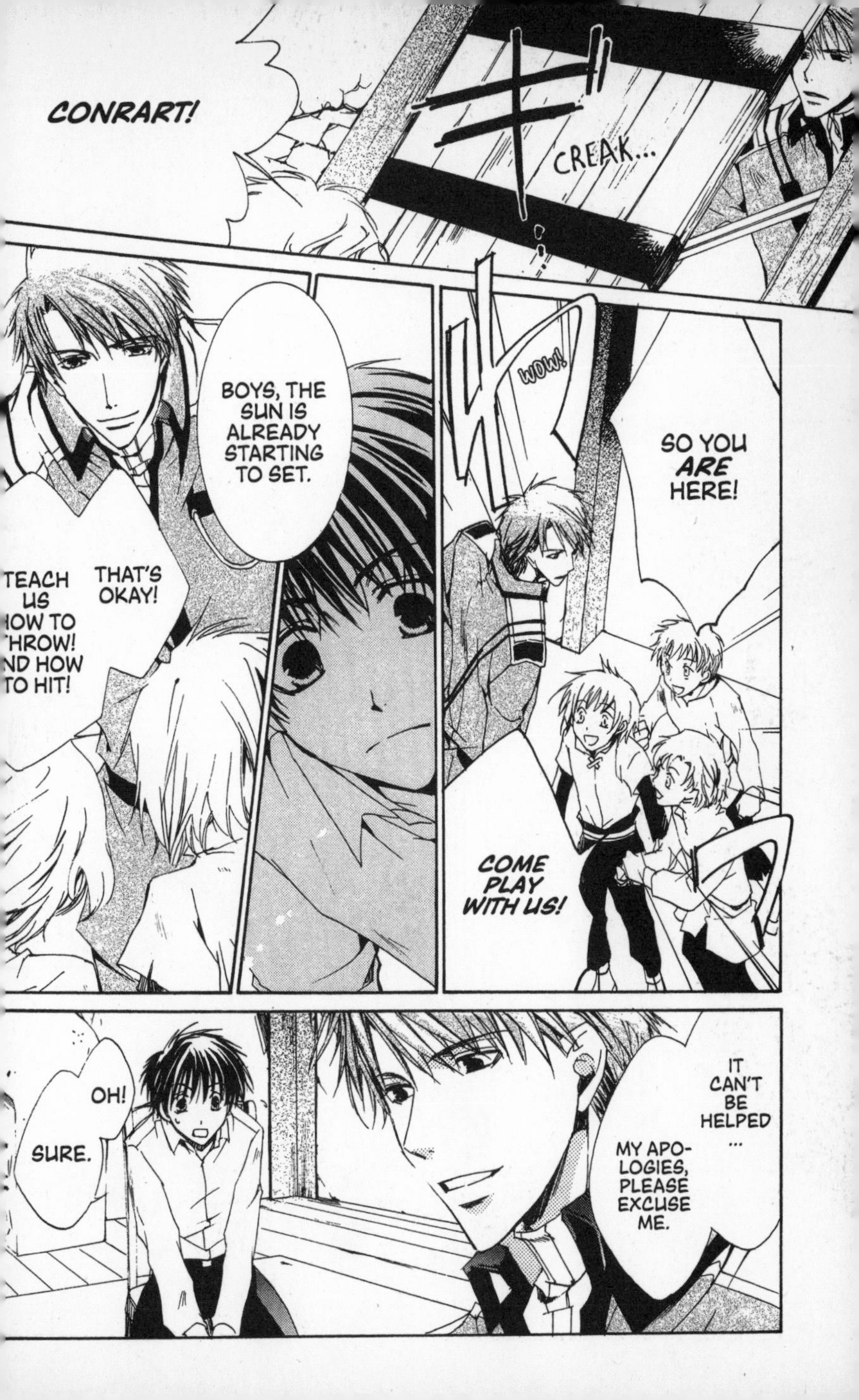
CREAK...
CONRART!
WOW!
SO YOU ARE HERE!
COME PLAY WITH US!
BOYS, THE SUN IS ALREADY STARTING TO SET.
THAT'S OKAY!
TEACH US HOW TO THROW! ND HOW TO HIT!
IT CAN'T BE HELPED...
MY APOLOGIES, PLEASE EXCUSE ME.
OH!
SURE.

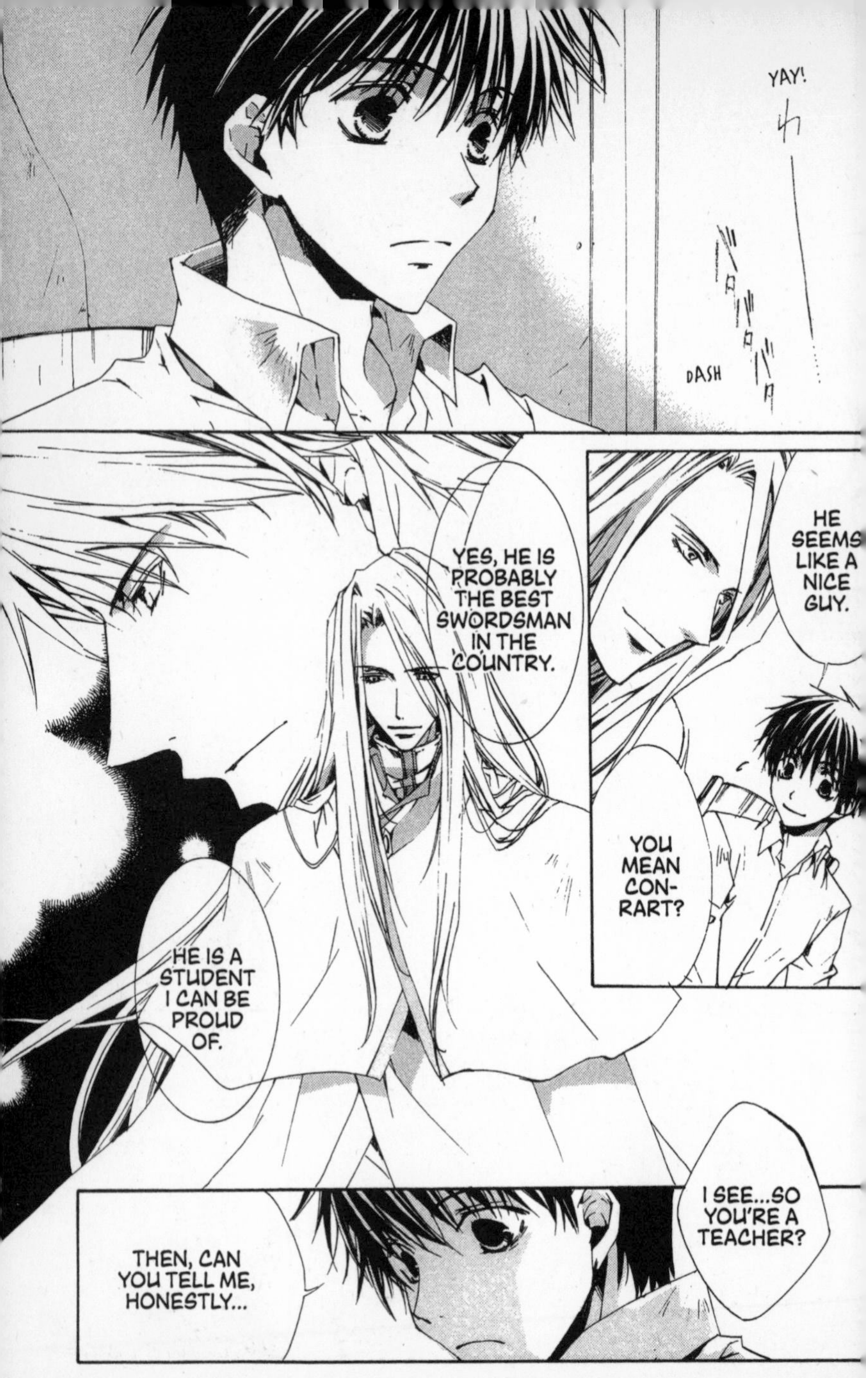
YAY!
DASH
HE SEEMS LIKE A NICE GUY.
YOU MEAN CON-RART?
YES, HE IS PROBABLY THE BEST SWORDSMAN IN THE COUNTRY.
HE IS A STUDENT I CAN BE PROUD OF.
I SEE...SO YOU'RE A TEACHER?
THEN, CAN YOU TELL ME, HONESTLY...

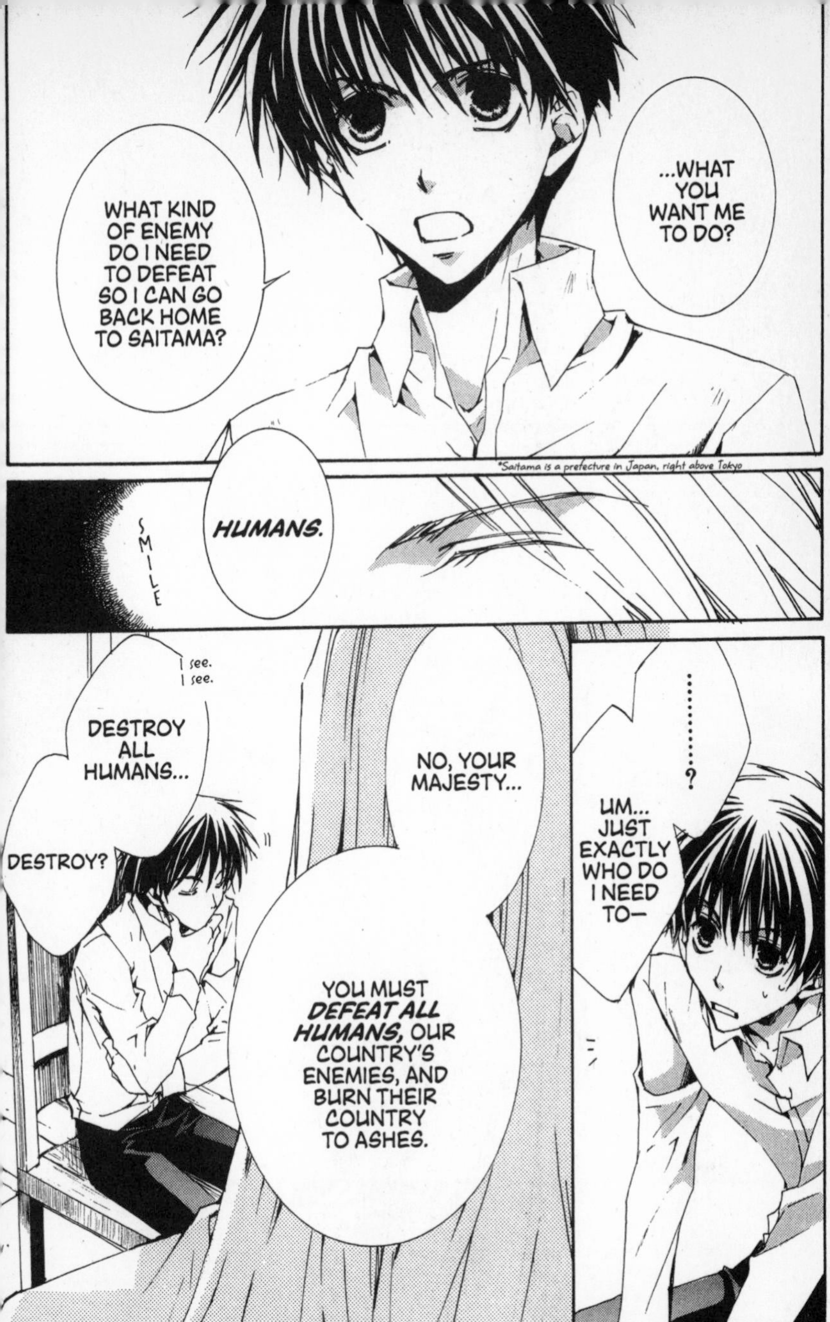
...WHAT YOU WANT ME TO DO?
WHAT KIND OF ENEMY DO I NEED TO DEFEAT SO I CAN GO BACK HOME TO SAITAMA?
*Saitama is a prefecture in Japan, right above Tokyo
HUMANS.
SMILE
.........?
UM... JUST EXACTLY WHO DO I NEED TO—
NO, YOUR MAJESTY...
YOU MUST DEFEAT ALL HUMANS, OUR COUNTRY'S ENEMIES, AND BURN THEIR COUNTRY TO ASHES.
I see. I see.
DESTROY ALL HUMANS...
DESTROY?

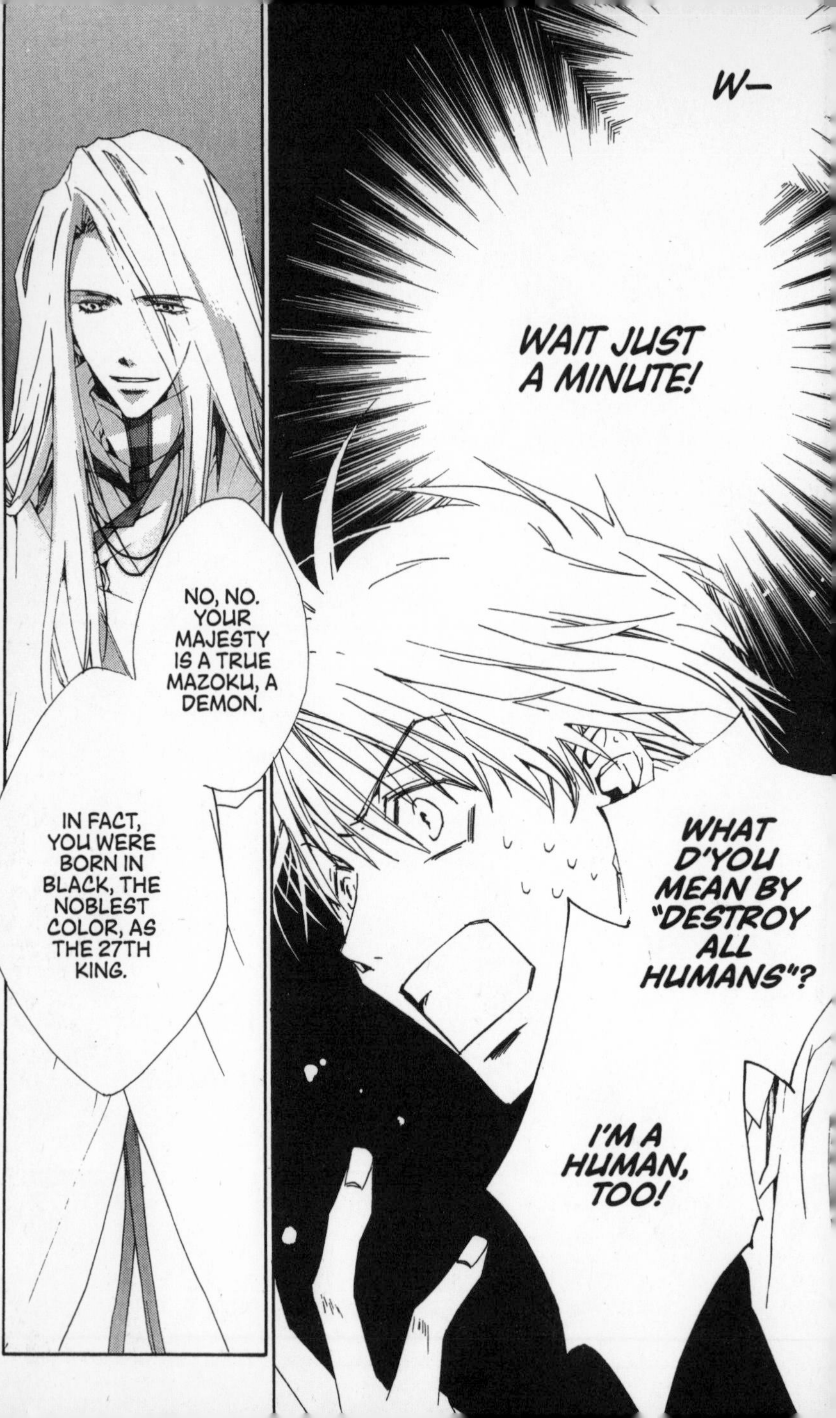
W—
WAIT JUST A MINUTE!
WHAT D'YOU MEAN BY "DESTROY ALL HUMANS"?
I'M A HUMAN, TOO!
NO, NO. YOUR MAJESTY IS A TRUE MAZOKU, A DEMON.
IN FACT, YOU WERE BORN IN BLACK, THE NOBLEST COLOR, AS THE 27TH KING.

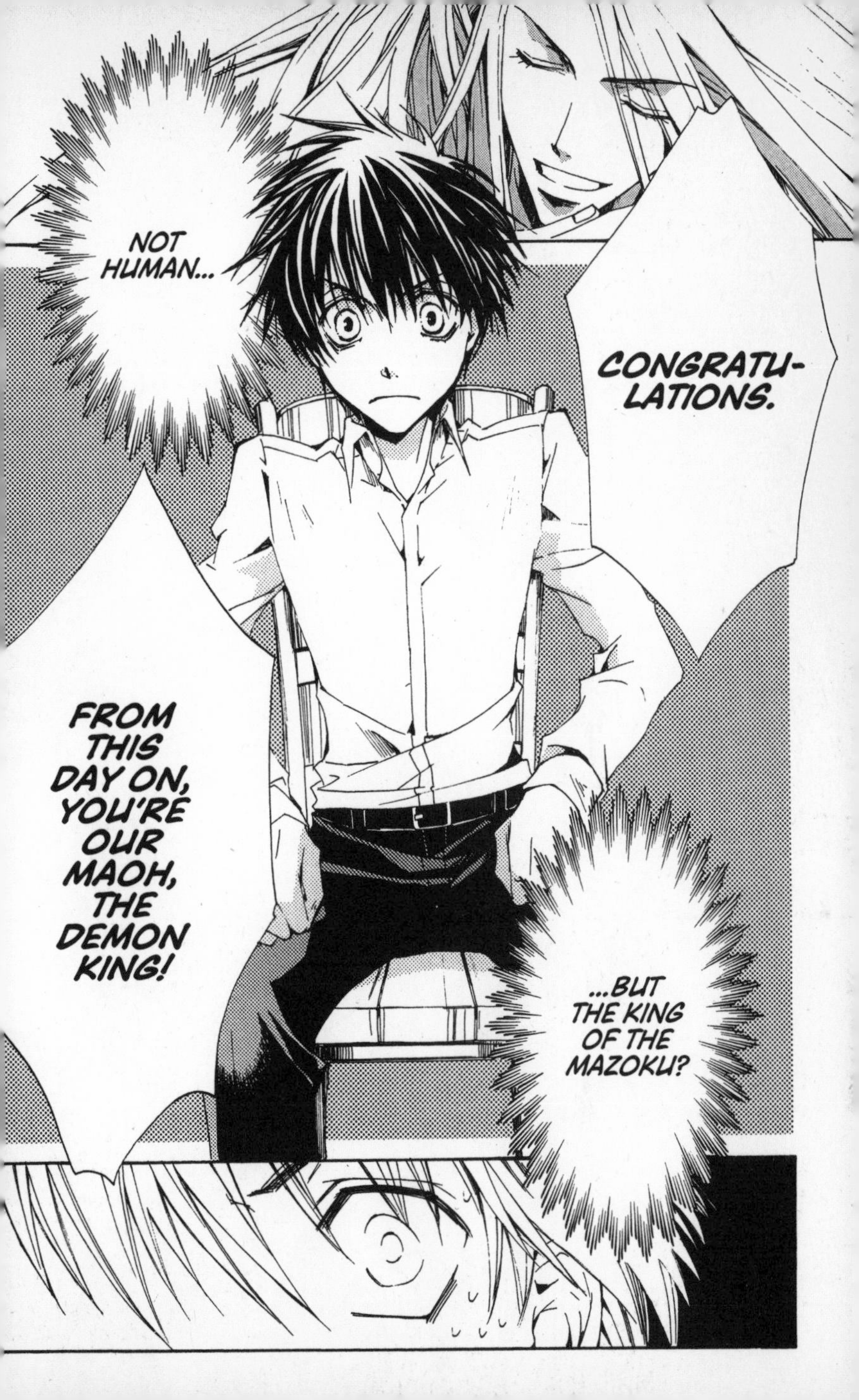
CONGRATULATIONS.
FROM THIS DAY ON, YOU'RE OUR MAOH, THE DEMON KING!
NOT HUMAN...
...BUT THE KING OF THE MAZOKU?

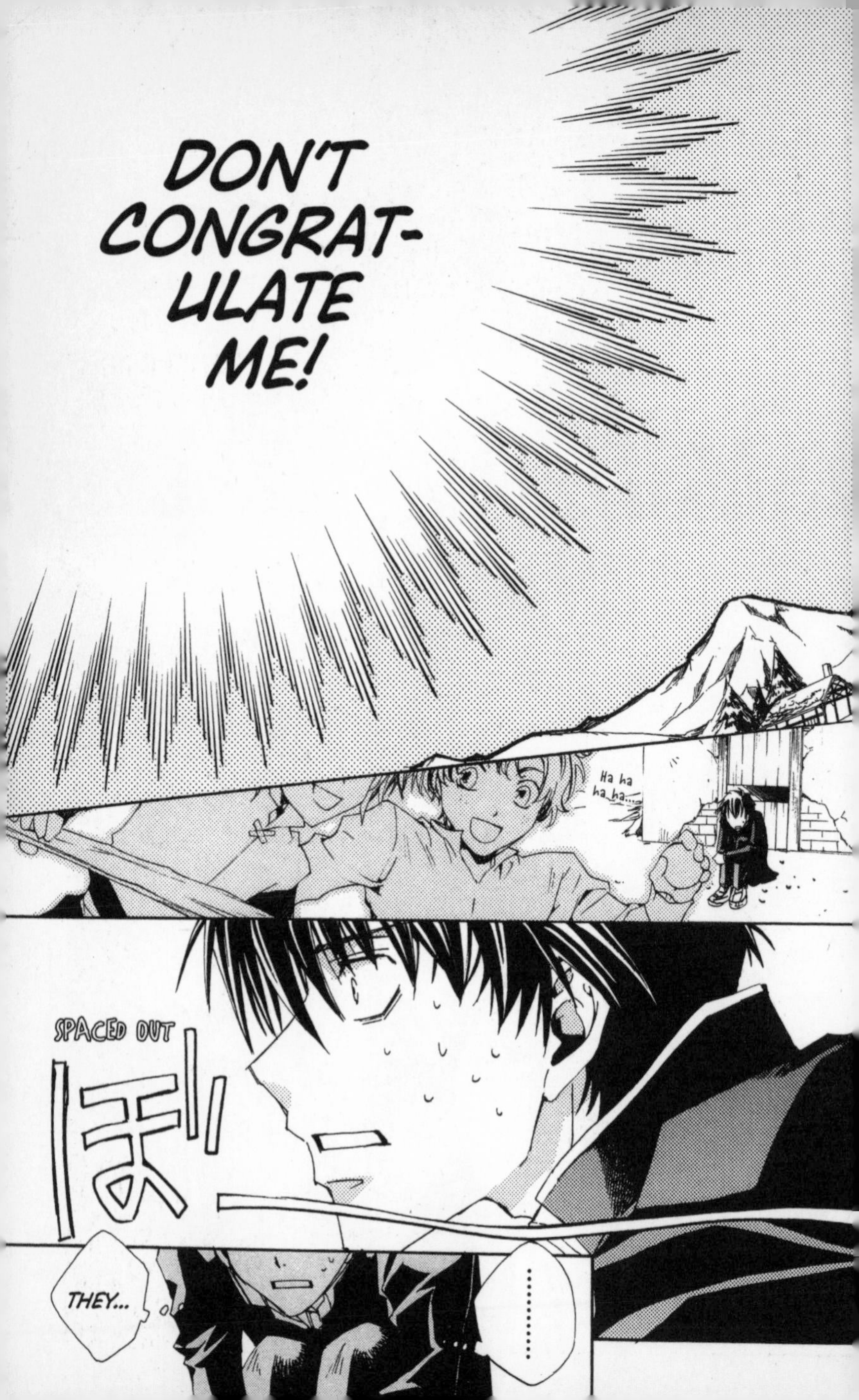
DON'T CONGRAT-ULATE ME!
Ha ha ha ha...
SPACED OUT
ぼー
....
THEY...

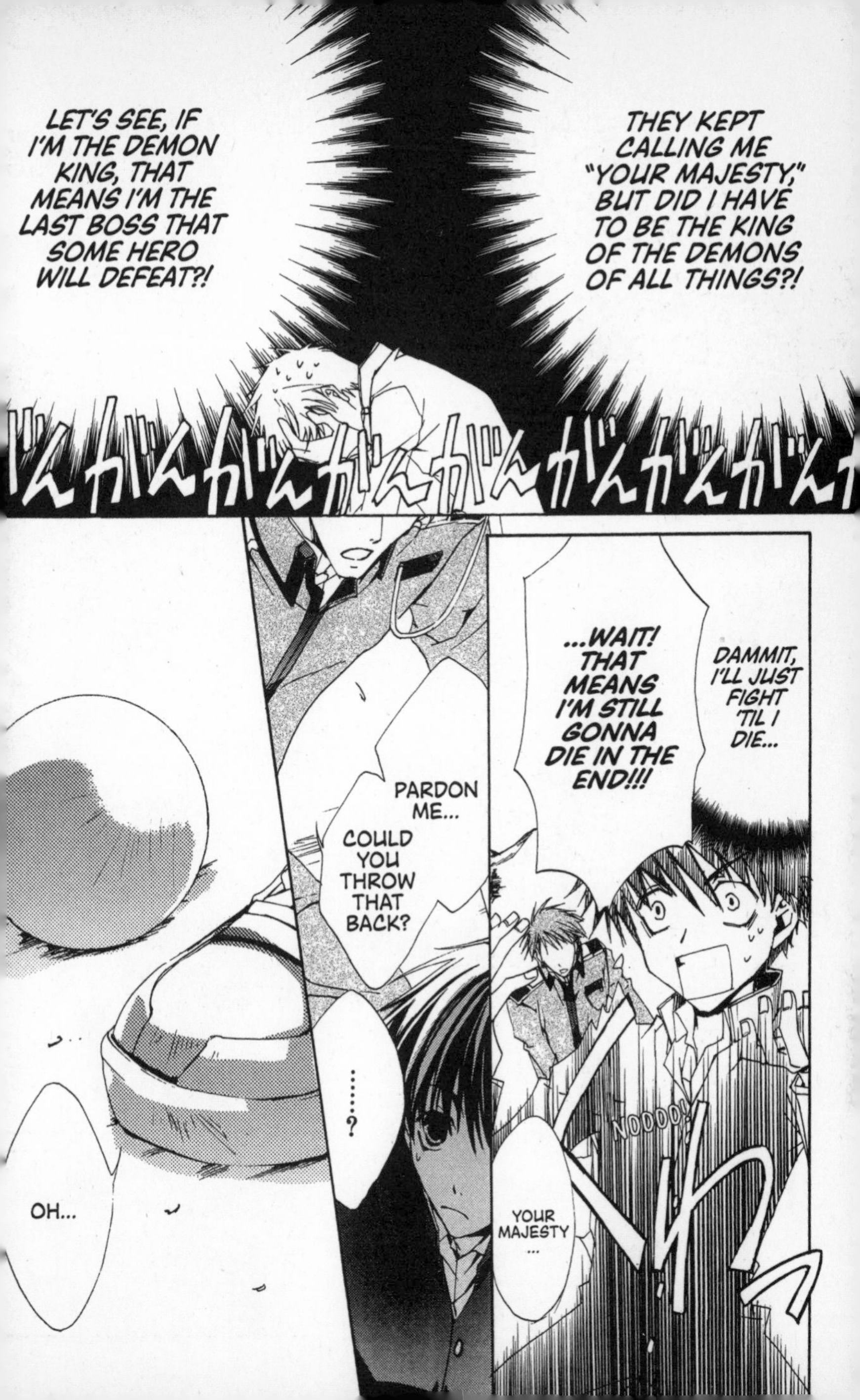
THEY KEPT CALLING ME "YOUR MAJESTY," BUT DID I HAVE TO BE THE KING OF THE DEMONS OF ALL THINGS?!
LET'S SEE, IF I'M THE DEMON KING, THAT MEANS I'M THE LAST BOSS THAT SOME HERO WILL DEFEAT?!
がんがんがんがんがんがんがんがん
DAMMIT, I'LL JUST FIGHT 'TIL I DIE...
...WAIT! THAT MEANS I'M STILL GONNA DIE IN THE END!!!
NOOOO!
YOUR MAJESTY...
PARDON ME...
COULD YOU THROW THAT BACK?
......?
OH...

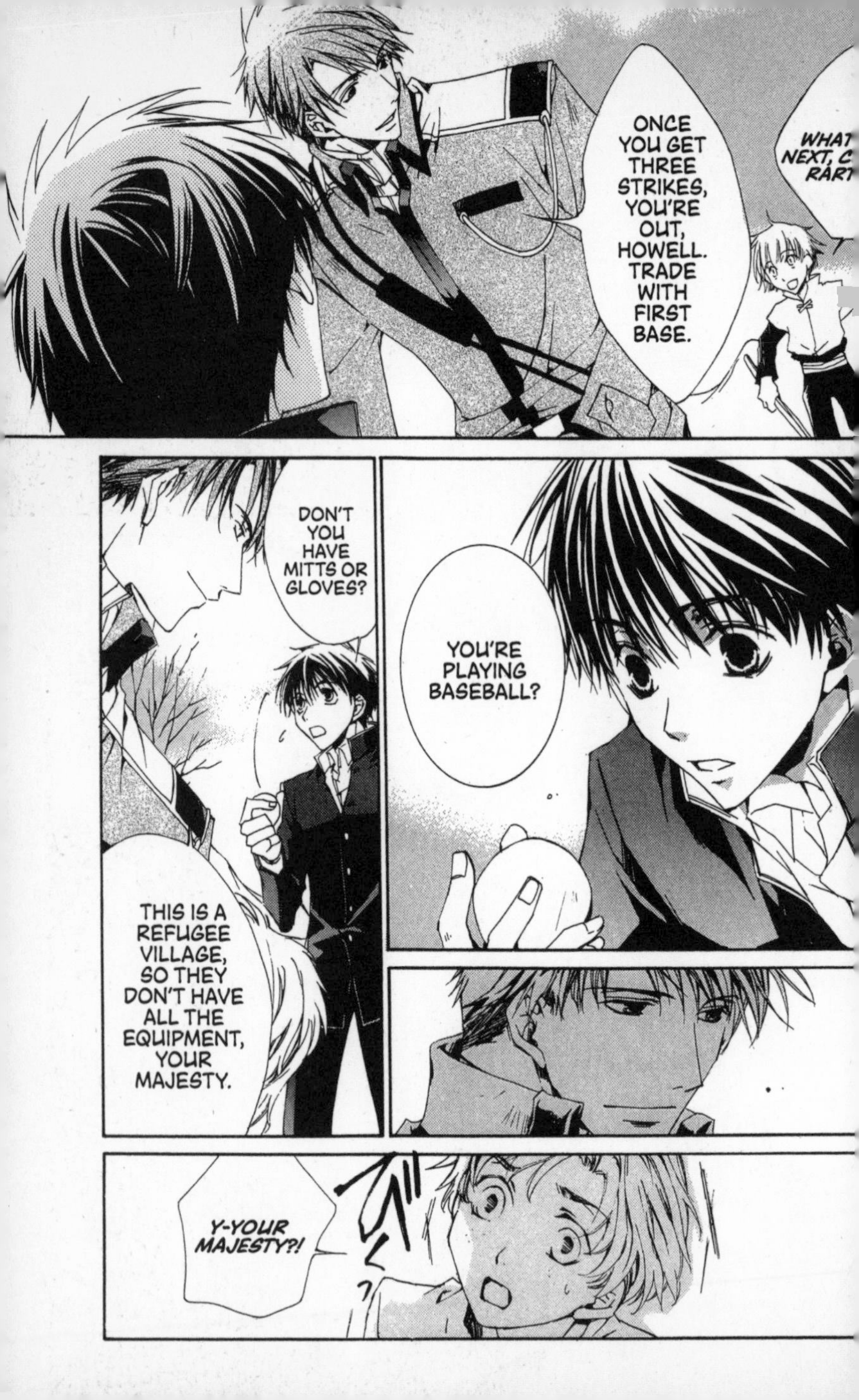

WHAT NEXT, C RART
ONCE YOU GET THREE STRIKES, YOU'RE OUT, HOWELL. TRADE WITH FIRST BASE.
YOU'RE PLAYING BASEBALL?
DON'T YOU HAVE MITTS OR GLOVES?
THIS IS A REFUGEE VILLAGE, SO THEY DON'T HAVE ALL THE EQUIPMENT, YOUR MAJESTY.
Y-YOUR MAJESTY?!

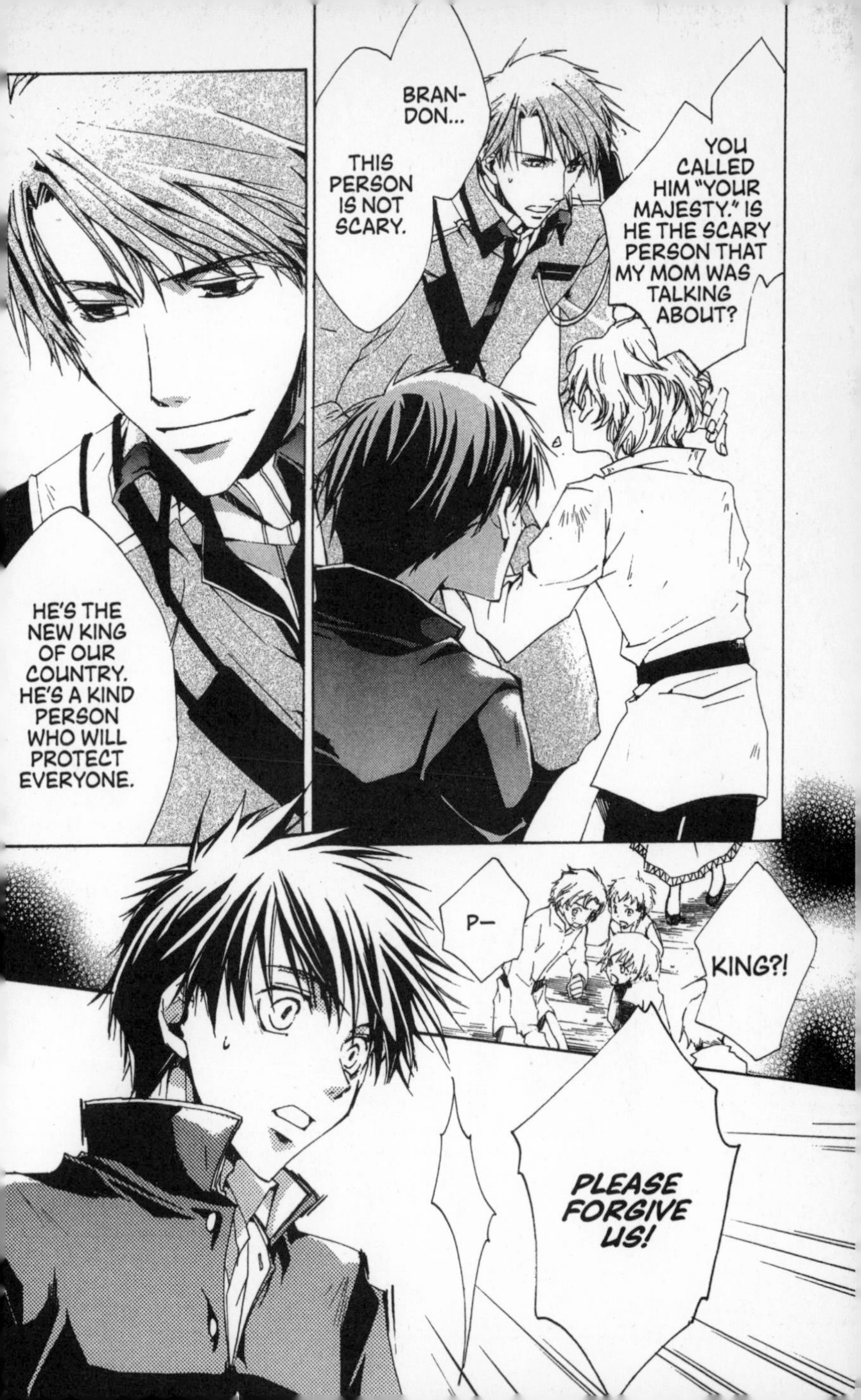
YOU CALLED HIM "YOUR MAJESTY." IS HE THE SCARY PERSON THAT MY MOM WAS TALKING ABOUT?
BRAN-DON...
THIS PERSON IS NOT SCARY.
HE'S THE NEW KING OF OUR COUNTRY. HE'S A KIND PERSON WHO WILL PROTECT EVERYONE.
P—
KING?!
PLEASE FORGIVE US!

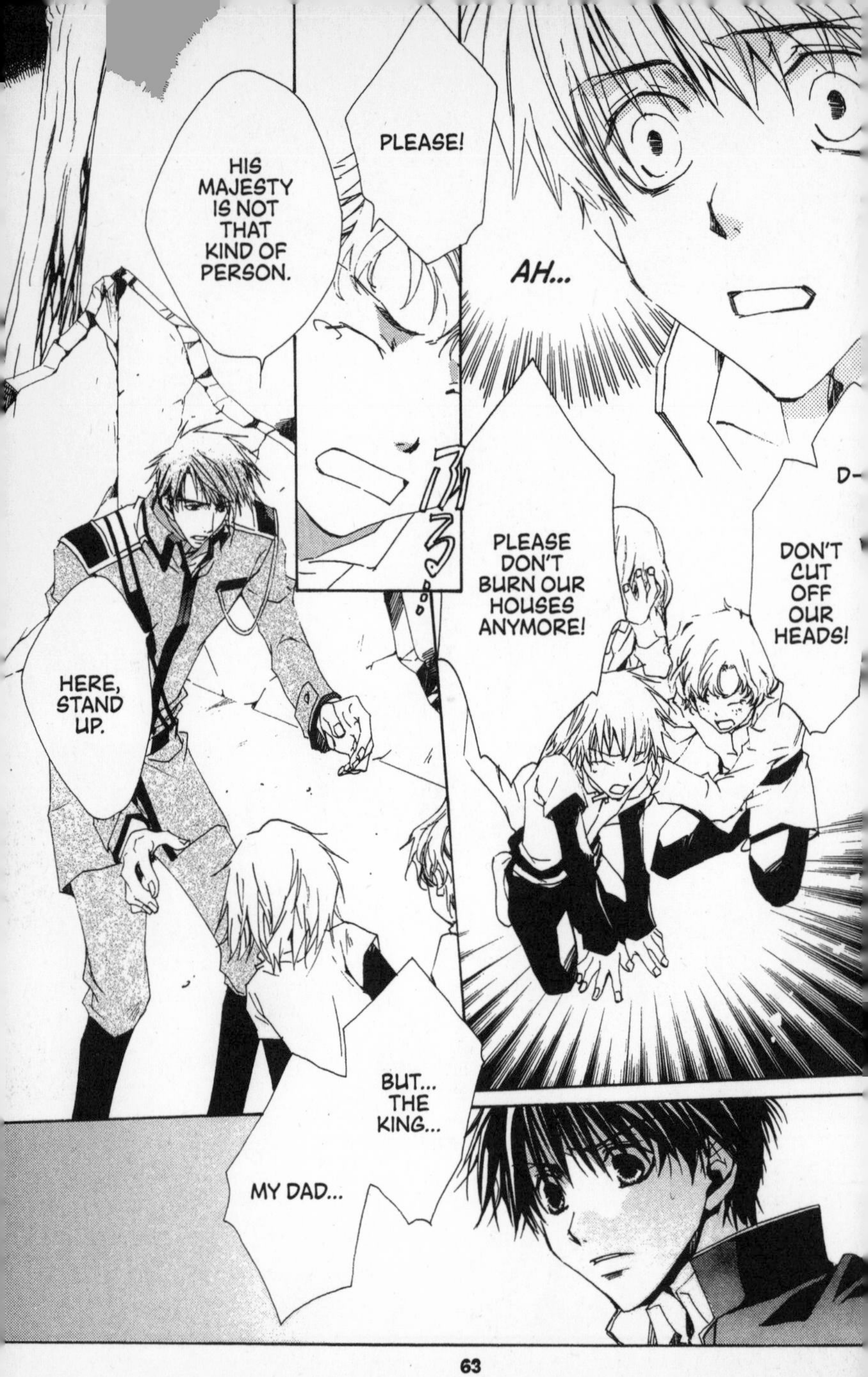
AH...
D-
DON'T CUT OFF OUR HEADS!
PLEASE DON'T BURN OUR HOUSES ANYMORE!
PLEASE!
HIS MAJESTY IS NOT THAT KIND OF PERSON.
HERE, STAND UP.
BUT... THE KING...
MY DAD...

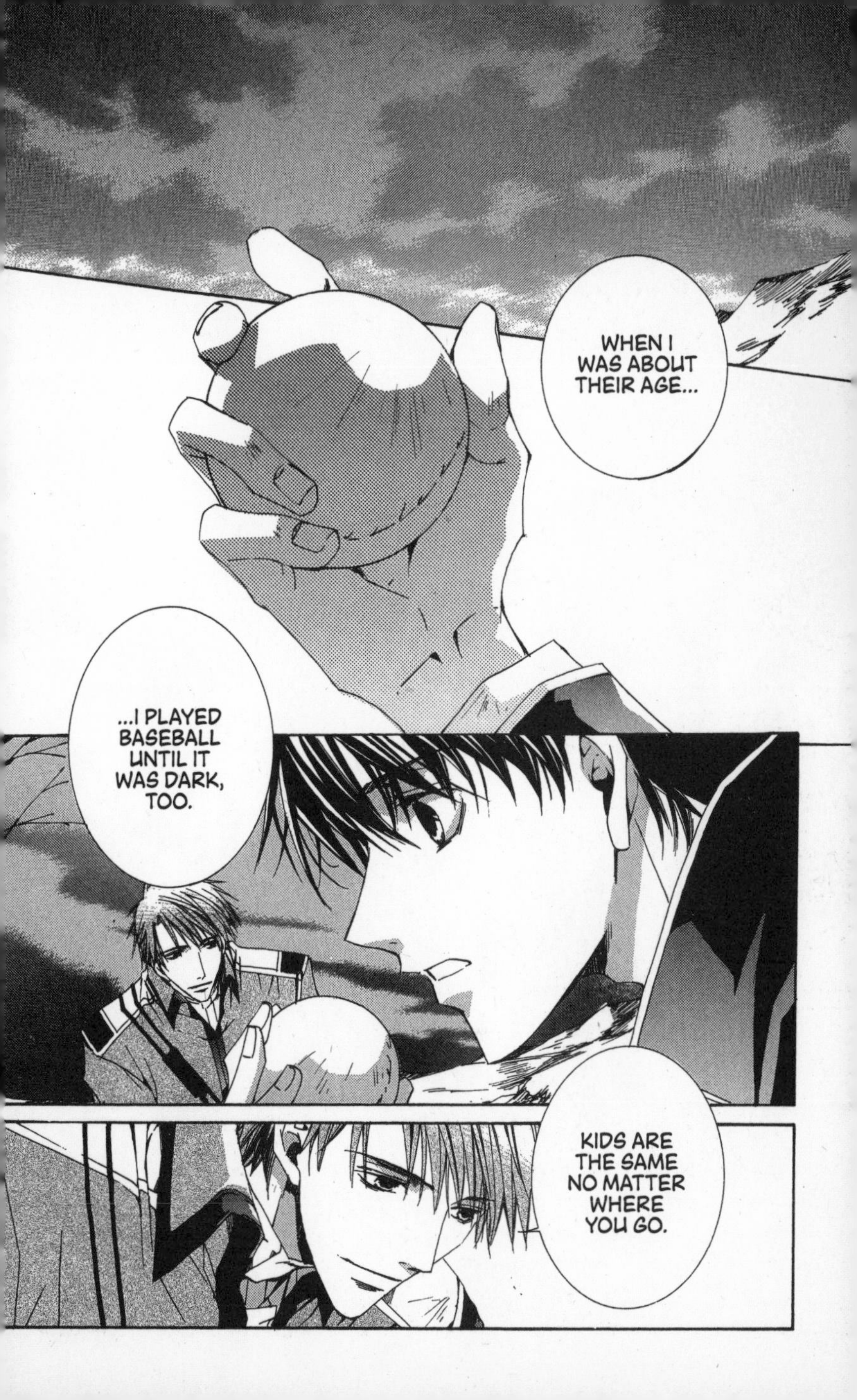
WHEN I WAS ABOUT THEIR AGE...
...I PLAYED BASEBALL UNTIL IT WAS DARK, TOO.
KIDS ARE THE SAME NO MATTER WHERE YOU GO.

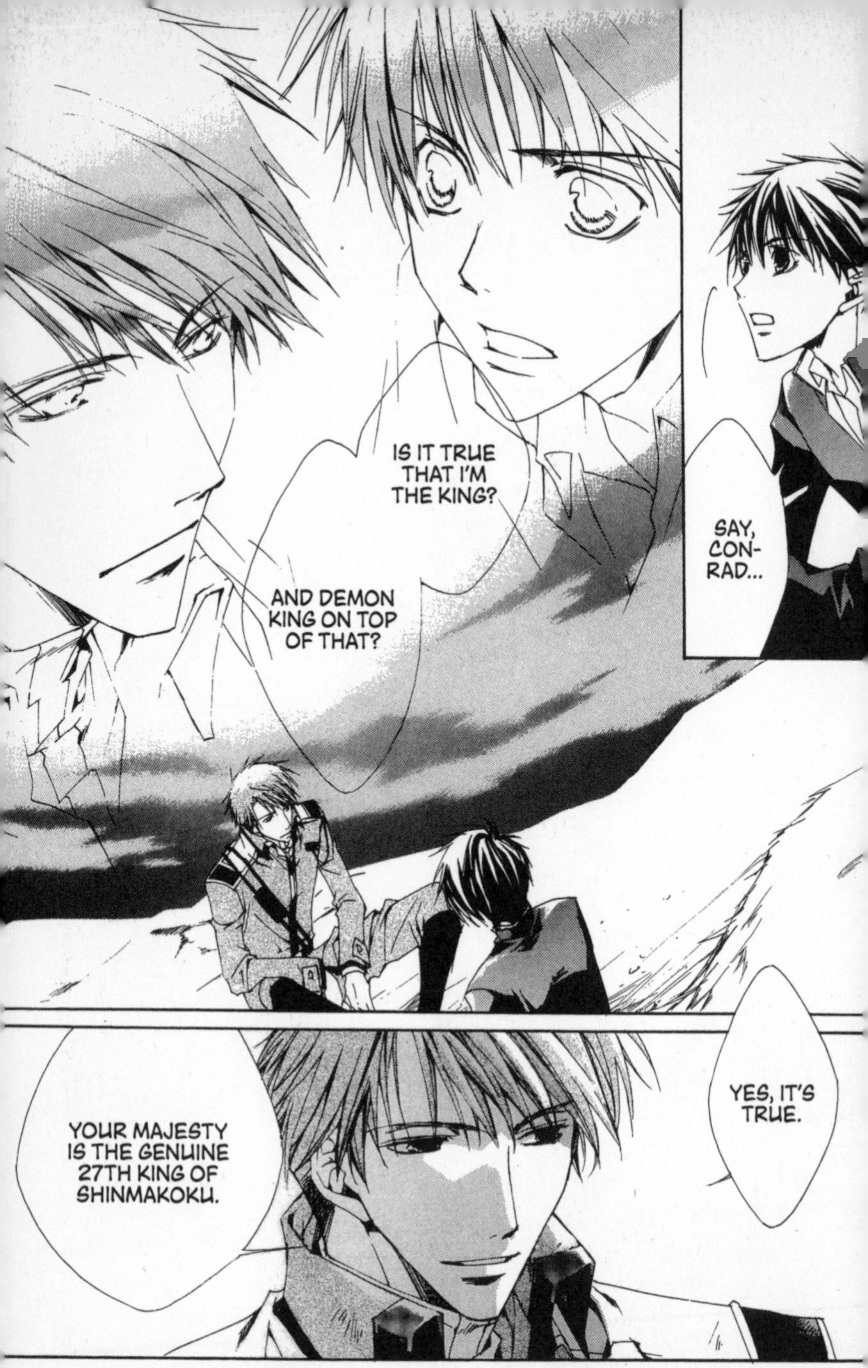
SAY, CON-RAD...
IS IT TRUE THAT I'M THE KING?
AND DEMON KING ON TOP OF THAT?
YES, IT'S TRUE.
YOUR MAJESTY IS THE GENUINE 27TH KING OF SHINMAKOKU.

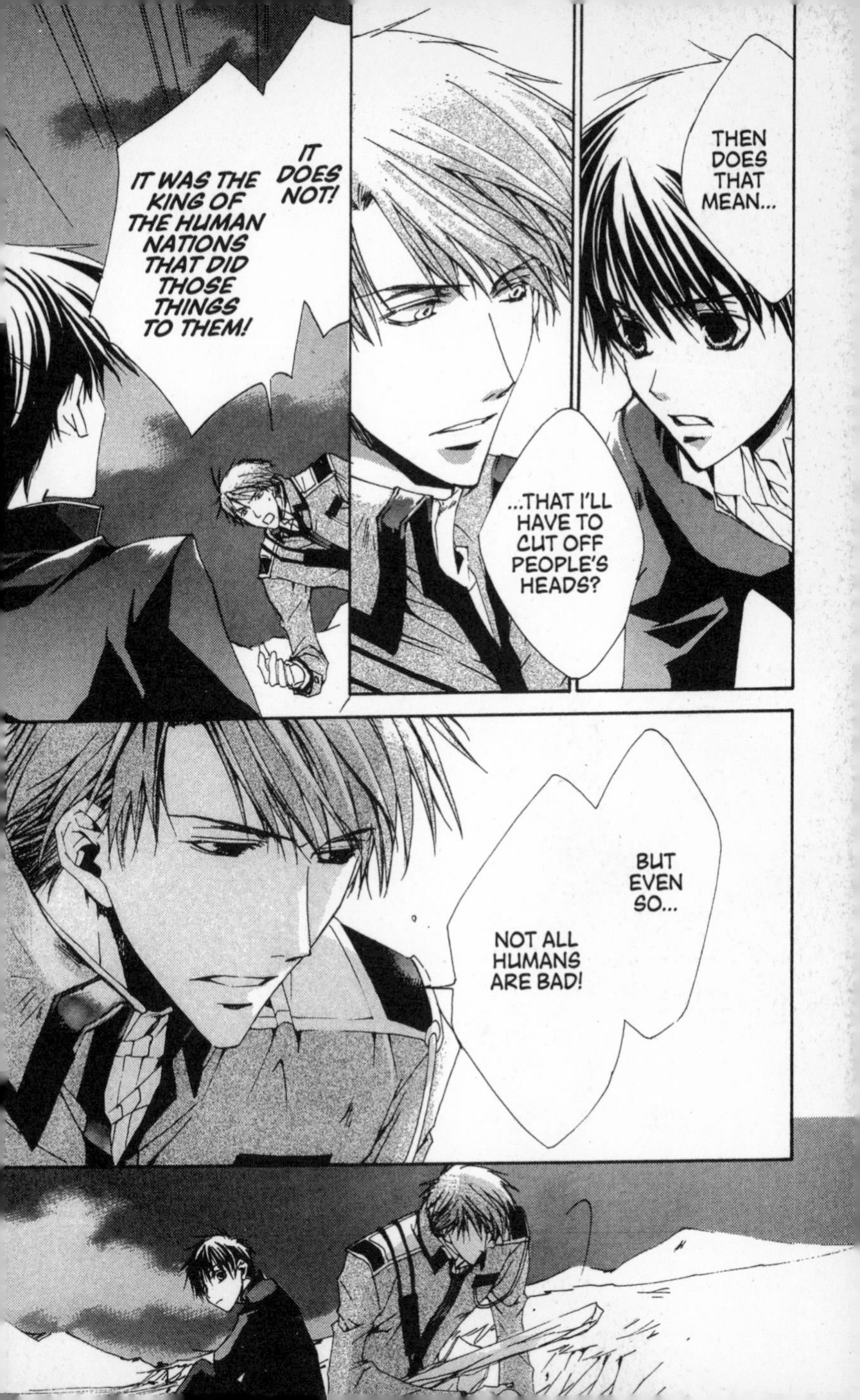
THEN DOES THAT MEAN...
...THAT I'LL HAVE TO CUT OFF PEOPLE'S HEADS?
IT DOES NOT!
IT WAS THE KING OF THE HUMAN NATIONS THAT DID THOSE THINGS TO THEM!
BUT EVEN SO...
NOT ALL HUMANS ARE BAD!

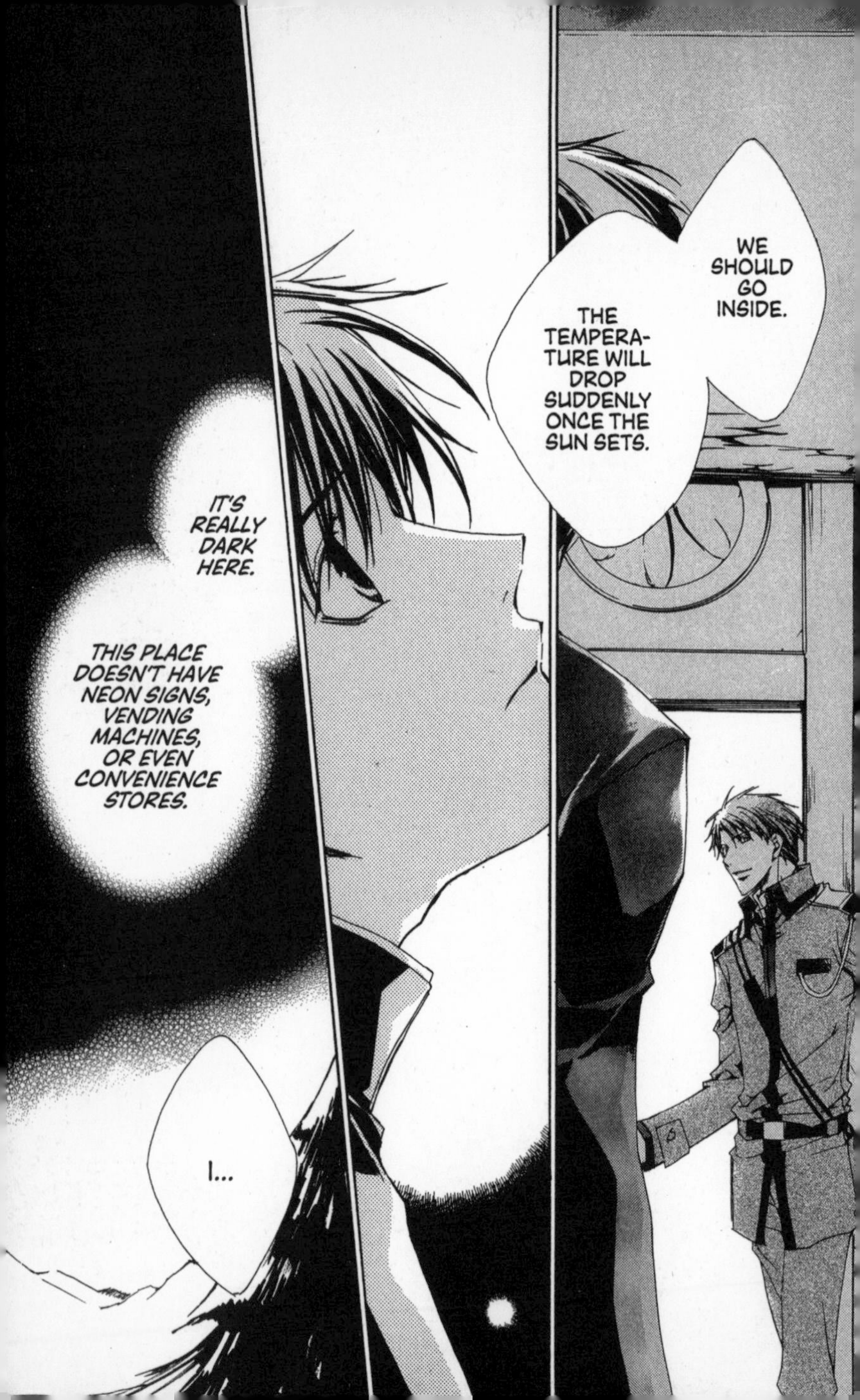
WE SHOULD GO INSIDE.
THE TEMPERATURE WILL DROP SUDDENLY ONCE THE SUN SETS.
IT'S REALLY DARK HERE.
THIS PLACE DOESN'T HAVE NEON SIGNS, VENDING MACHINES, OR EVEN CONVENIENCE STORES.
I...

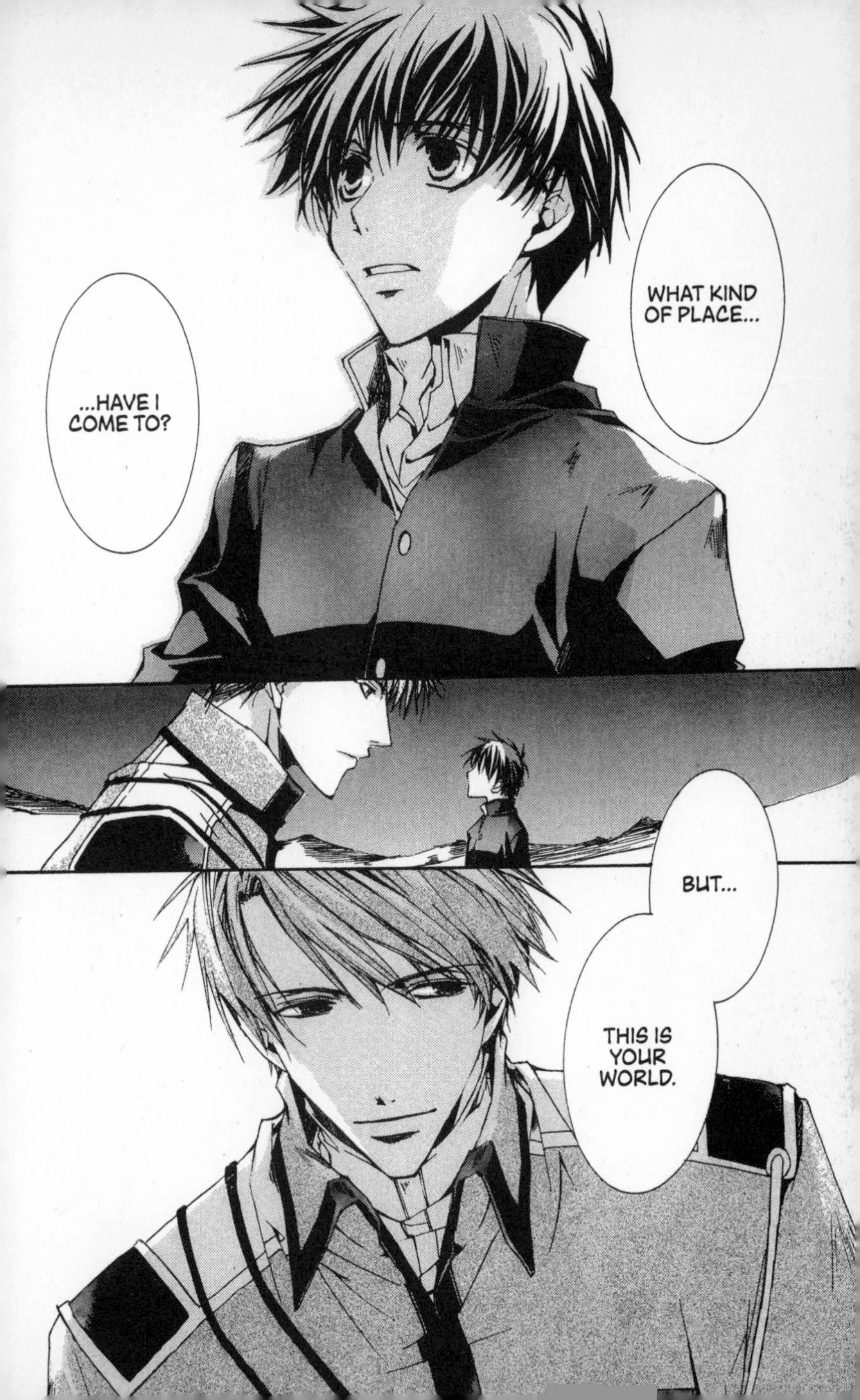
WHAT KIND OF PLACE...
...HAVE I COME TO?
BUT...
THIS IS YOUR WORLD.

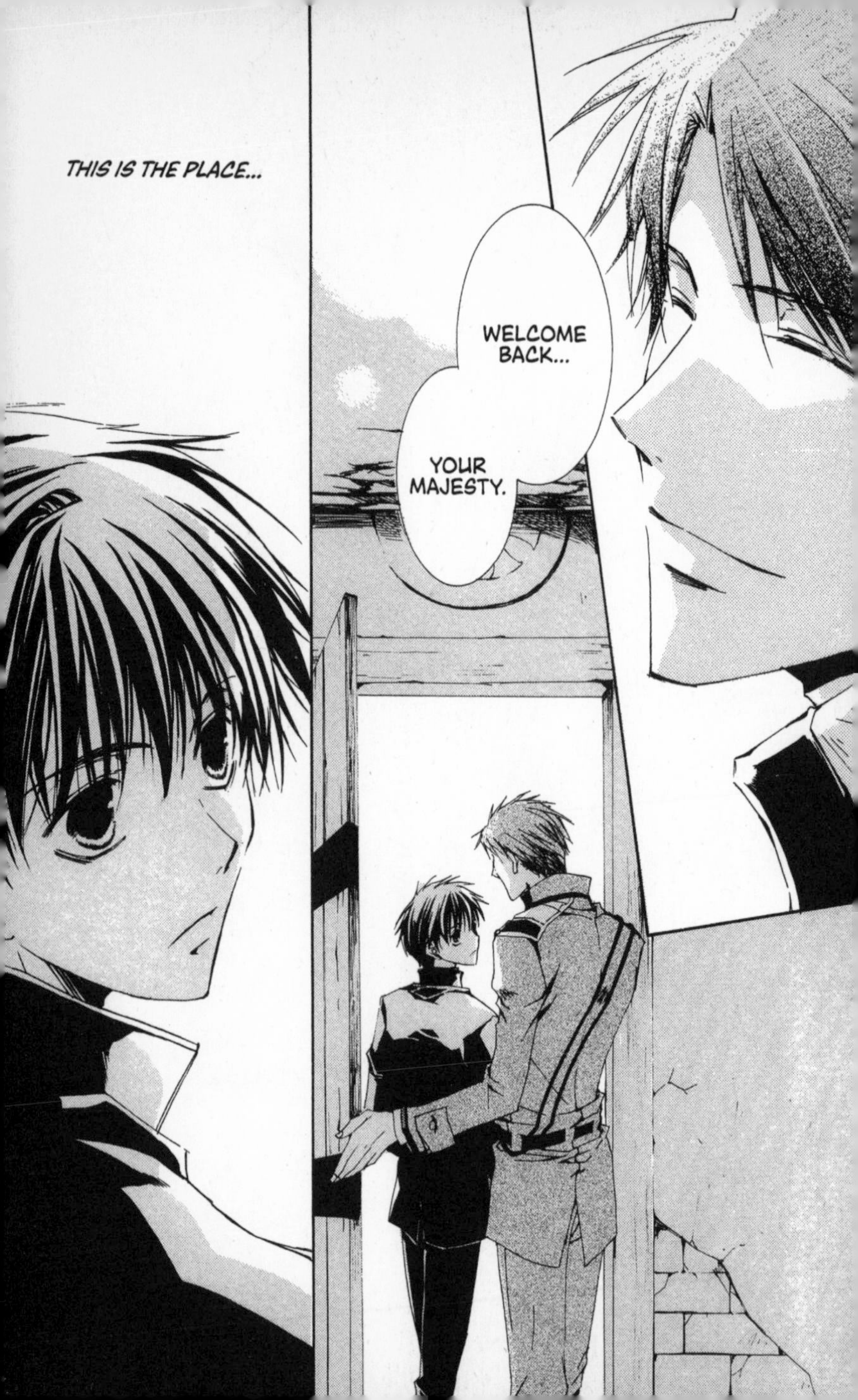
WELCOME BACK...
YOUR MAJESTY.
THIS IS THE PLACE...

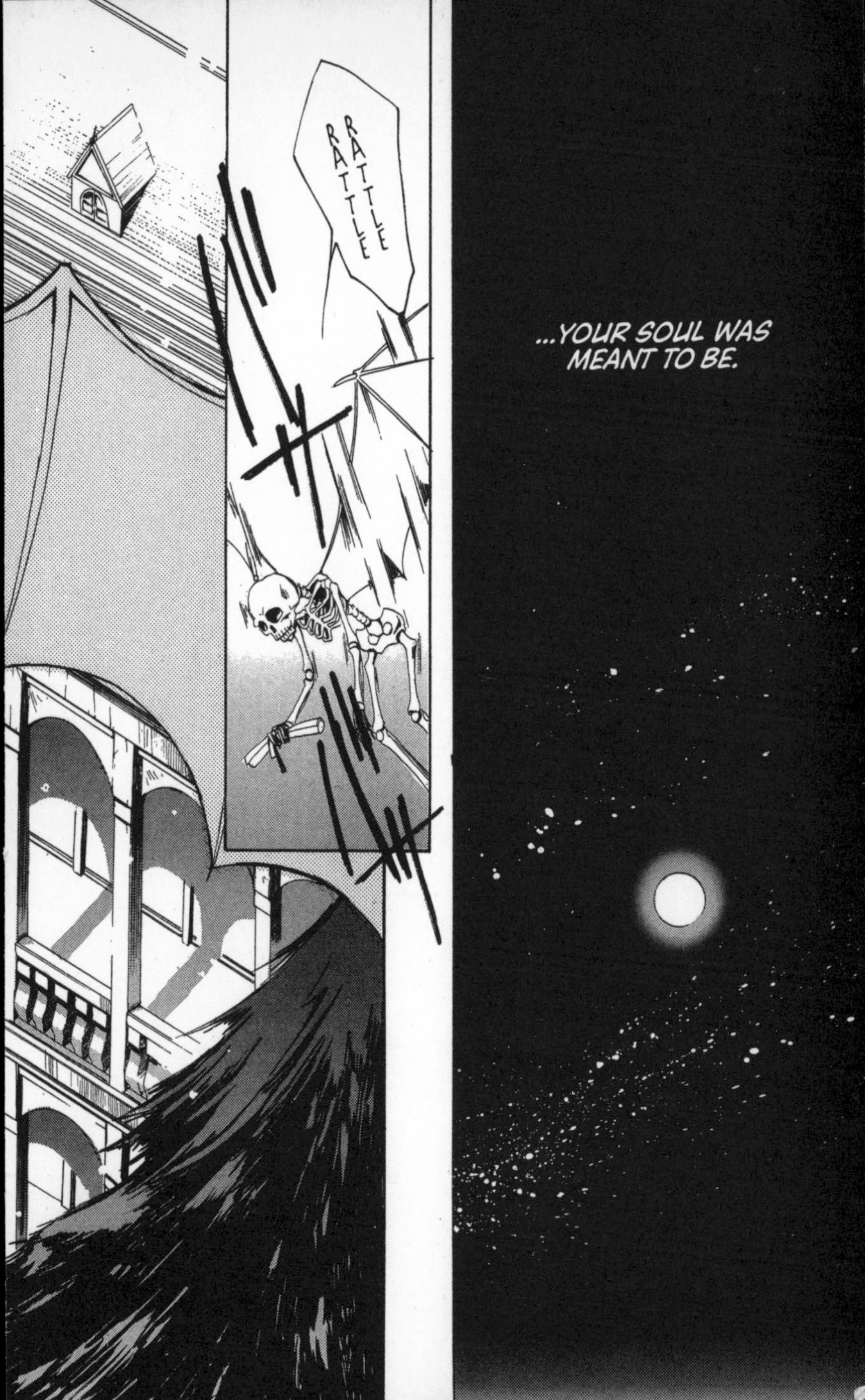
...YOUR SOUL WAS MEANT TO BE.
RATTLE RATTLE

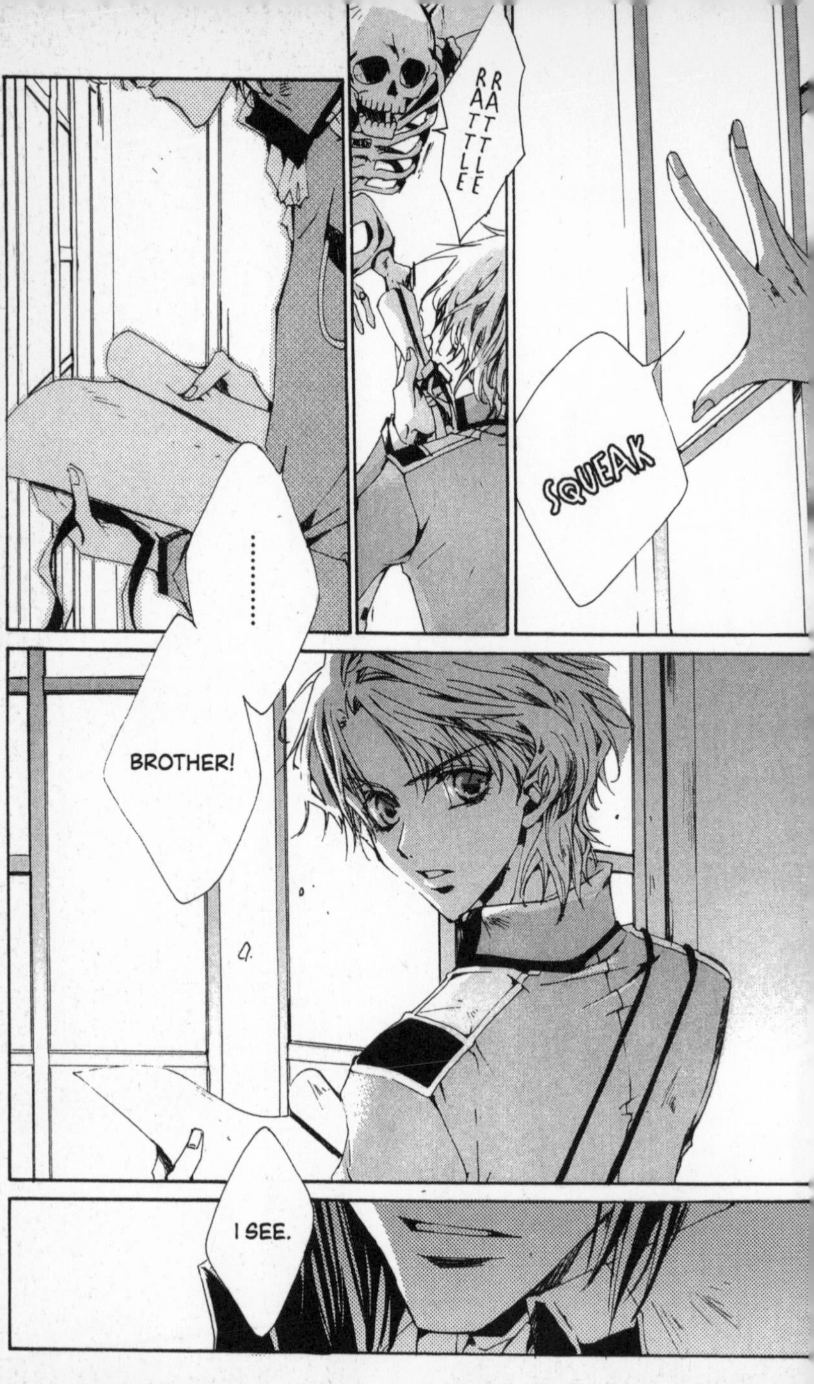
SQUEAK
RATTLE RATTLE
....
BROTHER!
I SEE.

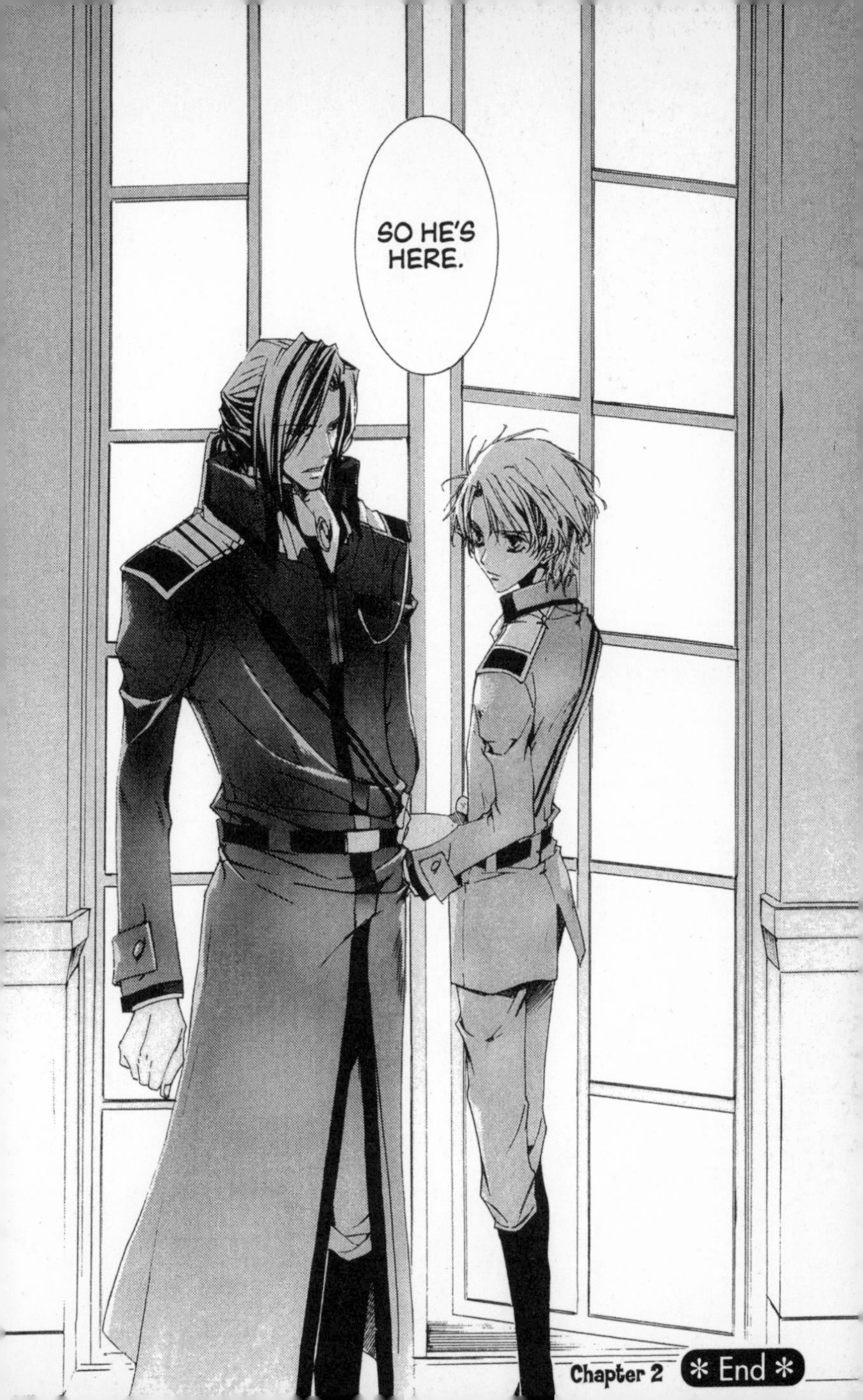
SO HE'S HERE.
Chapter 2 * End *

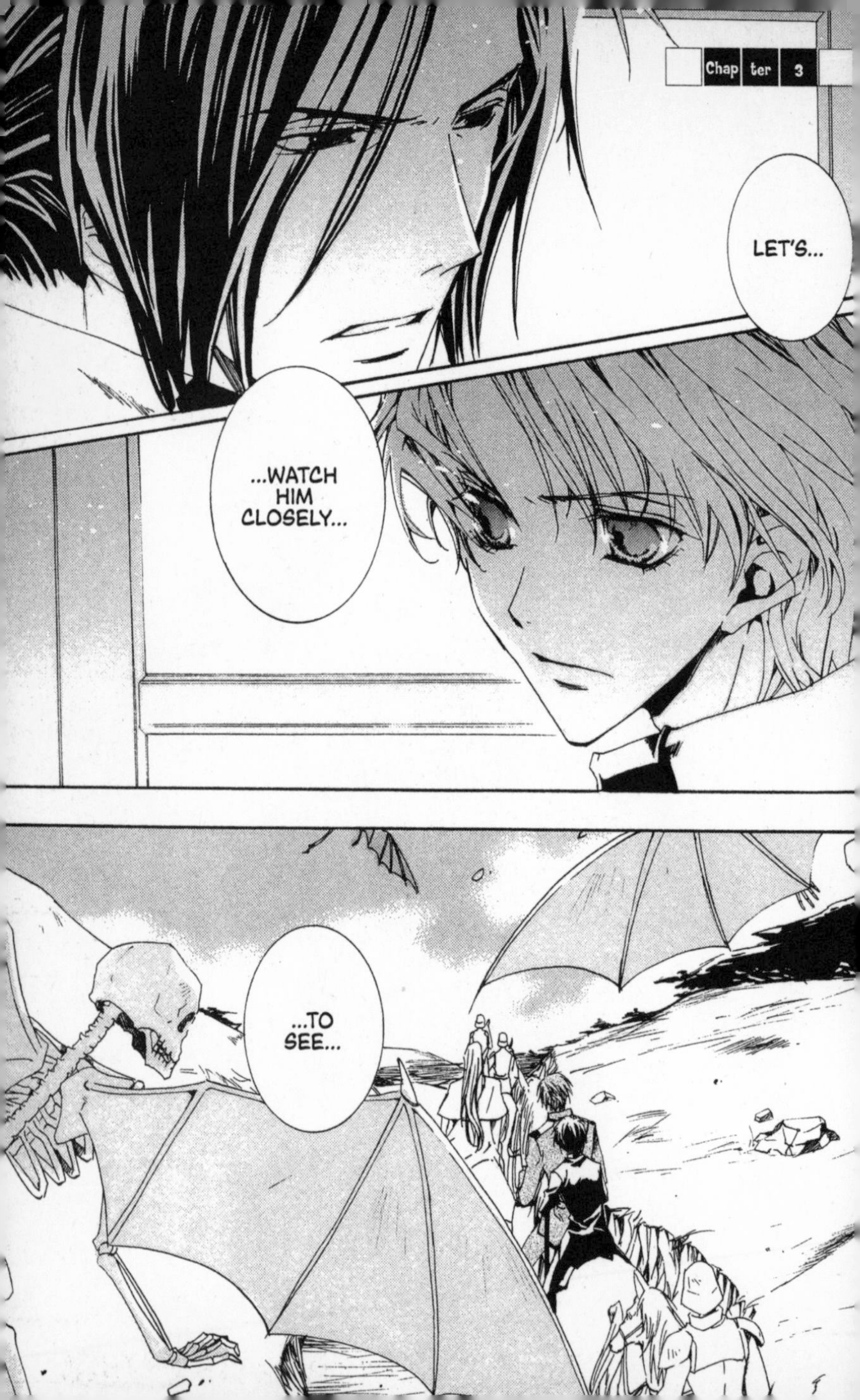
LET'S...
...WATCH HIM CLOSELY...
...TO SEE...

Chapter 3
Arrival at Blood-Pledge Castle?!

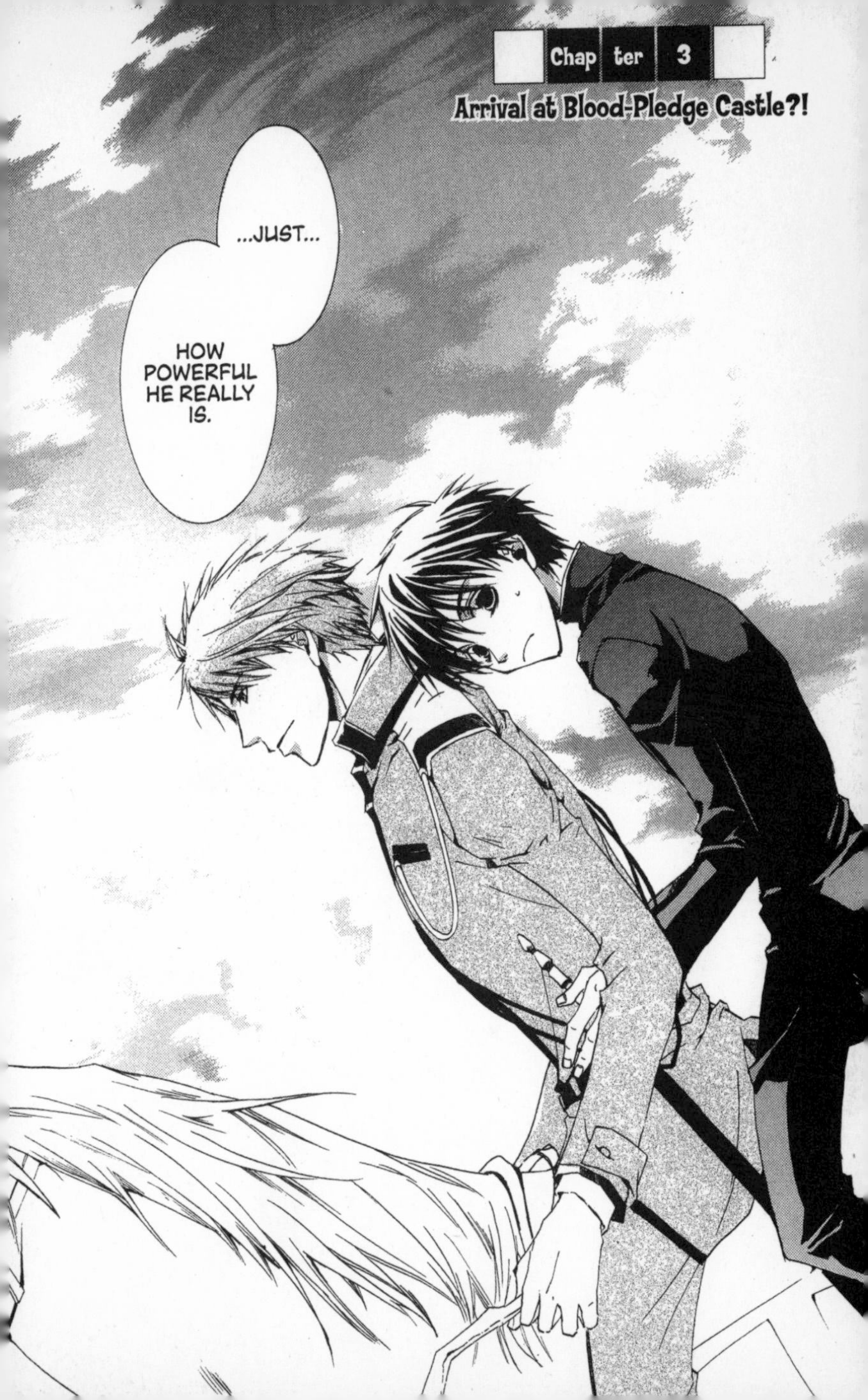
...JUST...
HOW POWERFUL HE REALLY IS.

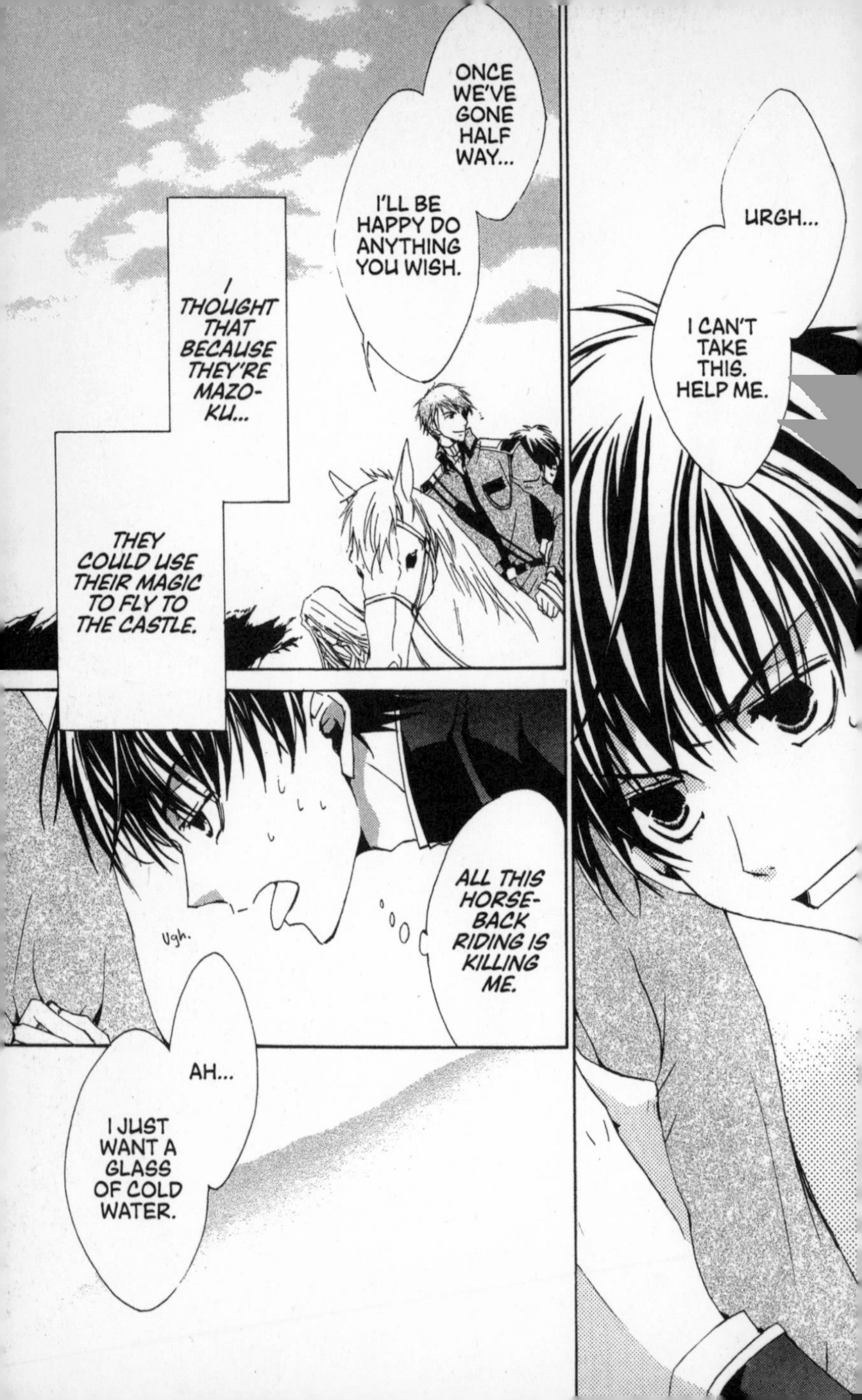
URGH...
I CAN'T TAKE THIS. HELP ME.
ONCE WE'VE GONE HALF WAY...
I'LL BE HAPPY DO ANYTHING YOU WISH.
I THOUGHT THAT BECAUSE THEY'RE MAZOKU...
THEY COULD USE THEIR MAGIC TO FLY TO THE CASTLE.
ALL THIS HORSEBACK RIDING IS KILLING ME.
Ugh.
AH...
I JUST WANT A GLASS OF COLD WATER.

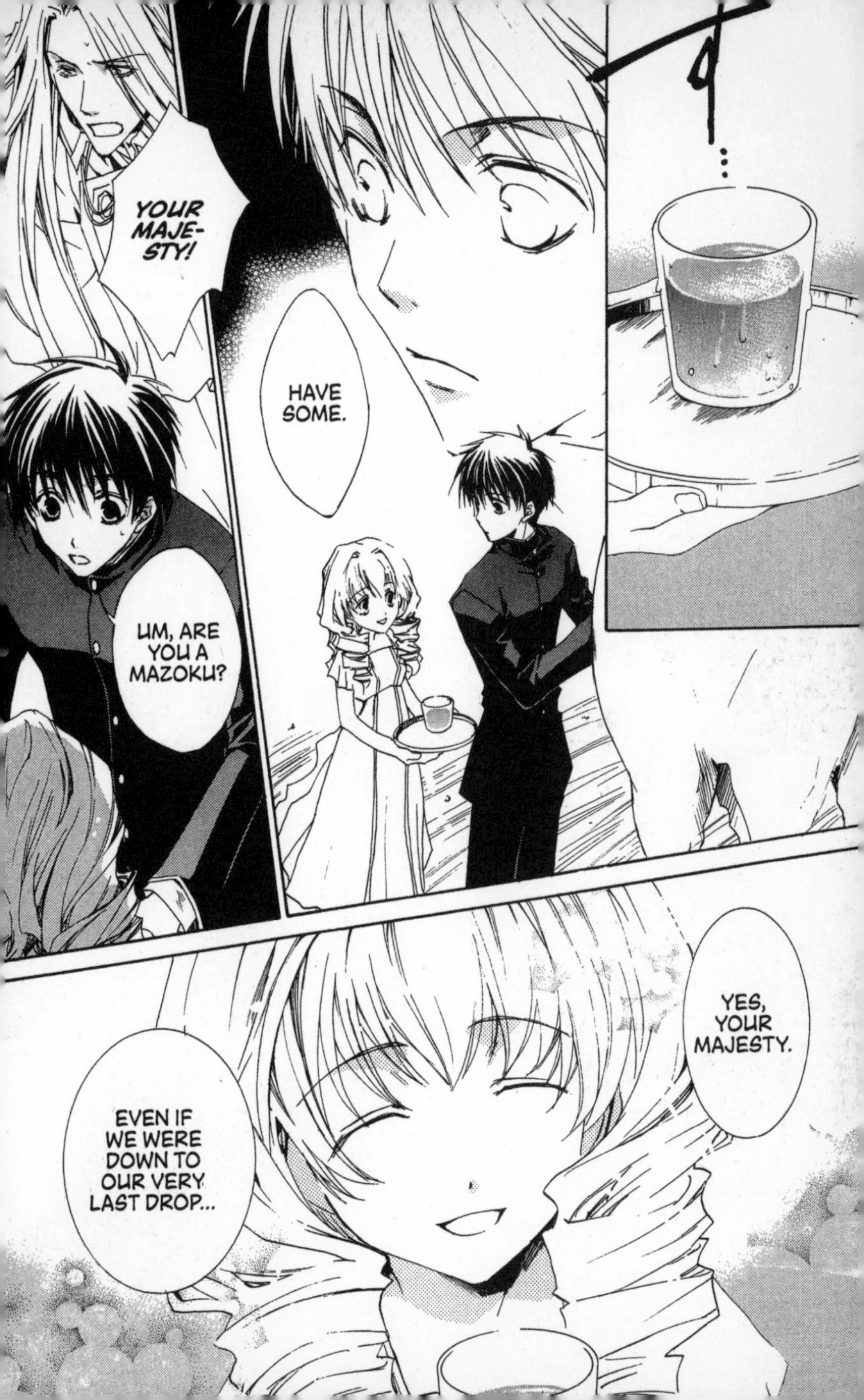
す
HAVE SOME.
YOUR MAJESTY!
UM, ARE YOU A MAZOKU?
YES, YOUR MAJESTY.
EVEN IF WE WERE DOWN TO OUR VERY LAST DROP...

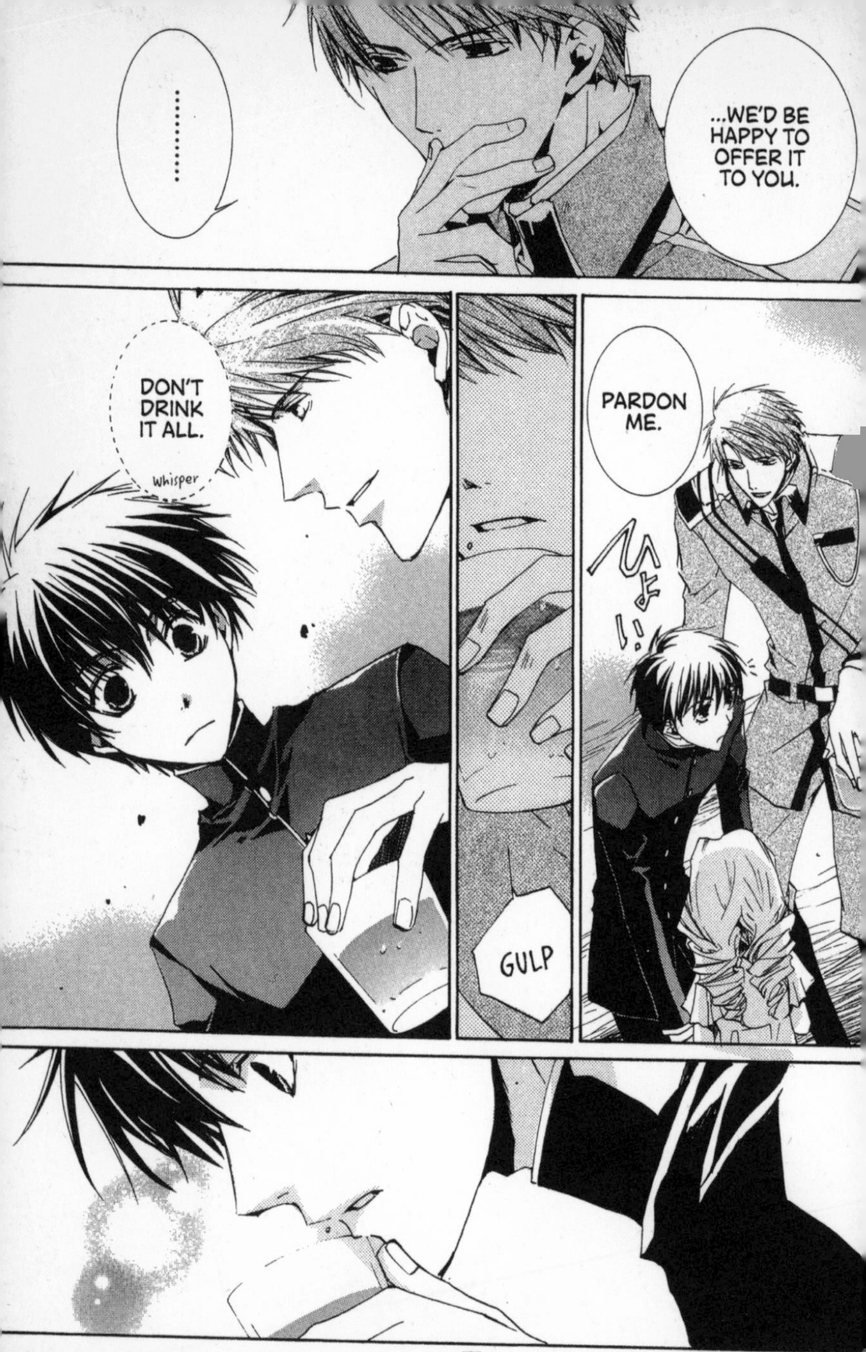
...WE'D BE HAPPY TO OFFER IT TO YOU.
......
PARDON ME.
ひょい!
GULP
DON'T DRINK IT ALL.
whisper

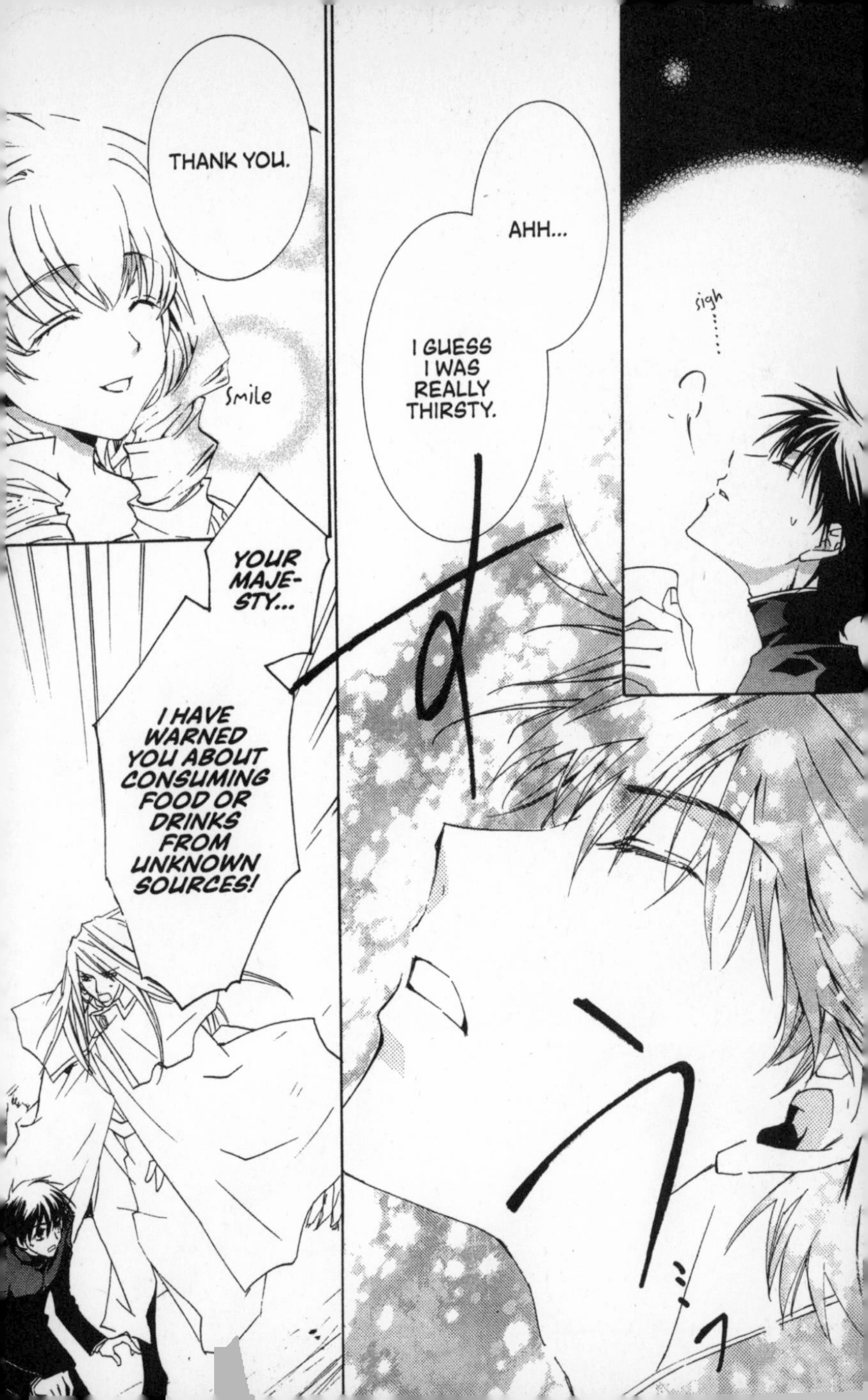
sigh......
AHH...
I GUESS I WAS REALLY THIRSTY.
THANK YOU.
Smile
YOUR MAJE-STY...
I HAVE WARNED YOU ABOUT CONSUMING FOOD OR DRINKS FROM UNKNOWN SOURCES!

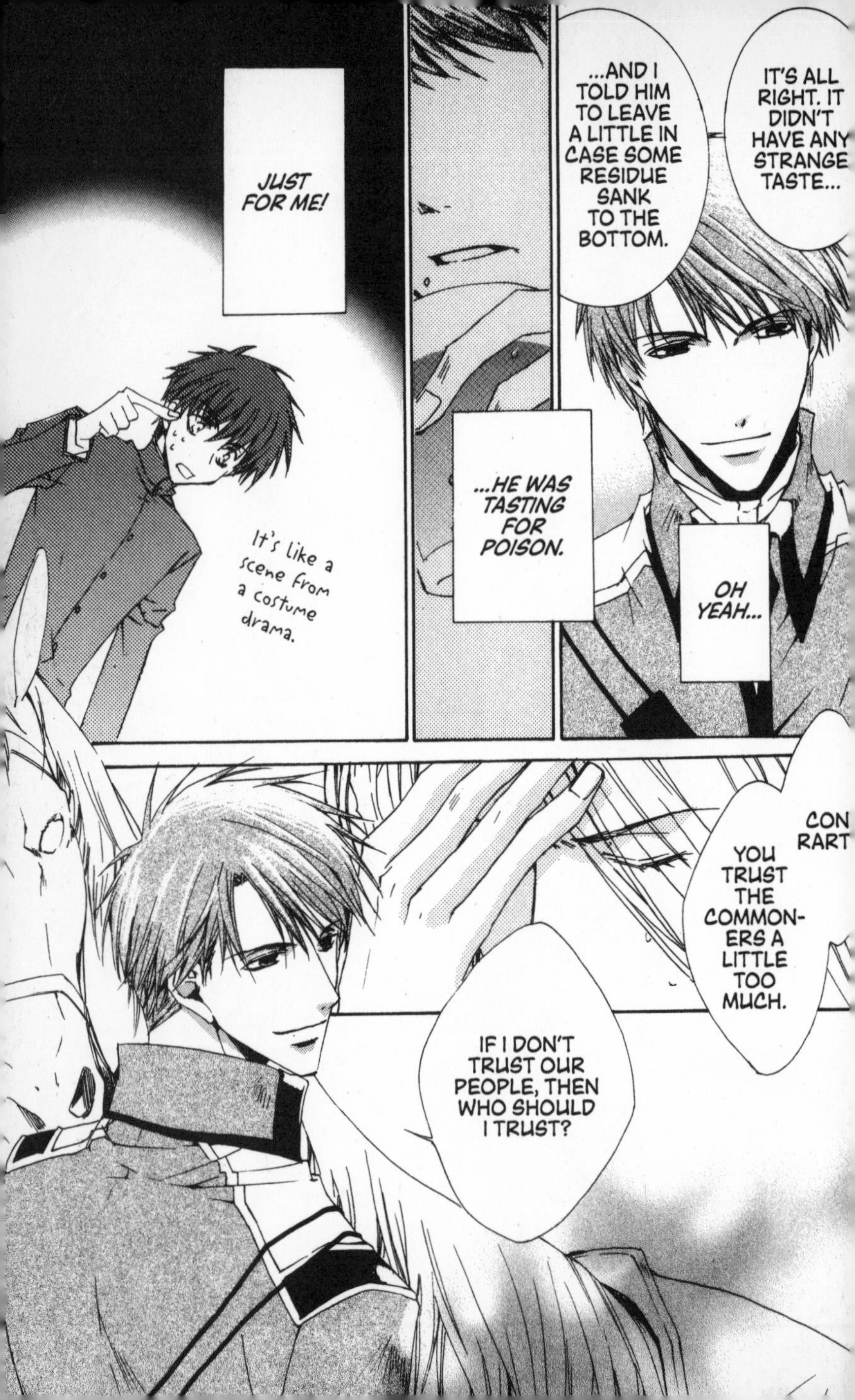
IT'S ALL RIGHT. IT DIDN'T HAVE ANY STRANGE TASTE...
...AND I TOLD HIM TO LEAVE A LITTLE IN CASE SOME RESIDUE SANK TO THE BOTTOM.
OH YEAH...
...HE WAS TASTING FOR POISON.
JUST FOR ME!
It's like a scene from a costume drama.
CONRART
YOU TRUST THE COMMONERS A LITTLE TOO MUCH.
IF I DON'T TRUST OUR PEOPLE, THEN WHO SHOULD I TRUST?

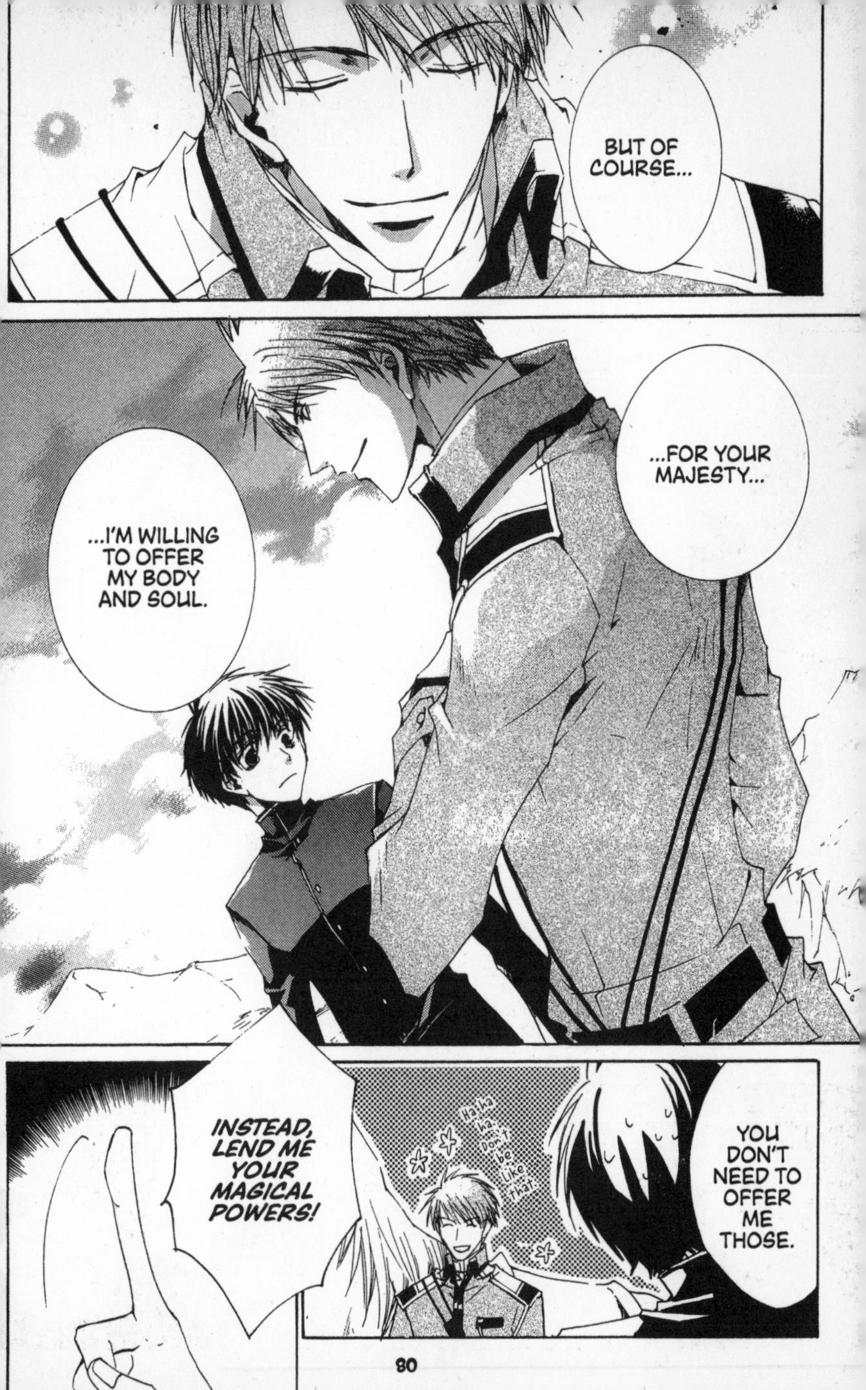
BUT OF COURSE...
...FOR YOUR MAJESTY...
...I'M WILLING TO OFFER MY BODY AND SOUL.
YOU DON'T NEED TO OFFER ME THOSE.
Ha ha ha. Don't be like that.
INSTEAD, LEND ME YOUR MAGICAL POWERS!

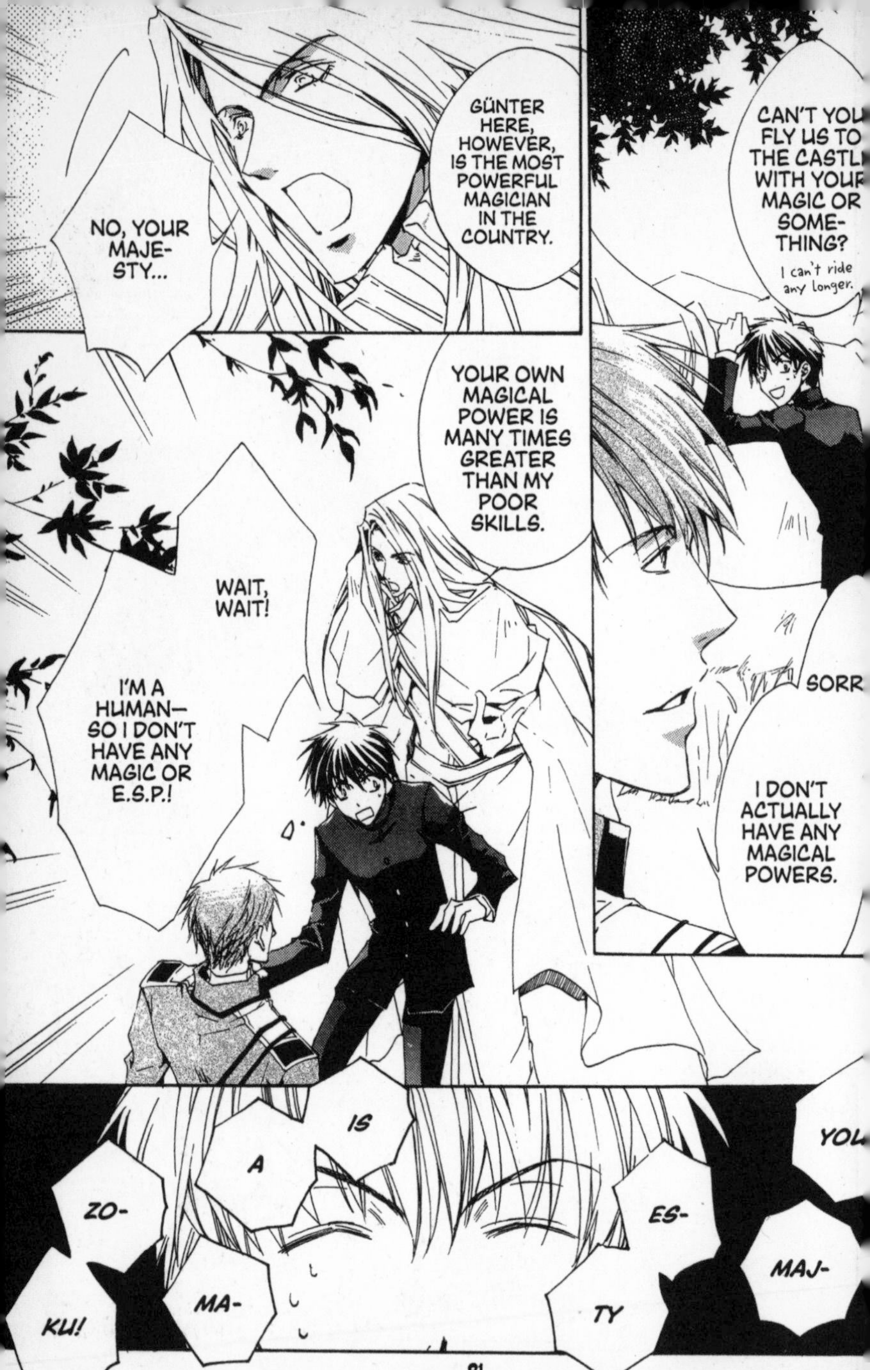
CAN'T YOU FLY US TO THE CASTLE WITH YOUR MAGIC OR SOME-THING?
I can't ride any longer.
SORR
I DON'T ACTUALLY HAVE ANY MAGICAL POWERS.
GÜNTER HERE, HOWEVER, IS THE MOST POWERFUL MAGICIAN IN THE COUNTRY.
NO, YOUR MAJE-STY...
YOUR OWN MAGICAL POWER IS MANY TIMES GREATER THAN MY POOR SKILLS.
WAIT, WAIT!
I'M A HUMAN— SO I DON'T HAVE ANY MAGIC OR E.S.P.!
YOU
MAJ-
ES-
TY
IS
A
ZO-
MA-
KU!

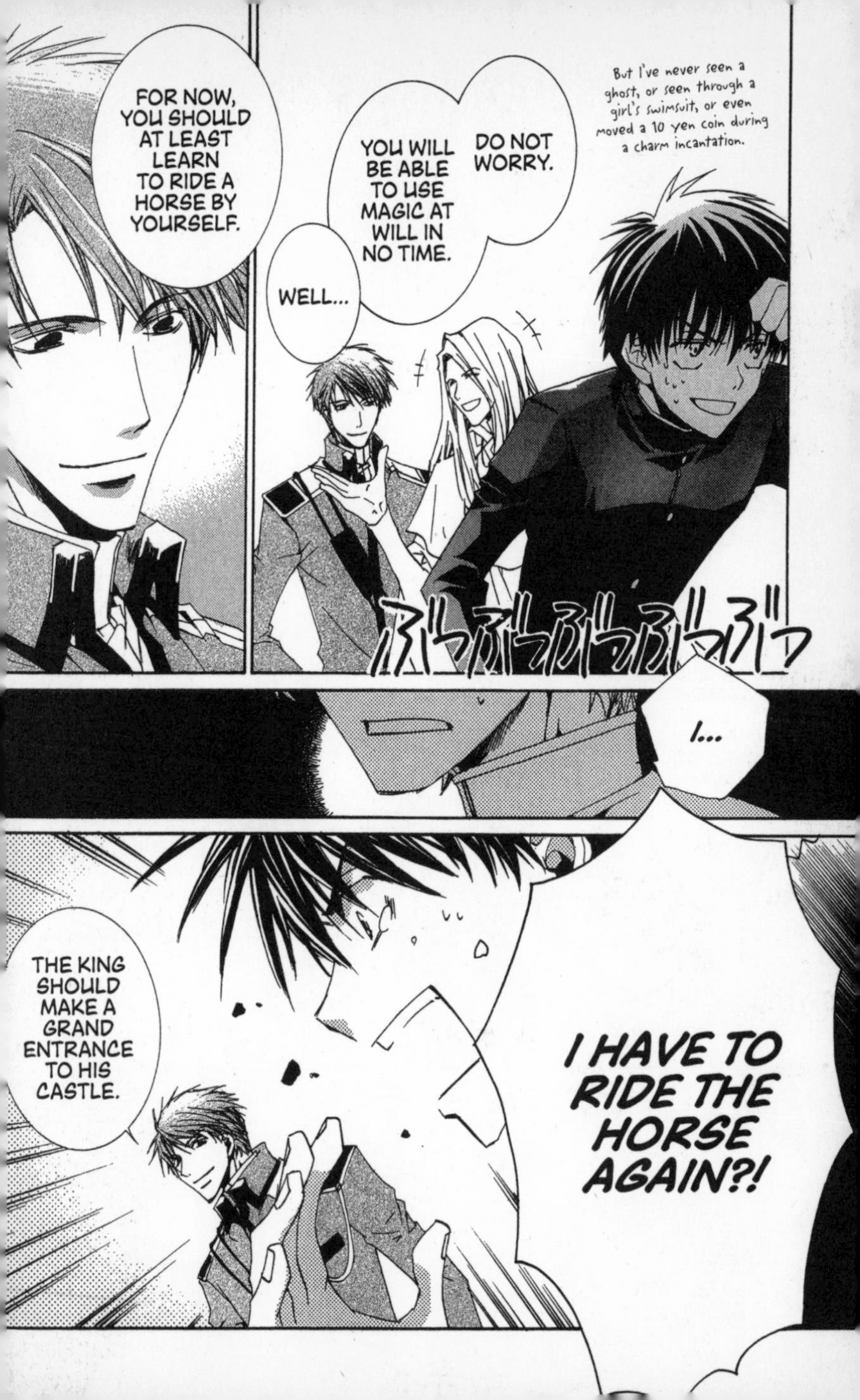
But I've never seen a ghost, or seen through a girl's swimsuit, or even moved a 10 yen coin during a charm incantation.
DO NOT WORRY.
YOU WILL BE ABLE TO USE MAGIC AT WILL IN NO TIME.
WELL...
FOR NOW, YOU SHOULD AT LEAST LEARN TO RIDE A HORSE BY YOURSELF.
I...
THE KING SHOULD MAKE A GRAND ENTRANCE TO HIS CASTLE.
I HAVE TO RIDE THE HORSE AGAIN?!

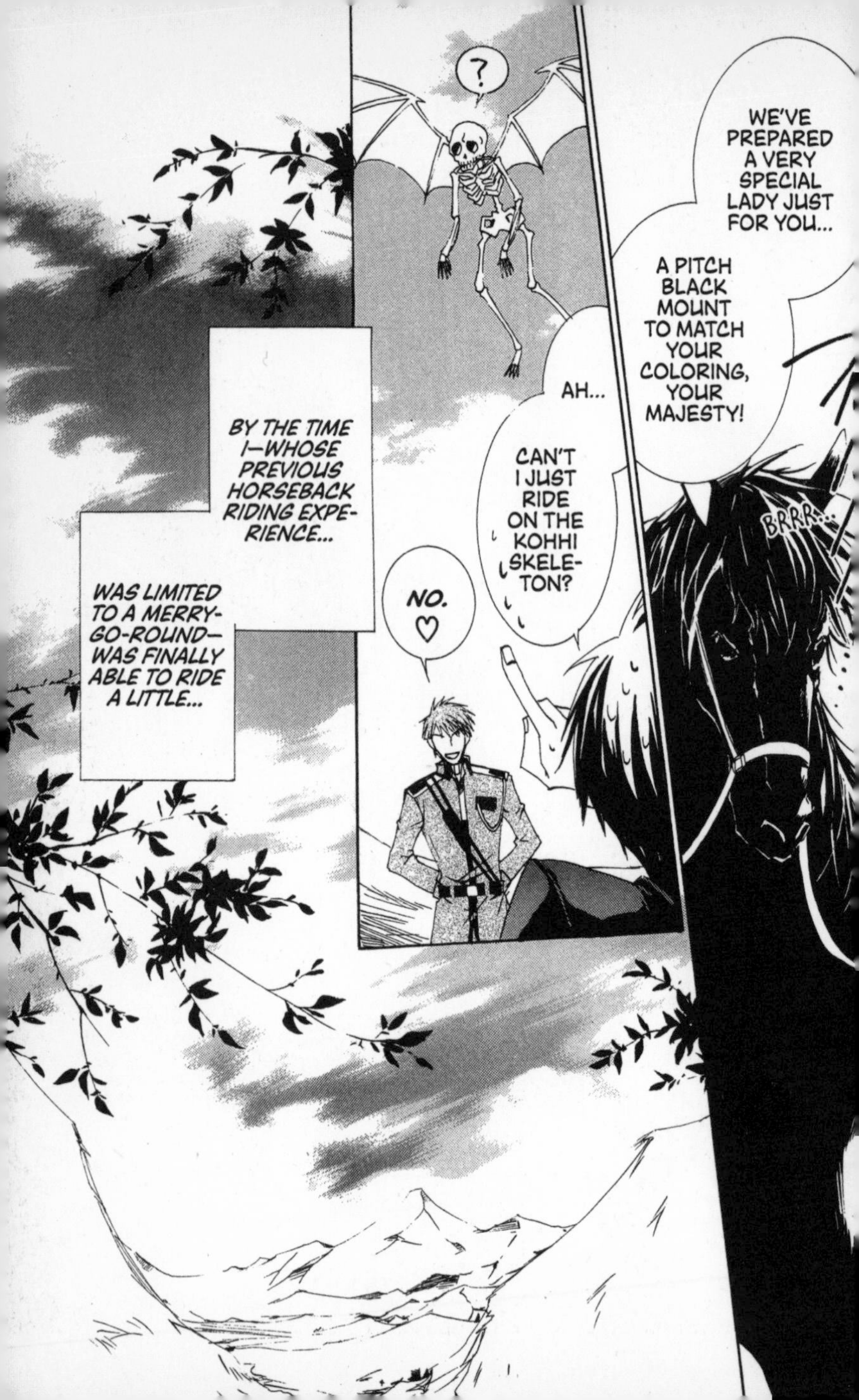
WE'VE PREPARED A VERY SPECIAL LADY JUST FOR YOU...
A PITCH BLACK MOUNT TO MATCH YOUR COLORING, YOUR MAJESTY!
BRRR...
?
AH...
CAN'T I JUST RIDE ON THE KOHHI SKELETON?
NO. ♥
BY THE TIME I—WHOSE PREVIOUS HORSEBACK RIDING EXPERIENCE...
WAS LIMITED TO A MERRY-GO-ROUND—WAS FINALLY ABLE TO RIDE A LITTLE...

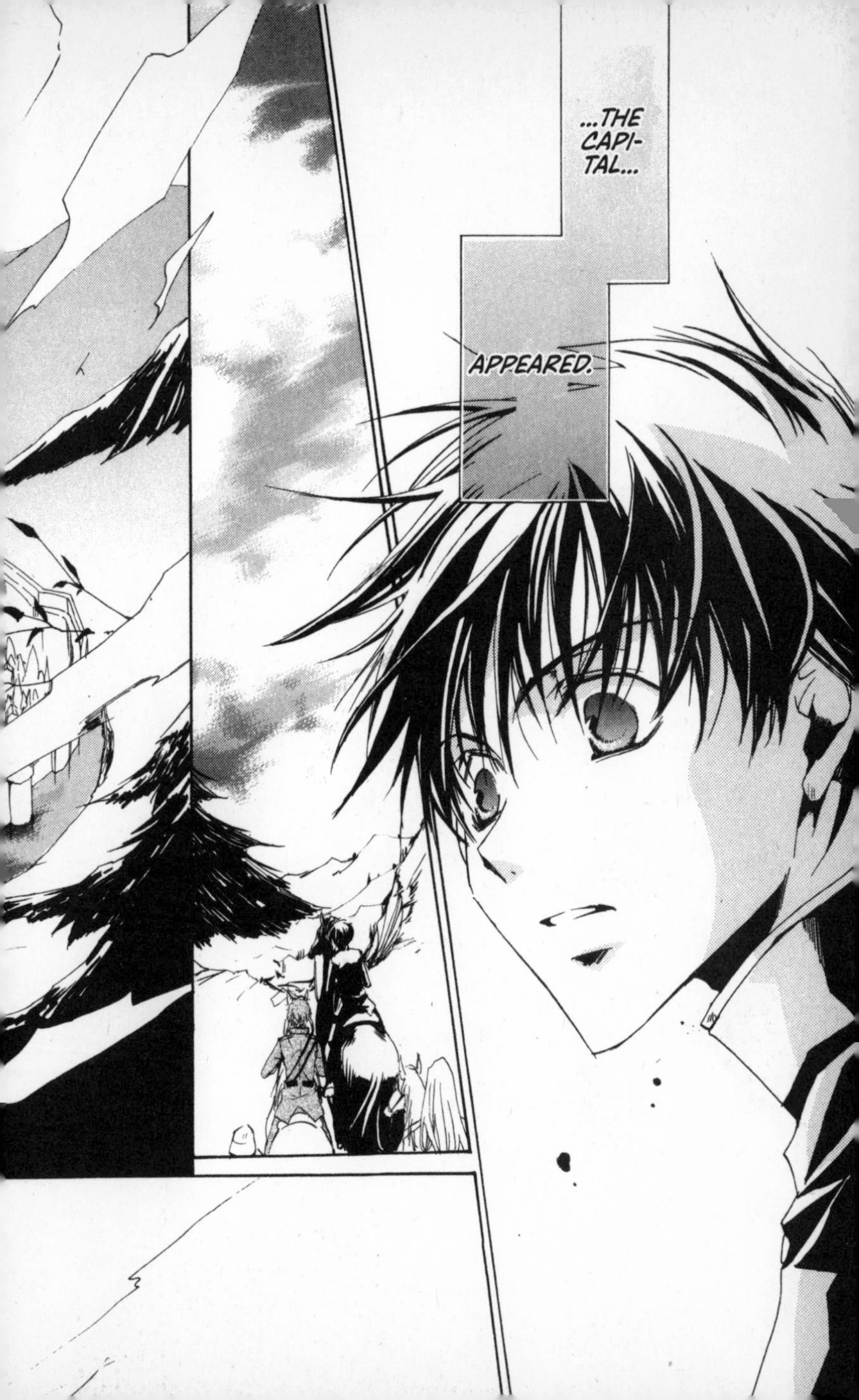
...THE CAPI-TAL...
APPEARED.

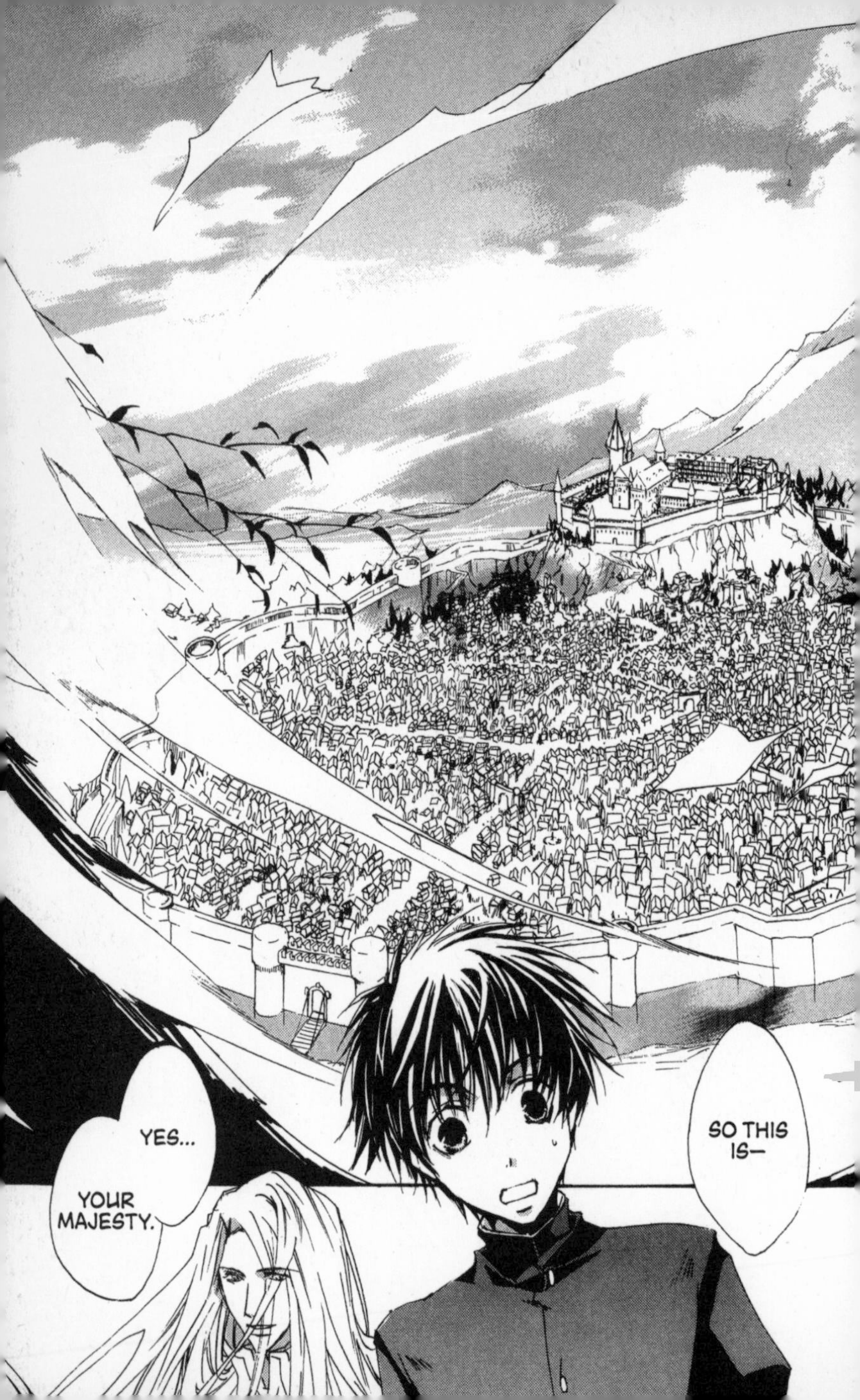
SO THIS IS—
YES...
YOUR MAJESTY.

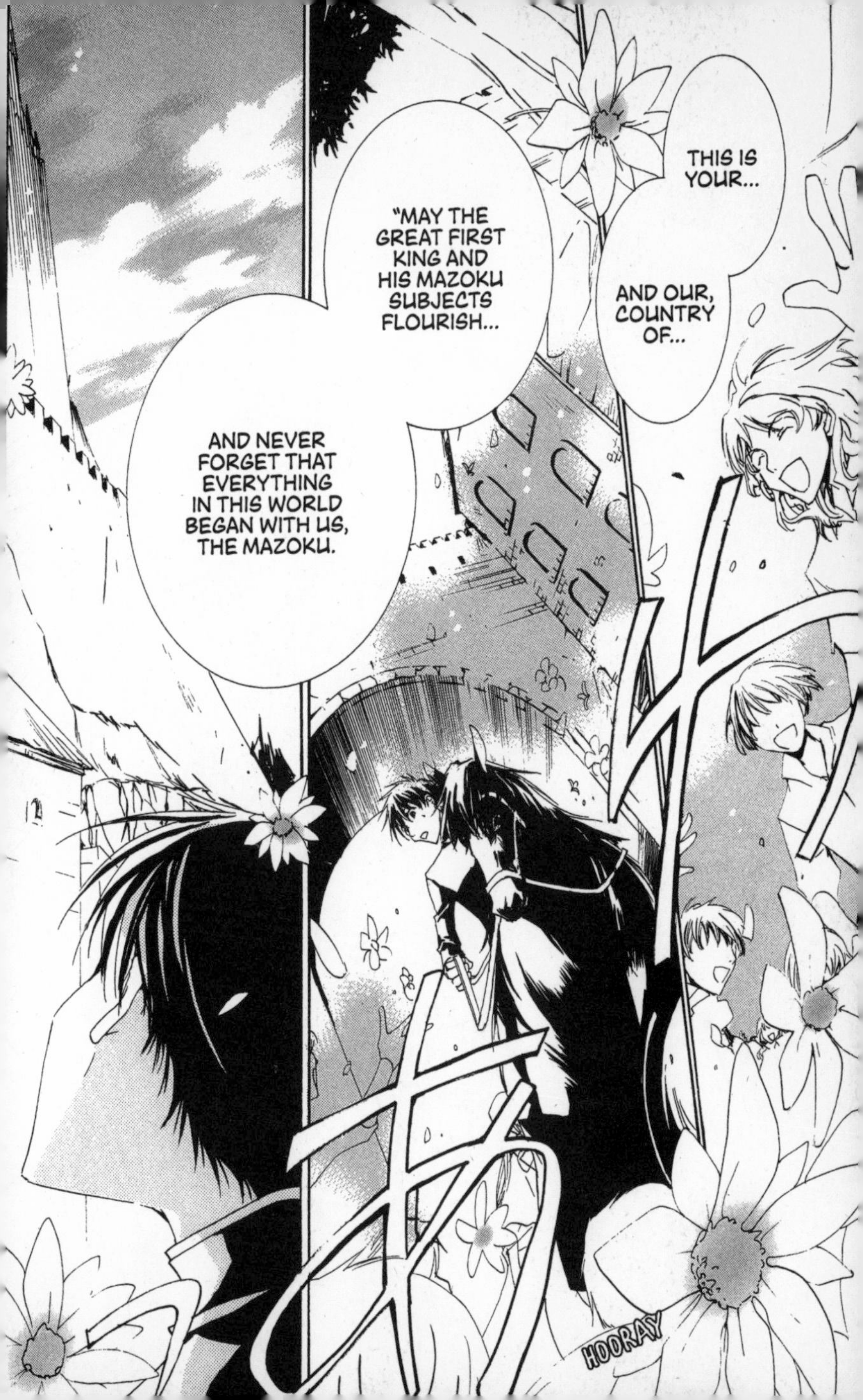
THIS IS YOUR...
AND OUR, COUNTRY OF...
"MAY THE GREAT FIRST KING AND HIS MAZOKU SUBJECTS FLOURISH...
AND NEVER FORGET THAT EVERYTHING IN THIS WORLD BEGAN WITH US, THE MAZOKU.
HOORAY

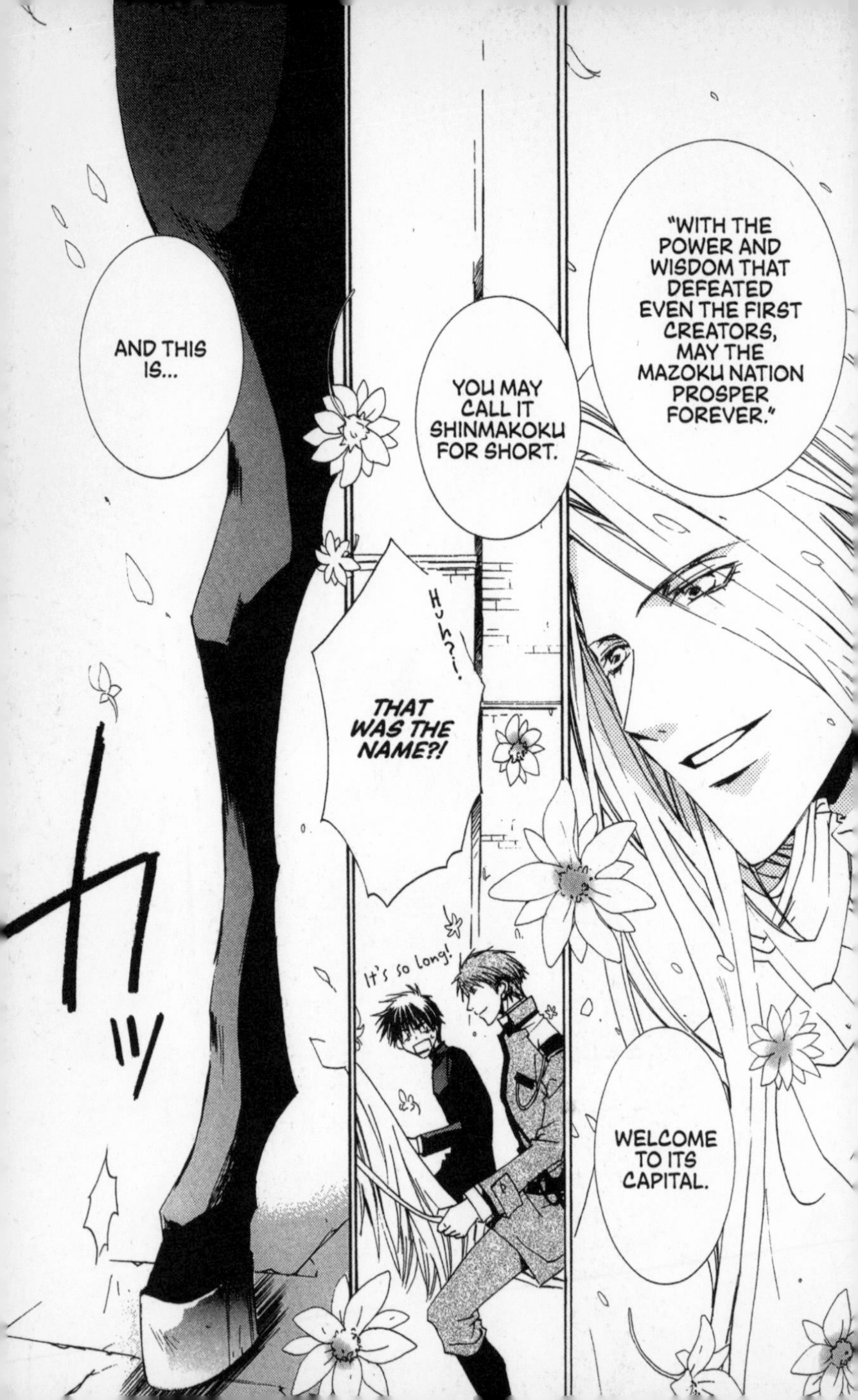
"WITH THE POWER AND WISDOM THAT DEFEATED EVEN THE FIRST CREATORS, MAY THE MAZOKU NATION PROSPER FOREVER."
WELCOME TO ITS CAPITAL.
YOU MAY CALL IT SHINMAKOKU FOR SHORT.
Huh?!
THAT WAS THE NAME?!
It's so long!
AND THIS IS...
カッ

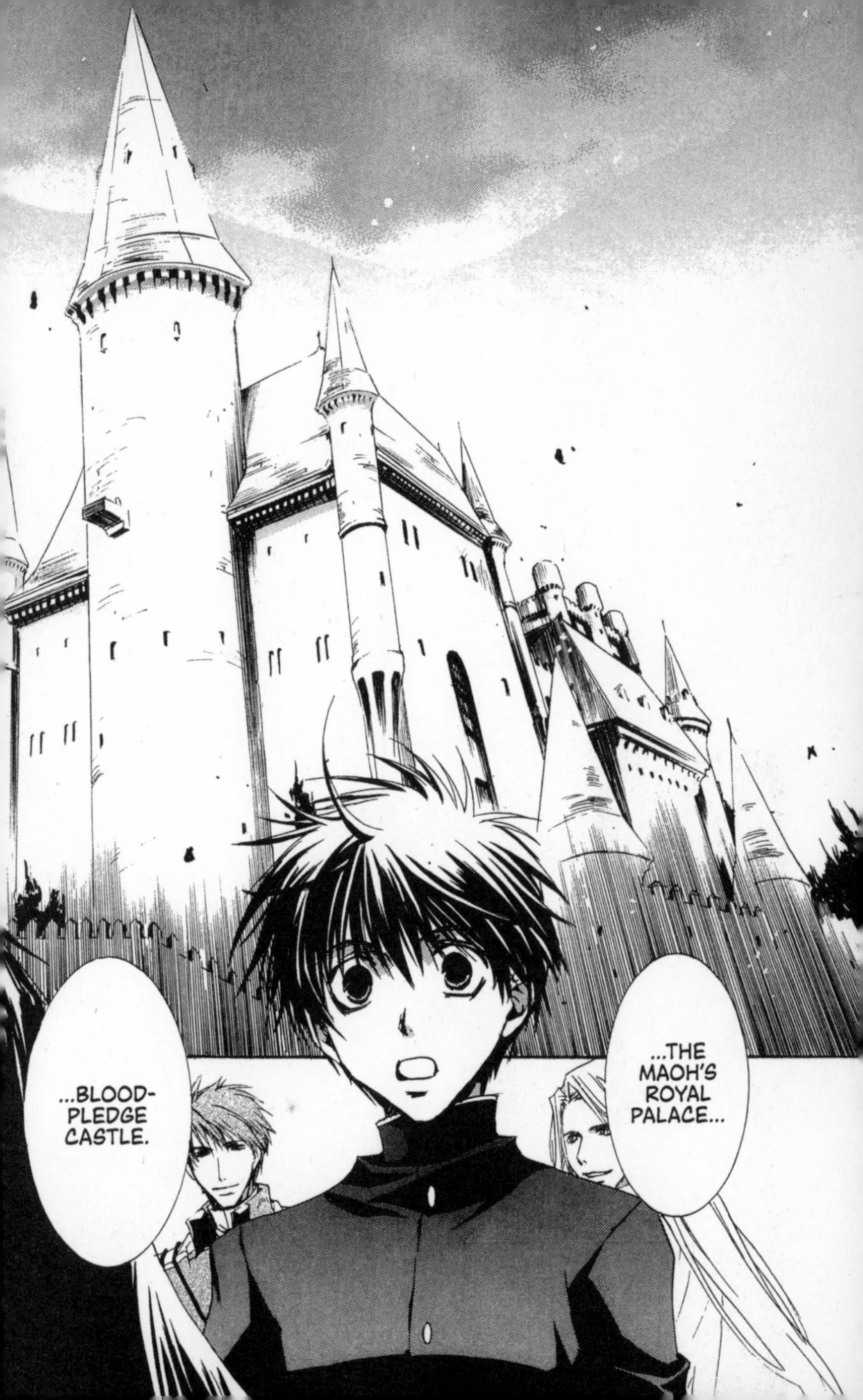
...THE MAOH'S ROYAL PALACE...
...BLOOD-PLEDGE CASTLE.

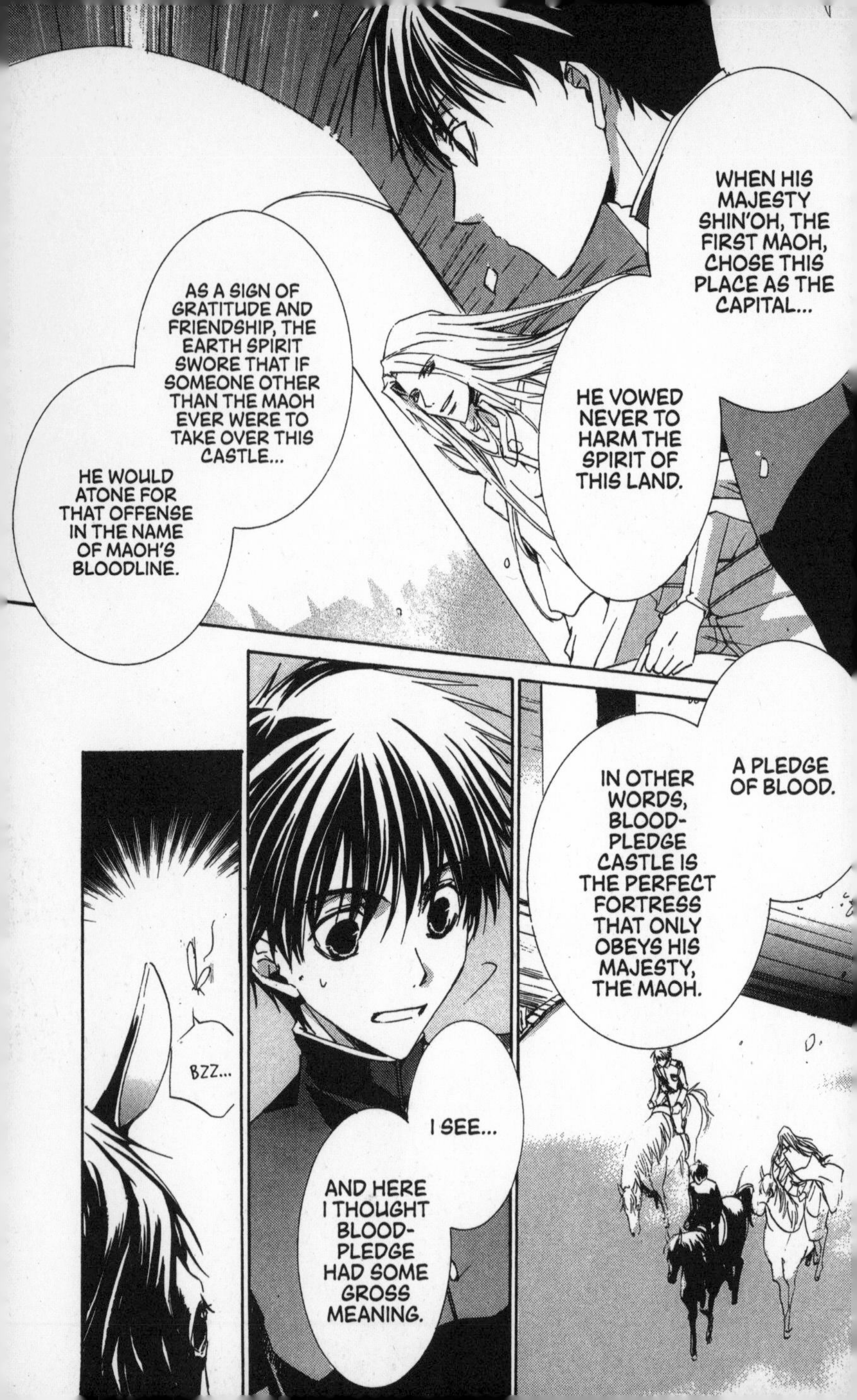
WHEN HIS MAJESTY SHIN'OH, THE FIRST MAOH, CHOSE THIS PLACE AS THE CAPITAL...
HE VOWED NEVER TO HARM THE SPIRIT OF THIS LAND.
AS A SIGN OF GRATITUDE AND FRIENDSHIP, THE EARTH SPIRIT SWORE THAT IF SOMEONE OTHER THAN THE MAOH EVER WERE TO TAKE OVER THIS CASTLE...
HE WOULD ATONE FOR THAT OFFENSE IN THE NAME OF MAOH'S BLOODLINE.
A PLEDGE OF BLOOD.
IN OTHER WORDS, BLOOD-PLEDGE CASTLE IS THE PERFECT FORTRESS THAT ONLY OBEYS HIS MAJESTY, THE MAOH.
I SEE...
AND HERE I THOUGHT BLOOD-PLEDGE HAD SOME GROSS MEANING.
BZZ...

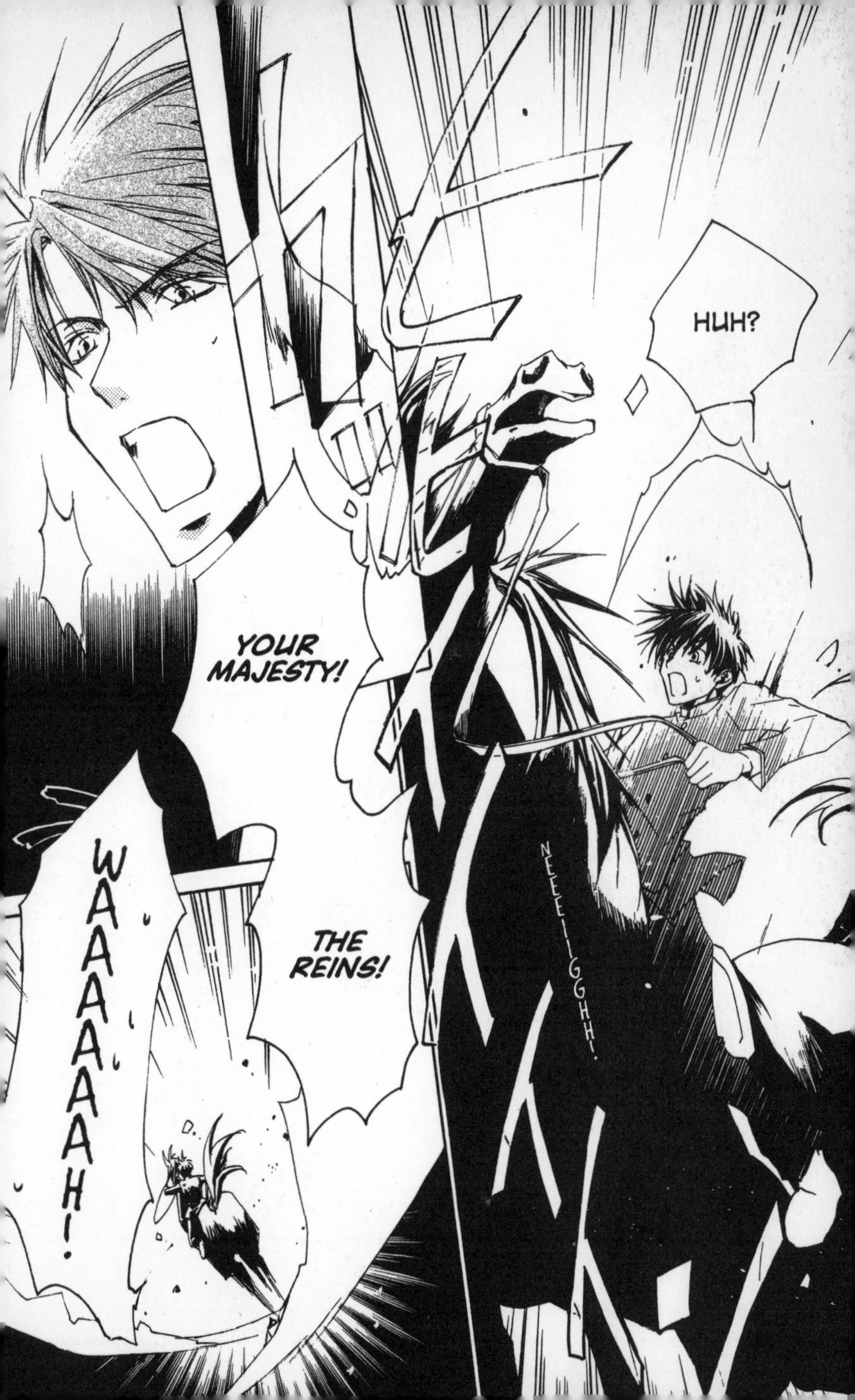
HUH?
YOUR MAJESTY!
NEEEIIGGH!
THE REINS!
WAAAAAAH!

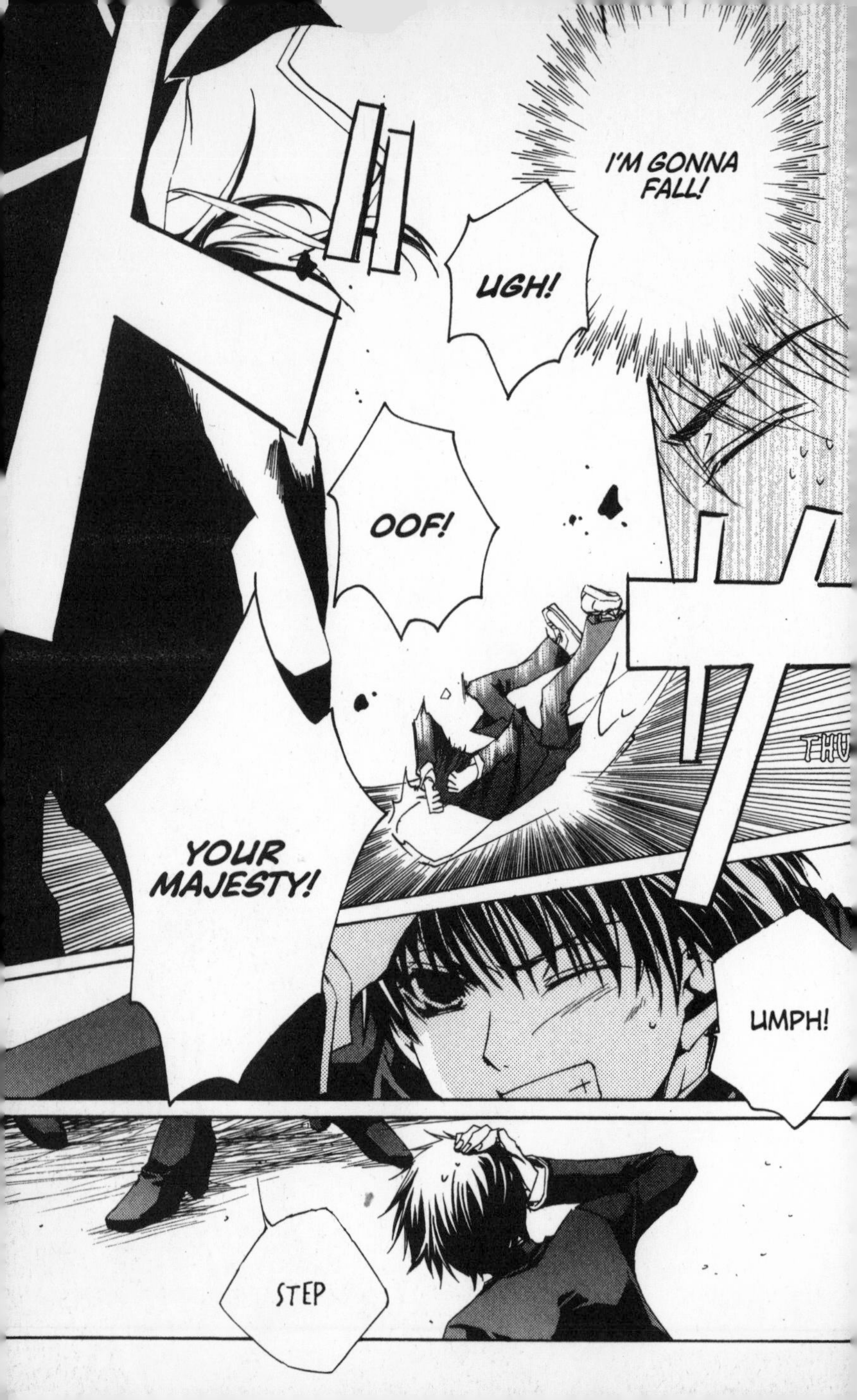
I'M GONNA FALL!
UGH!
OOF!
THU
YOUR MAJESTY!
UMPH!
STEP

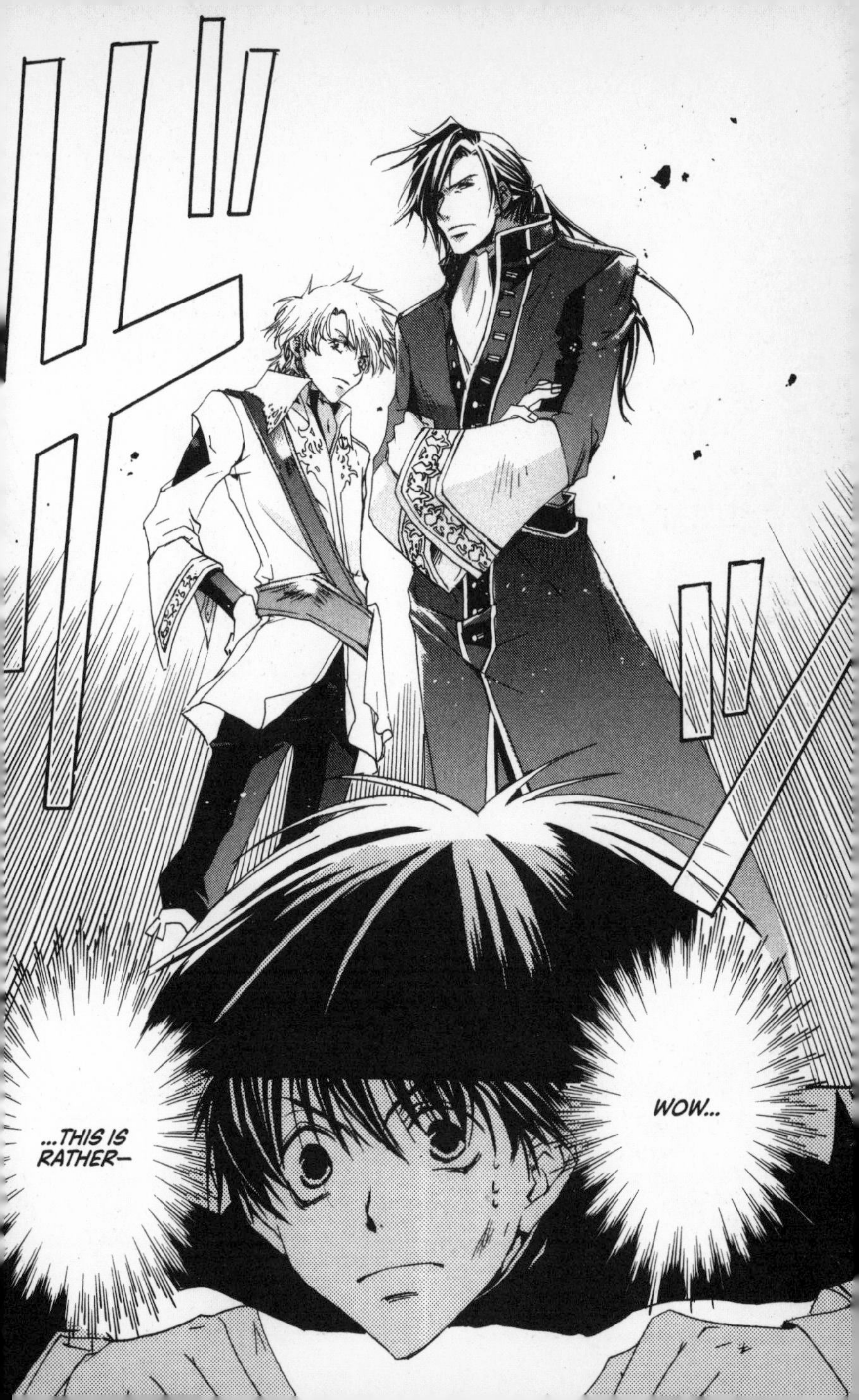
WOW...
...THIS IS RATHER—

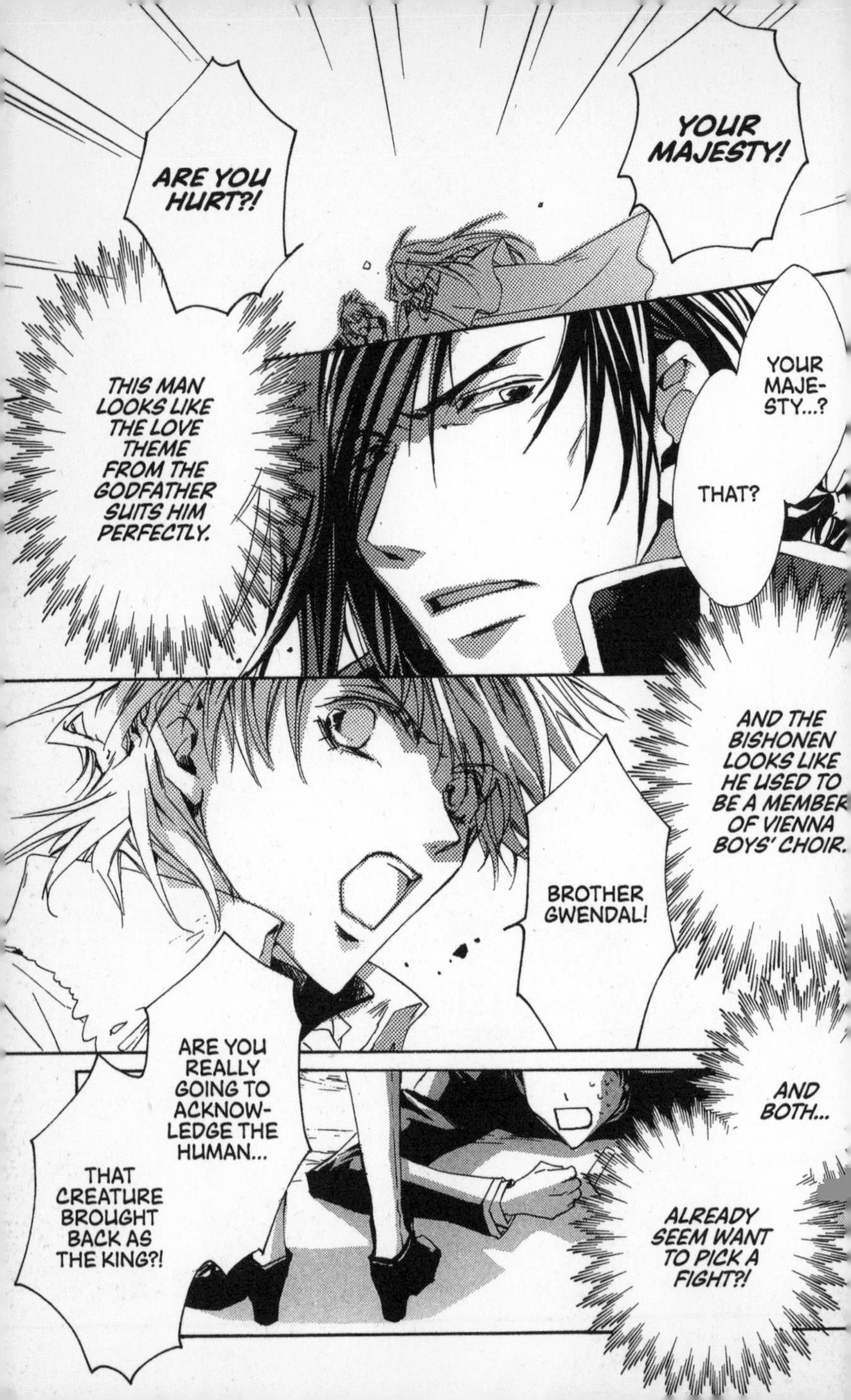
YOUR MAJESTY!
ARE YOU HURT?!
YOUR MAJE-STY...?
THAT?
THIS MAN LOOKS LIKE THE LOVE THEME FROM THE GODFATHER SUITS HIM PERFECTLY.
AND THE BISHONEN LOOKS LIKE HE USED TO BE A MEMBER OF VIENNA BOYS' CHOIR.
BROTHER GWENDAL!
AND BOTH...
ALREADY SEEM WANT TO PICK A FIGHT?!
ARE YOU REALLY GOING TO ACKNOW-LEDGE THE HUMAN...
THAT CREATURE BROUGHT BACK AS THE KING?!

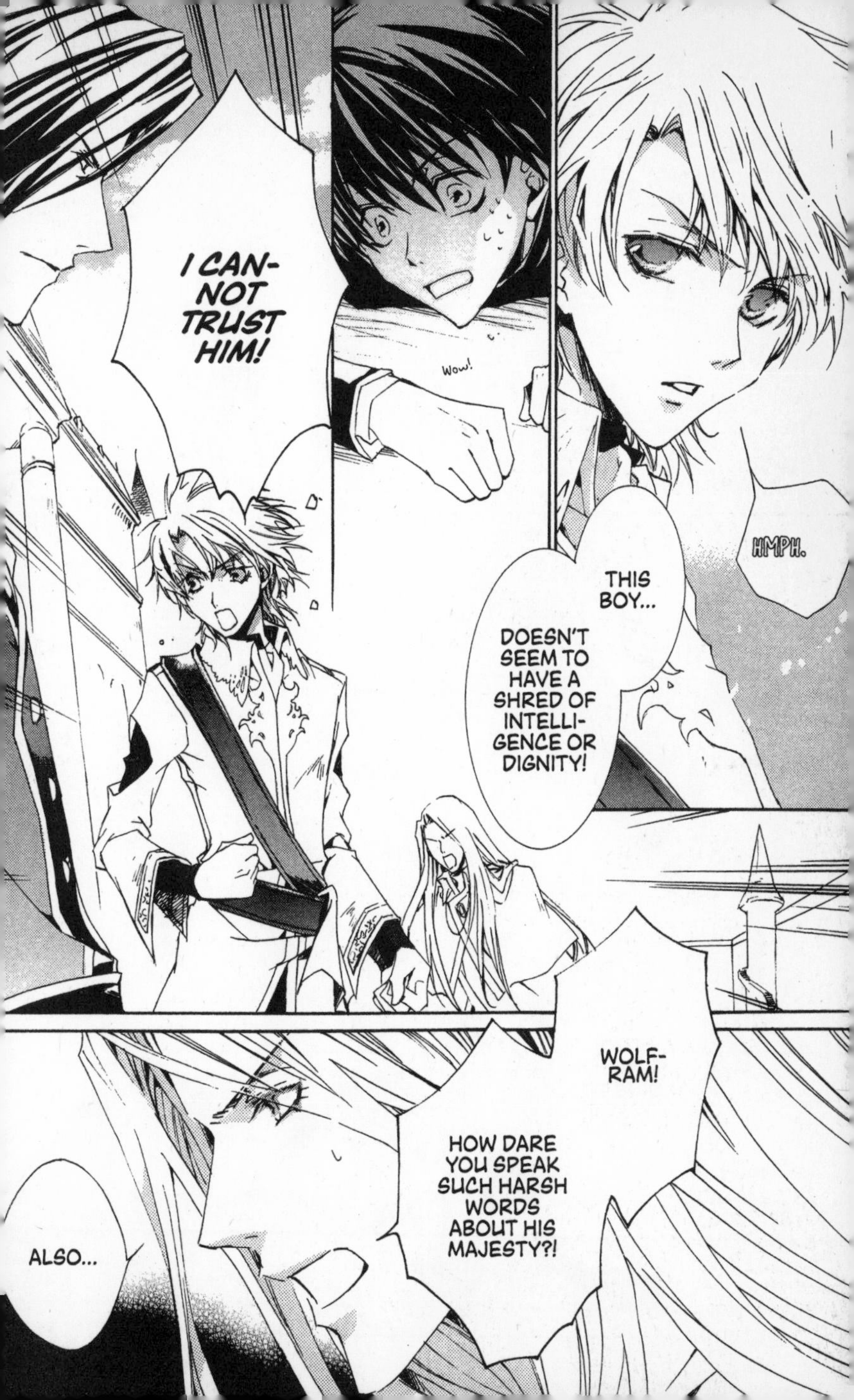

HMPH.
THIS BOY...
DOESN'T SEEM TO HAVE A SHRED OF INTELLI-GENCE OR DIGNITY!
Wow!
I CAN-NOT TRUST HIM!
WOLF-RAM!
HOW DARE YOU SPEAK SUCH HARSH WORDS ABOUT HIS MAJESTY?!
ALSO...

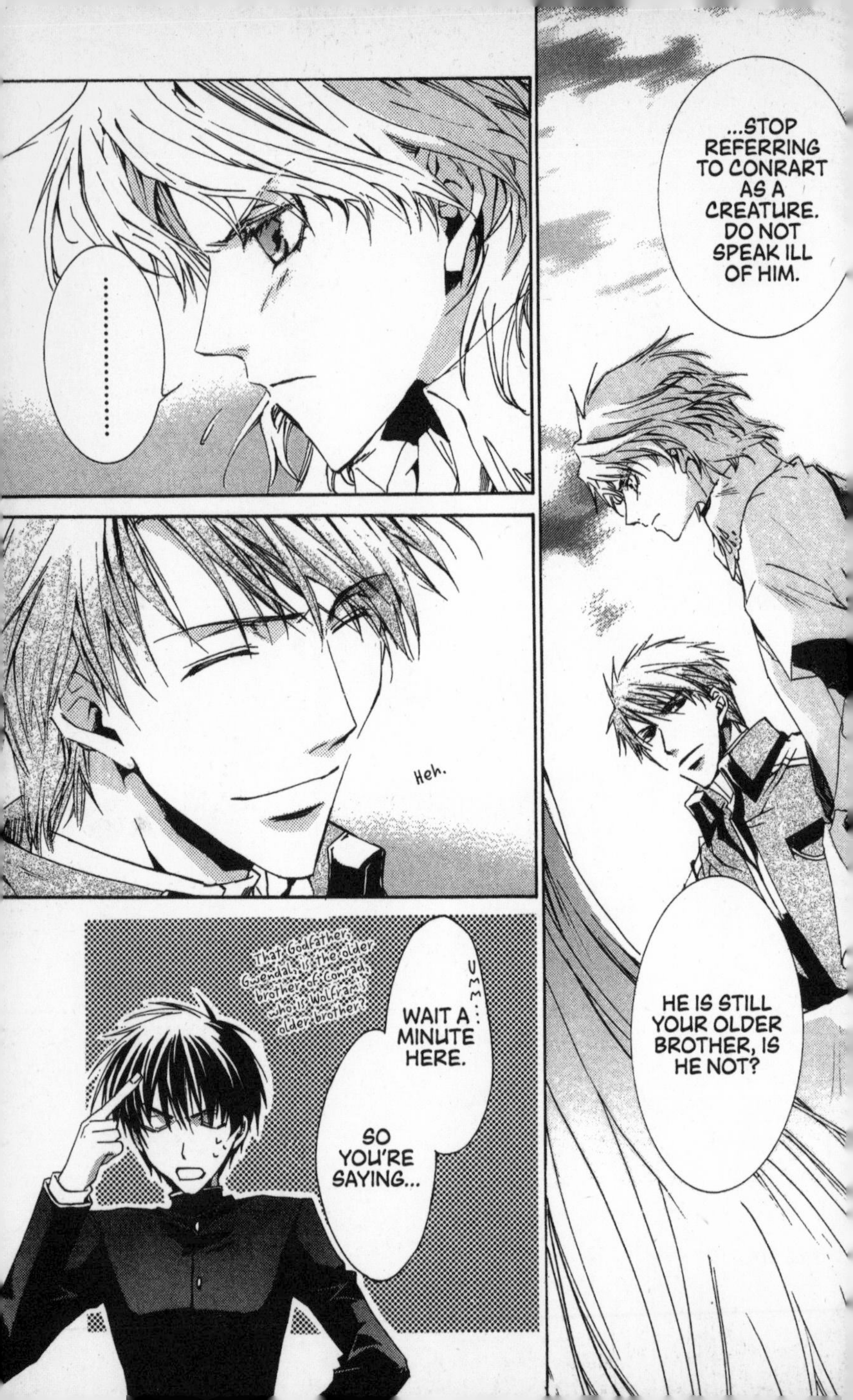
...STOP REFERRING TO CONRART AS A CREATURE. DO NOT SPEAK ILL OF HIM.
HE IS STILL YOUR OLDER BROTHER, IS HE NOT?
......
Heh.
UMM...
WAIT A MINUTE HERE.
That Godfather, Gwendal, is the older brother of Conrad, who is Wolfram's older brother?
SO YOU'RE SAYING...

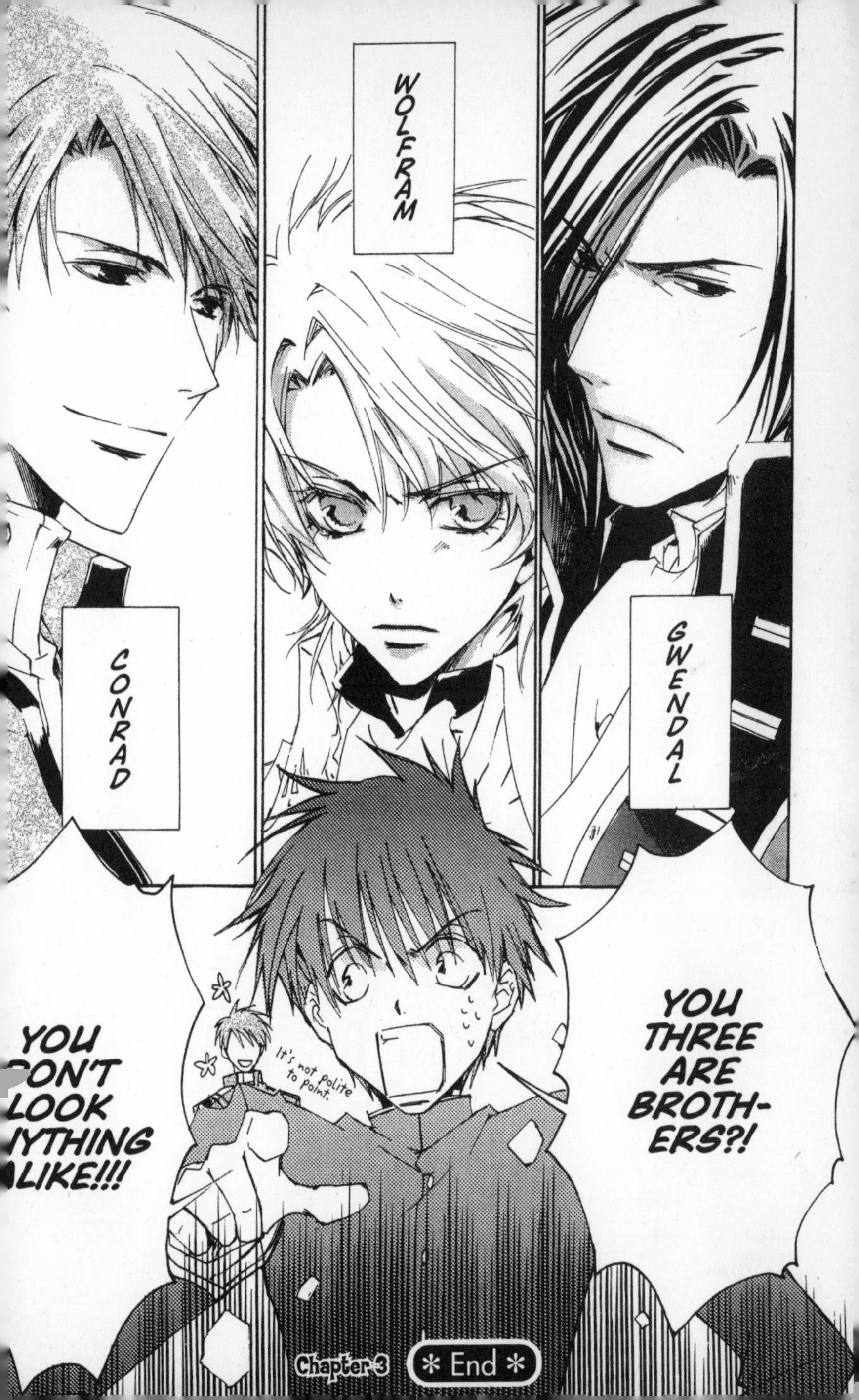
GWENDAL
WOLFRAM
CONRAD
YOU THREE ARE BROTH-ERS?!
It's not polite to point.
YOU ON'T LOOK YTHING LIKE!!!
Chapter 3 * End *

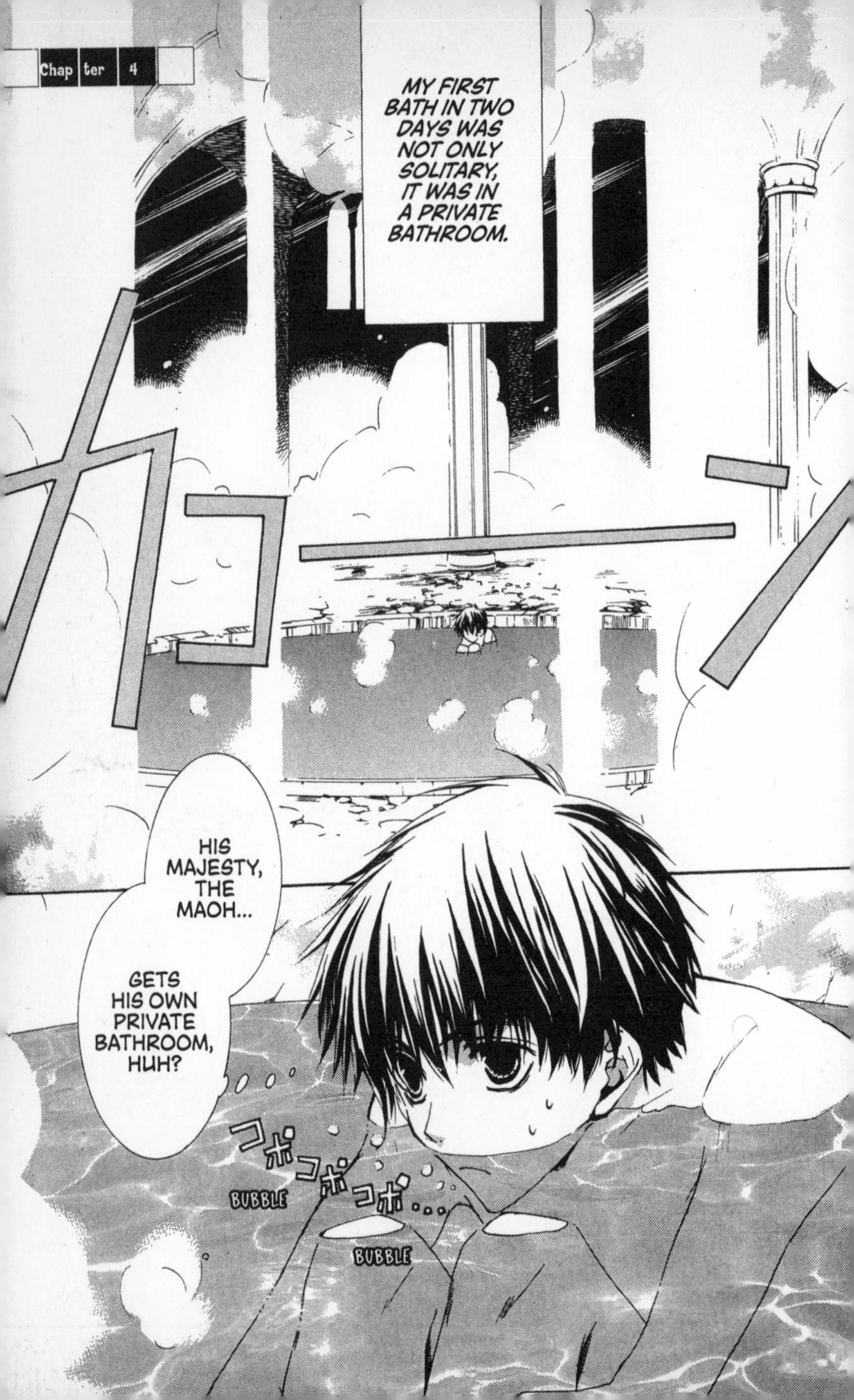
Chapter 4
MY FIRST BATH IN TWO DAYS WAS NOT ONLY SOLITARY, IT WAS IN A PRIVATE BATHROOM.
HIS MAJESTY, THE MAOH...
GETS HIS OWN PRIVATE BATHROOM, HUH?
BUBBLE
BUBBLE

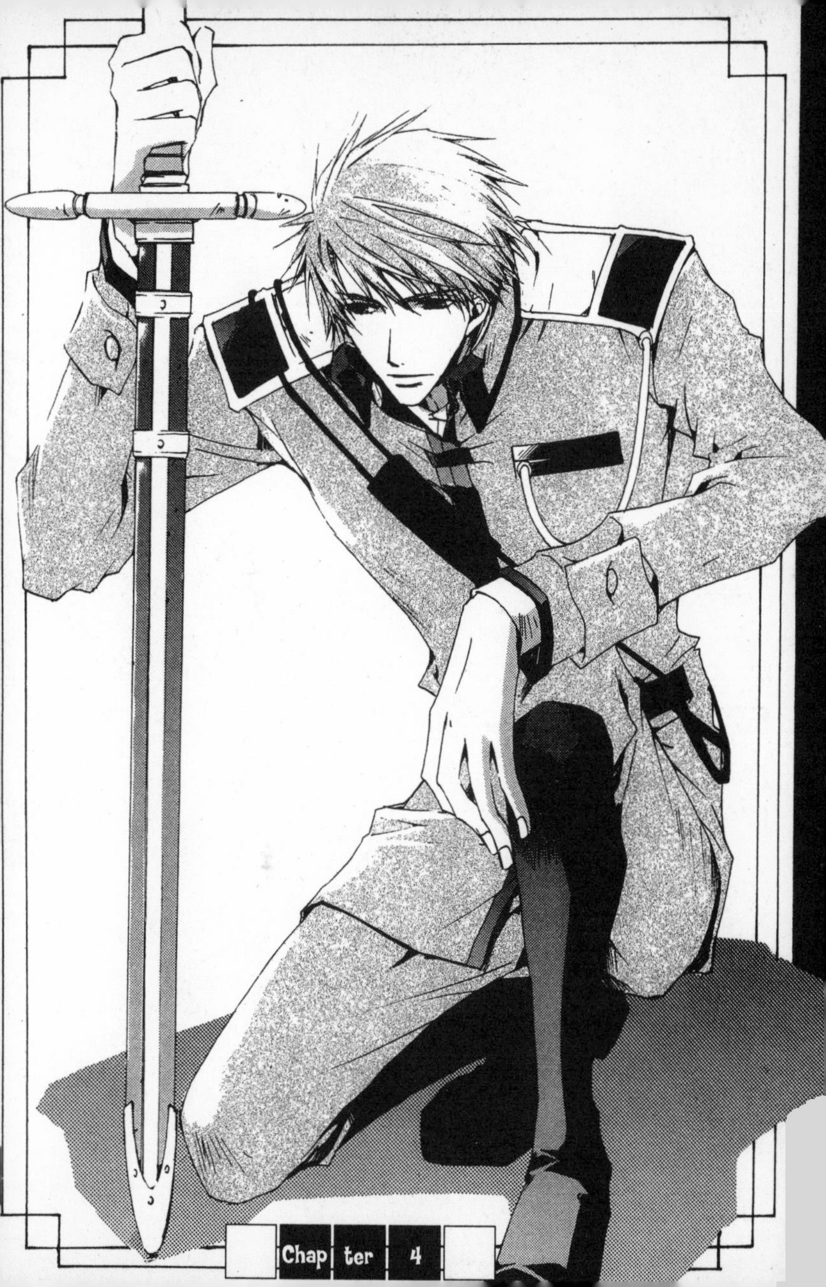
Chap ter 4

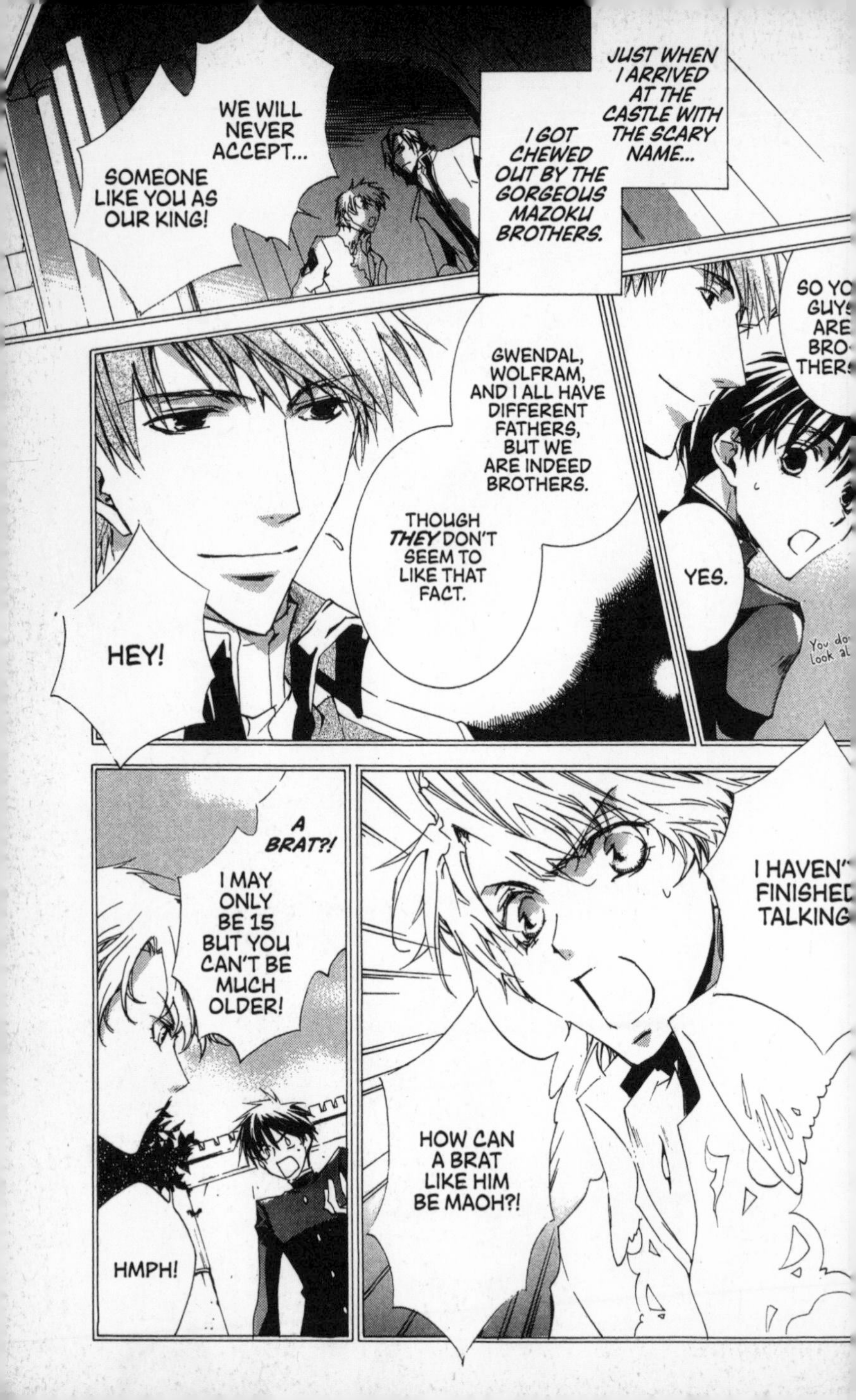
JUST WHEN I ARRIVED AT THE CASTLE WITH THE SCARY NAME...
I GOT CHEWED OUT BY THE GORGEOUS MAZOKU BROTHERS.
WE WILL NEVER ACCEPT...
SOMEONE LIKE YOU AS OUR KING!
SO YO GUYS ARE BRO- THERS
YES.
You do look al
GWENDAL, WOLFRAM, AND I ALL HAVE DIFFERENT FATHERS, BUT WE ARE INDEED BROTHERS.
THOUGH *THEY* DON'T SEEM TO LIKE THAT FACT.
HEY!
I HAVEN' FINISHED TALKING
HOW CAN A BRAT LIKE HIM BE MAOH?!
A BRAT?!
I MAY ONLY BE 15 BUT YOU CAN'T BE MUCH OLDER!
HMPH!

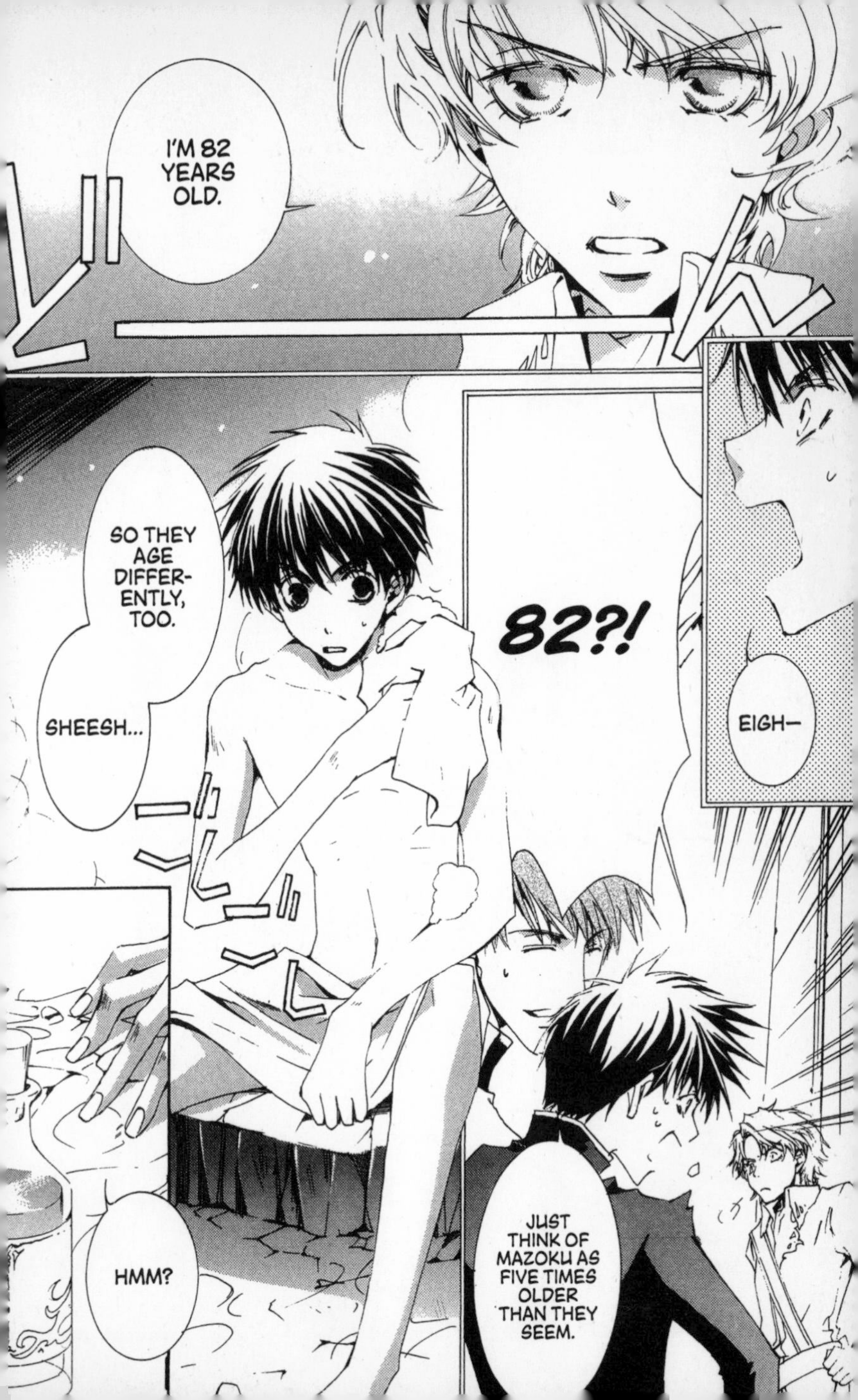
I'M 82 YEARS OLD.
EIGH—
82?!
SO THEY AGE DIFFERENTLY, TOO.
SHEESH...
JUST THINK OF MAZOKU AS FIVE TIMES OLDER THAN THEY SEEM.
HMM?

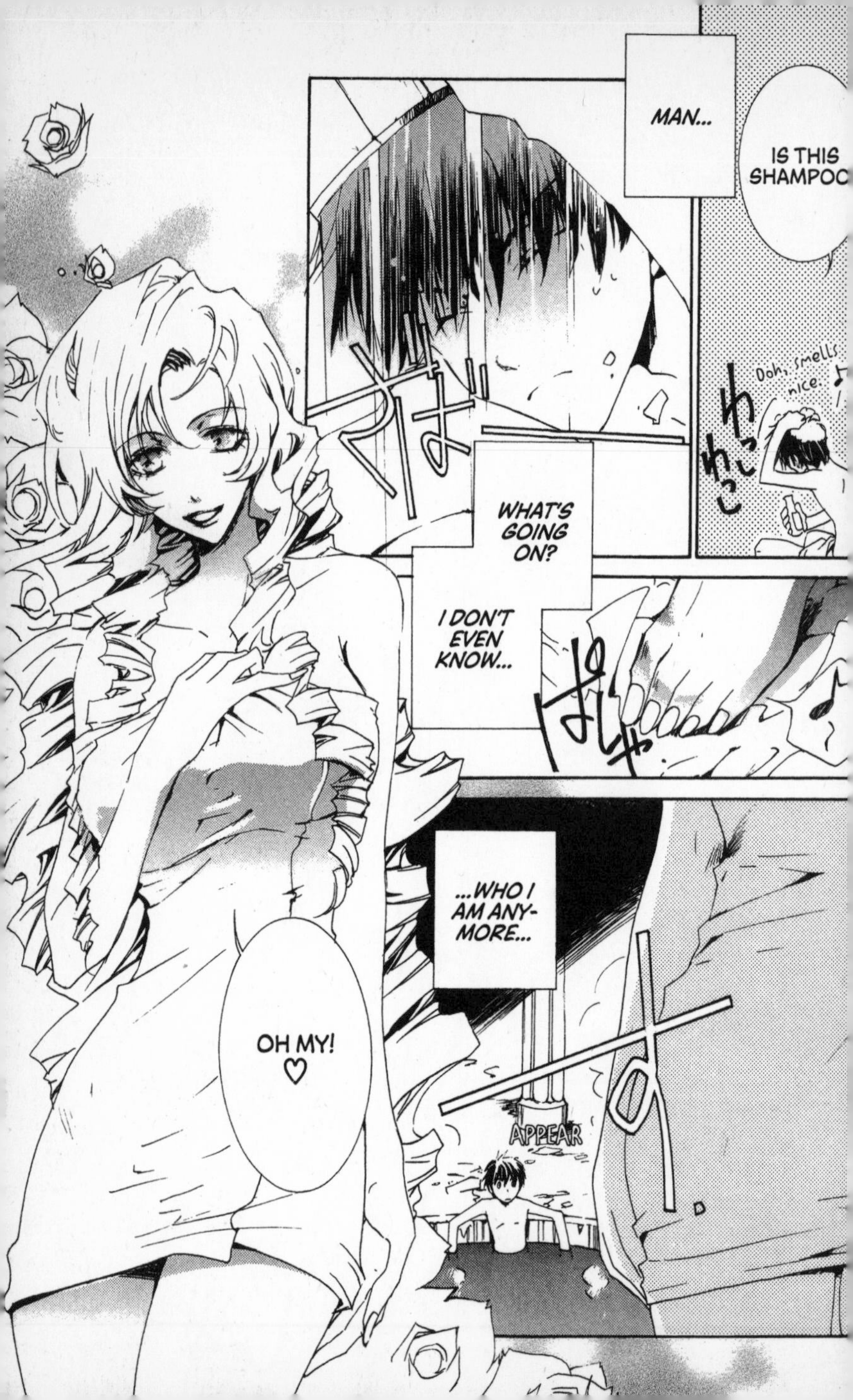

IS THIS SHAMPOO
Ooh, smells nice. ♪
MAN...
WHAT'S GOING ON?
I DON'T EVEN KNOW...
...WHO I AM ANYMORE...
APPEAR
OH MY! ♡

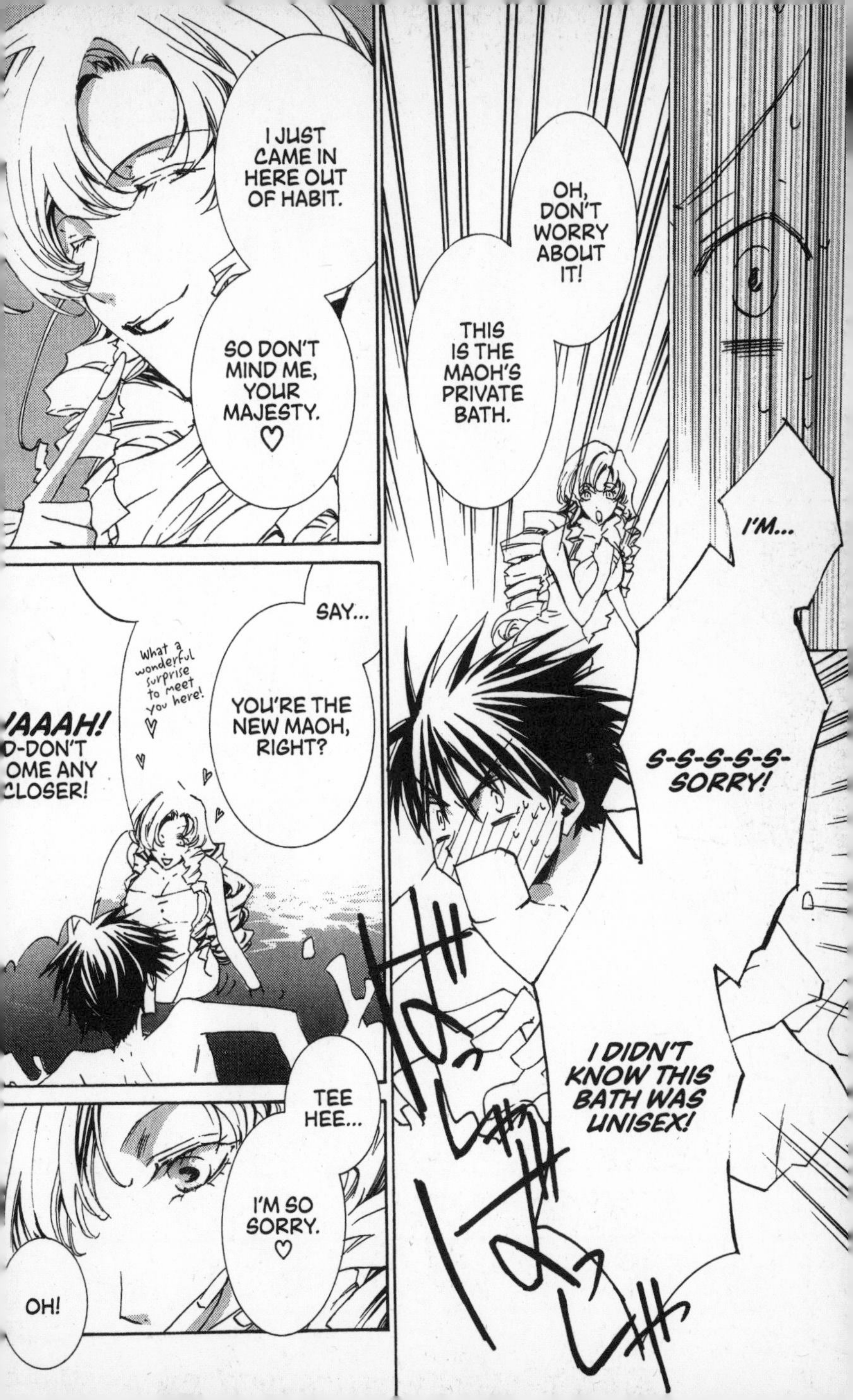
OH, DON'T WORRY ABOUT IT!
THIS IS THE MAOH'S PRIVATE BATH.
I'M...
S-S-S-S-S-SORRY!
I DIDN'T KNOW THIS BATH WAS UNISEX!
I JUST CAME IN HERE OUT OF HABIT.
SO DON'T MIND ME, YOUR MAJESTY. ♡
SAY...
YOU'RE THE NEW MAOH, RIGHT?
What a wonderful surprise to meet you here! ♡
AAAH! D-DON'T OME ANY CLOSER!
TEE HEE...
I'M SO SORRY. ♡
OH!

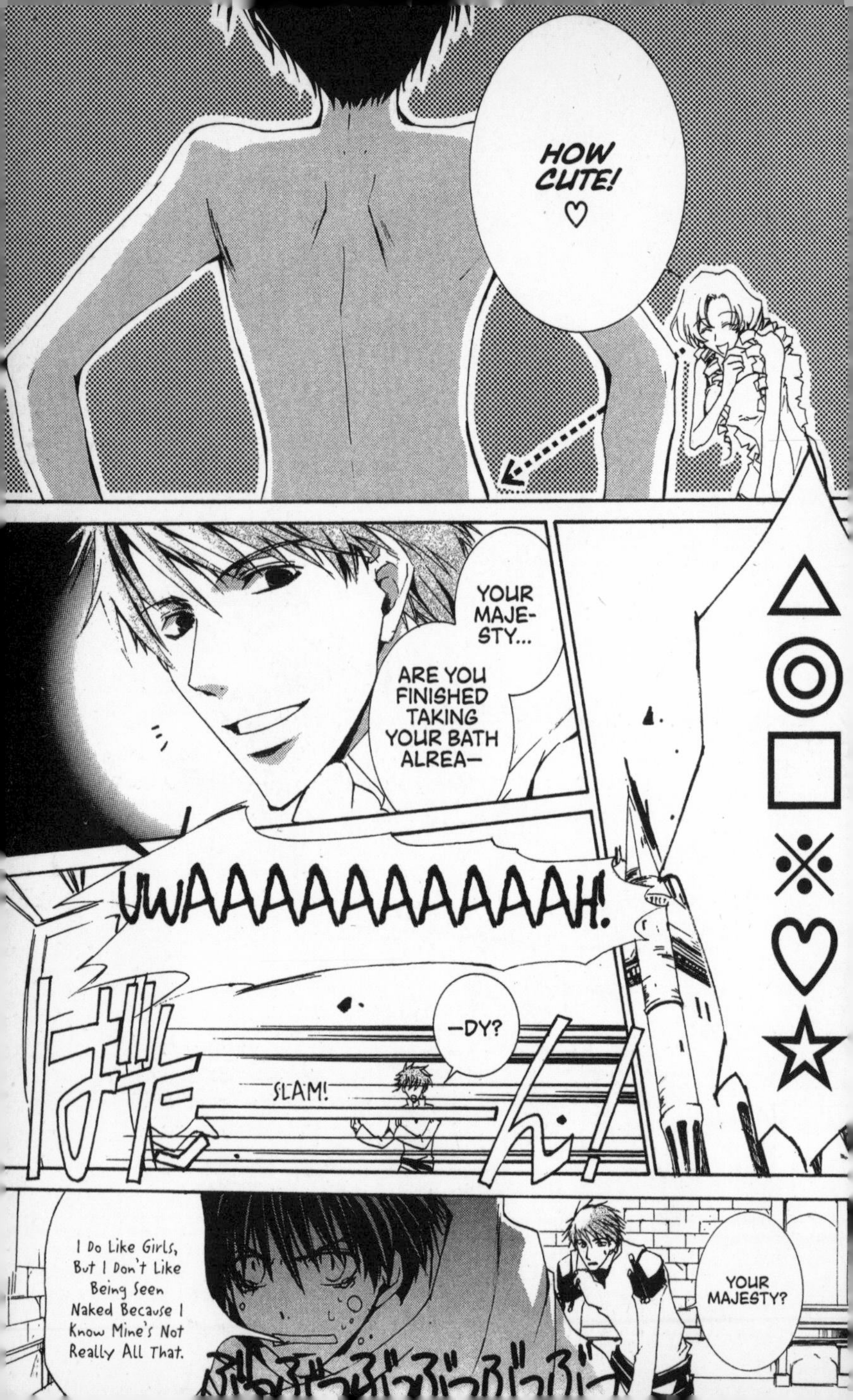
HOW CUTE! ♡
△ ◎ □ ※ ♡ ☆
YOUR MAJESTY...
ARE YOU FINISHED TAKING YOUR BATH ALREA—
UWAAAAAAAAAAAAH!
—DY?
SLAM!
YOUR MAJESTY?
I Do Like Girls, But I Don't Like Being Seen Naked Because I Know Mine's Not Really All That.

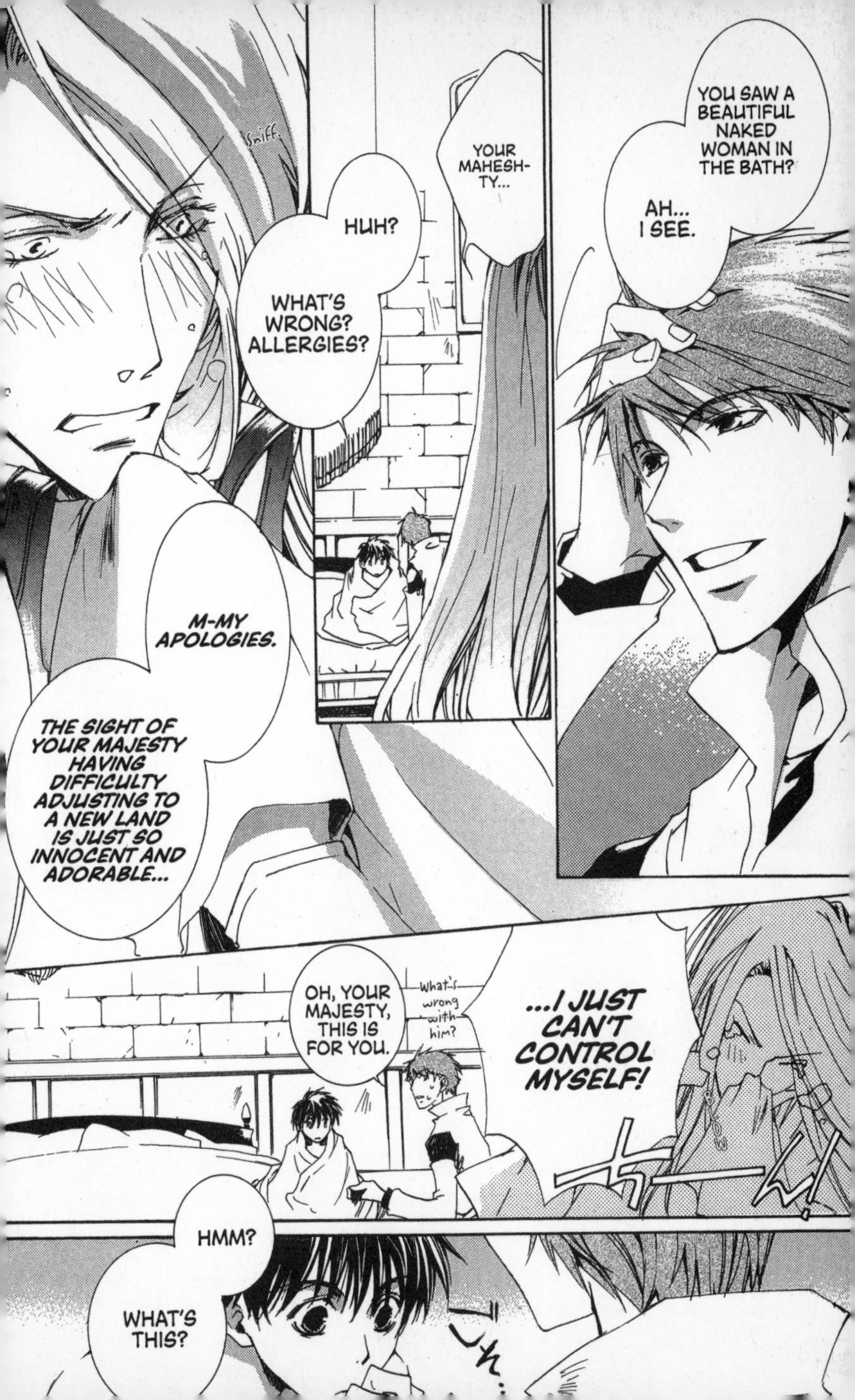
YOU SAW A BEAUTIFUL NAKED WOMAN IN THE BATH?
AH... I SEE.
YOUR MAHESH-TY...
HUH?
WHAT'S WRONG? ALLERGIES?
Sniff.
M-MY APOLOGIES.
THE SIGHT OF YOUR MAJESTY HAVING DIFFICULTY ADJUSTING TO A NEW LAND IS JUST SO INNOCENT AND ADORABLE...
...I JUST CAN'T CONTROL MYSELF!
What's wrong with him?
OH, YOUR MAJESTY, THIS IS FOR YOU.
HMM?
WHAT'S THIS?

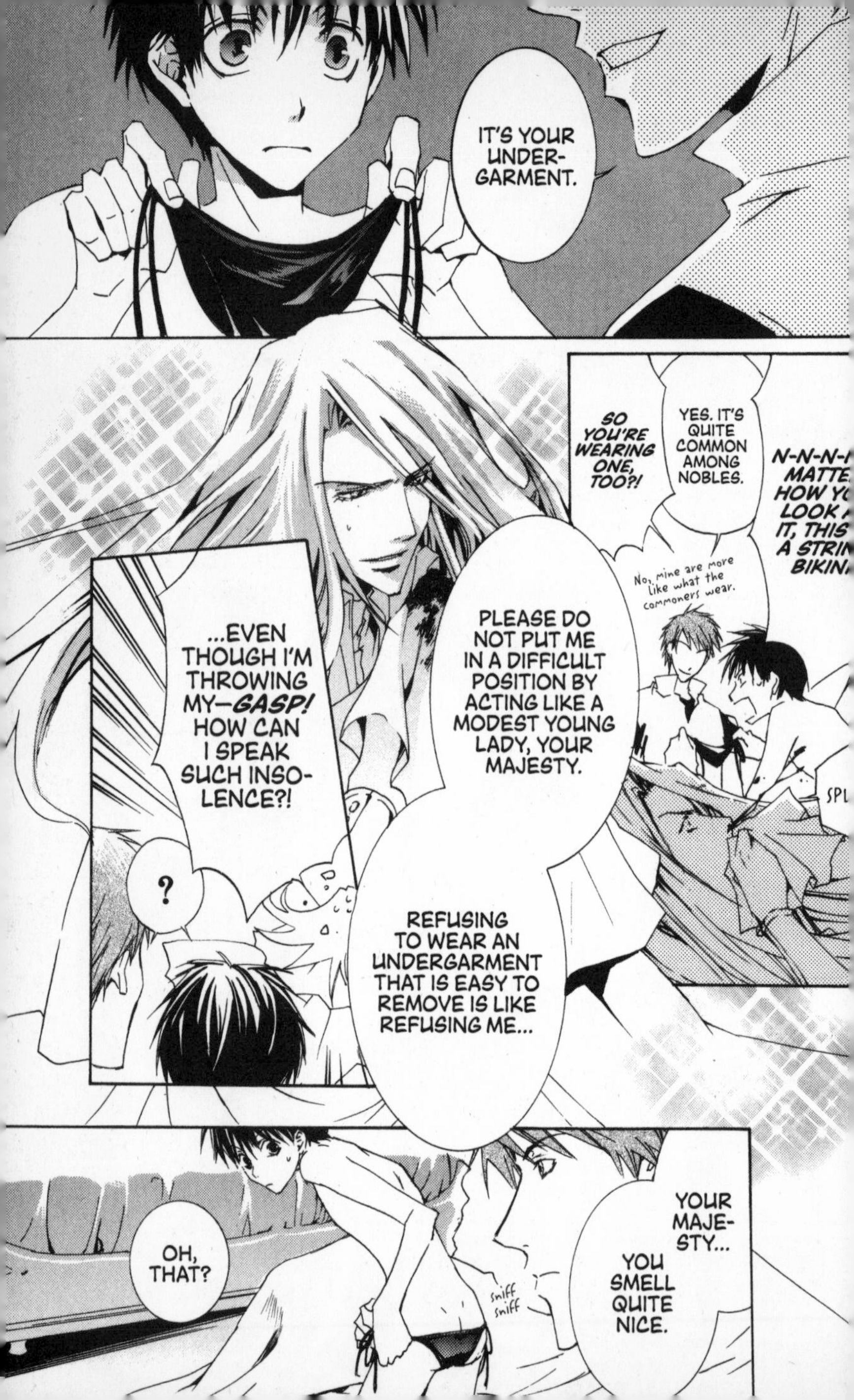

IT'S YOUR UNDER-GARMENT.
N-N-N-N MATTE HOW Y LOOK A IT, THIS A STRIN BIKIN
YES. IT'S QUITE COMMON AMONG NOBLES.
SO YOU'RE WEARING ONE, TOO?!
No, mine are more like what the commoners wear.
SPL
PLEASE DO NOT PUT ME IN A DIFFICULT POSITION BY ACTING LIKE A MODEST YOUNG LADY, YOUR MAJESTY.
...EVEN THOUGH I'M THROWING MY—*GASP!* HOW CAN I SPEAK SUCH INSO-LENCE?!
?
REFUSING TO WEAR AN UNDERGARMENT THAT IS EASY TO REMOVE IS LIKE REFUSING ME...
YOUR MAJE-STY... YOU SMELL QUITE NICE.
sniff sniff
OH, THAT?

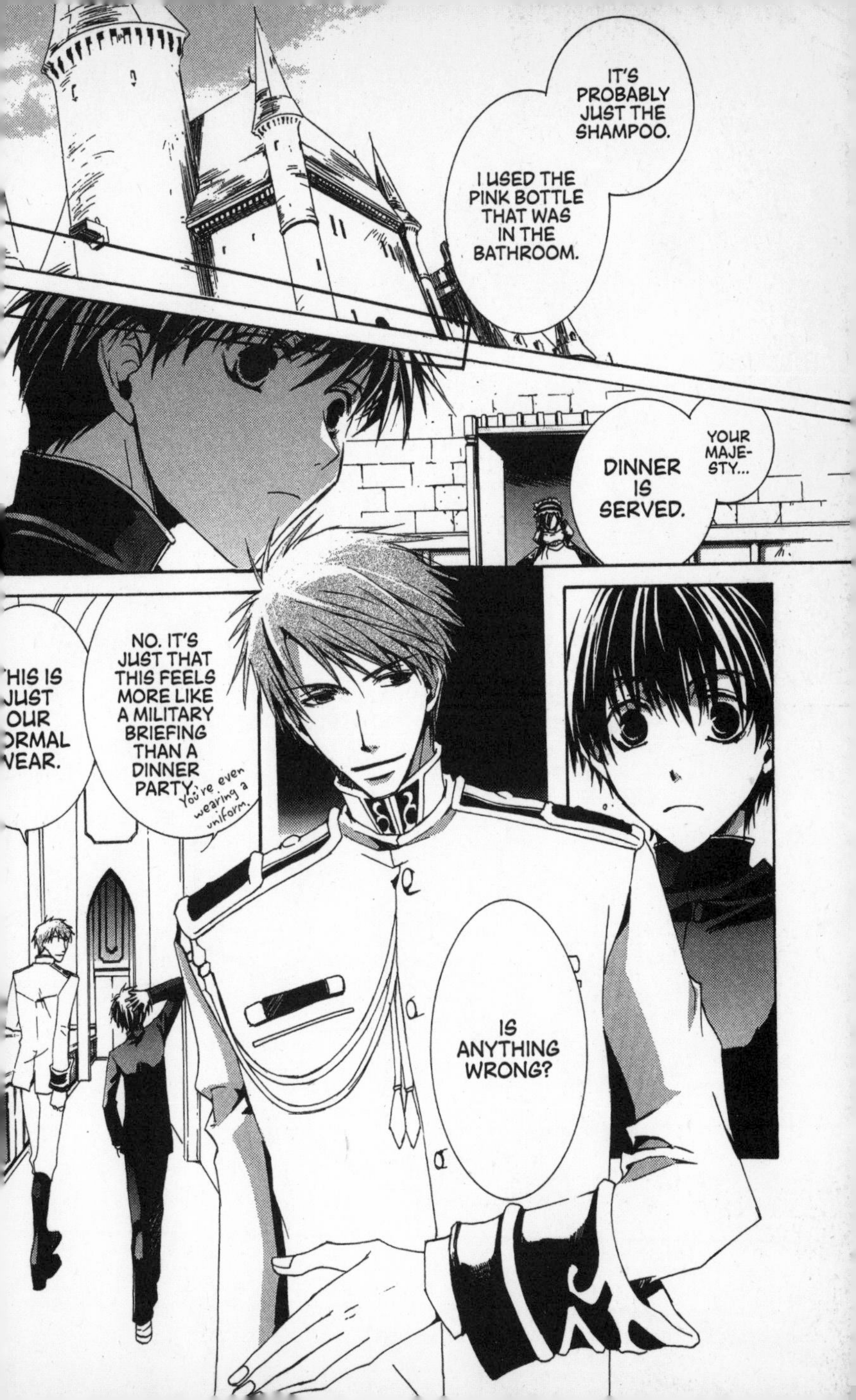
IT'S PROBABLY JUST THE SHAMPOO.
I USED THE PINK BOTTLE THAT WAS IN THE BATHROOM.
YOUR MAJESTY...
DINNER IS SERVED.
IS ANYTHING WRONG?
NO. IT'S JUST THAT THIS FEELS MORE LIKE A MILITARY BRIEFING THAN A DINNER PARTY.
You're even wearing a uniform.
HIS IS JUST OUR RMAL VEAR.

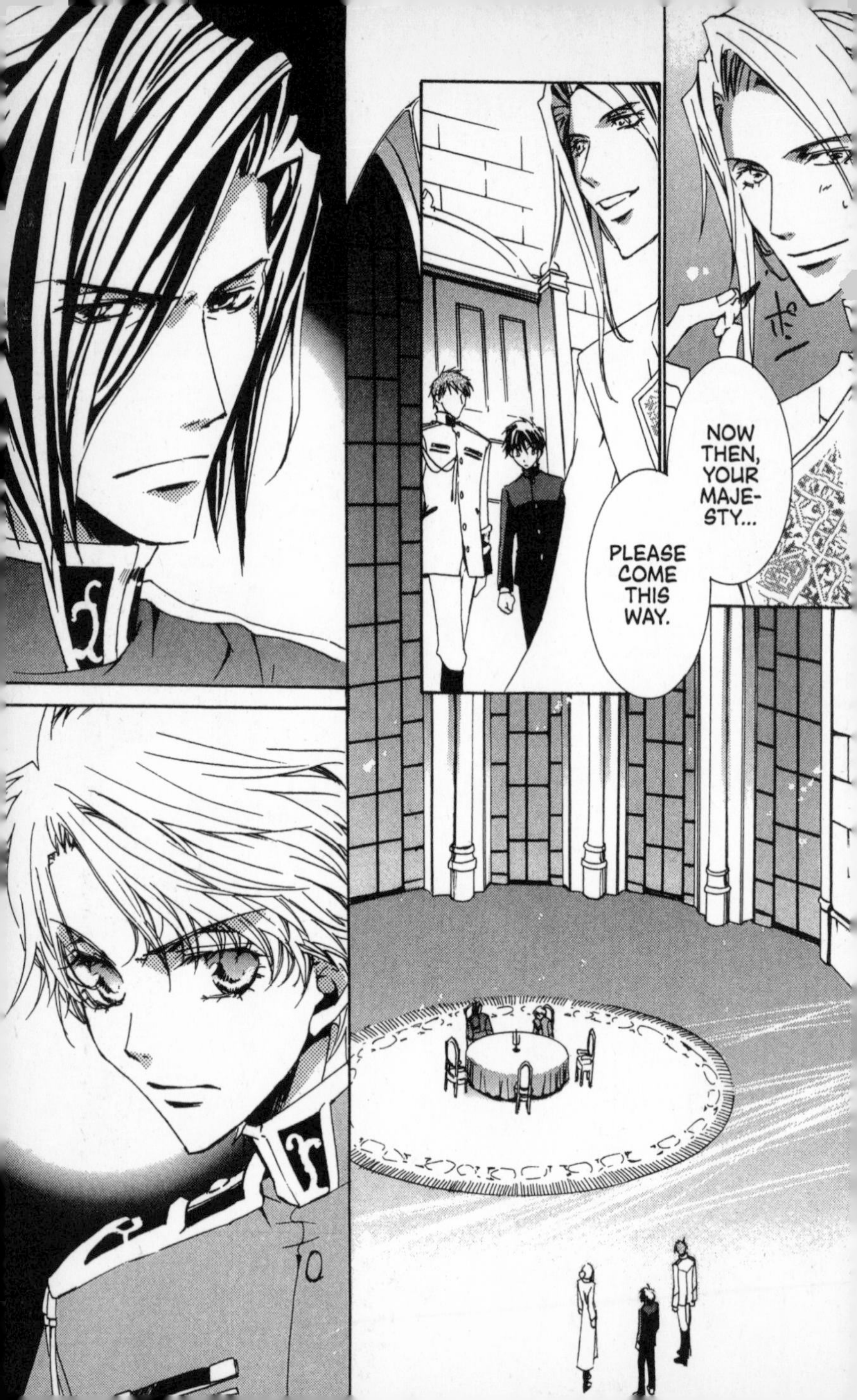
NOW THEN, YOUR MAJESTY...
PLEASE COME THIS WAY.

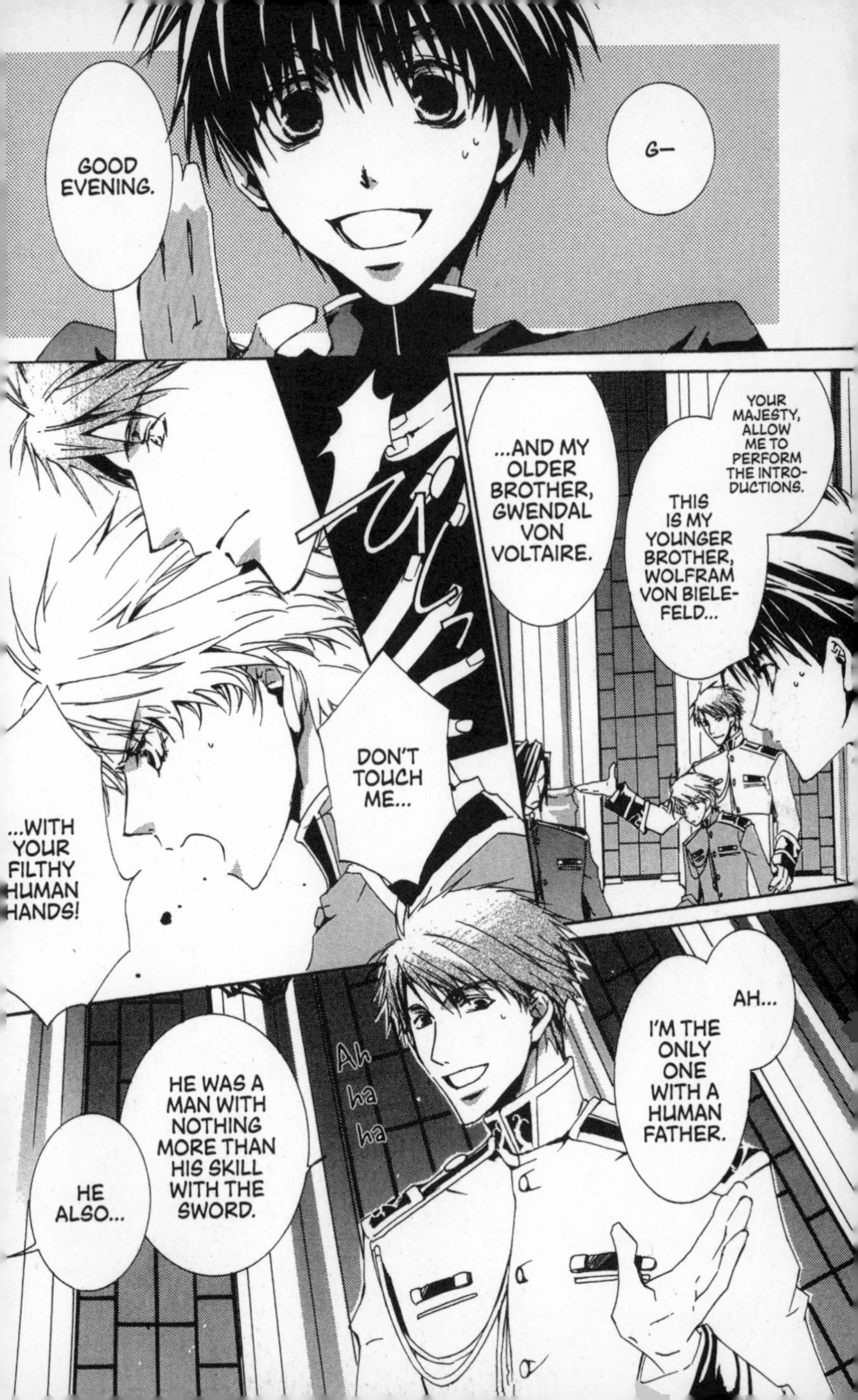
G—
GOOD EVENING.
YOUR MAJESTY, ALLOW ME TO PERFORM THE INTRO-DUCTIONS.
THIS IS MY YOUNGER BROTHER, WOLFRAM VON BIELE-FELD...
...AND MY OLDER BROTHER, GWENDAL VON VOLTAIRE.
DON'T TOUCH ME...
...WITH YOUR FILTHY HUMAN HANDS!
AH...
I'M THE ONLY ONE WITH A HUMAN FATHER.
Ah ha ha
HE WAS A MAN WITH NOTHING MORE THAN HIS SKILL WITH THE SWORD.
HE ALSO...

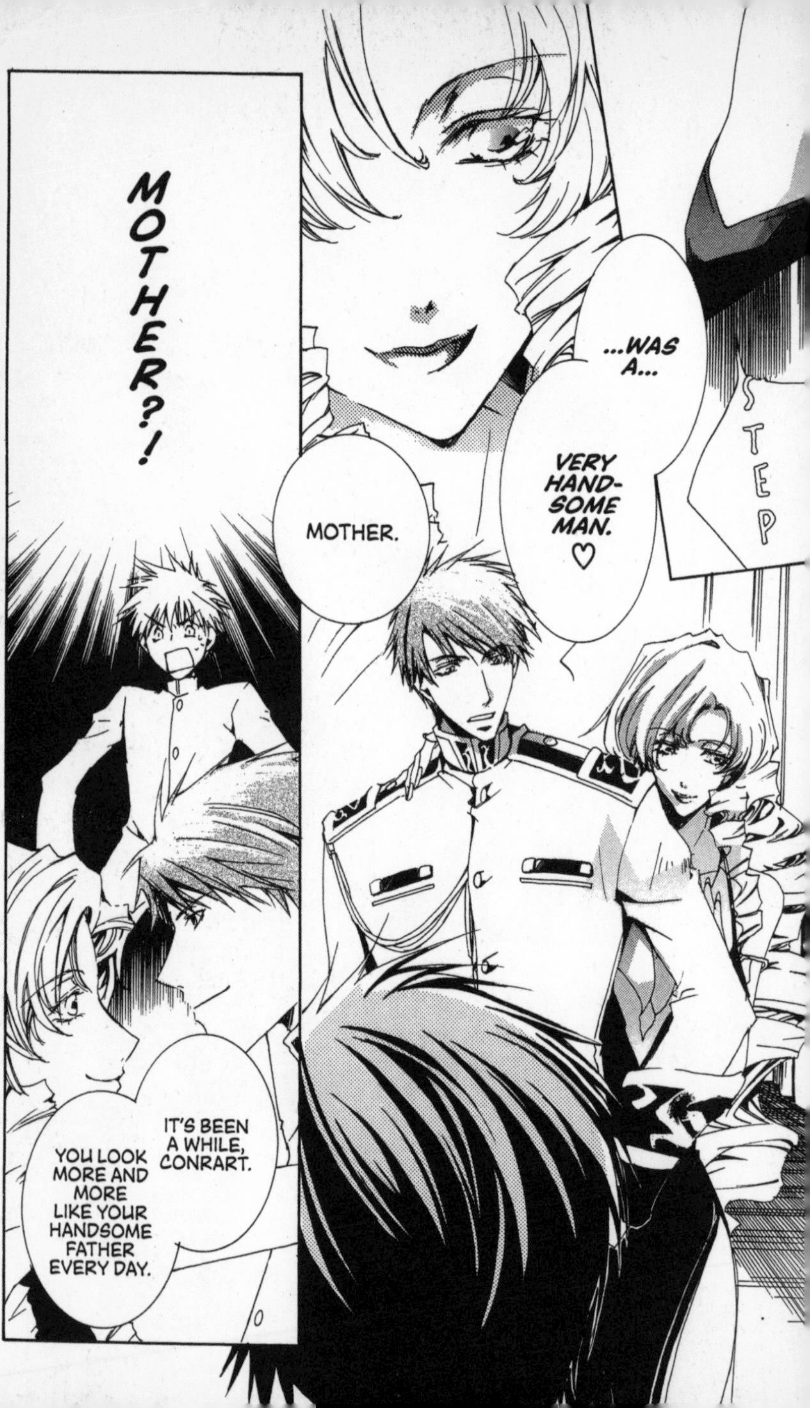
...WAS A...
VERY HAND-SOME MAN. ♡
STEP
MOTHER.
MOTHER?!
IT'S BEEN A WHILE, CONRART.
YOU LOOK MORE AND MORE LIKE YOUR HANDSOME FATHER EVERY DAY.

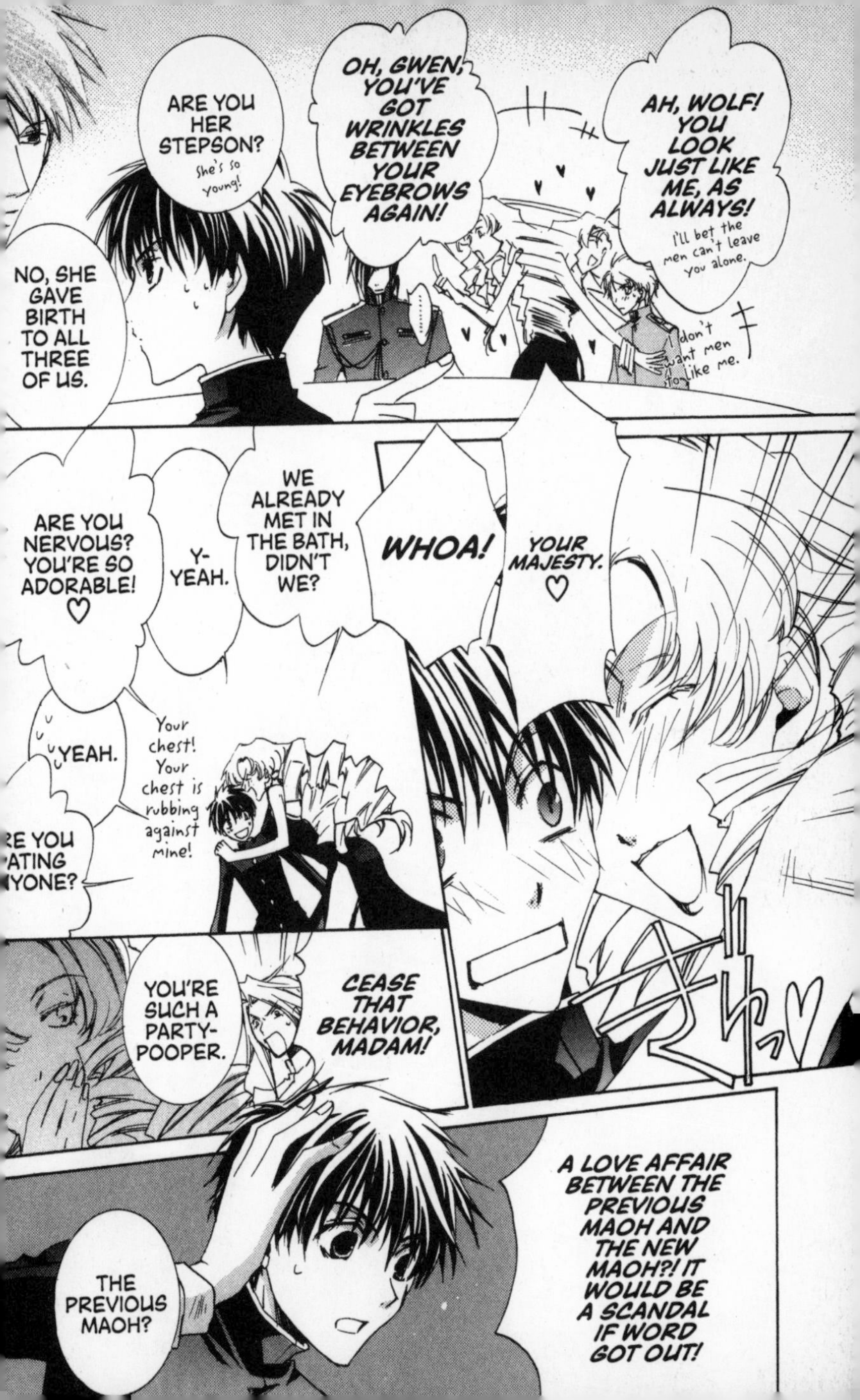

AH, WOLF! YOU LOOK JUST LIKE ME, AS ALWAYS!
I'll bet the men can't leave you alone.
I don't want men to like me.
OH, GWEN, YOU'VE GOT WRINKLES BETWEEN YOUR EYEBROWS AGAIN!
ARE YOU HER STEPSON?
She's so young!
NO, SHE GAVE BIRTH TO ALL THREE OF US.
YOUR MAJESTY. ♡
WHOA!
WE ALREADY MET IN THE BATH, DIDN'T WE?
Y-YEAH.
ARE YOU NERVOUS? YOU'RE SO ADORABLE! ♡
Your chest! Your chest is rubbing against mine!
YEAH.
RE YOU ATING YONE?
CEASE THAT BEHAVIOR, MADAM!
YOU'RE SUCH A PARTY-POOPER.
A LOVE AFFAIR BETWEEN THE PREVIOUS MAOH AND THE NEW MAOH?! IT WOULD BE A SCANDAL IF WORD GOT OUT!
THE PREVIOUS MAOH?

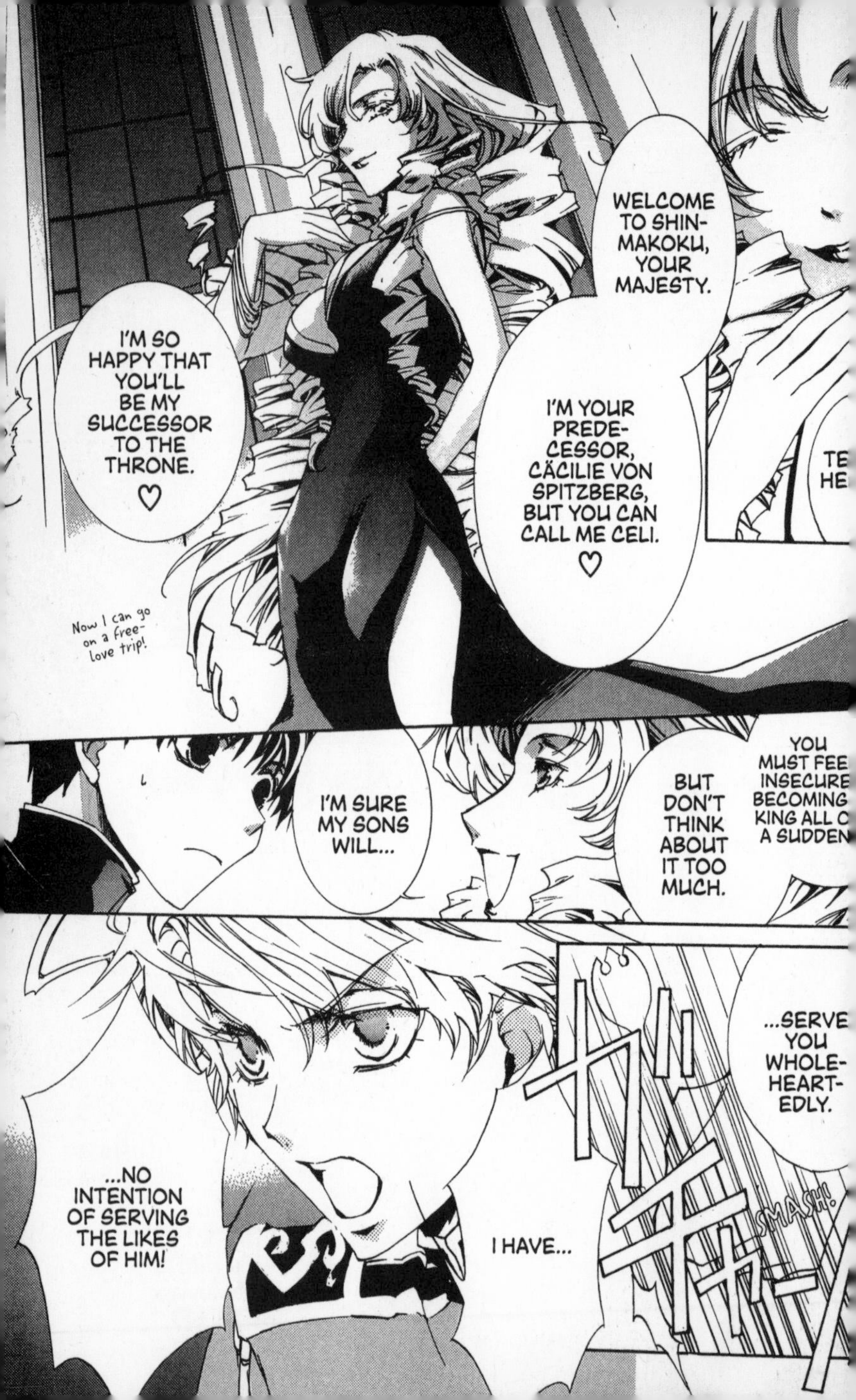
WELCOME TO SHIN-MAKOKU, YOUR MAJESTY.
I'M YOUR PREDE-CESSOR, CÄCILIE VON SPITZBERG, BUT YOU CAN CALL ME CELI. ♡
TE HE
I'M SO HAPPY THAT YOU'LL BE MY SUCCESSOR TO THE THRONE. ♡
Now I can go on a free-love trip!
YOU MUST FEE INSECURE BECOMING KING ALL O A SUDDEN
BUT DON'T THINK ABOUT IT TOO MUCH.
I'M SURE MY SONS WILL...
...SERVE YOU WHOLE-HEART-EDLY.
SMASH!
I HAVE...
...NO INTENTION OF SERVING THE LIKES OF HIM!

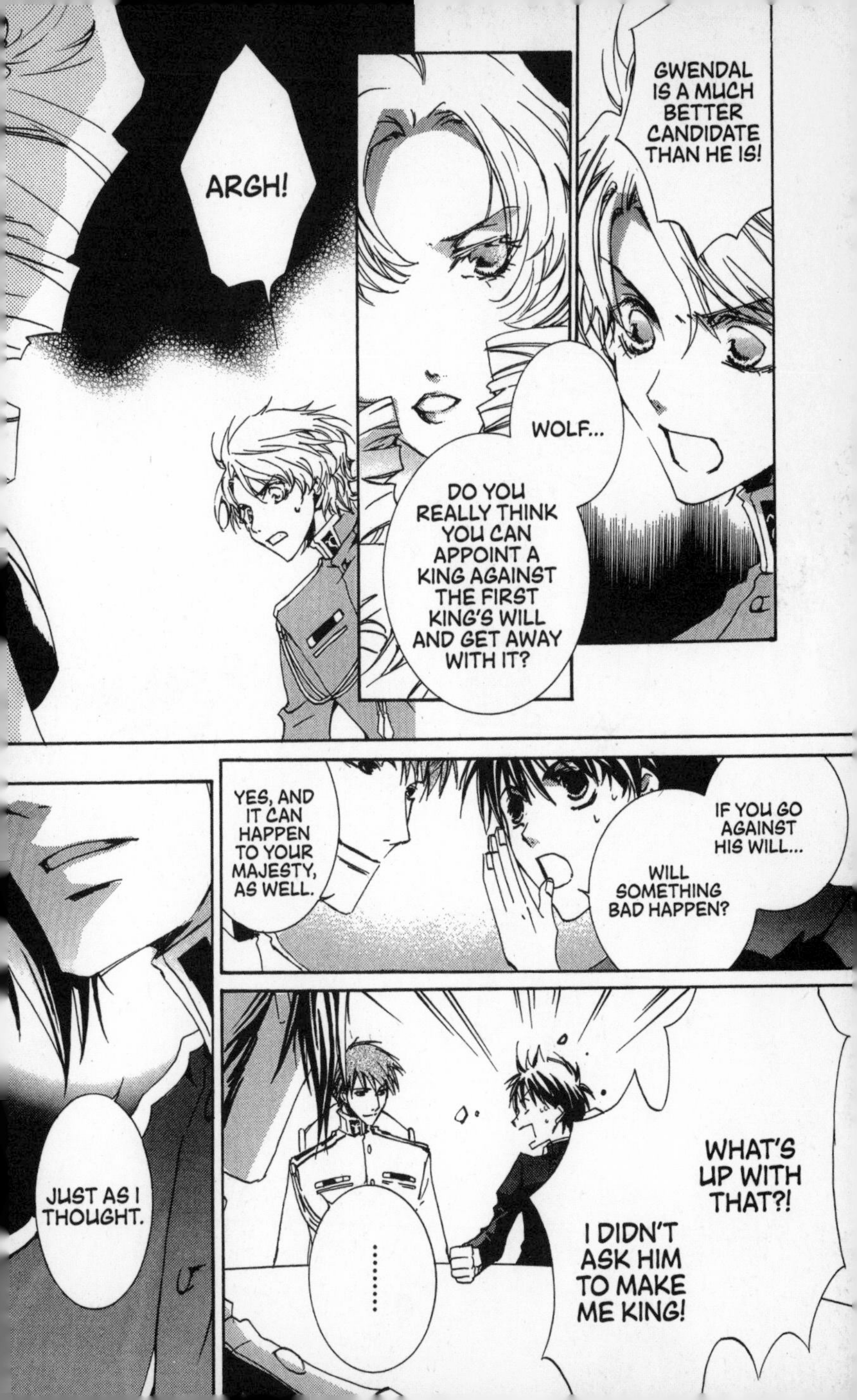
GWENDAL IS A MUCH BETTER CANDIDATE THAN HE IS!
WOLF...
DO YOU REALLY THINK YOU CAN APPOINT A KING AGAINST THE FIRST KING'S WILL AND GET AWAY WITH IT?
ARGH!
IF YOU GO AGAINST HIS WILL...
WILL SOMETHING BAD HAPPEN?
YES, AND IT CAN HAPPEN TO YOUR MAJESTY, AS WELL.
WHAT'S UP WITH THAT?!
I DIDN'T ASK HIM TO MAKE ME KING!
....
JUST AS I THOUGHT.

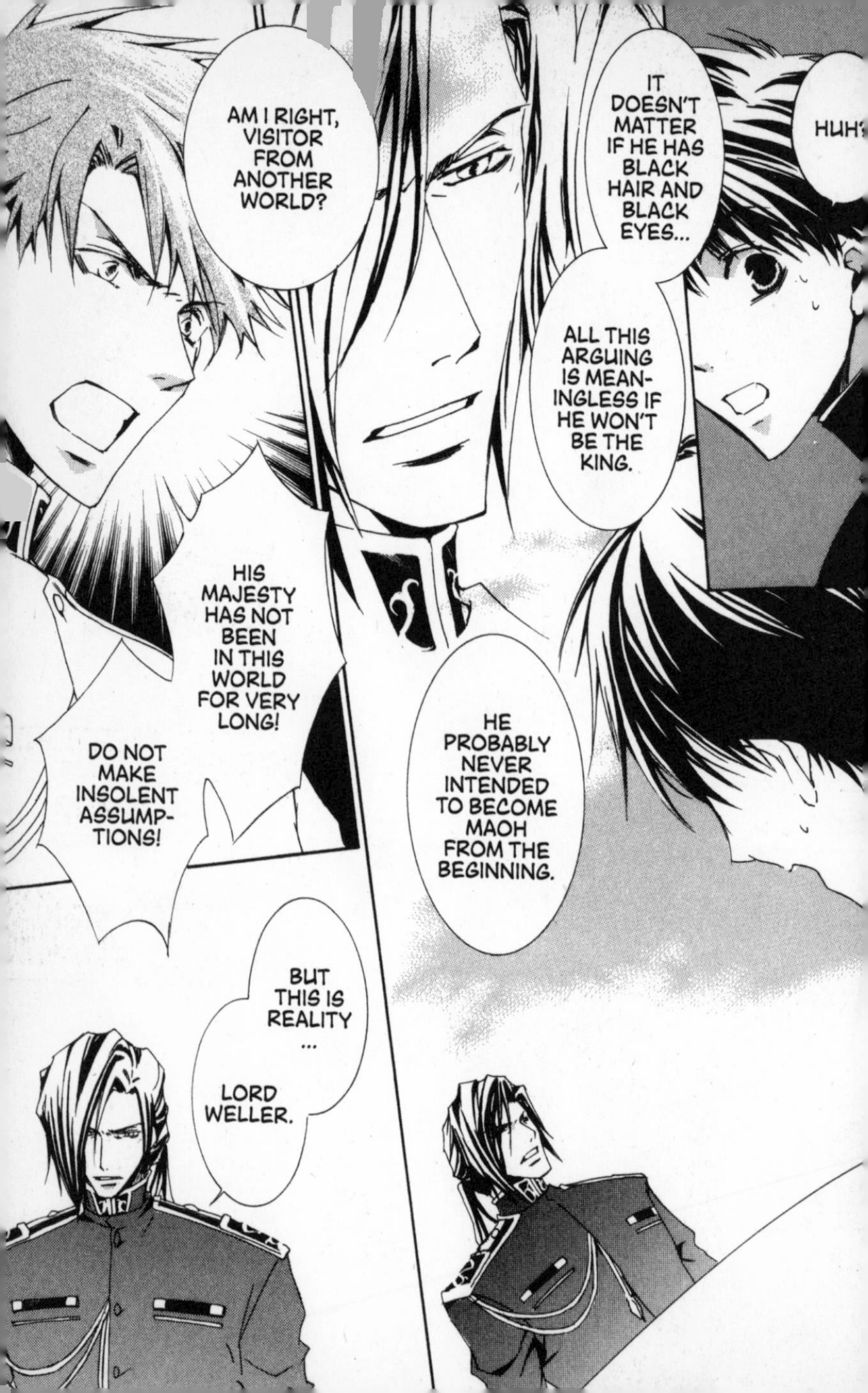
IT DOESN'T MATTER IF HE HAS BLACK HAIR AND BLACK EYES...
ALL THIS ARGUING IS MEAN-INGLESS IF HE WON'T BE THE KING.
HE PROBABLY NEVER INTENDED TO BECOME MAOH FROM THE BEGINNING.
AM I RIGHT, VISITOR FROM ANOTHER WORLD?
HUH?
HIS MAJESTY HAS NOT BEEN IN THIS WORLD FOR VERY LONG!
DO NOT MAKE INSOLENT ASSUMP-TIONS!
BUT THIS IS REALITY...
LORD WELLER.

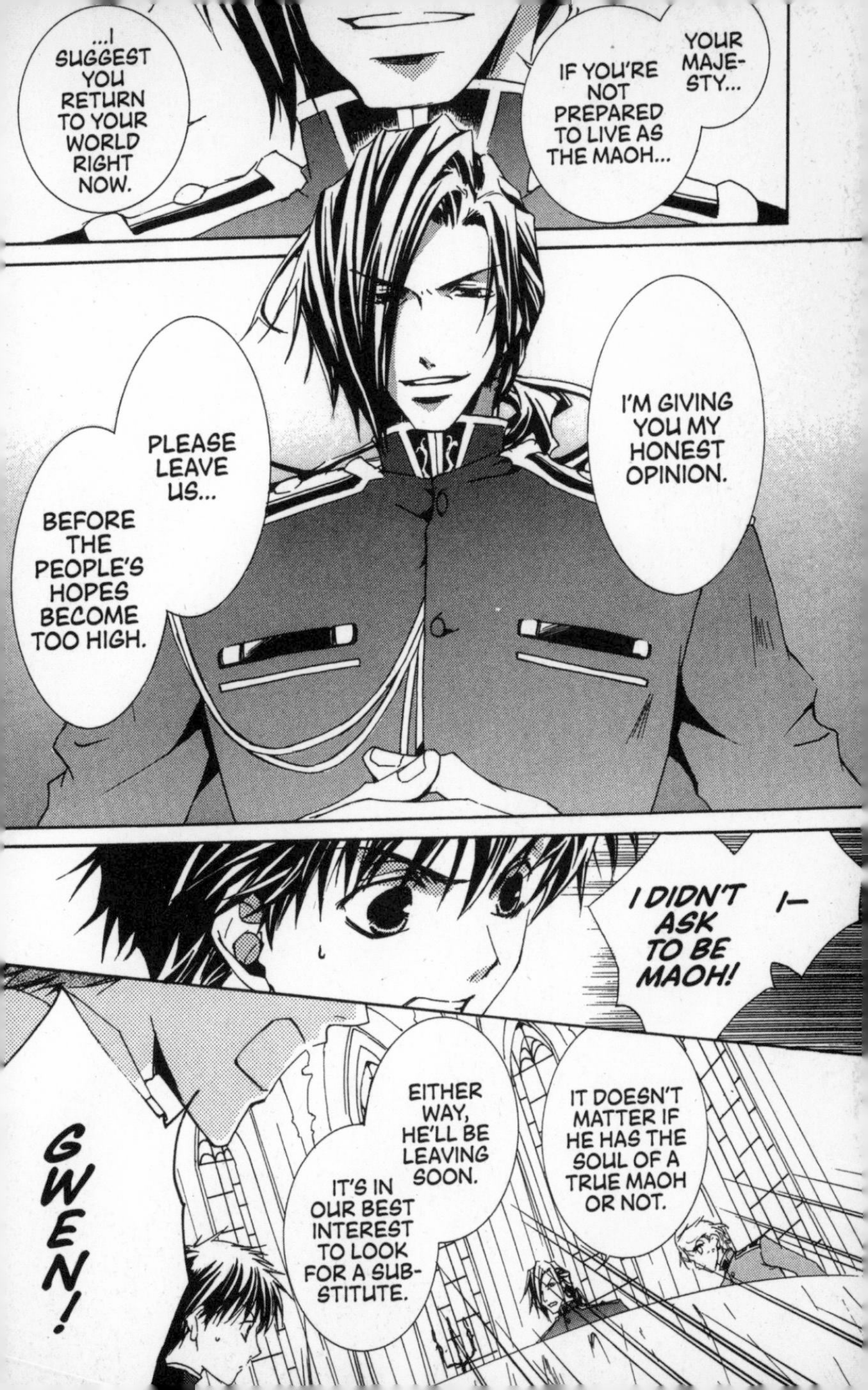
YOUR MAJESTY...
IF YOU'RE NOT PREPARED TO LIVE AS THE MAOH...
...I SUGGEST YOU RETURN TO YOUR WORLD RIGHT NOW.
I'M GIVING YOU MY HONEST OPINION.
PLEASE LEAVE US...
BEFORE THE PEOPLE'S HOPES BECOME TOO HIGH.
I—
I DIDN'T ASK TO BE MAOH!
IT DOESN'T MATTER IF HE HAS THE SOUL OF A TRUE MAOH OR NOT.
EITHER WAY, HE'LL BE LEAVING SOON.
IT'S IN OUR BEST INTEREST TO LOOK FOR A SUBSTITUTE.
GWEN!

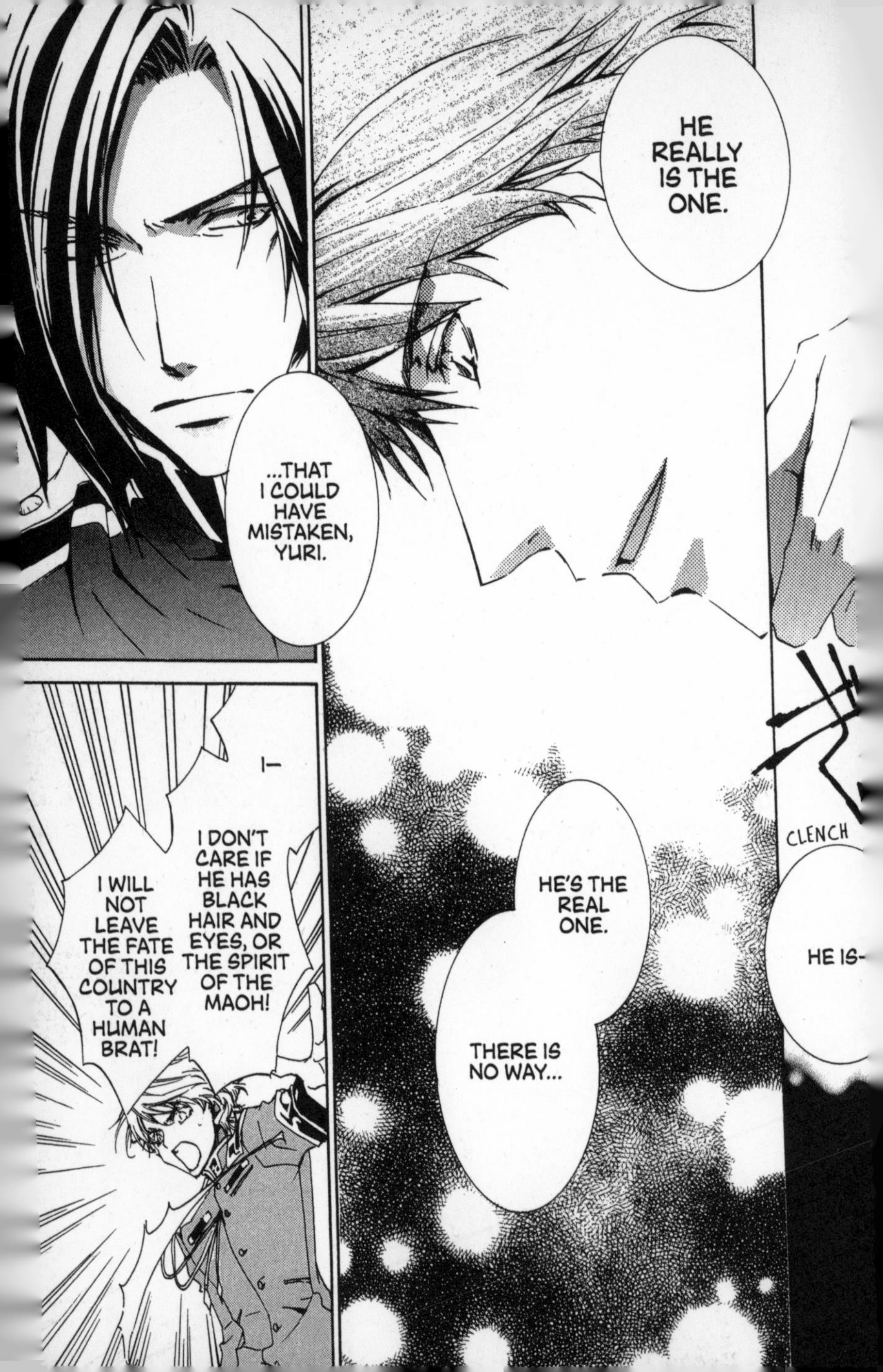
CLENCH
HE IS-
HE REALLY IS THE ONE.
HE'S THE REAL ONE.
THERE IS NO WAY...
...THAT I COULD HAVE MISTAKEN, YURI.
I—
I DON'T CARE IF HE HAS BLACK HAIR AND EYES, OR THE SPIRIT OF THE MAOH!
I WILL NOT LEAVE THE FATE OF THIS COUNTRY TO A HUMAN BRAT!

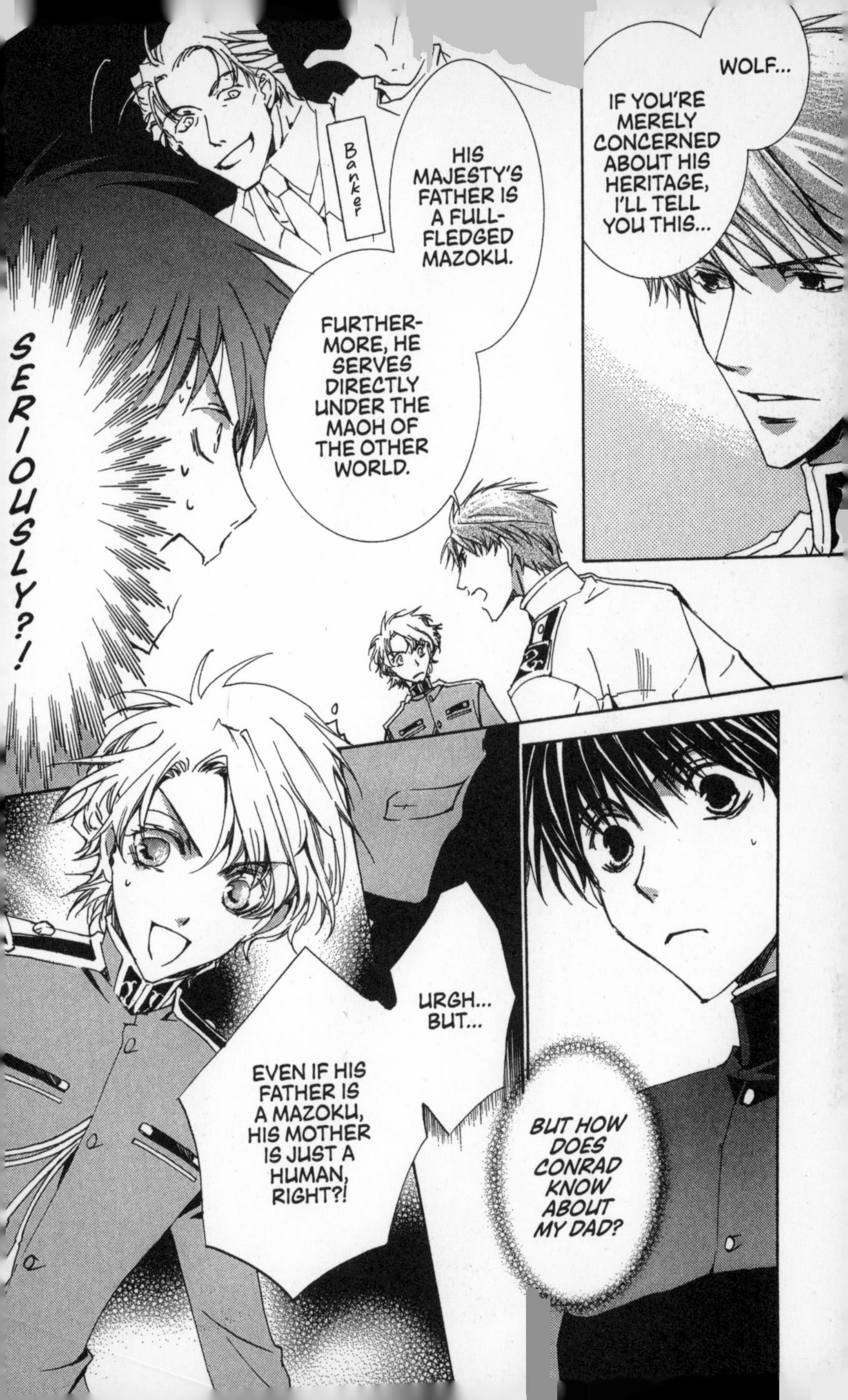
WOLF...
IF YOU'RE MERELY CONCERNED ABOUT HIS HERITAGE, I'LL TELL YOU THIS...
HIS MAJESTY'S FATHER IS A FULL-FLEDGED MAZOKU.
Banker
FURTHER-MORE, HE SERVES DIRECTLY UNDER THE MAOH OF THE OTHER WORLD.
SERIOUSLY?!
BUT HOW DOES CONRAD KNOW ABOUT MY DAD?
URGH... BUT...
EVEN IF HIS FATHER IS A MAZOKU, HIS MOTHER IS JUST A HUMAN, RIGHT?!

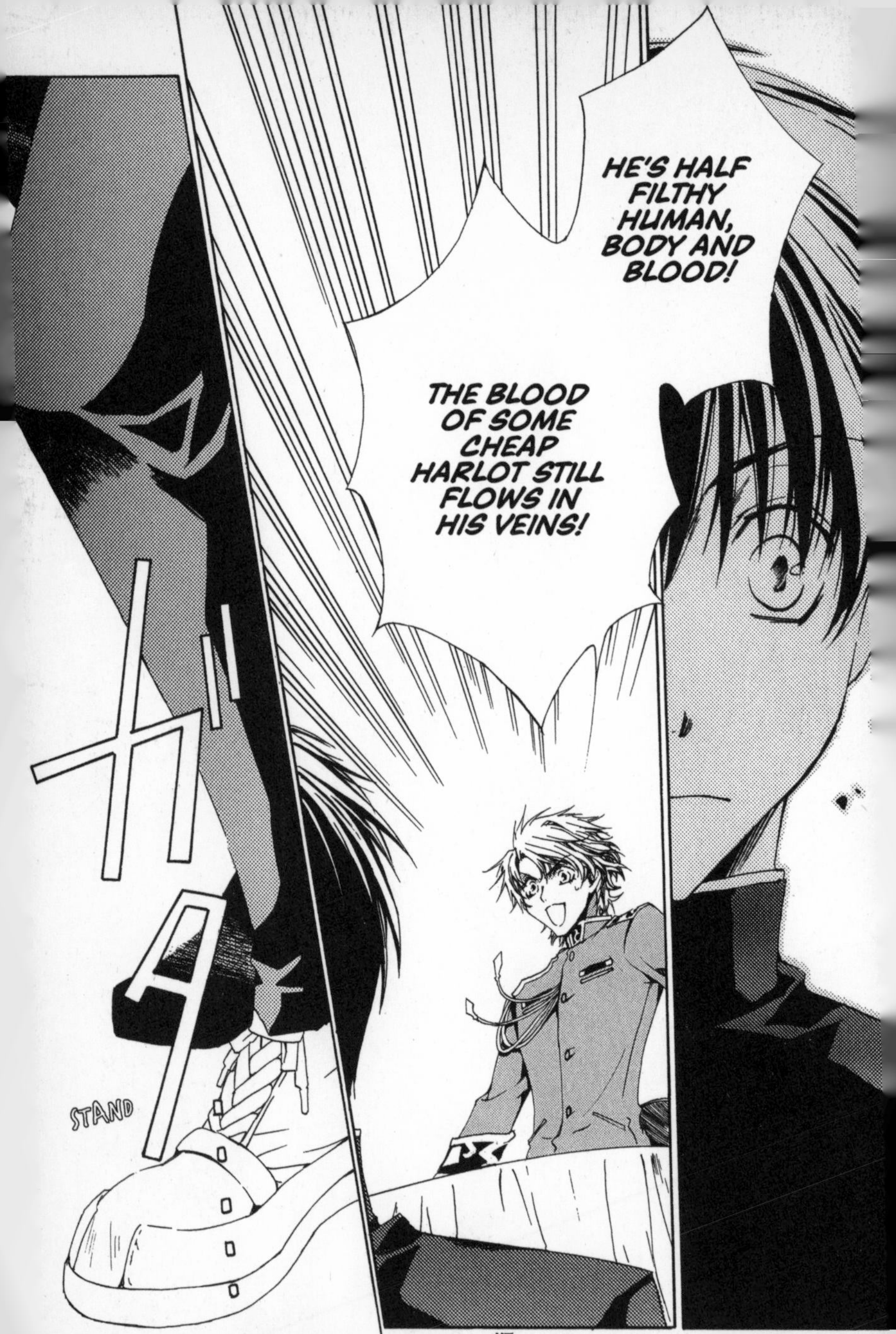
HE'S HALF FILTHY HUMAN, BODY AND BLOOD!
THE BLOOD OF SOME CHEAP HARLOT STILL FLOWS IN HIS VEINS!
STAND

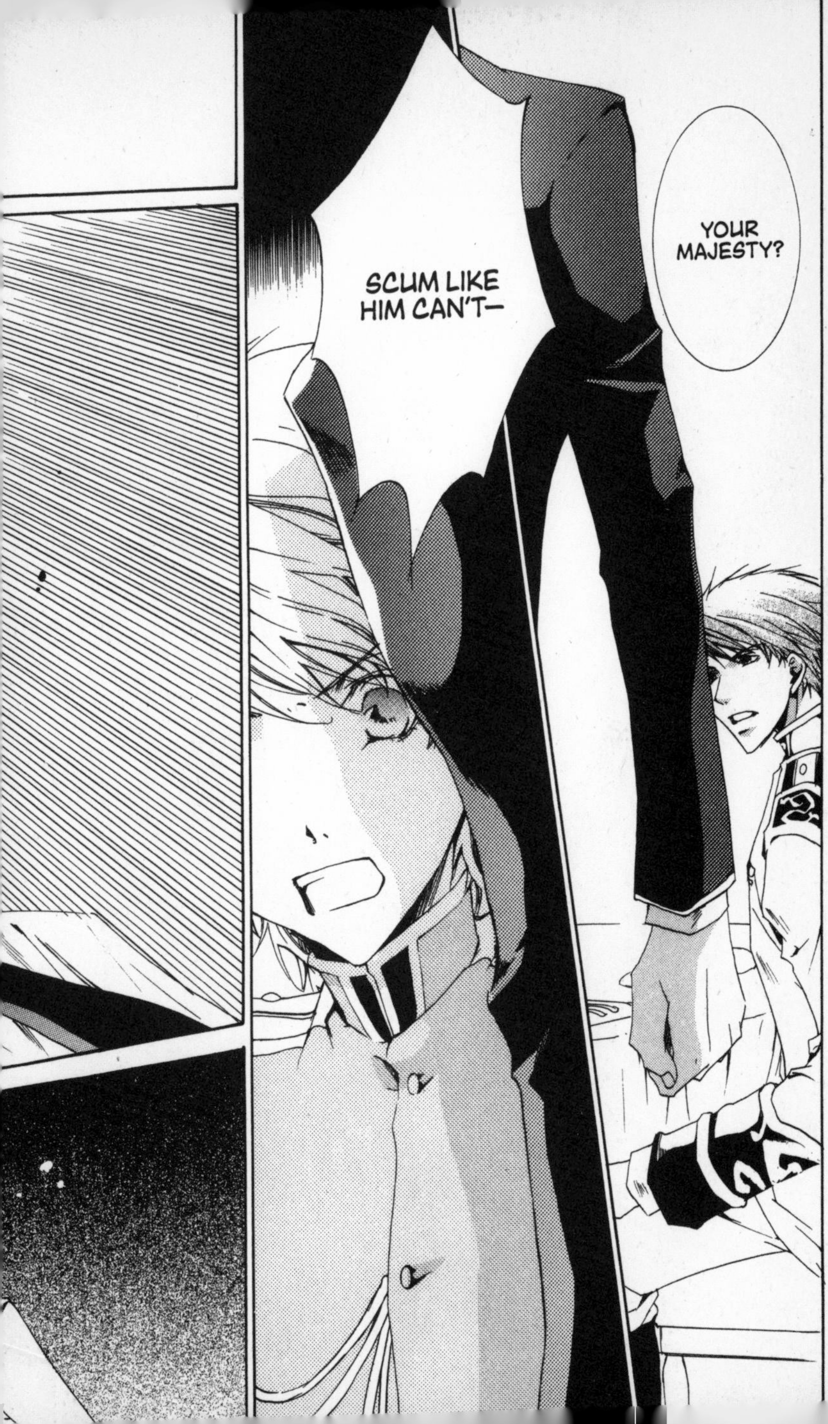
YOUR MAJESTY?
SCUM LIKE HIM CAN'T—

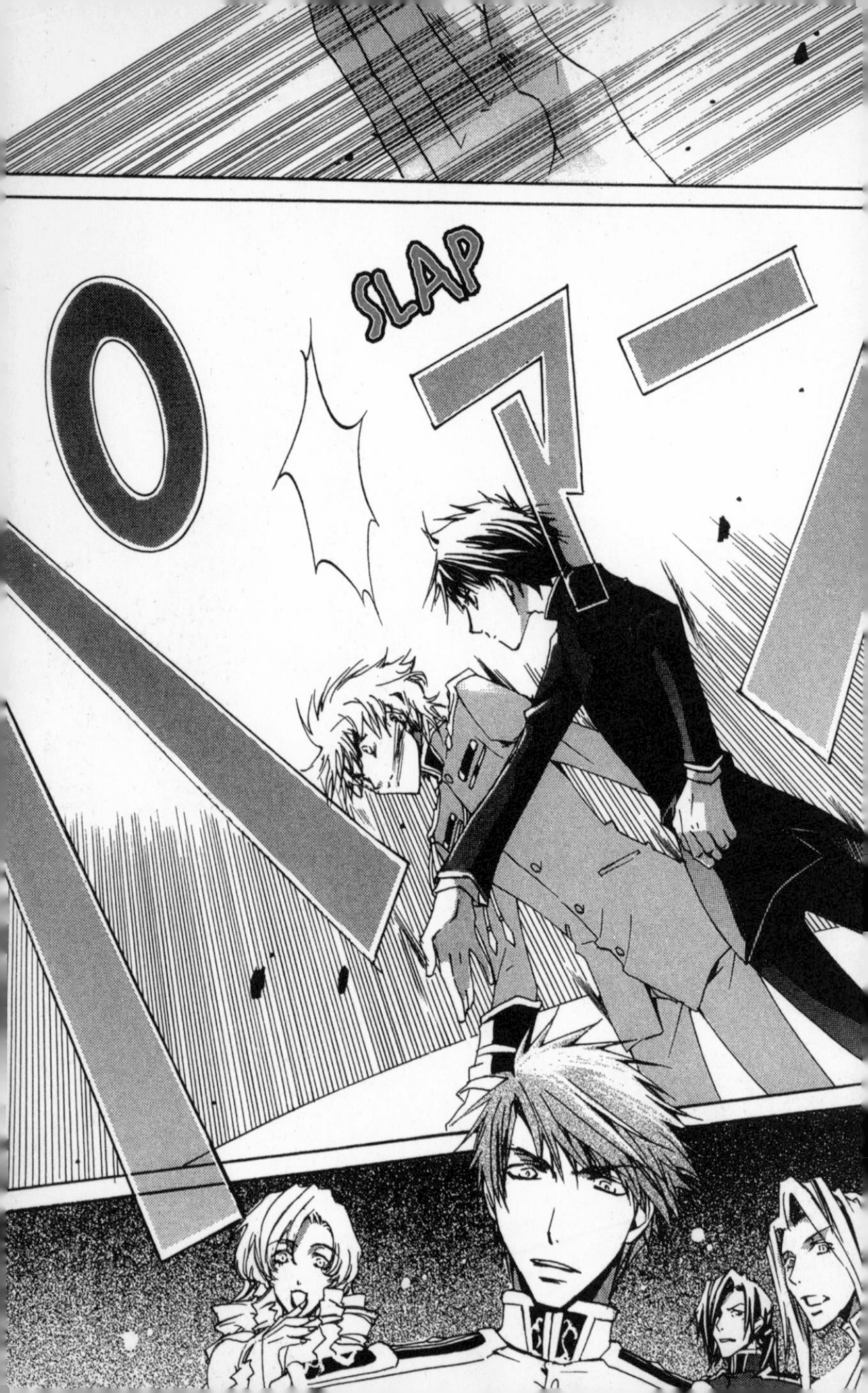
SLAP

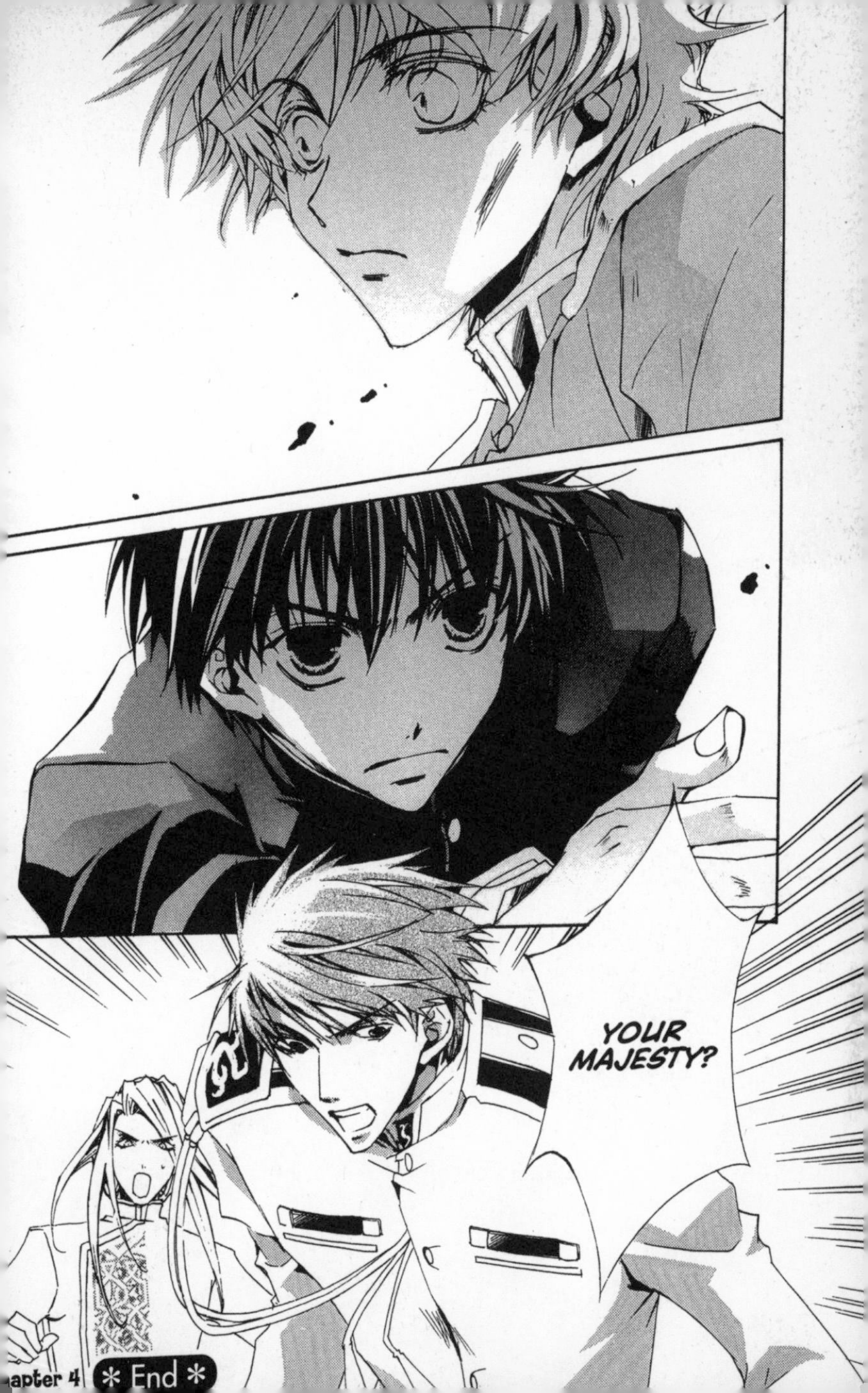
YOUR MAJESTY?
apter 4 * End *

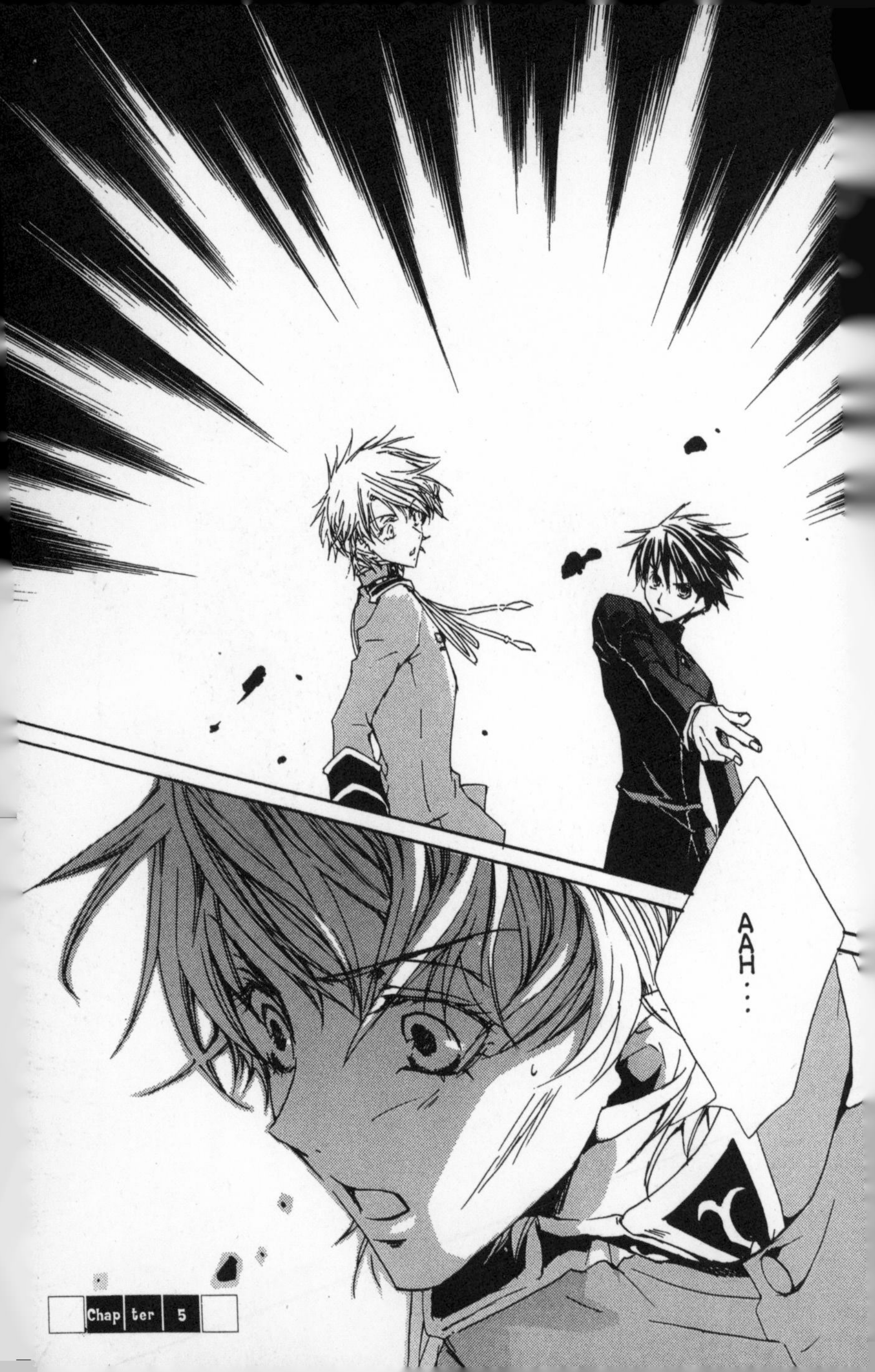
AAH...
Chapter 5

Chapter 5

Bishonen vs. The Baseball Kid

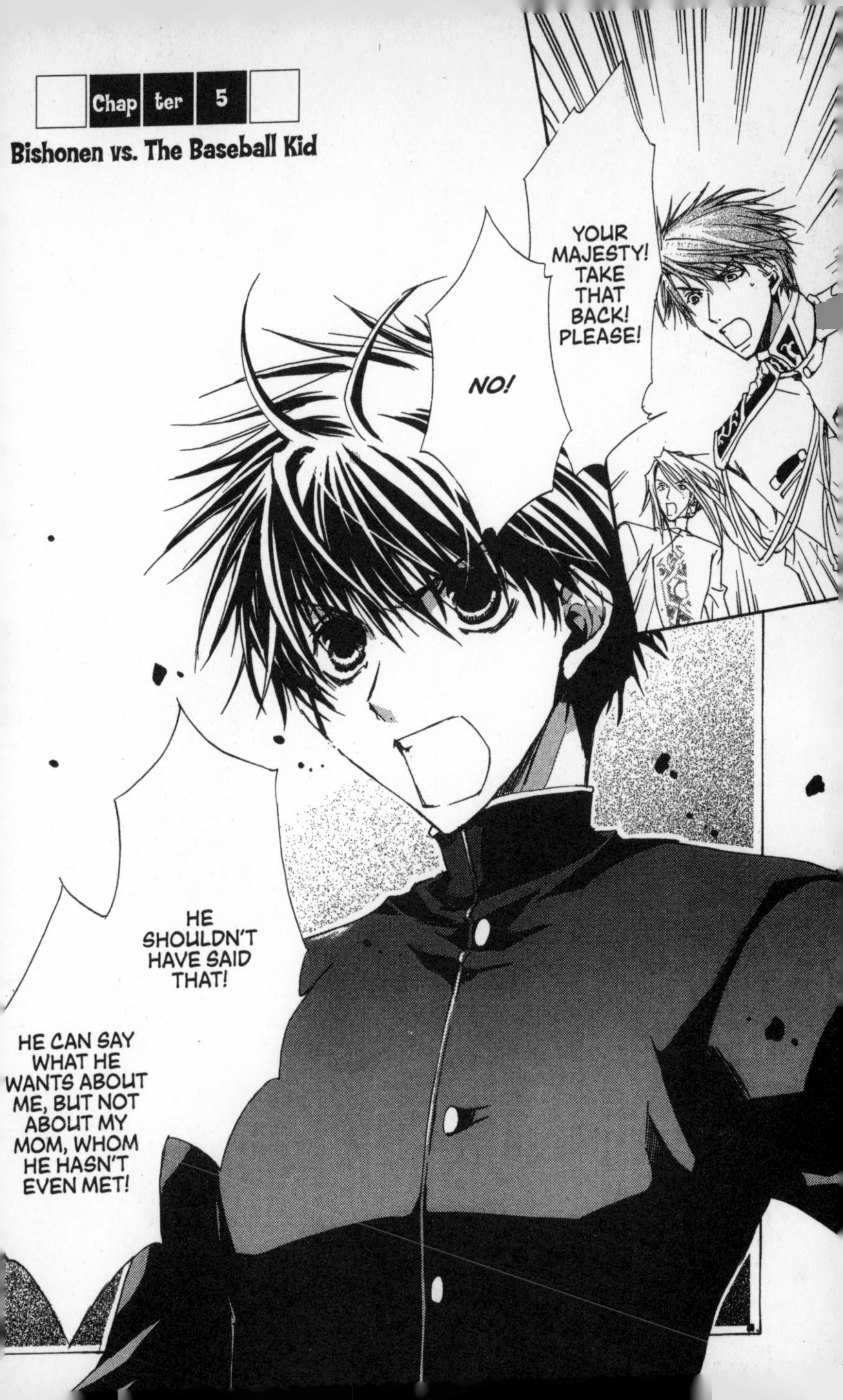
YOUR MAJESTY! TAKE THAT BACK! PLEASE!
NO!
HE SHOULDN'T HAVE SAID THAT!
HE CAN SAY WHAT HE WANTS ABOUT ME, BUT NOT ABOUT MY MOM, WHOM HE HASN'T EVEN MET!

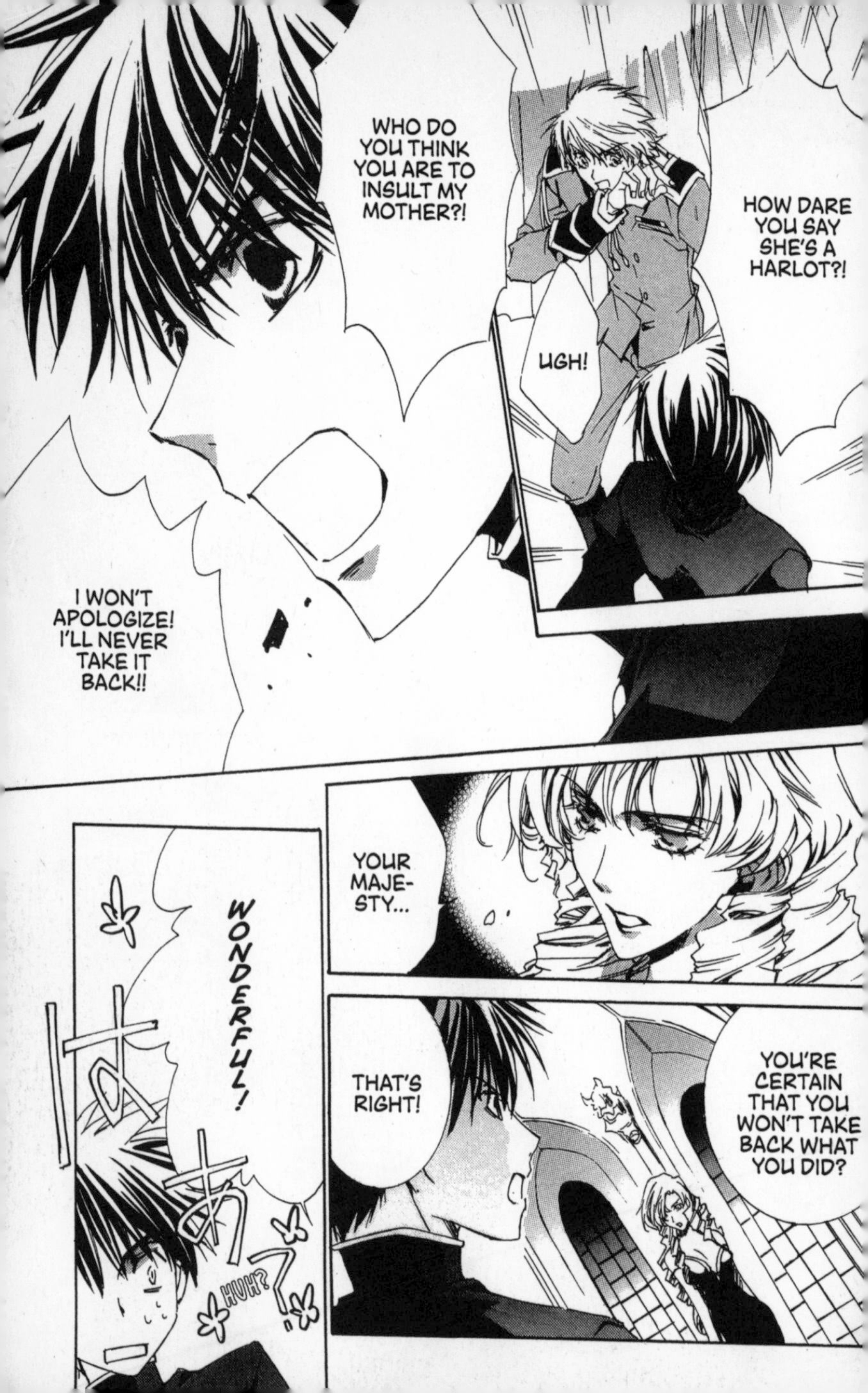
WHO DO YOU THINK YOU ARE TO INSULT MY MOTHER?!
HOW DARE YOU SAY SHE'S A HARLOT?!
UGH!
I WON'T APOLOGIZE! I'LL NEVER TAKE IT BACK!!
YOUR MAJE-STY...
YOU'RE CERTAIN THAT YOU WON'T TAKE BACK WHAT YOU DID?
THAT'S RIGHT!
WONDERFUL!
はあ
HUH?

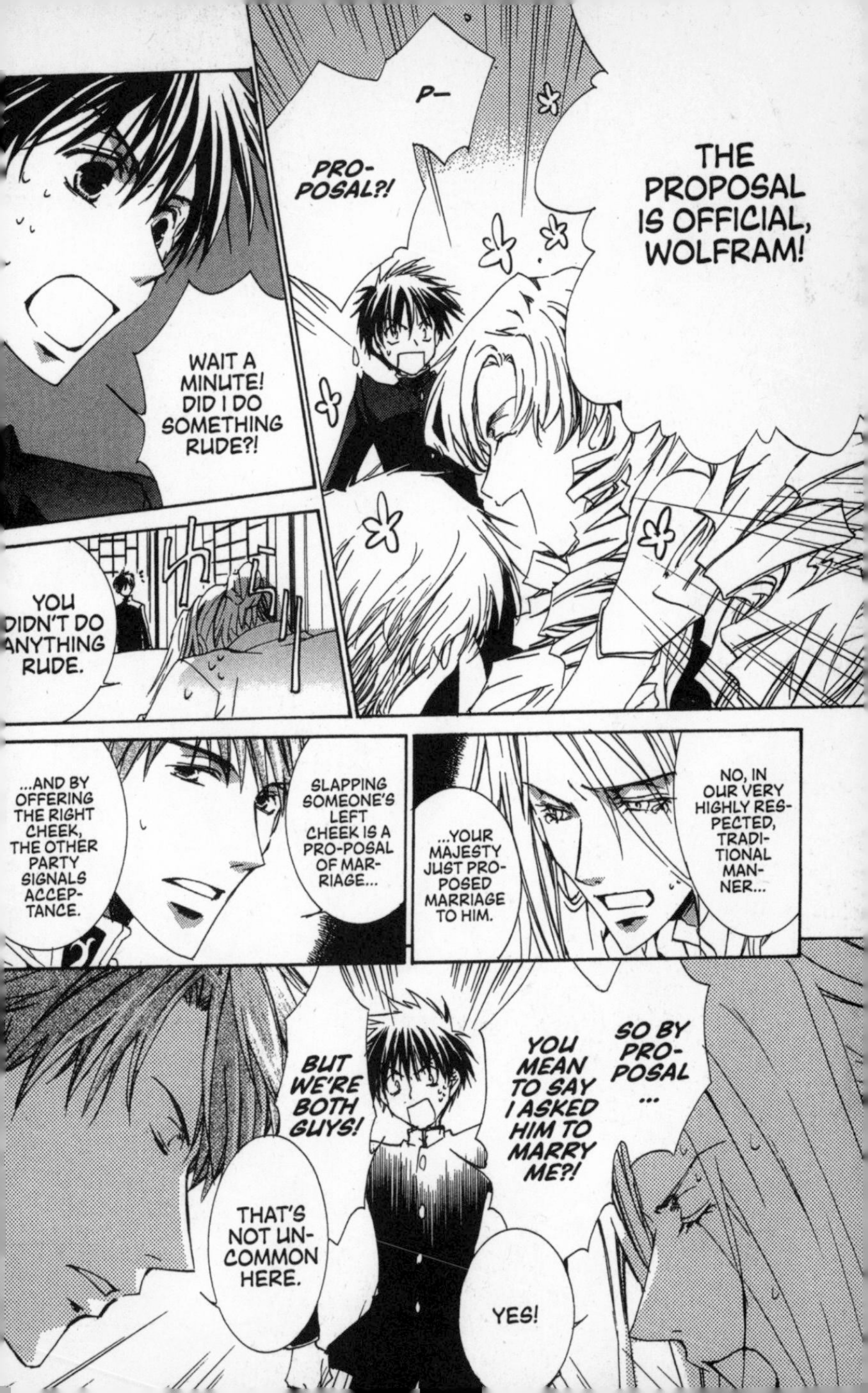
THE PROPOSAL IS OFFICIAL, WOLFRAM!
P—
PRO-POSAL?!
WAIT A MINUTE! DID I DO SOMETHING RUDE?!
YOU DIDN'T DO ANYTHING RUDE.
NO, IN OUR VERY HIGHLY RES-PECTED, TRADI-TIONAL MAN-NER...
...YOUR MAJESTY JUST PRO-POSED MARRIAGE TO HIM.
SLAPPING SOMEONE'S LEFT CHEEK IS A PRO-POSAL OF MAR-RIAGE...
...AND BY OFFERING THE RIGHT CHEEK, THE OTHER PARTY SIGNALS ACCEP-TANCE.
SO BY PRO-POSAL...
YOU MEAN TO SAY I ASKED HIM TO MARRY ME?!
YES!
BUT WE'RE BOTH GUYS!
THAT'S NOT UN-COMMON HERE.

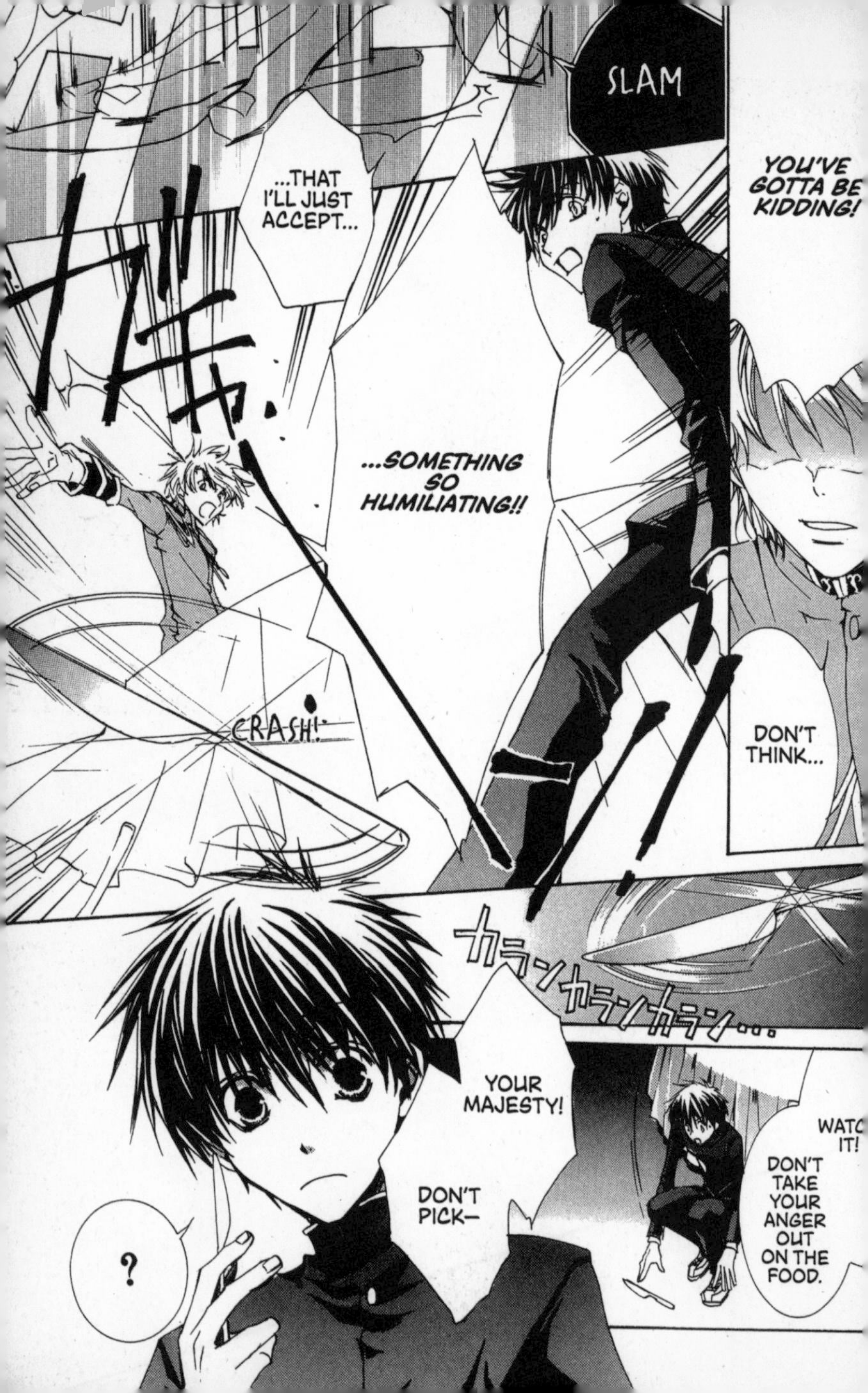
YOU'VE GOTTA BE KIDDING!
DON'T THINK...
SLAM
...THAT I'LL JUST ACCEPT...
...SOMETHING SO HUMILIATING!!
CRASH!
カランカランカラン…
WATC IT!
DON'T TAKE YOUR ANGER OUT ON THE FOOD.
YOUR MAJESTY!
DON'T PICK–
?

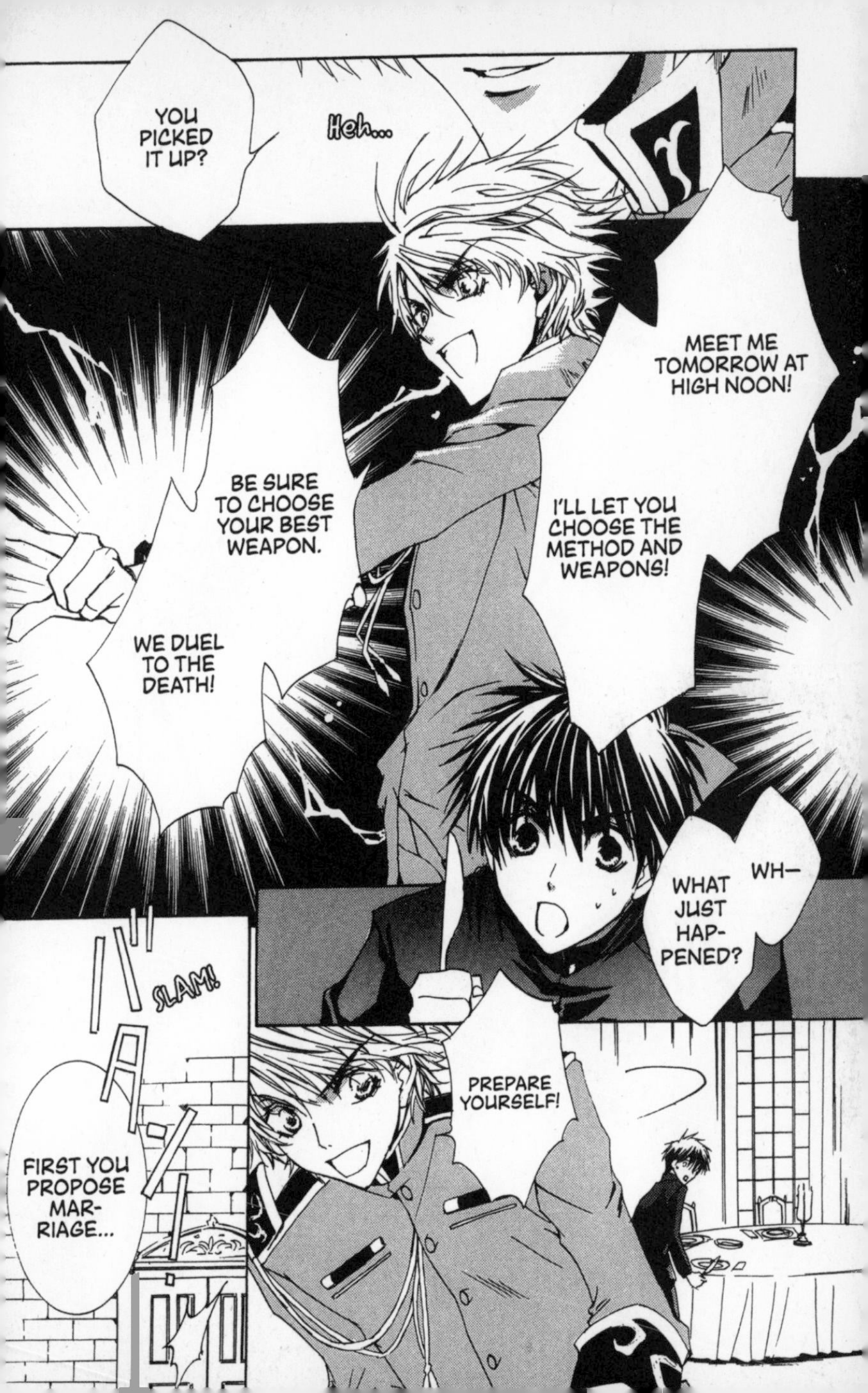
Heh...
YOU PICKED IT UP?
MEET ME TOMORROW AT HIGH NOON!
I'LL LET YOU CHOOSE THE METHOD AND WEAPONS!
BE SURE TO CHOOSE YOUR BEST WEAPON.
WE DUEL TO THE DEATH!
WH—
WHAT JUST HAP-PENED?
PREPARE YOURSELF!
SLAM!
FIRST YOU PROPOSE MAR-RIAGE...

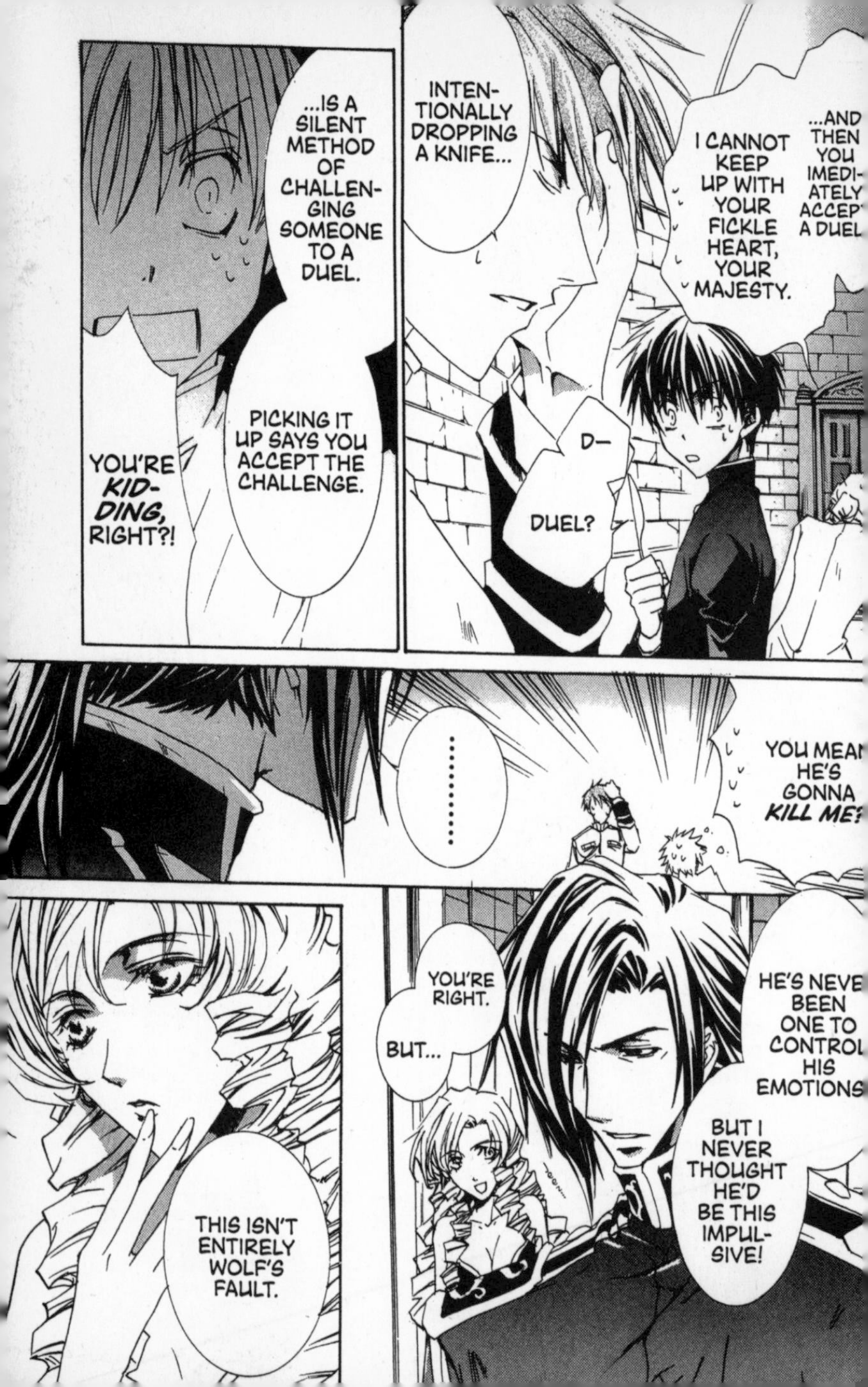
...AND THEN YOU IMEDIATELY ACCEP A DUEL
I CANNOT KEEP UP WITH YOUR FICKLE HEART, YOUR MAJESTY.
INTENTIONALLY DROPPING A KNIFE...
D—
DUEL?
...IS A SILENT METHOD OF CHALLENGING SOMEONE TO A DUEL.
PICKING IT UP SAYS YOU ACCEPT THE CHALLENGE.
YOU'RE *KIDDING,* RIGHT?!
YOU MEA HE'S GONNA *KILL ME*
....
HE'S NEVE BEEN ONE TO CONTROL HIS EMOTIONS
BUT I NEVER THOUGHT HE'D BE THIS IMPULSIVE!
YOU'RE RIGHT.
BUT...
THIS ISN'T ENTIRELY WOLF'S FAULT.

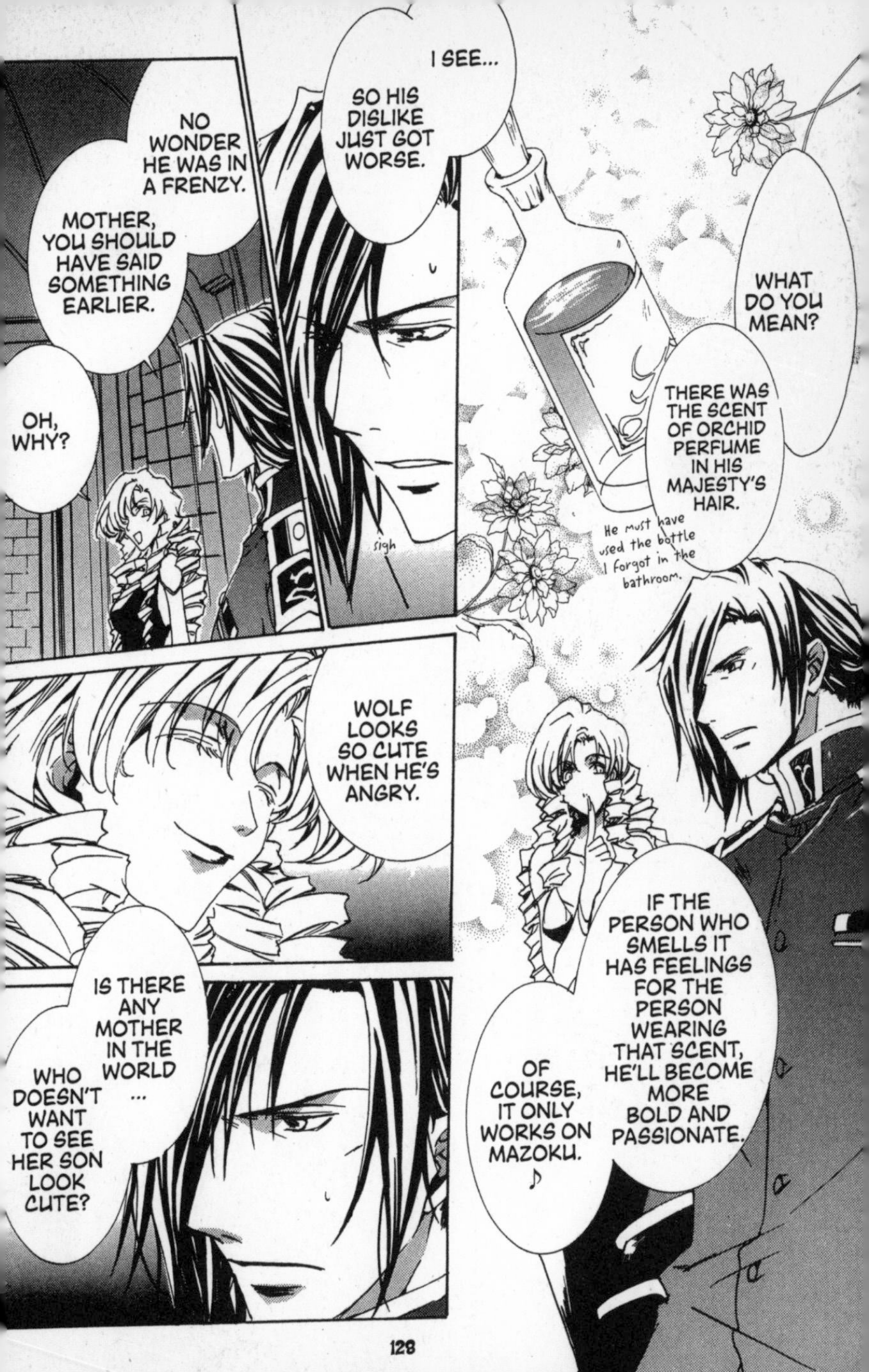
WHAT DO YOU MEAN?
THERE WAS THE SCENT OF ORCHID PERFUME IN HIS MAJESTY'S HAIR.
He must have used the bottle I forgot in the bathroom.
IF THE PERSON WHO SMELLS IT HAS FEELINGS FOR THE PERSON WEARING THAT SCENT, HE'LL BECOME MORE BOLD AND PASSIONATE.
OF COURSE, IT ONLY WORKS ON MAZOKU. ♪
I SEE...
SO HIS DISLIKE JUST GOT WORSE.
sigh
NO WONDER HE WAS IN A FRENZY.
MOTHER, YOU SHOULD HAVE SAID SOMETHING EARLIER.
OH, WHY?
WOLF LOOKS SO CUTE WHEN HE'S ANGRY.
IS THERE ANY MOTHER IN THE WORLD ...
WHO DOESN'T WANT TO SEE HER SON LOOK CUTE?

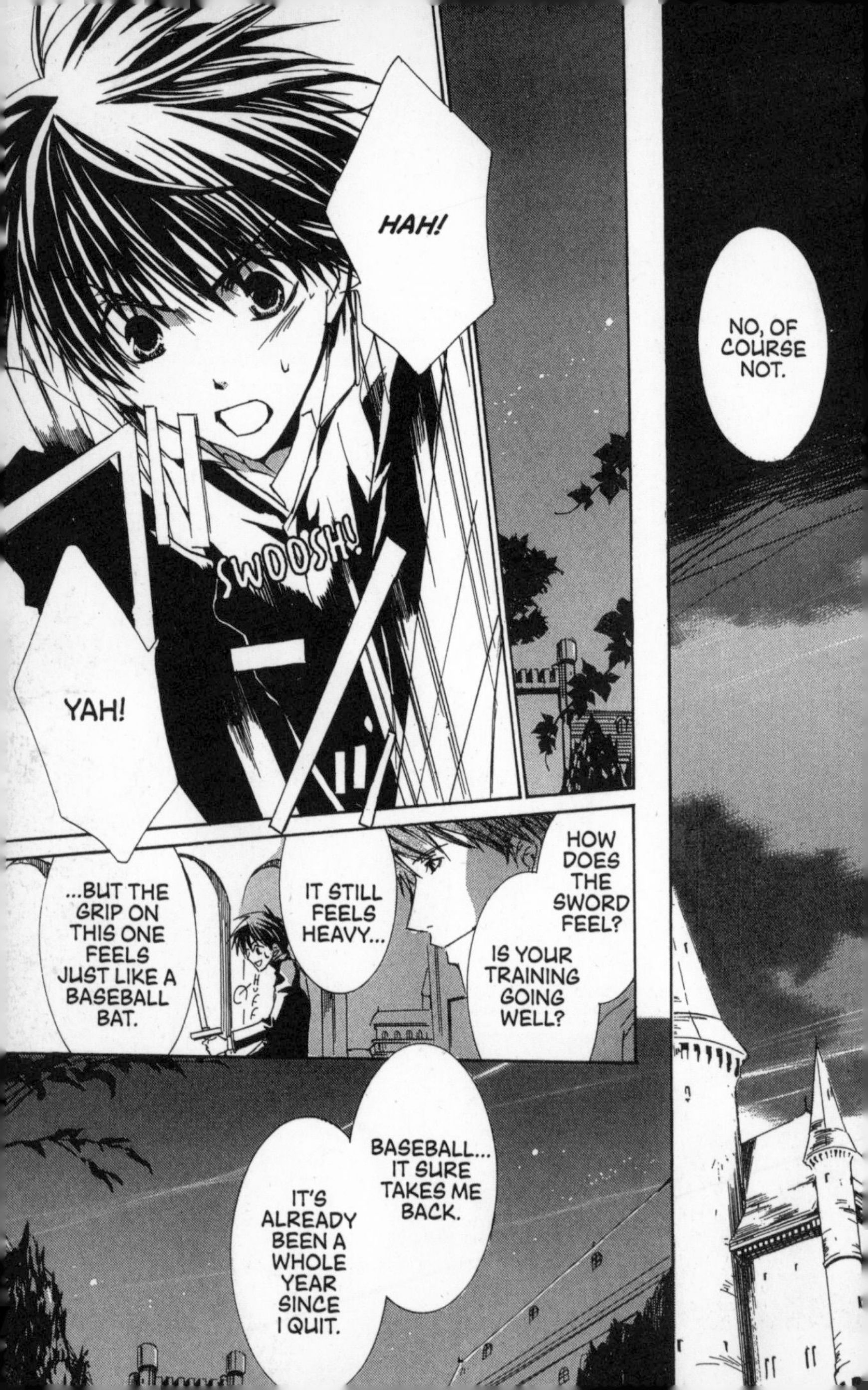
NO, OF COURSE NOT.
HAH!
SWOOSH!
YAH!
HOW DOES THE SWORD FEEL?
IS YOUR TRAINING GOING WELL?
IT STILL FEELS HEAVY...
...BUT THE GRIP ON THIS ONE FEELS JUST LIKE A BASEBALL BAT.
HUFF
BASEBALL... IT SURE TAKES ME BACK.
IT'S ALREADY BEEN A WHOLE YEAR SINCE I QUIT.

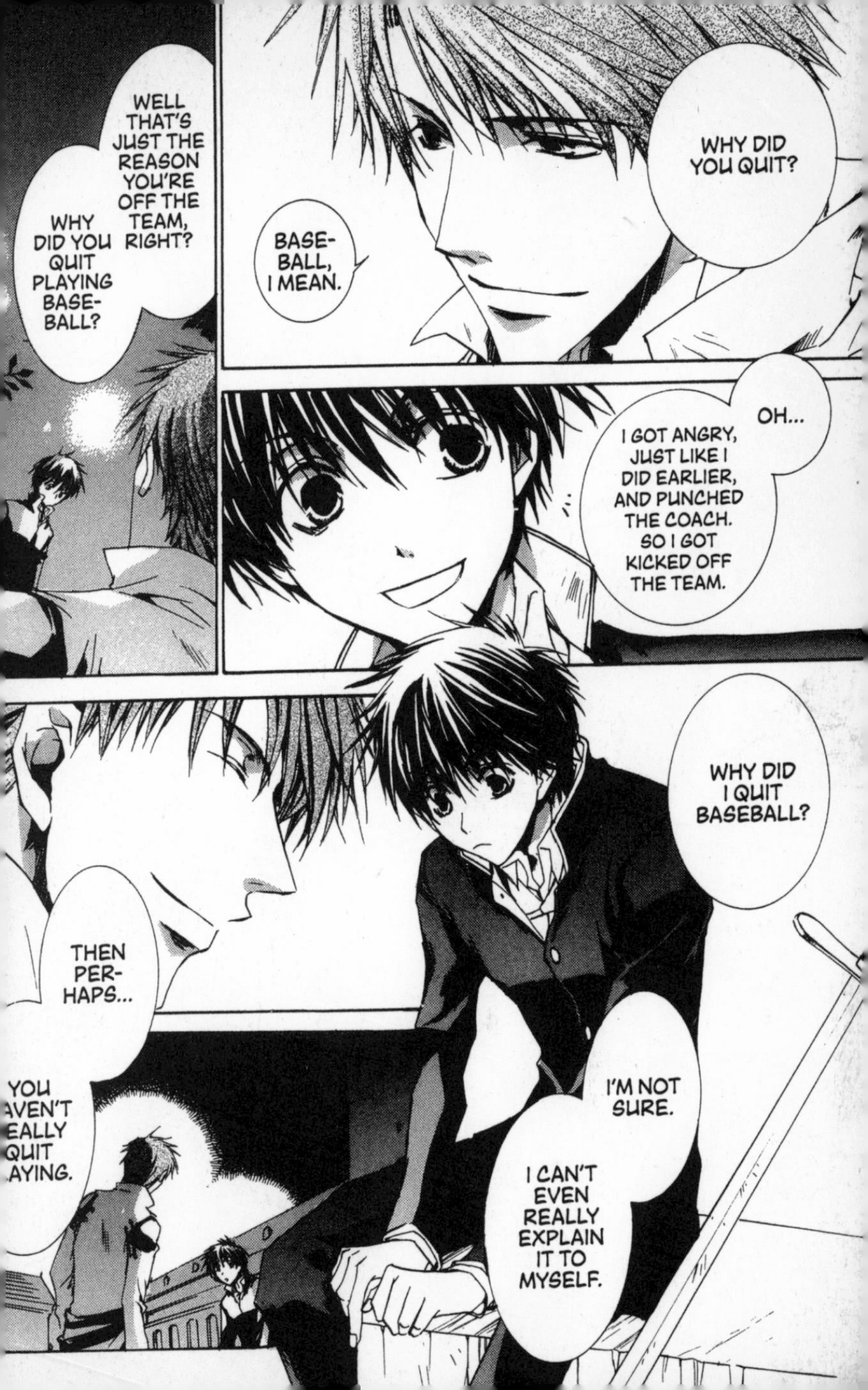
WHY DID YOU QUIT?
BASE-BALL, I MEAN.
OH...
I GOT ANGRY, JUST LIKE I DID EARLIER, AND PUNCHED THE COACH. SO I GOT KICKED OFF THE TEAM.
WELL THAT'S JUST THE REASON YOU'RE OFF THE TEAM, RIGHT?
WHY DID YOU QUIT PLAYING BASE-BALL?
WHY DID I QUIT BASEBALL?
I'M NOT SURE.
I CAN'T EVEN REALLY EXPLAIN IT TO MYSELF.
THEN PER-HAPS...
YOU AVEN'T EALLY QUIT AYING.

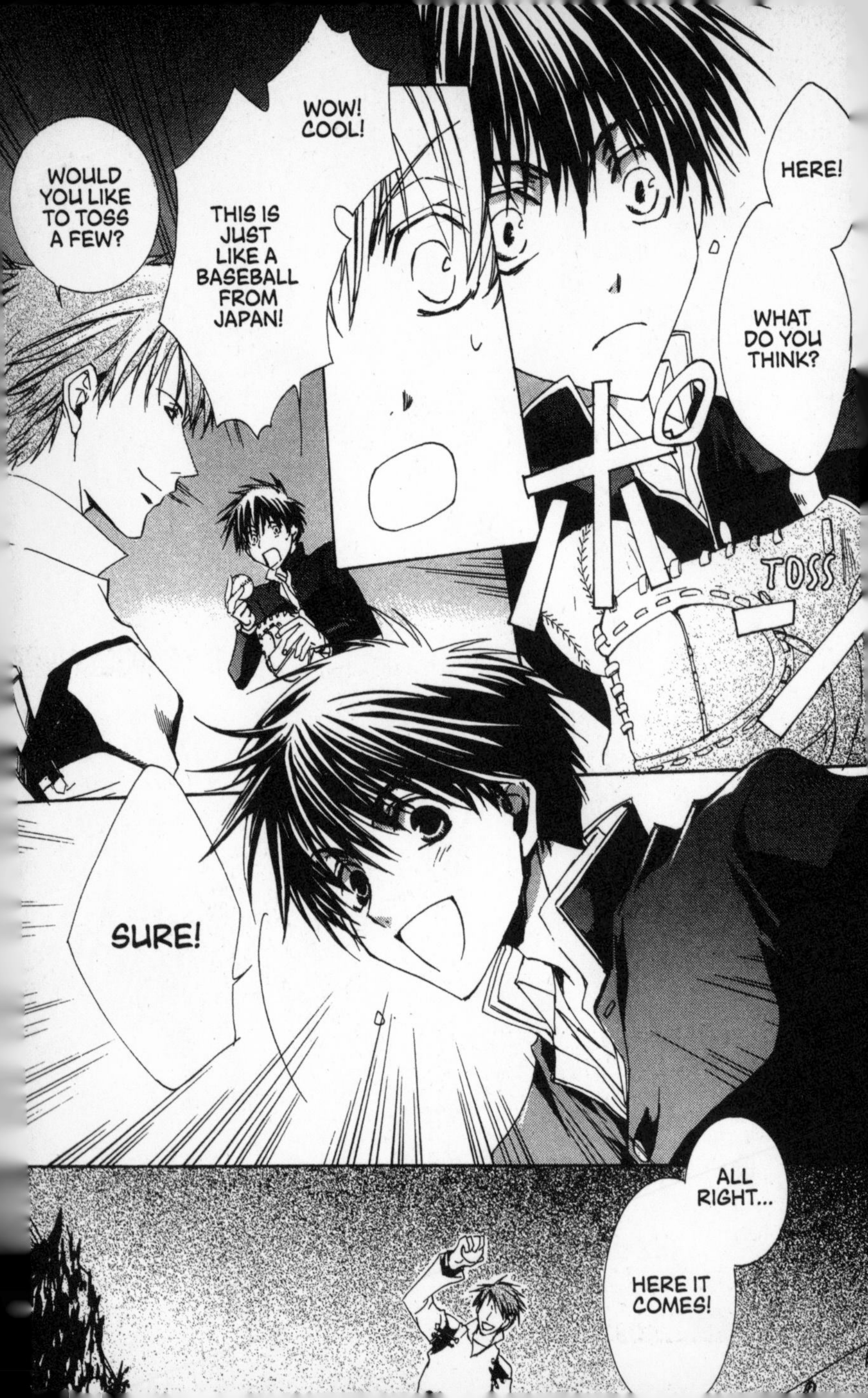
HERE!
WHAT DO YOU THINK?
WOW! COOL!
THIS IS JUST LIKE A BASEBALL FROM JAPAN!
WOULD YOU LIKE TO TOSS A FEW?
TOSS
SURE!
ALL RIGHT...
HERE IT COMES!

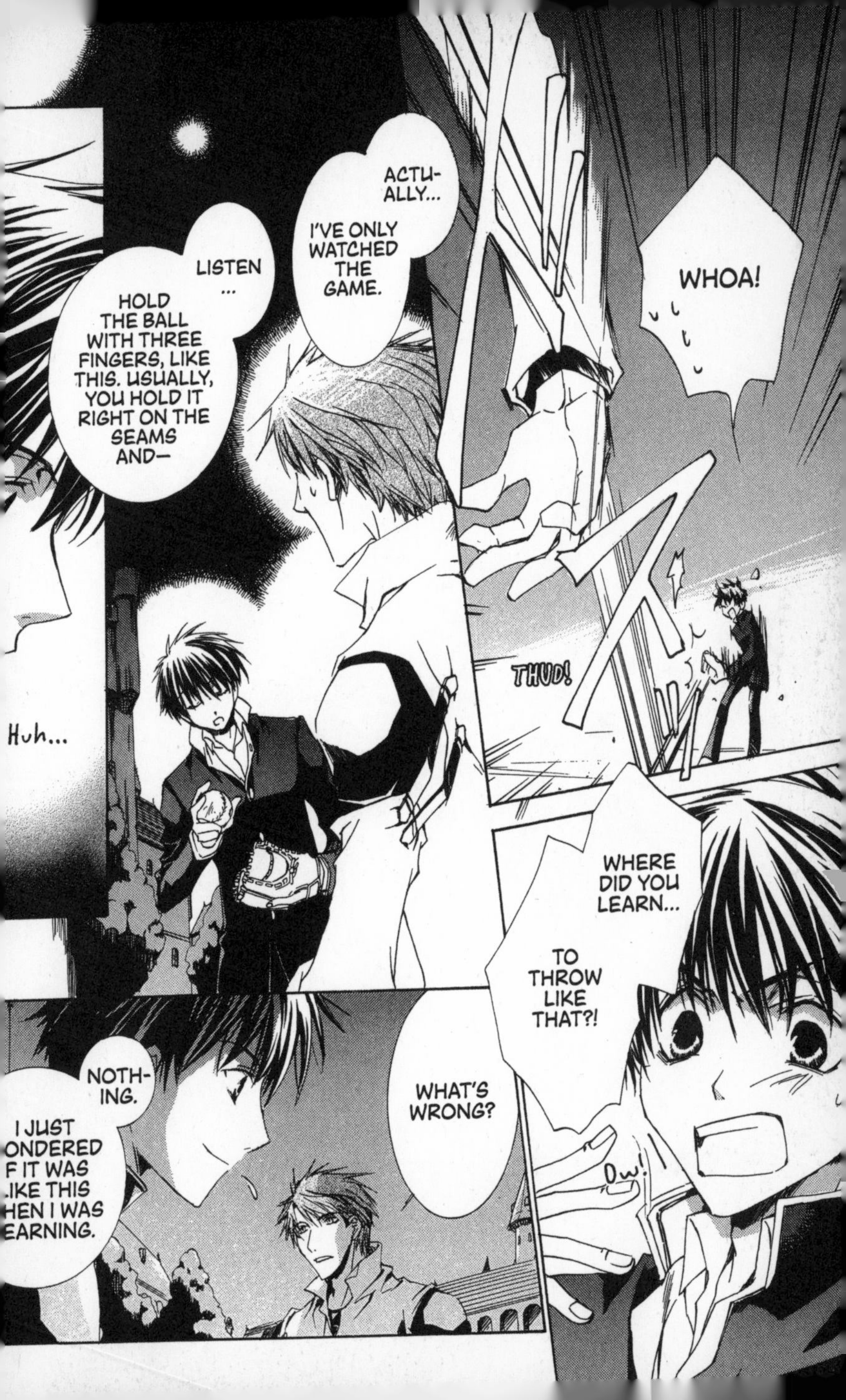
WHOA!
THUD!
WHERE DID YOU LEARN...
TO THROW LIKE THAT?!
Ow!
ACTU-ALLY...
I'VE ONLY WATCHED THE GAME.
LISTEN ...
HOLD THE BALL WITH THREE FINGERS, LIKE THIS. USUALLY, YOU HOLD IT RIGHT ON THE SEAMS AND—
Huh...
WHAT'S WRONG?
NOTH-ING.
I JUST ONDERED F IT WAS IKE THIS HEN I WAS EARNING.

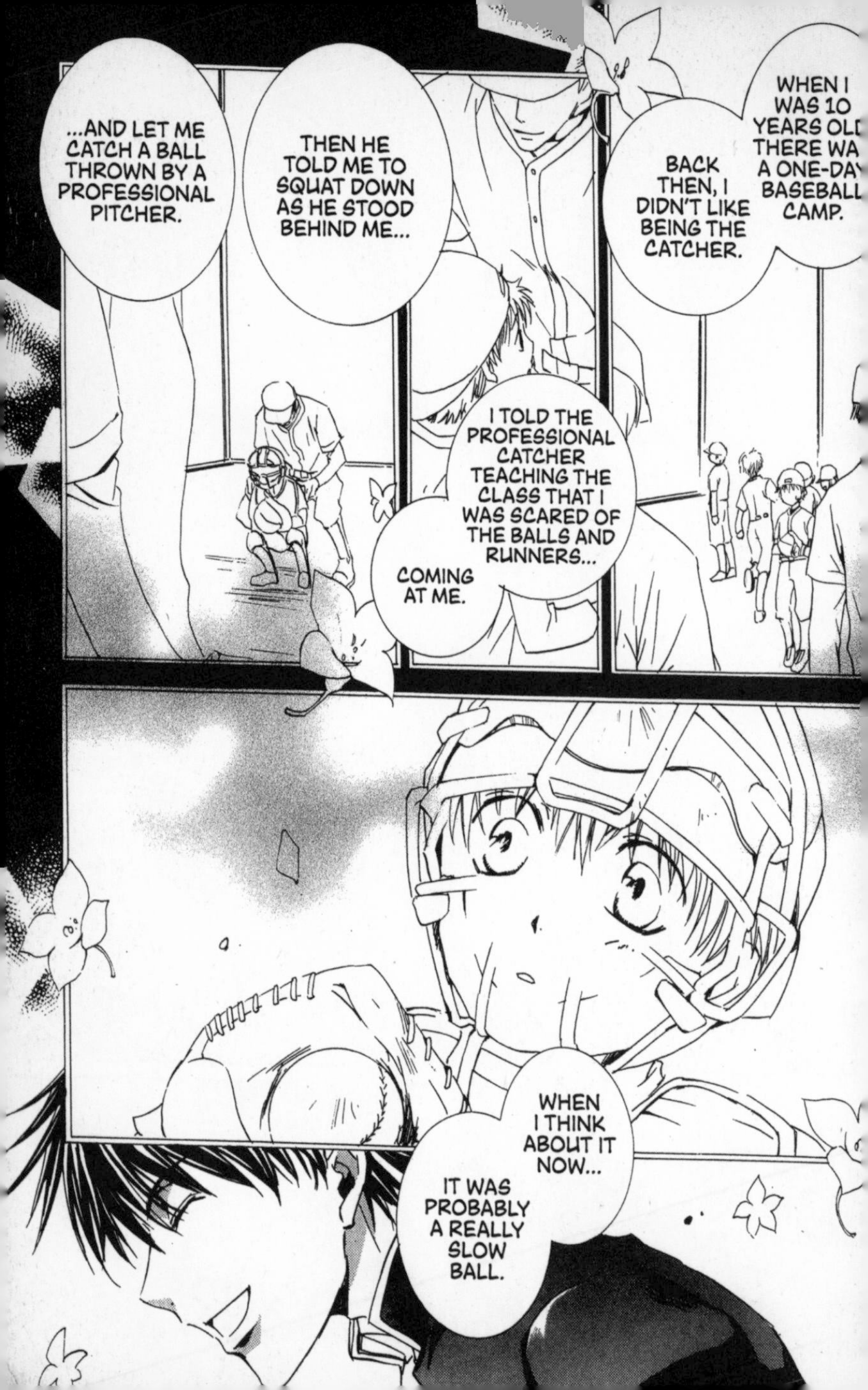
WHEN I WAS 10 YEARS OLD THERE WA A ONE-DAY BASEBALL CAMP.
BACK THEN, I DIDN'T LIKE BEING THE CATCHER.
I TOLD THE PROFESSIONAL CATCHER TEACHING THE CLASS THAT I WAS SCARED OF THE BALLS AND RUNNERS...
COMING AT ME.
THEN HE TOLD ME TO SQUAT DOWN AS HE STOOD BEHIND ME...
...AND LET ME CATCH A BALL THROWN BY A PROFESSIONAL PITCHER.
WHEN I THINK ABOUT IT NOW...
IT WAS PROBABLY A REALLY SLOW BALL.

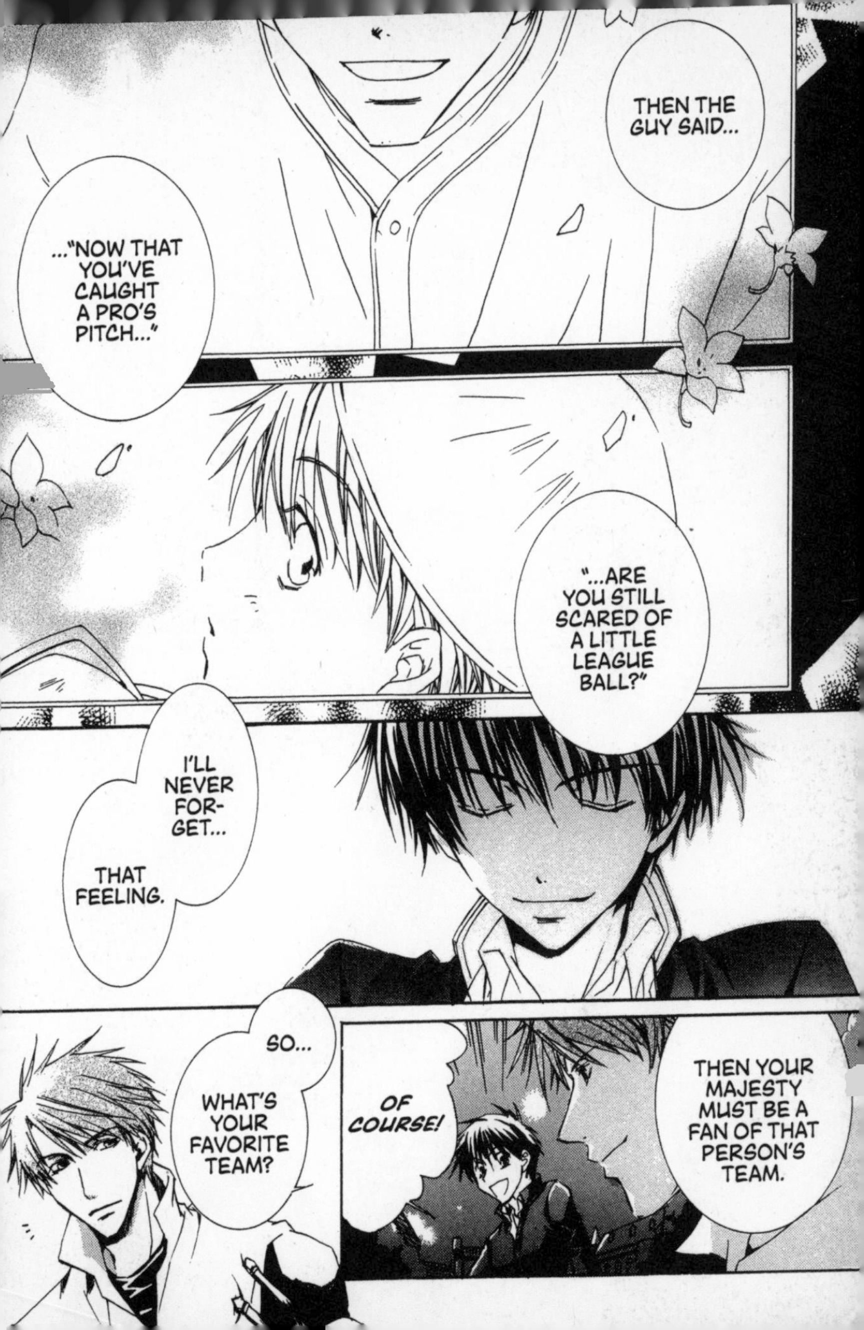
THEN THE GUY SAID...
..."NOW THAT YOU'VE CAUGHT A PRO'S PITCH..."
"...ARE YOU STILL SCARED OF A LITTLE LEAGUE BALL?"
I'LL NEVER FOR-GET...
THAT FEELING.
THEN YOUR MAJESTY MUST BE A FAN OF THAT PERSON'S TEAM.
OF COURSE!
SO...
WHAT'S YOUR FAVORITE TEAM?

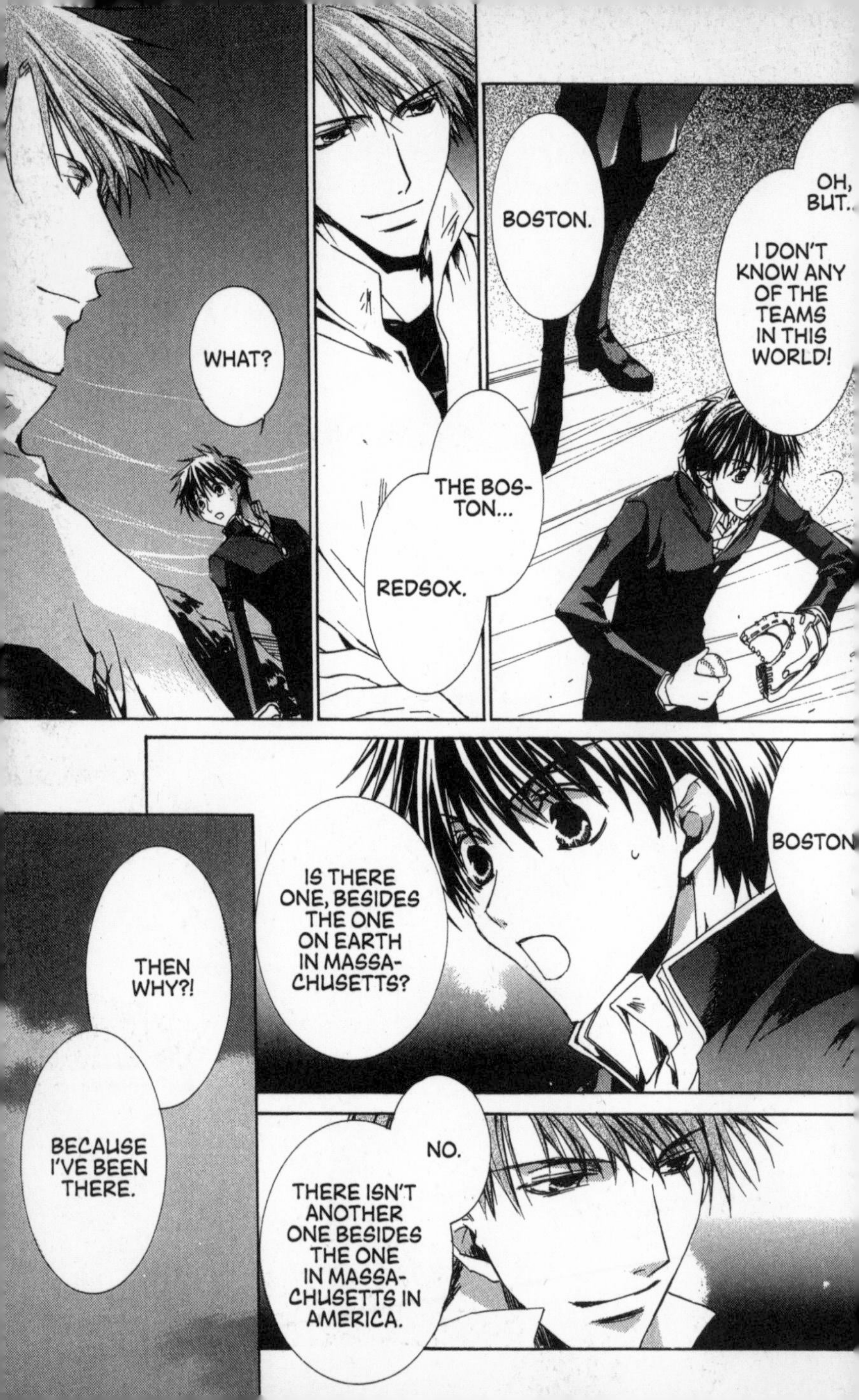
OH, BUT..
I DON'T KNOW ANY OF THE TEAMS IN THIS WORLD!
BOSTON.
THE BOS-TON...
REDSOX.
WHAT?
BOSTON
IS THERE ONE, BESIDES THE ONE ON EARTH IN MASSA-CHUSETTS?
NO.
THERE ISN'T ANOTHER ONE BESIDES THE ONE IN MASSA-CHUSETTS IN AMERICA.
THEN WHY?!
BECAUSE I'VE BEEN THERE.

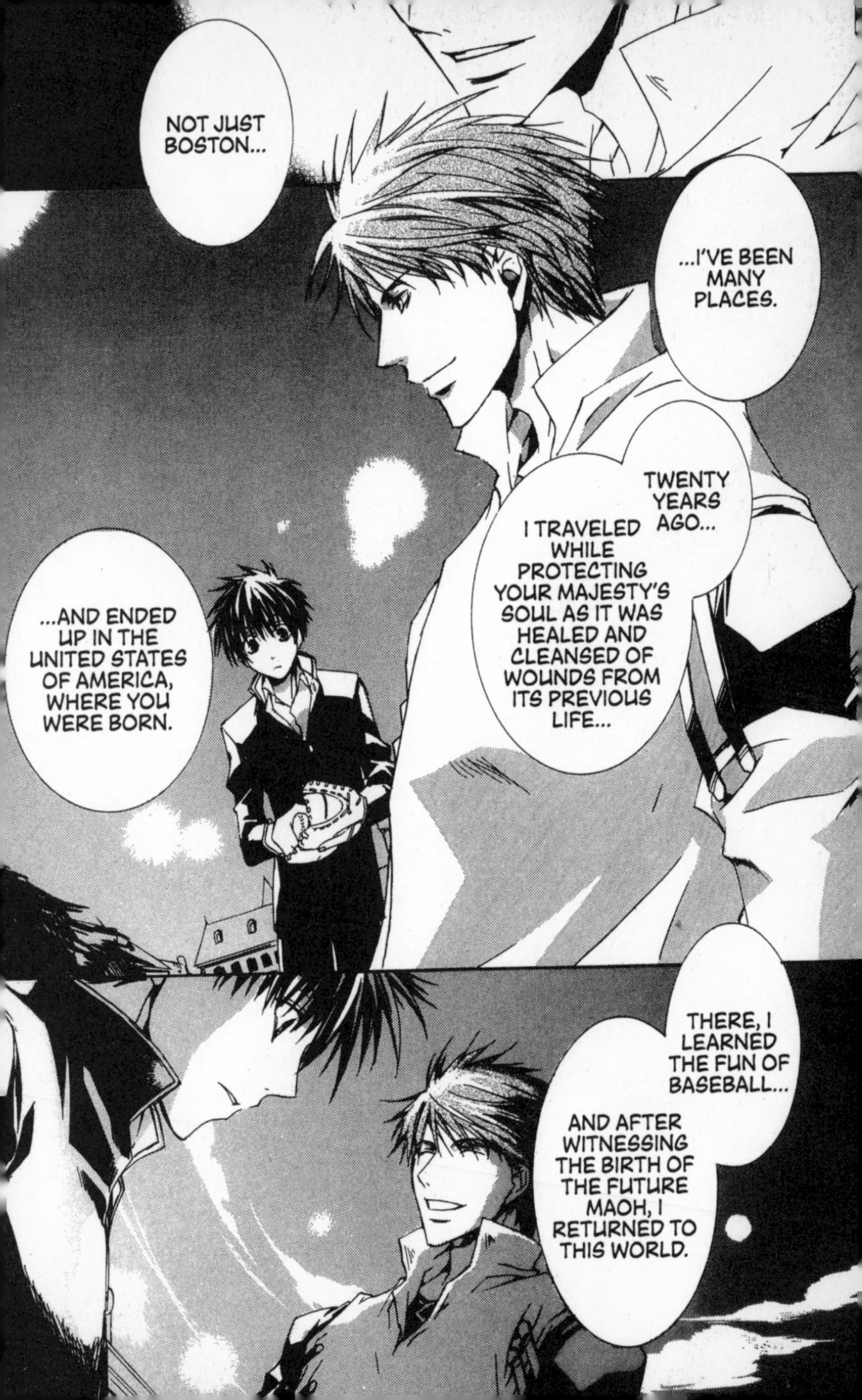
NOT JUST BOSTON...
...I'VE BEEN MANY PLACES.
TWENTY YEARS AGO... I TRAVELED WHILE PROTECTING YOUR MAJESTY'S SOUL AS IT WAS HEALED AND CLEANSED OF WOUNDS FROM ITS PREVIOUS LIFE...
...AND ENDED UP IN THE UNITED STATES OF AMERICA, WHERE YOU WERE BORN.
THERE, I LEARNED THE FUN OF BASEBALL...
AND AFTER WITNESSING THE BIRTH OF THE FUTURE MAOH, I RETURNED TO THIS WORLD.

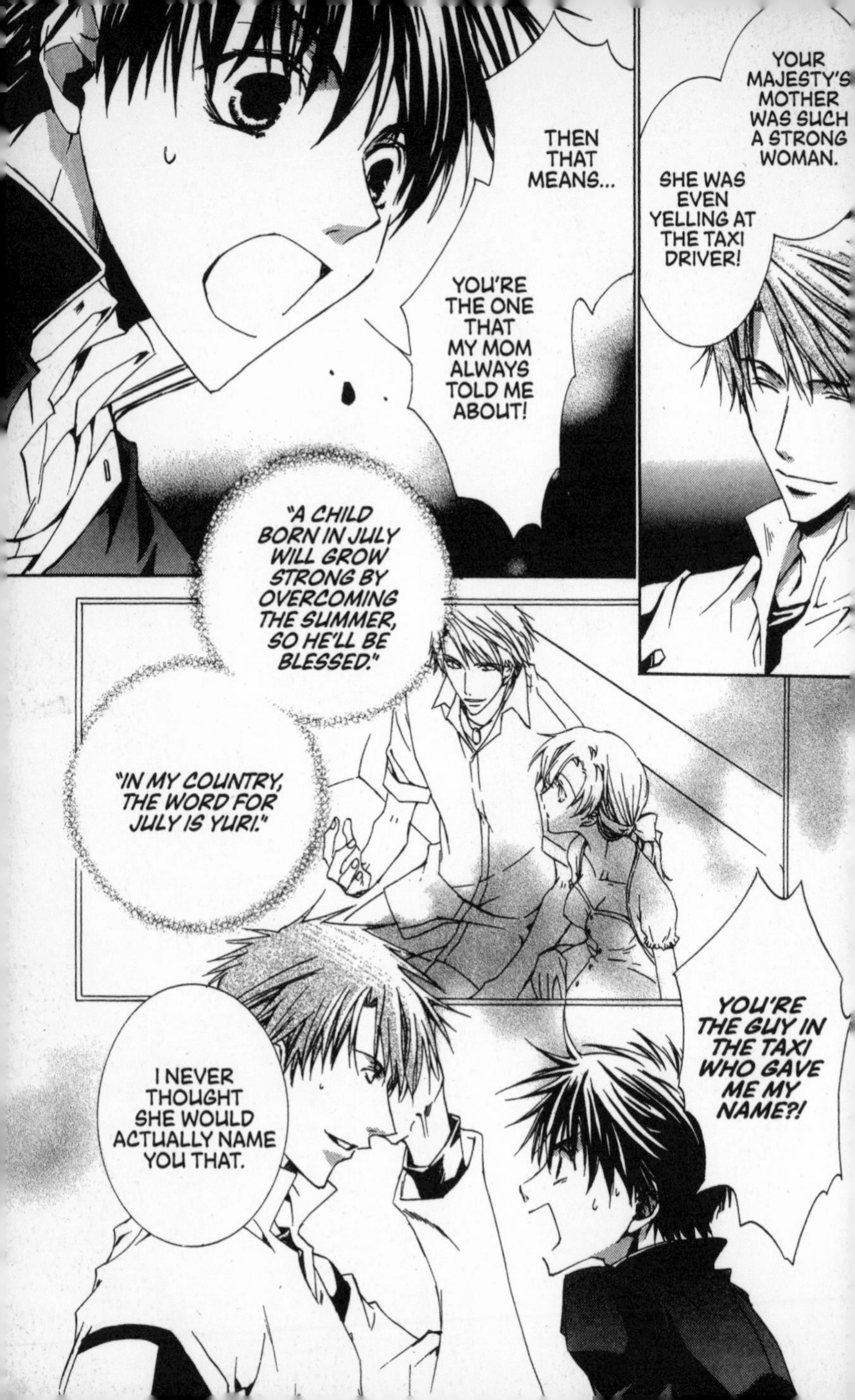
YOUR MAJESTY'S MOTHER WAS SUCH A STRONG WOMAN.
SHE WAS EVEN YELLING AT THE TAXI DRIVER!
THEN THAT MEANS...
YOU'RE THE ONE THAT MY MOM ALWAYS TOLD ME ABOUT!
"A CHILD BORN IN JULY WILL GROW STRONG BY OVERCOMING THE SUMMER, SO HE'LL BE BLESSED."
"IN MY COUNTRY, THE WORD FOR JULY IS YURI."
YOU'RE THE GUY IN THE TAXI WHO GAVE ME MY NAME?!
I NEVER THOUGHT SHE WOULD ACTUALLY NAME YOU THAT.

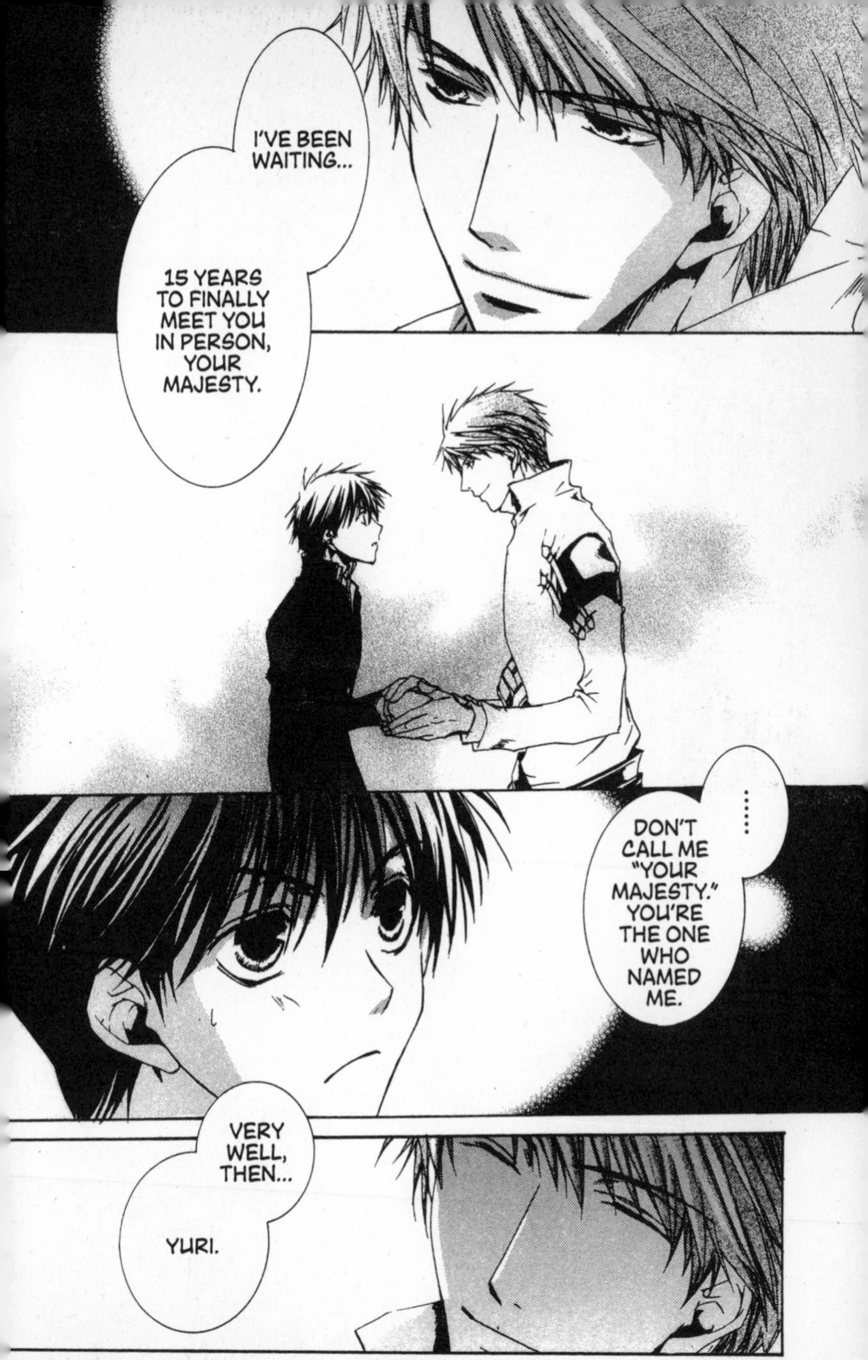
I'VE BEEN WAITING...
15 YEARS TO FINALLY MEET YOU IN PERSON, YOUR MAJESTY.
......
DON'T CALL ME "YOUR MAJESTY." YOU'RE THE ONE WHO NAMED ME.
VERY WELL, THEN...
YURI.

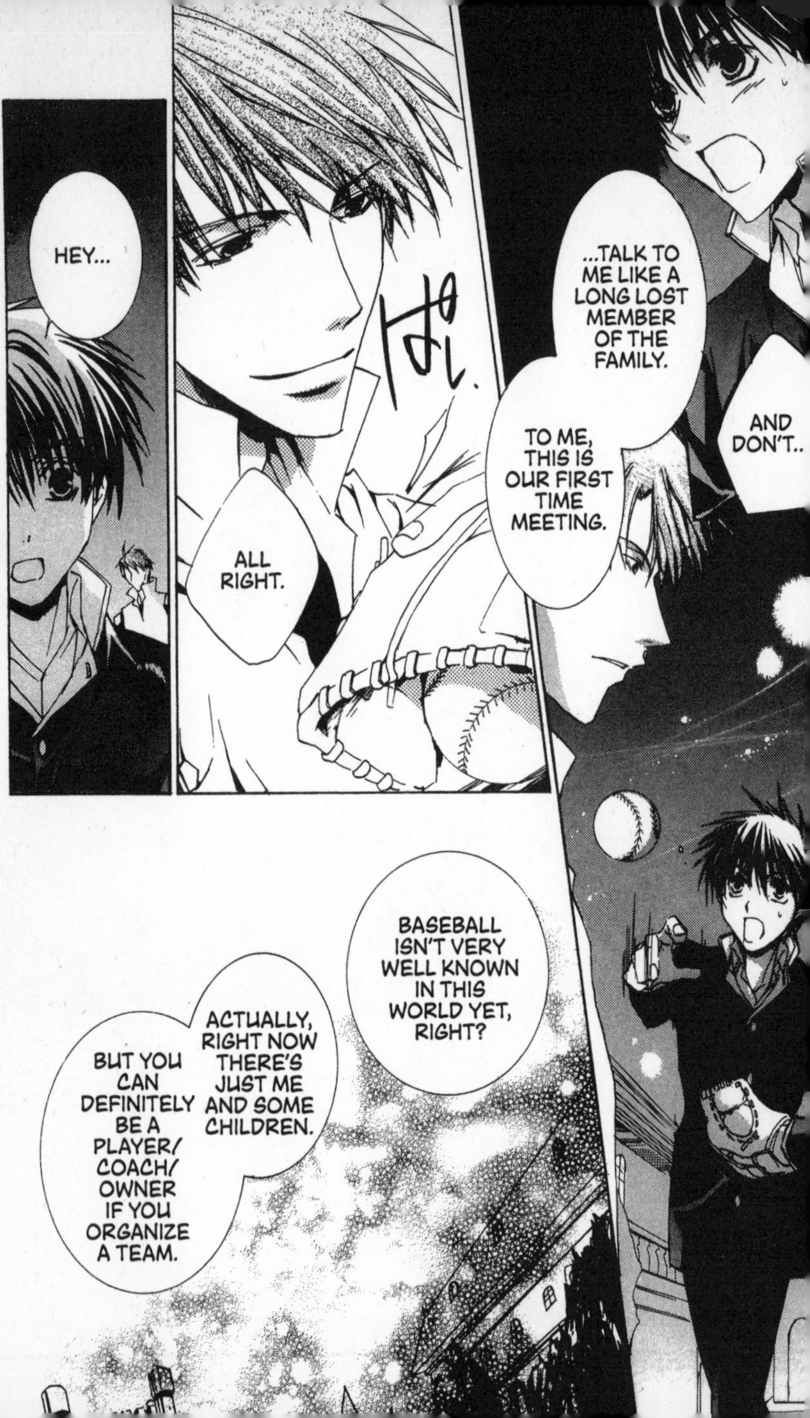
AND DON'T..
...TALK TO ME LIKE A LONG LOST MEMBER OF THE FAMILY.
TO ME, THIS IS OUR FIRST TIME MEETING.
ぱし.
ALL RIGHT.
HEY...
BASEBALL ISN'T VERY WELL KNOWN IN THIS WORLD YET, RIGHT?
ACTUALLY, RIGHT NOW THERE'S JUST ME AND SOME CHILDREN.
BUT YOU CAN DEFINITELY BE A PLAYER/ COACH/ OWNER IF YOU ORGANIZE A TEAM.

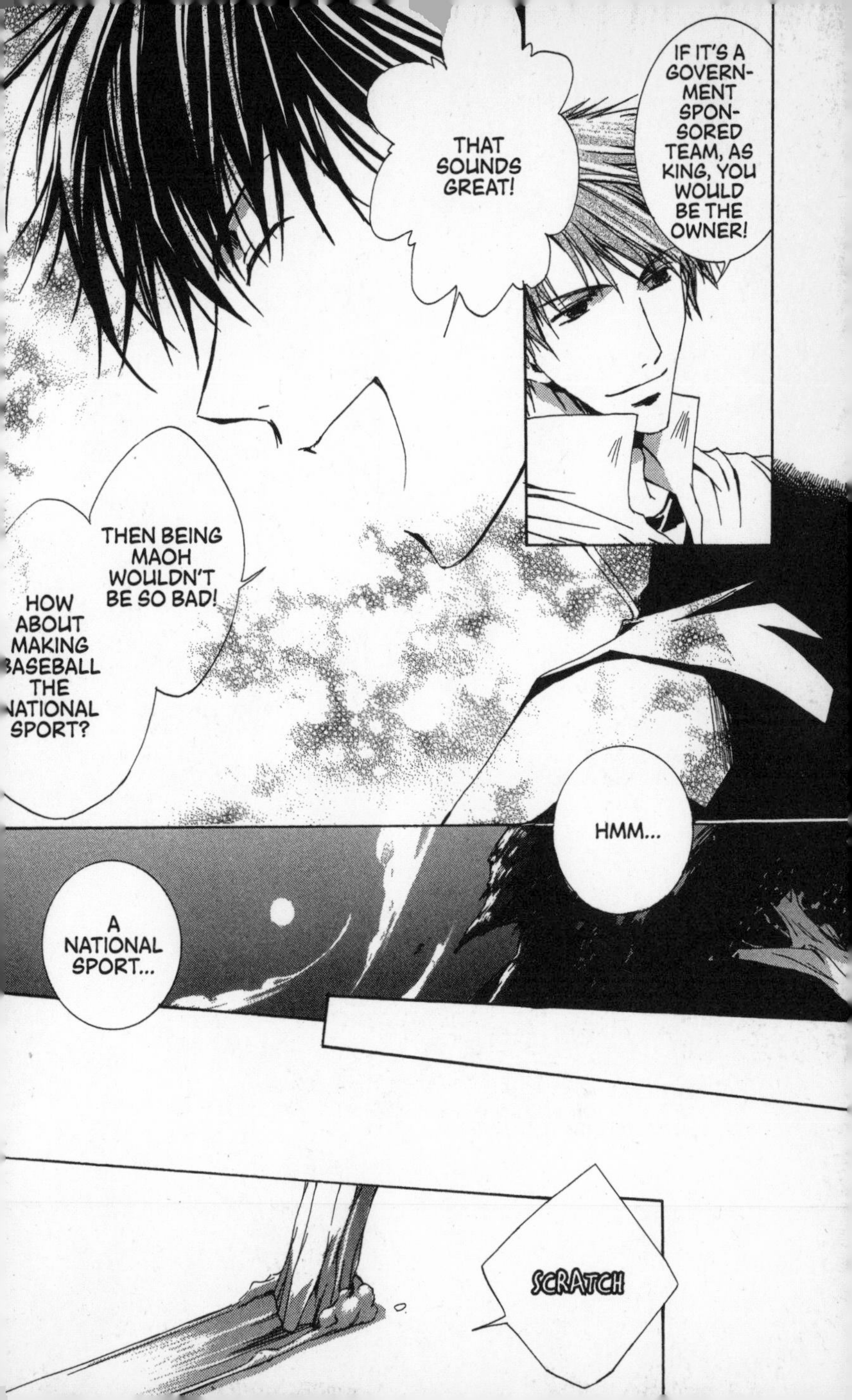
IF IT'S A GOVERNMENT-SPONSORED TEAM, AS KING, YOU WOULD BE THE OWNER!
THAT SOUNDS GREAT!
THEN BEING MAOH WOULDN'T BE SO BAD!
HOW ABOUT MAKING BASEBALL THE NATIONAL SPORT?
HMM...
A NATIONAL SPORT...
SCRATCH

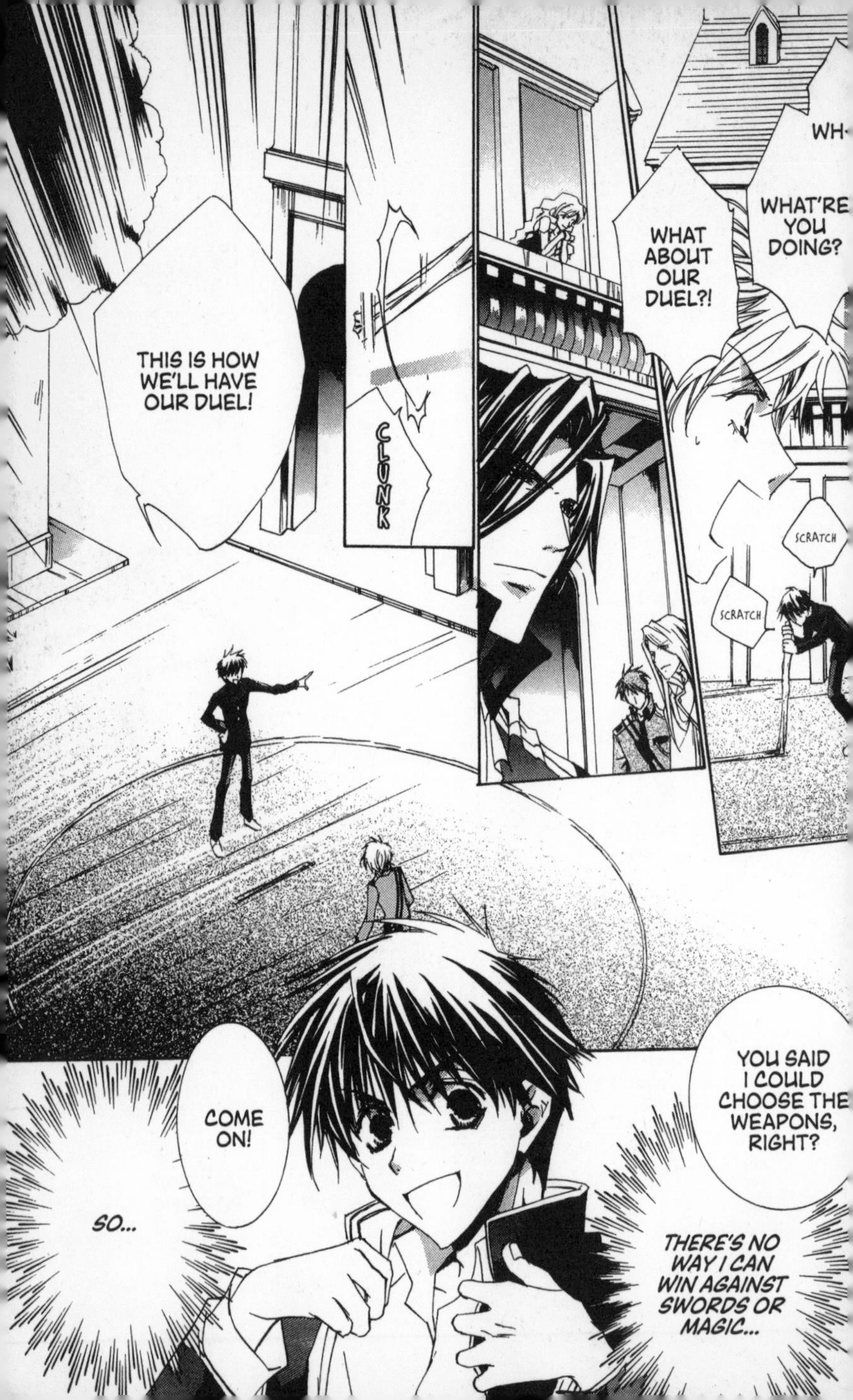
WH-
WHAT'RE YOU DOING?
WHAT ABOUT OUR DUEL?!
SCRATCH
SCRATCH
CLUNK
THIS IS HOW WE'LL HAVE OUR DUEL!
YOU SAID I COULD CHOOSE THE WEAPONS, RIGHT?
COME ON!
THERE'S NO WAY I CAN WIN AGAINST SWORDS OR MAGIC...
SO...

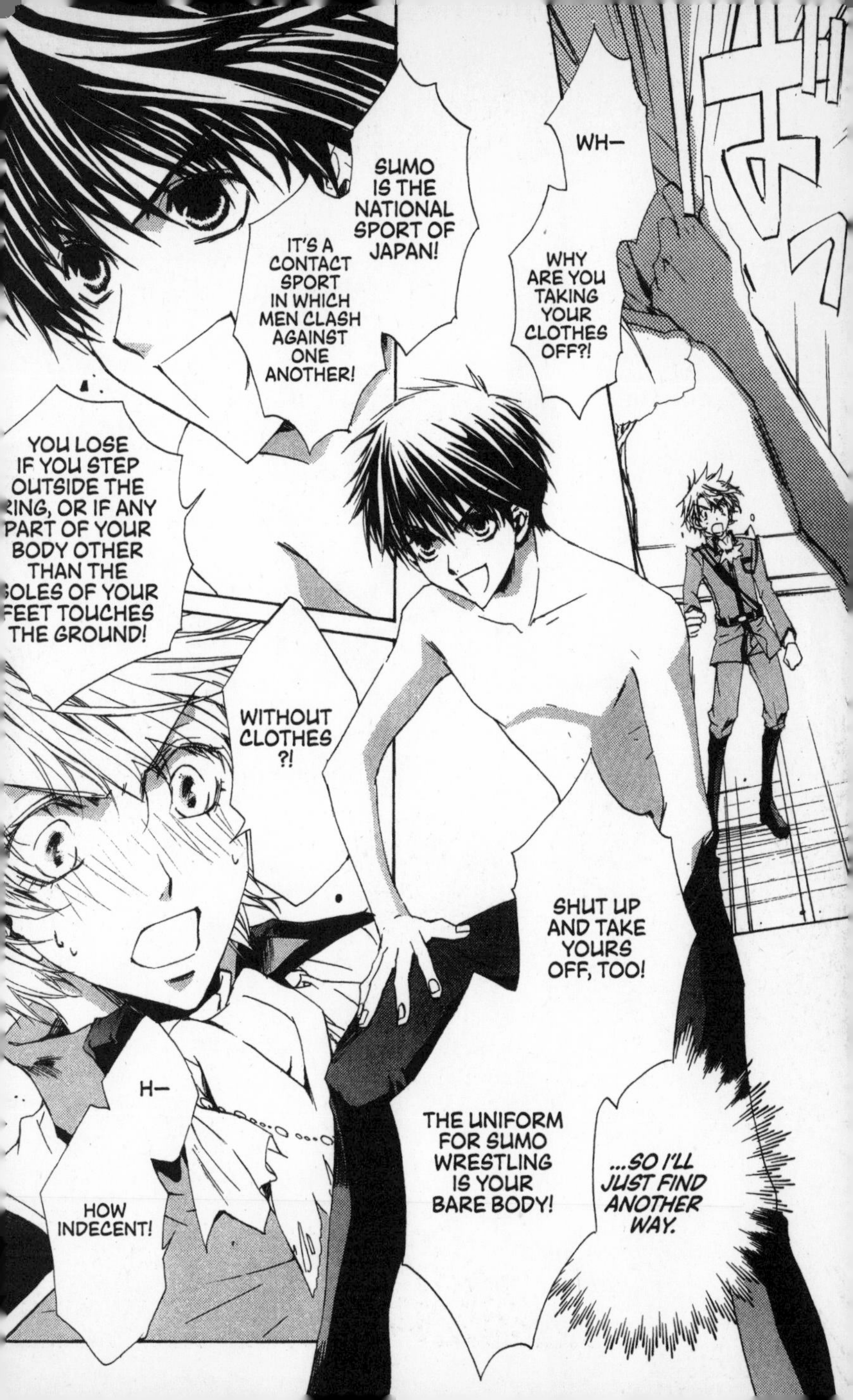
WH—
WHY ARE YOU TAKING YOUR CLOTHES OFF?!
SUMO IS THE NATIONAL SPORT OF JAPAN!
IT'S A CONTACT SPORT IN WHICH MEN CLASH AGAINST ONE ANOTHER!
YOU LOSE IF YOU STEP OUTSIDE THE RING, OR IF ANY PART OF YOUR BODY OTHER THAN THE SOLES OF YOUR FEET TOUCHES THE GROUND!
SHUT UP AND TAKE YOURS OFF, TOO!
WITHOUT CLOTHES ?!
...SO I'LL JUST FIND ANOTHER WAY.
THE UNIFORM FOR SUMO WRESTLING IS YOUR BARE BODY!
H—
HOW INDECENT!

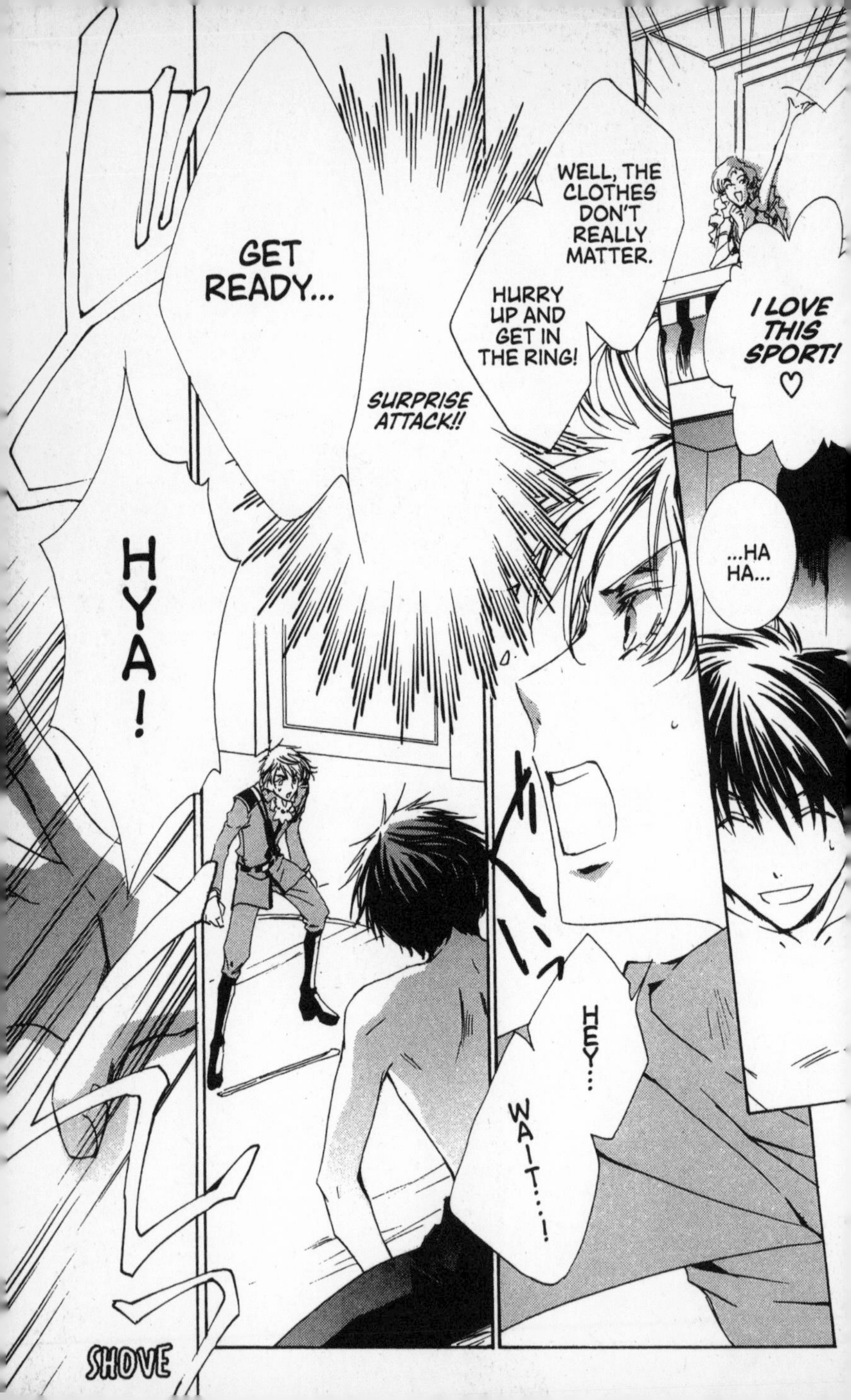
WELL, THE CLOTHES DON'T REALLY MATTER.
HURRY UP AND GET IN THE RING!
I LOVE THIS SPORT! ♡
...HA HA...
SURPRISE ATTACK!!
GET READY...
HEY... WAIT...!
HYA!
SHOVE

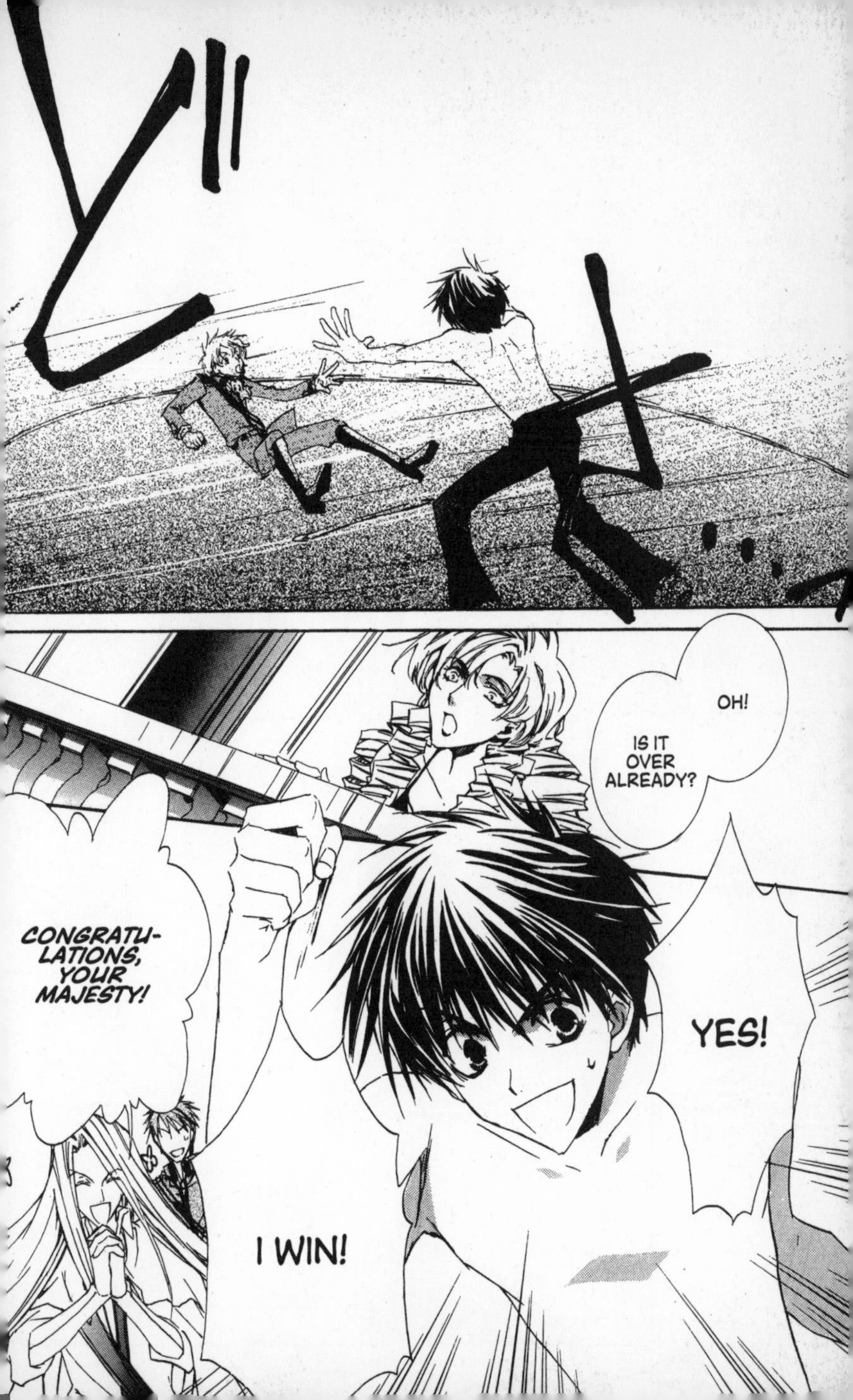
OH!
IS IT OVER ALREADY?
YES!
CONGRATU-LATIONS, YOUR MAJESTY!
I WIN!

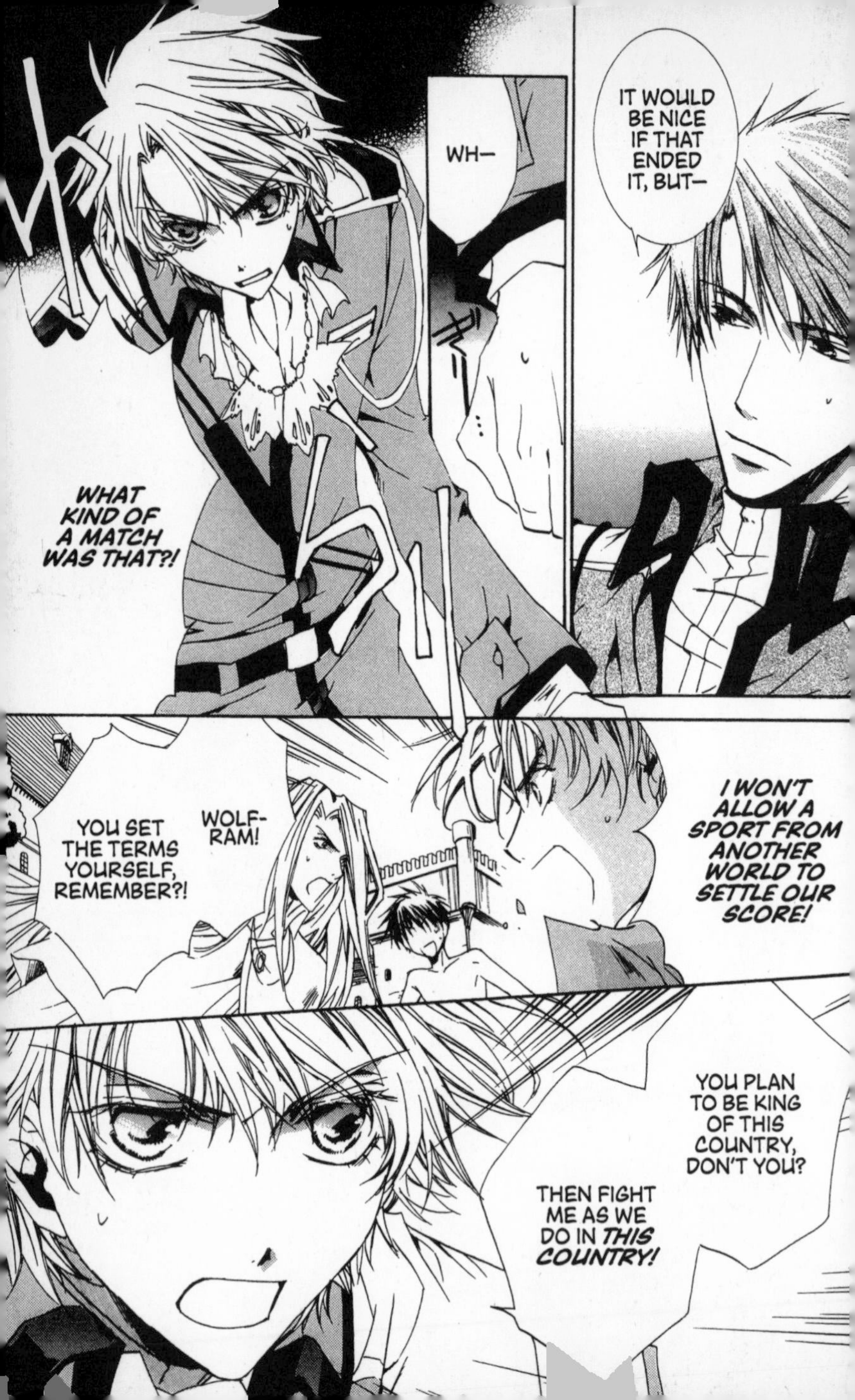
IT WOULD BE NICE IF THAT ENDED IT, BUT—
WH—
WHAT KIND OF A MATCH WAS THAT?!
I WON'T ALLOW A SPORT FROM ANOTHER WORLD TO SETTLE OUR SCORE!
WOLF-RAM!
YOU SET THE TERMS YOURSELF, REMEMBER?!
YOU PLAN TO BE KING OF THIS COUNTRY, DON'T YOU?
THEN FIGHT ME AS WE DO IN THIS COUNTRY!

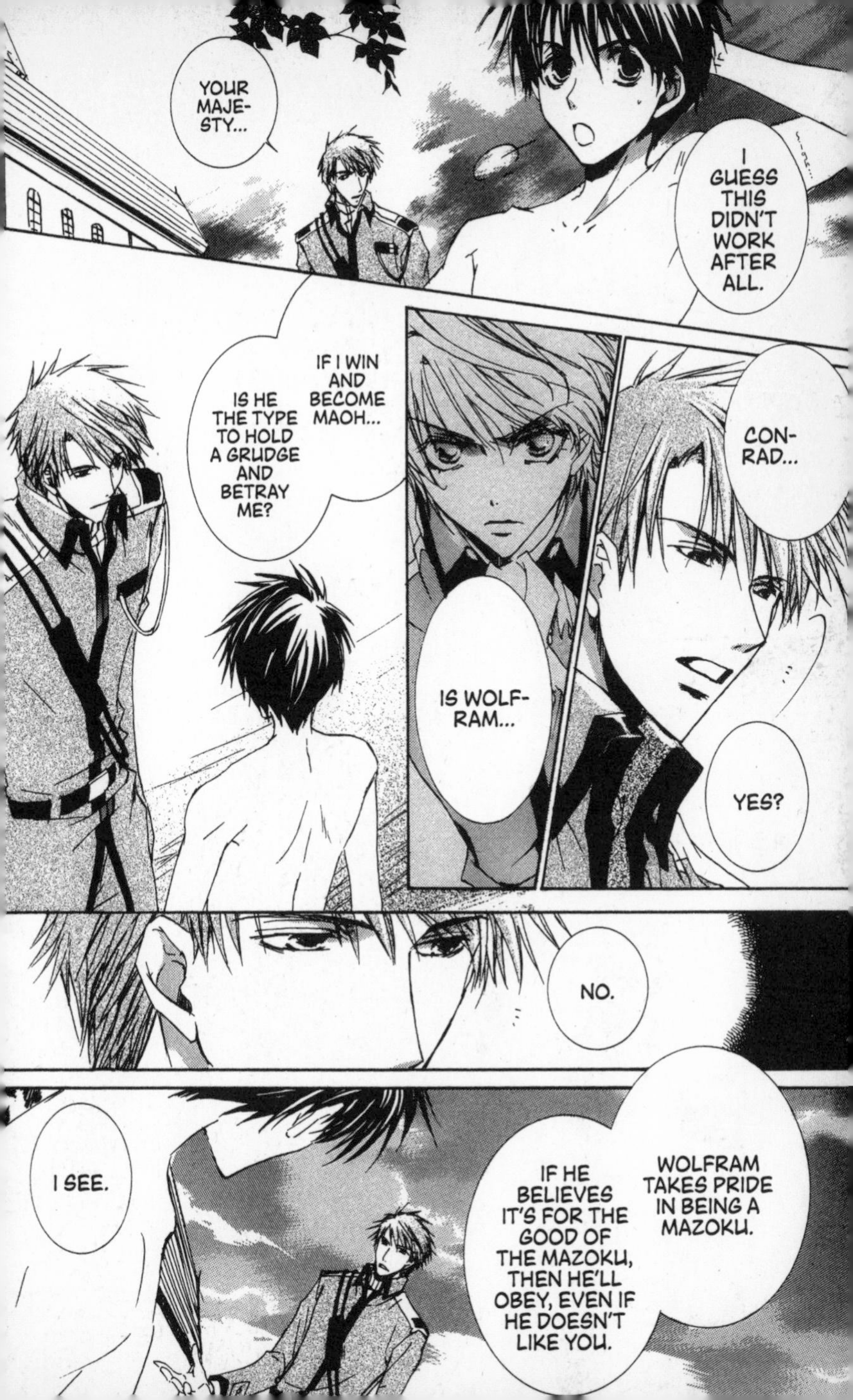
I GUESS THIS DIDN'T WORK AFTER ALL.
YOUR MAJESTY...
CONRAD...
YES?
IS WOLFRAM...
IF I WIN AND BECOME MAOH...
IS HE THE TYPE TO HOLD A GRUDGE AND BETRAY ME?
NO.
WOLFRAM TAKES PRIDE IN BEING A MAZOKU.
IF HE BELIEVES IT'S FOR THE GOOD OF THE MAZOKU, THEN HE'LL OBEY, EVEN IF HE DOESN'T LIKE YOU.
I SEE.

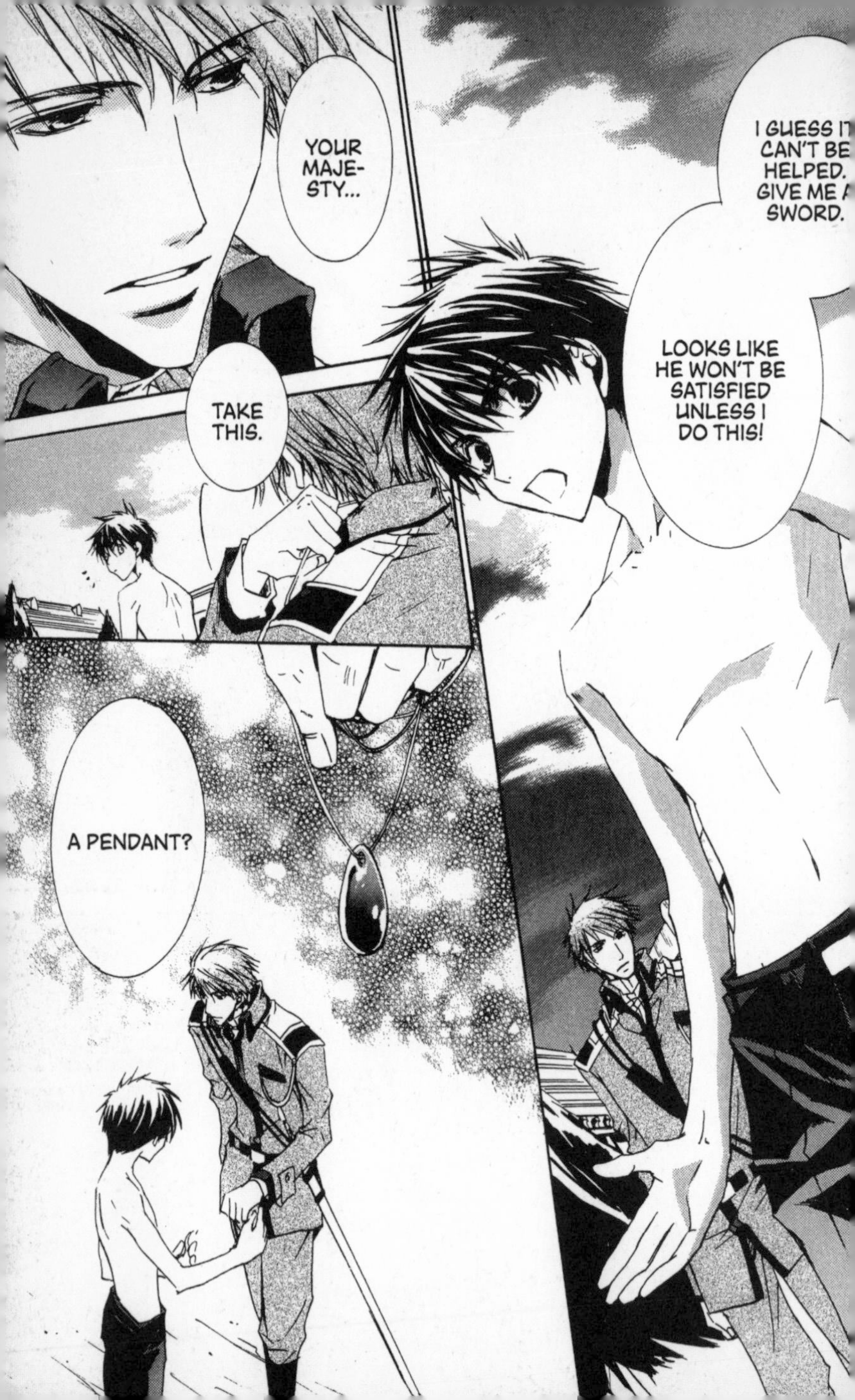
I GUESS IT CAN'T BE HELPED. GIVE ME A SWORD.
LOOKS LIKE HE WON'T BE SATISFIED UNLESS I DO THIS!
YOUR MAJESTY...
TAKE THIS.
A PENDANT?

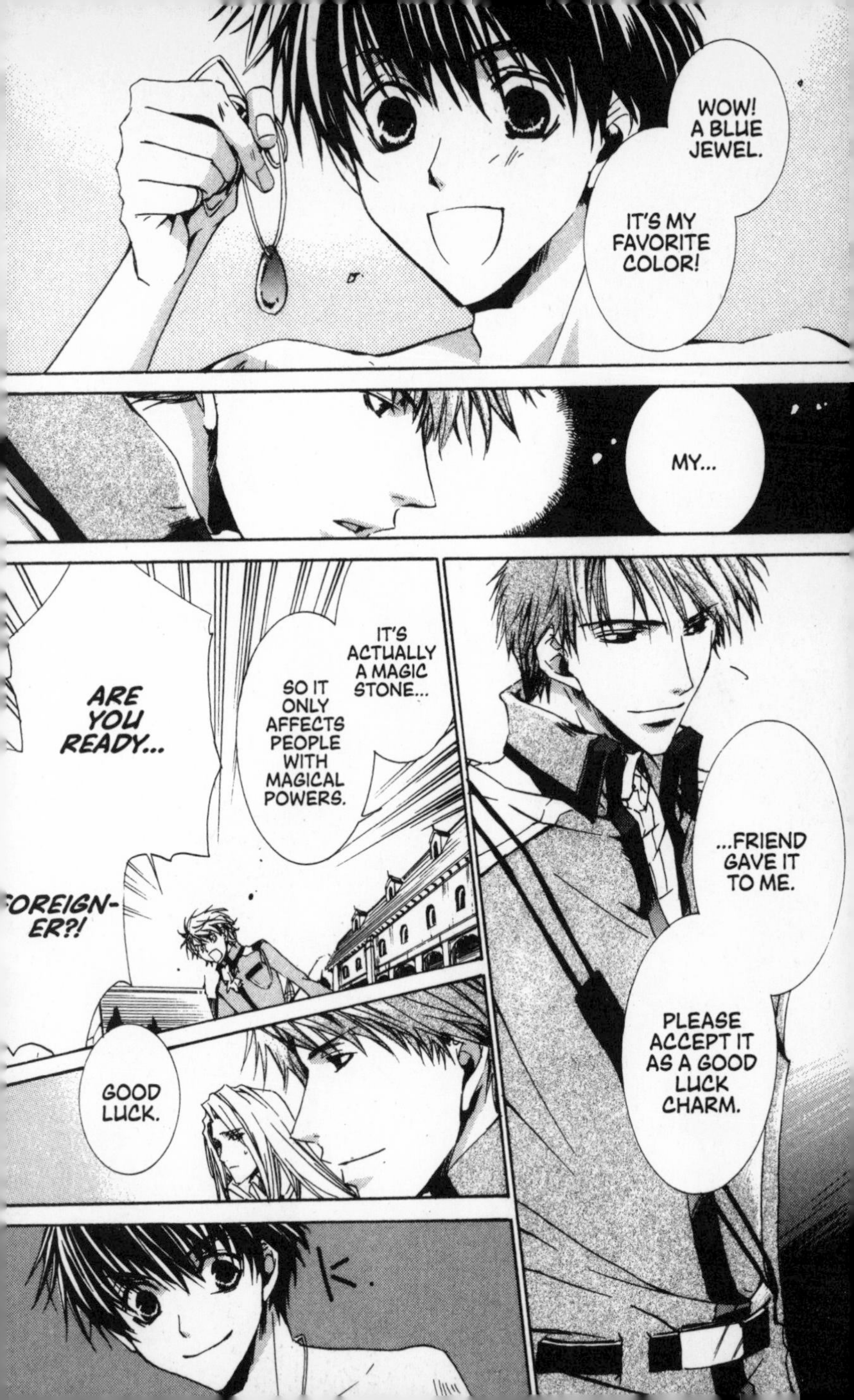
WOW! A BLUE JEWEL.
IT'S MY FAVORITE COLOR!
MY...
...FRIEND GAVE IT TO ME.
PLEASE ACCEPT IT AS A GOOD LUCK CHARM.
IT'S ACTUALLY A MAGIC STONE...
SO IT ONLY AFFECTS PEOPLE WITH MAGICAL POWERS.
ARE YOU READY...
FOREIGNER?!
GOOD LUCK.

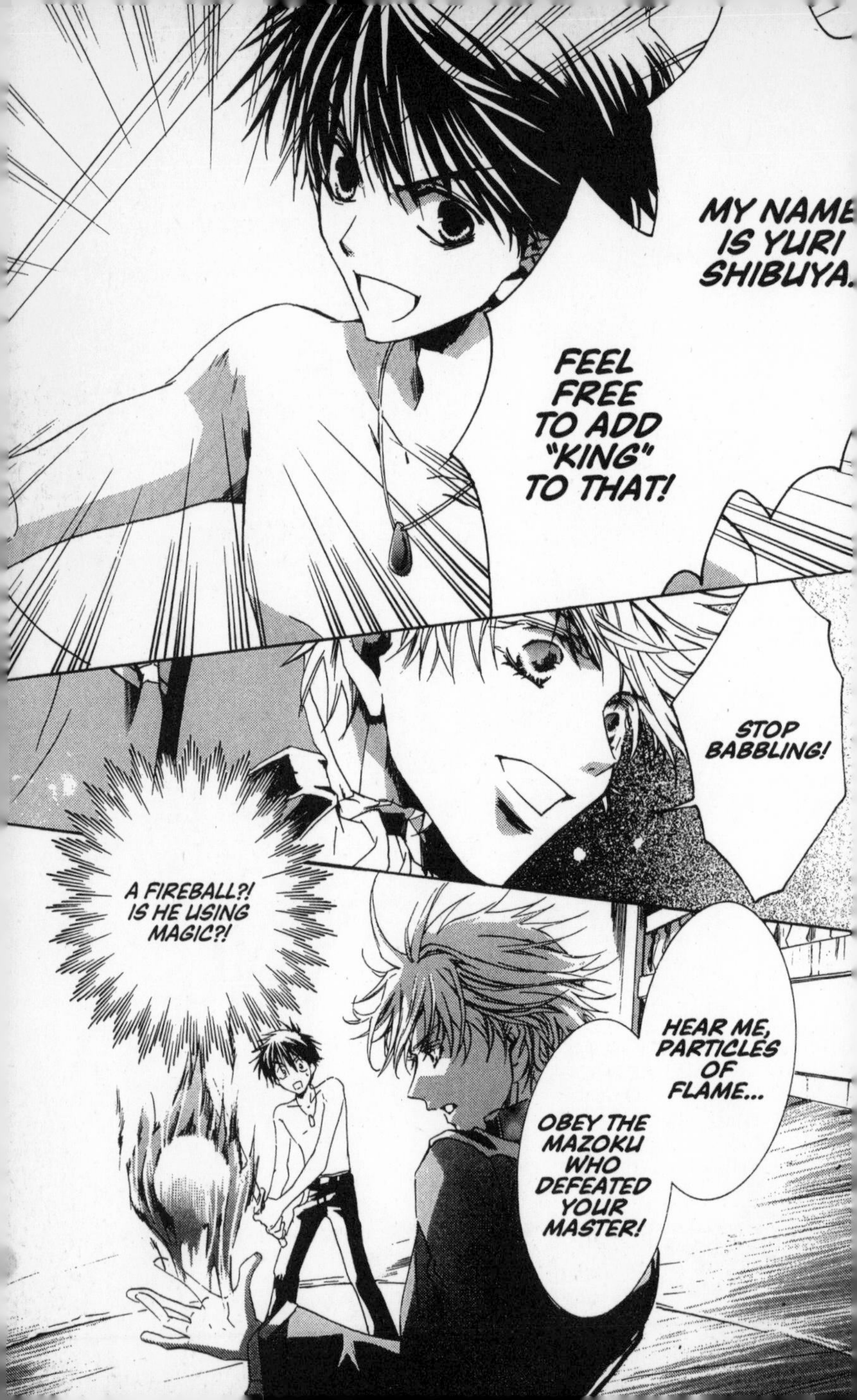
MY NAME IS YURI SHIBUYA...
FEEL FREE TO ADD "KING" TO THAT!
STOP BABBLING!
HEAR ME, PARTICLES OF FLAME...
OBEY THE MAZOKU WHO DEFEATED YOUR MASTER!
A FIREBALL?! IS HE USING MAGIC?!

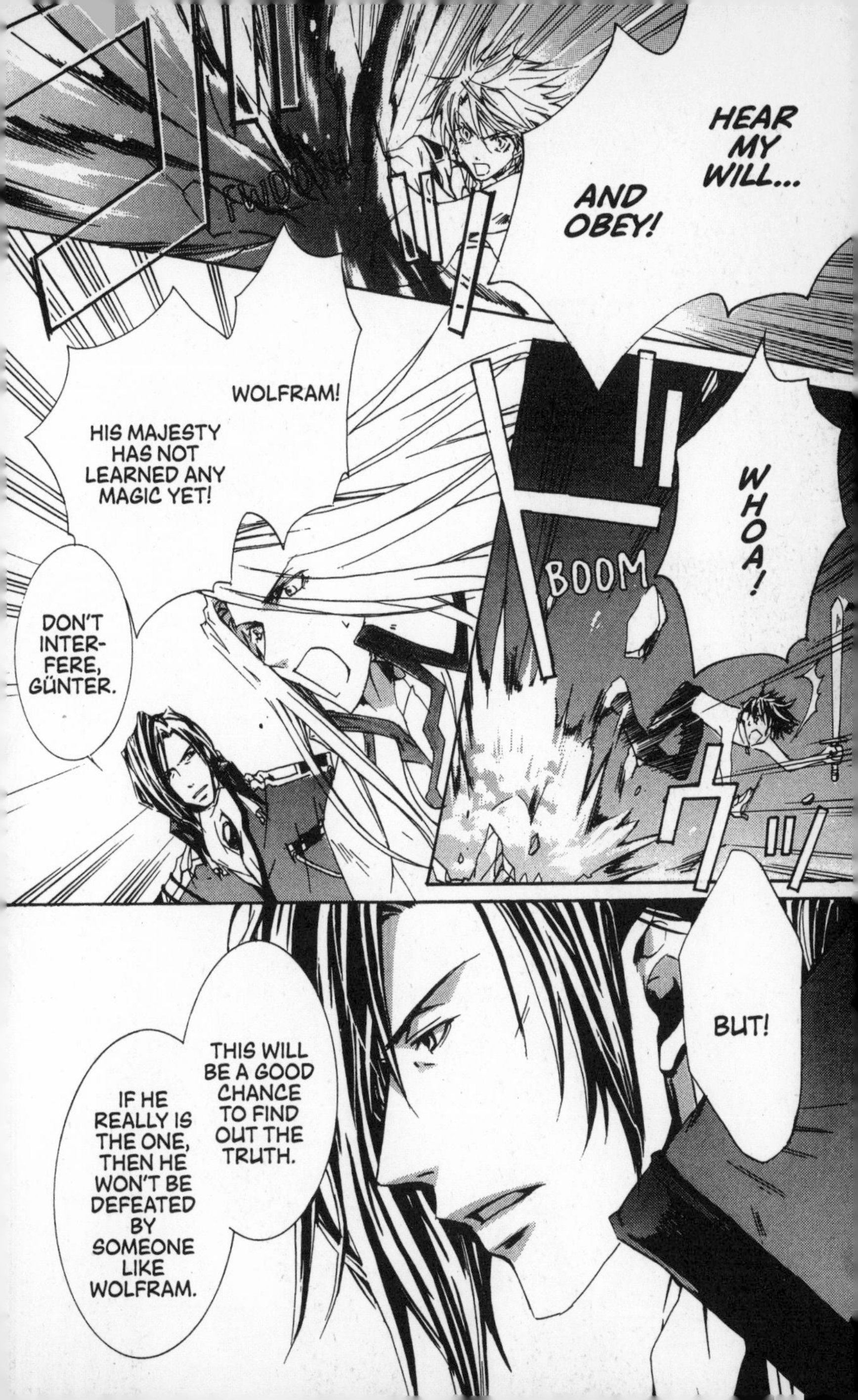
HEAR MY WILL...
AND OBEY!
WHOA!
BOOM
WOLFRAM!
HIS MAJESTY HAS NOT LEARNED ANY MAGIC YET!
DON'T INTER-FERE, GÜNTER.
BUT!
THIS WILL BE A GOOD CHANCE TO FIND OUT THE TRUTH.
IF HE REALLY IS THE ONE, THEN HE WON'T BE DEFEATED BY SOMEONE LIKE WOLFRAM.

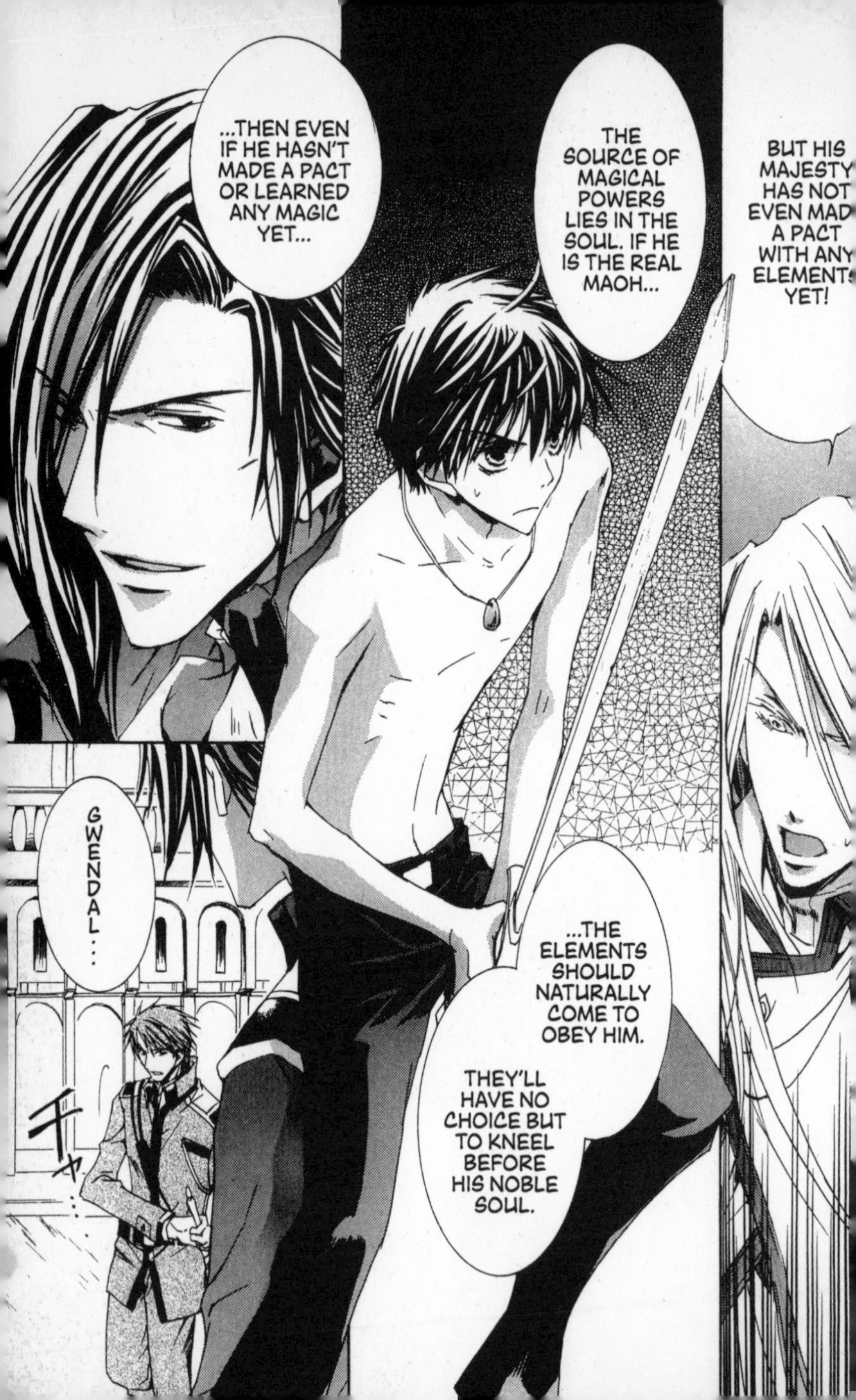
BUT HIS MAJESTY HAS NOT EVEN MAD A PACT WITH ANY ELEMENTS YET!
THE SOURCE OF MAGICAL POWERS LIES IN THE SOUL. IF HE IS THE REAL MAOH...
...THEN EVEN IF HE HASN'T MADE A PACT OR LEARNED ANY MAGIC YET...
...THE ELEMENTS SHOULD NATURALLY COME TO OBEY HIM.
THEY'LL HAVE NO CHOICE BUT TO KNEEL BEFORE HIS NOBLE SOUL.
GWENDAL...
チャ...

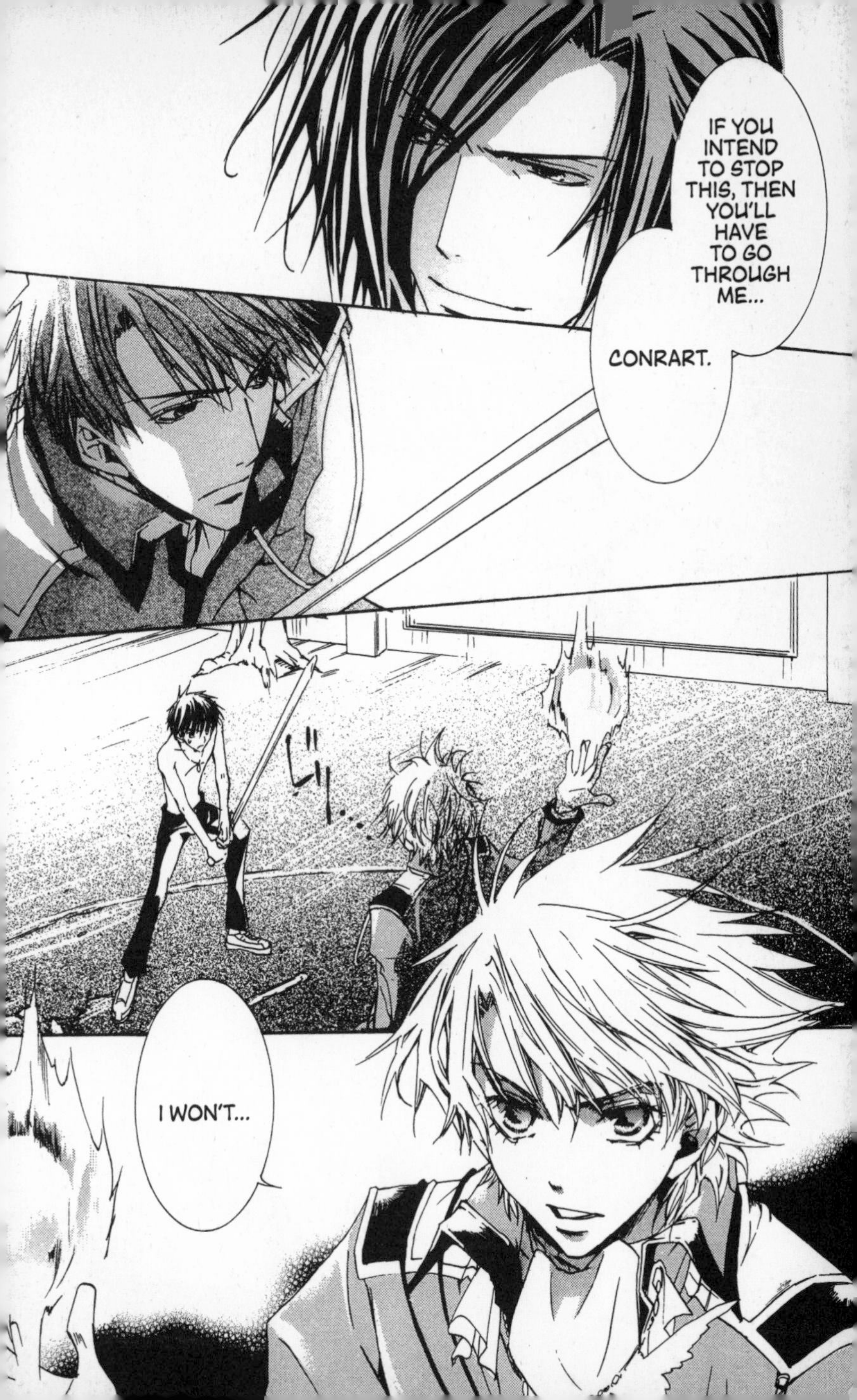
IF YOU INTEND TO STOP THIS, THEN YOU'LL HAVE TO GO THROUGH ME...
CONRART.
I WON'T...

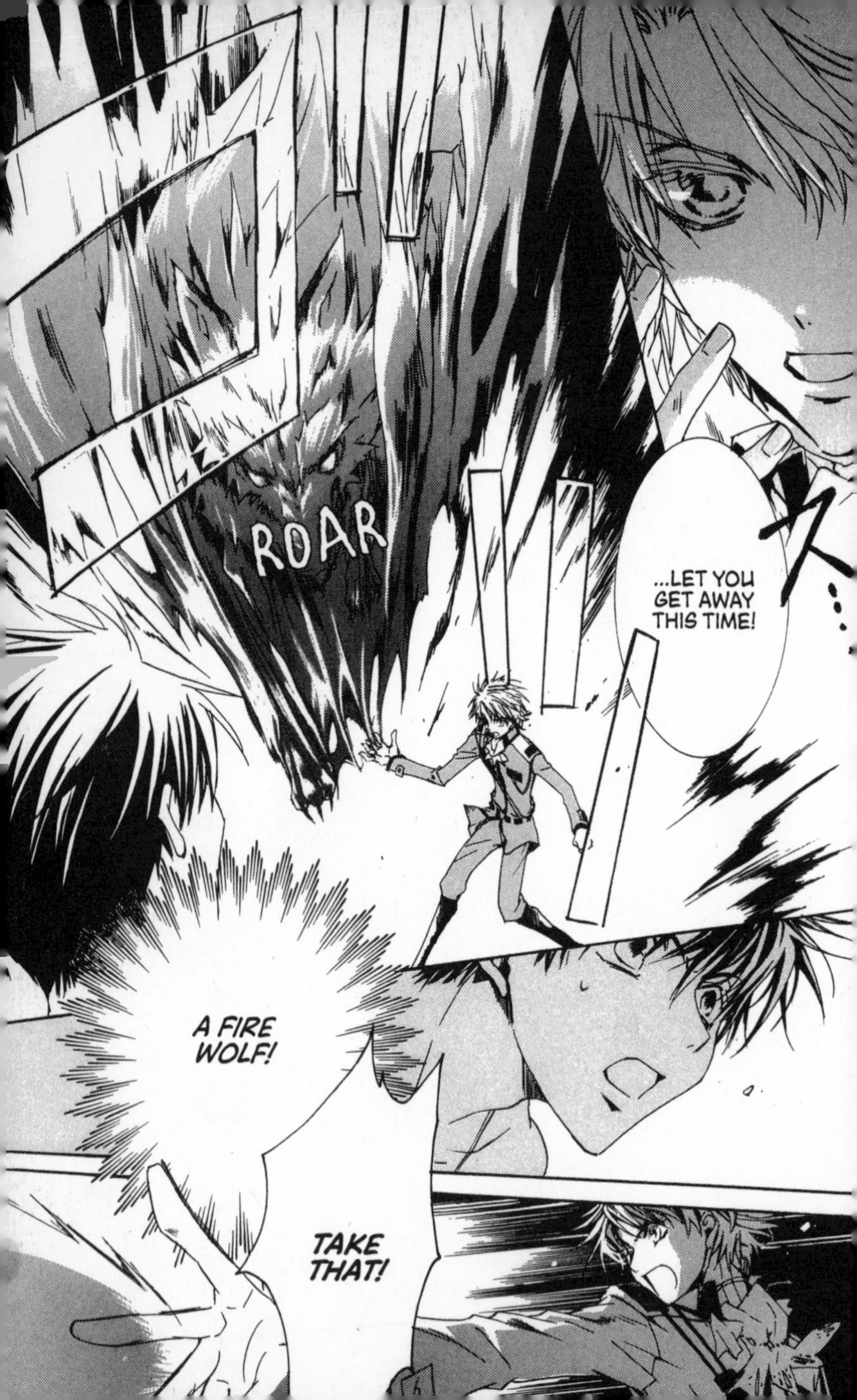
...LET YOU GET AWAY THIS TIME!
ROAR
A FIRE WOLF!
TAKE THAT!

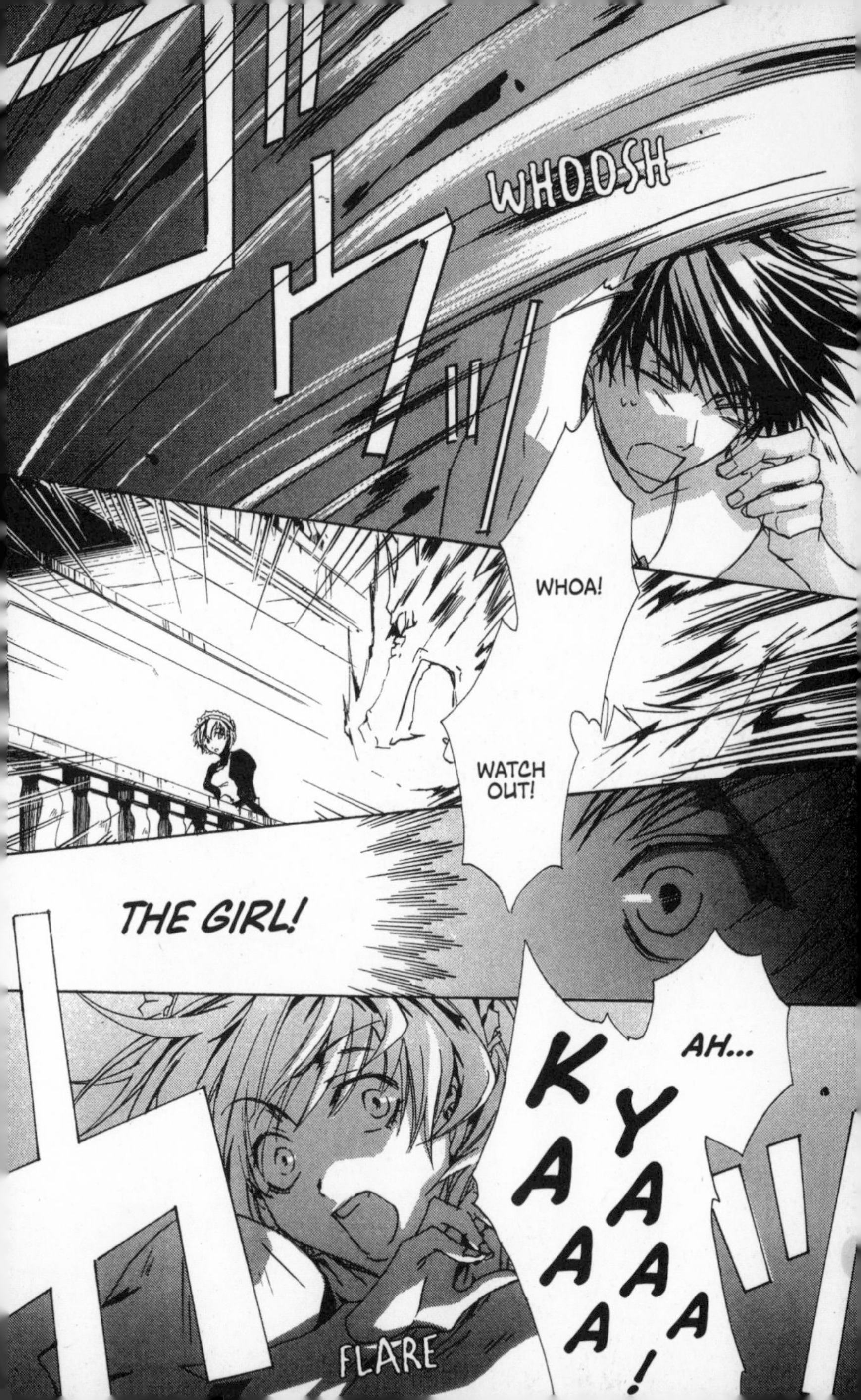
WHOOSH
WHOA!
WATCH OUT!
THE GIRL!
AH...
KYAAAAAA!
FLARE

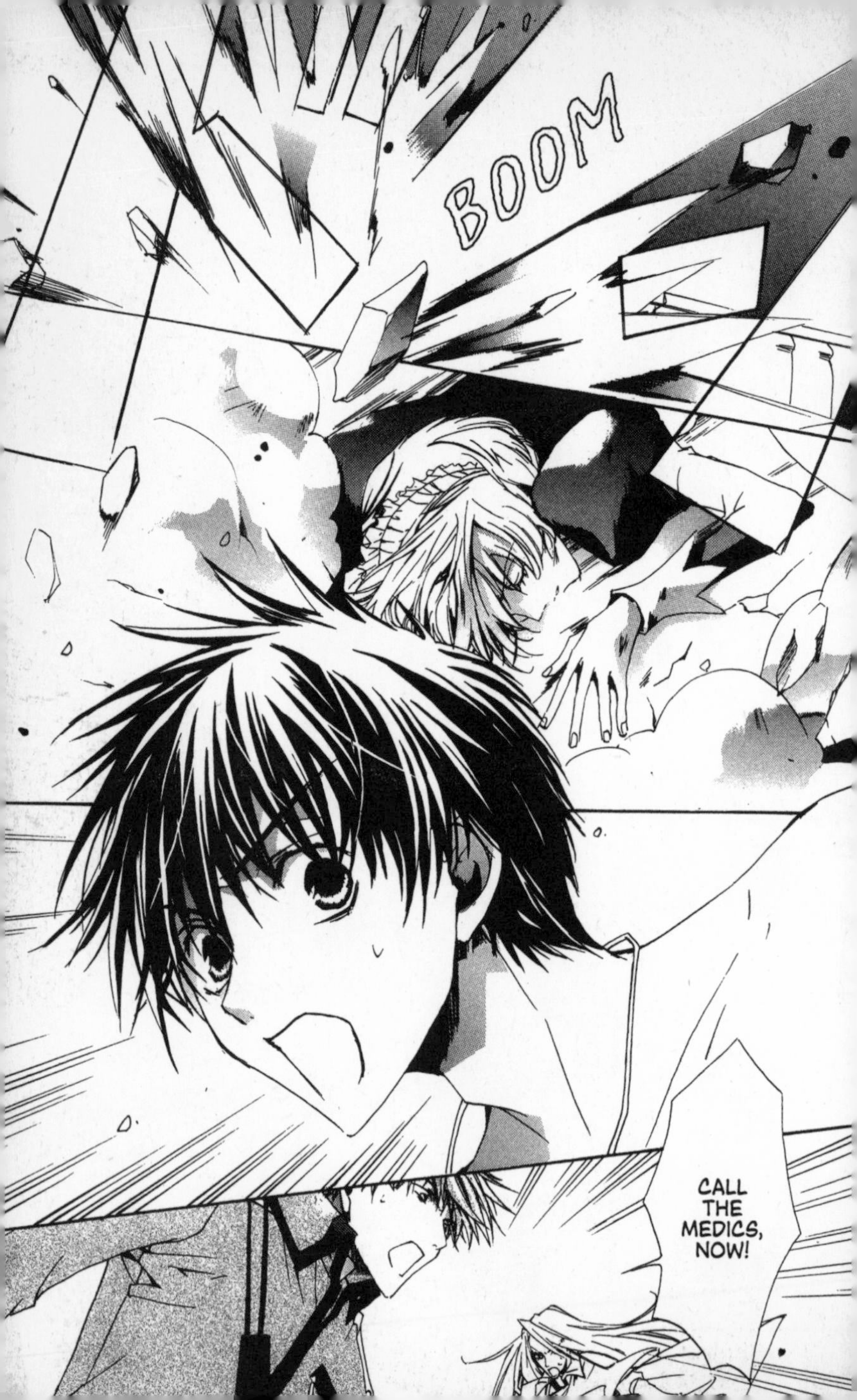
BOOM
CALL THE MEDICS, NOW!

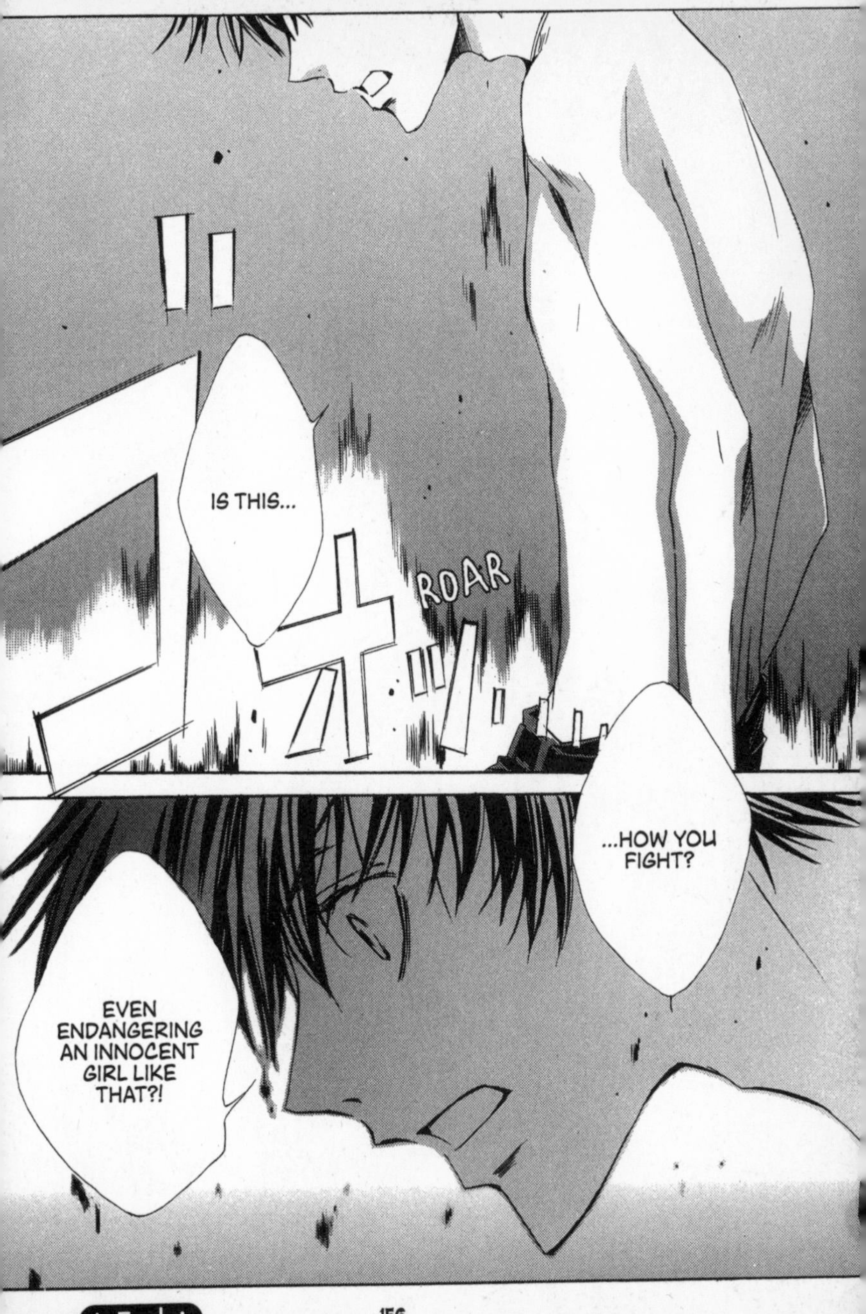
IS THIS...
ROAR
...HOW YOU FIGHT?
EVEN ENDANGERING AN INNOCENT GIRL LIKE THAT?!

apter 5 * End *

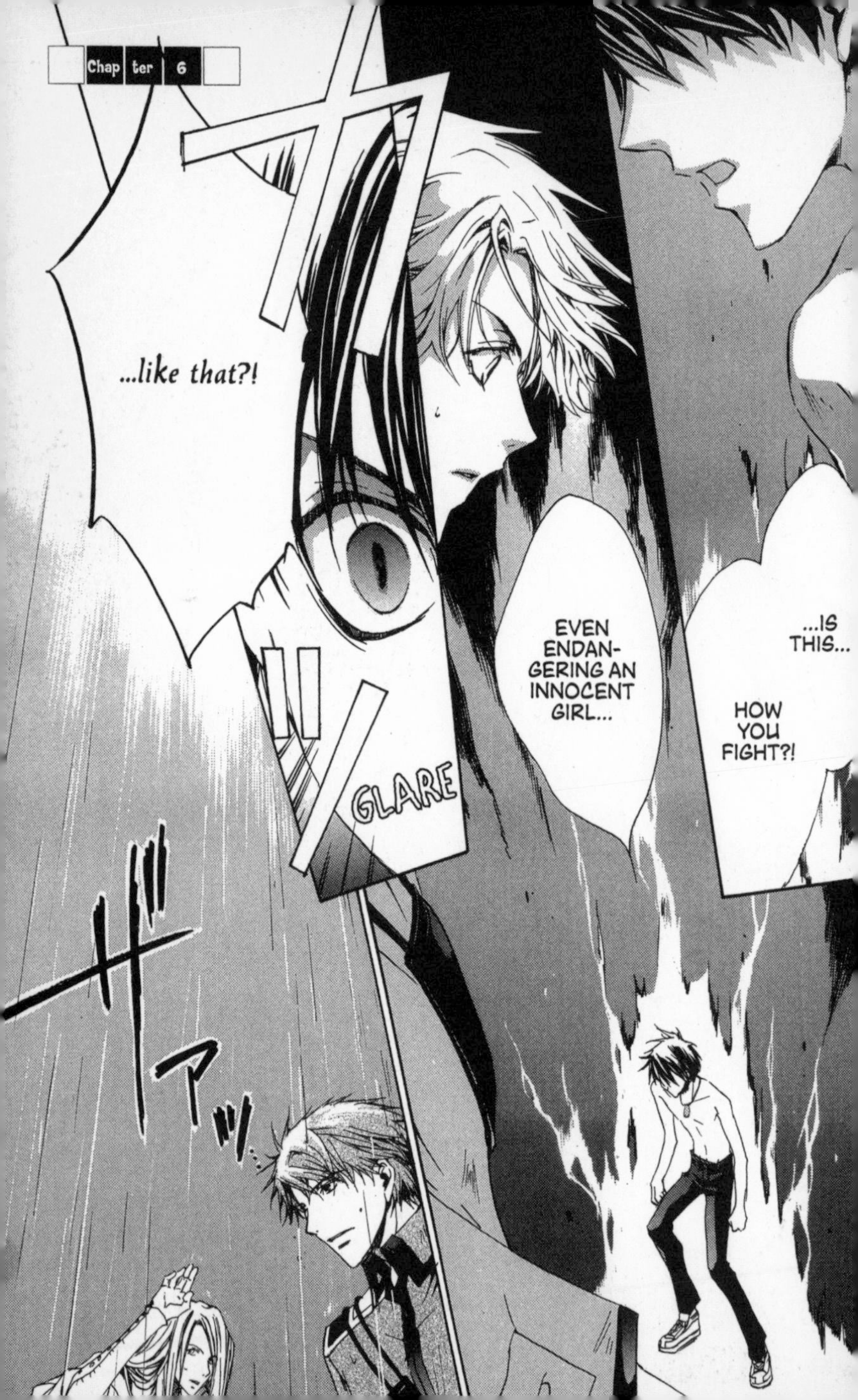
EVEN ENDANGERING AN INNOCENT GIRL...
...IS THIS... HOW YOU FIGHT?!
...like that?!
GLARE
ザァッ

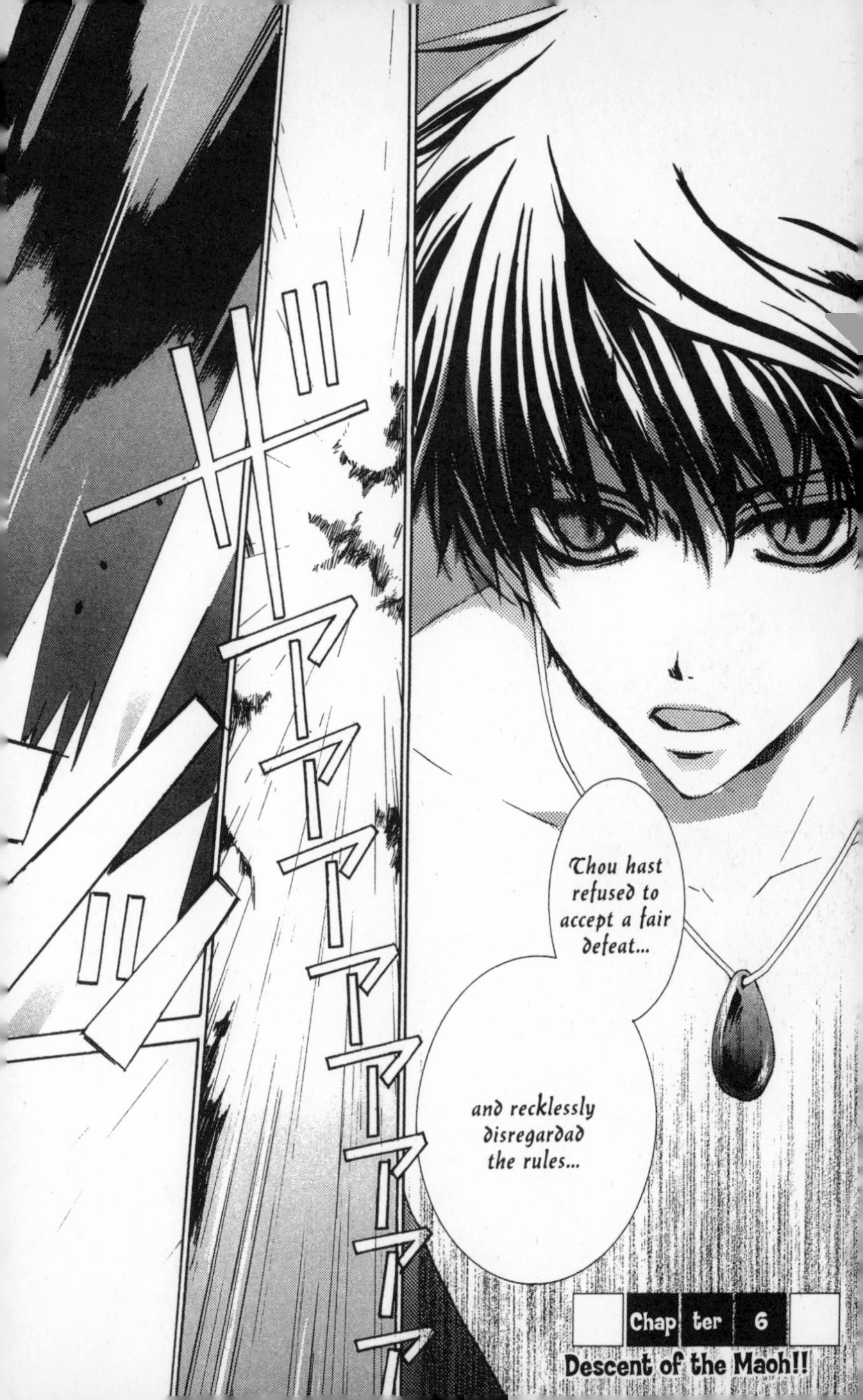
Thou hast refused to accept a fair defeat...
and recklessly disregardad the rules...
Chapter 6
Descent of the Maoh!!

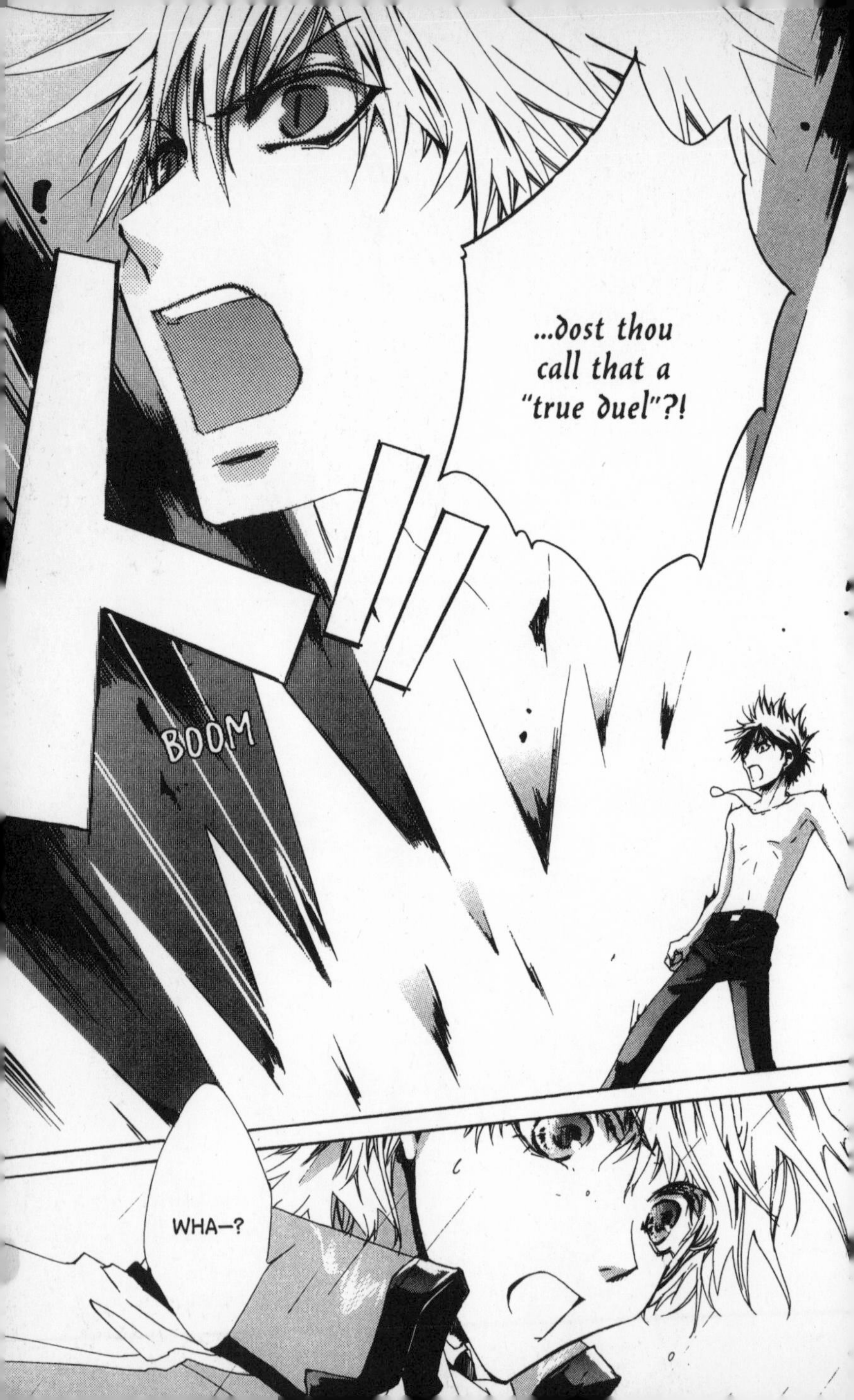
...dost thou call that a "true duel"?!
BOOM
WHA—?

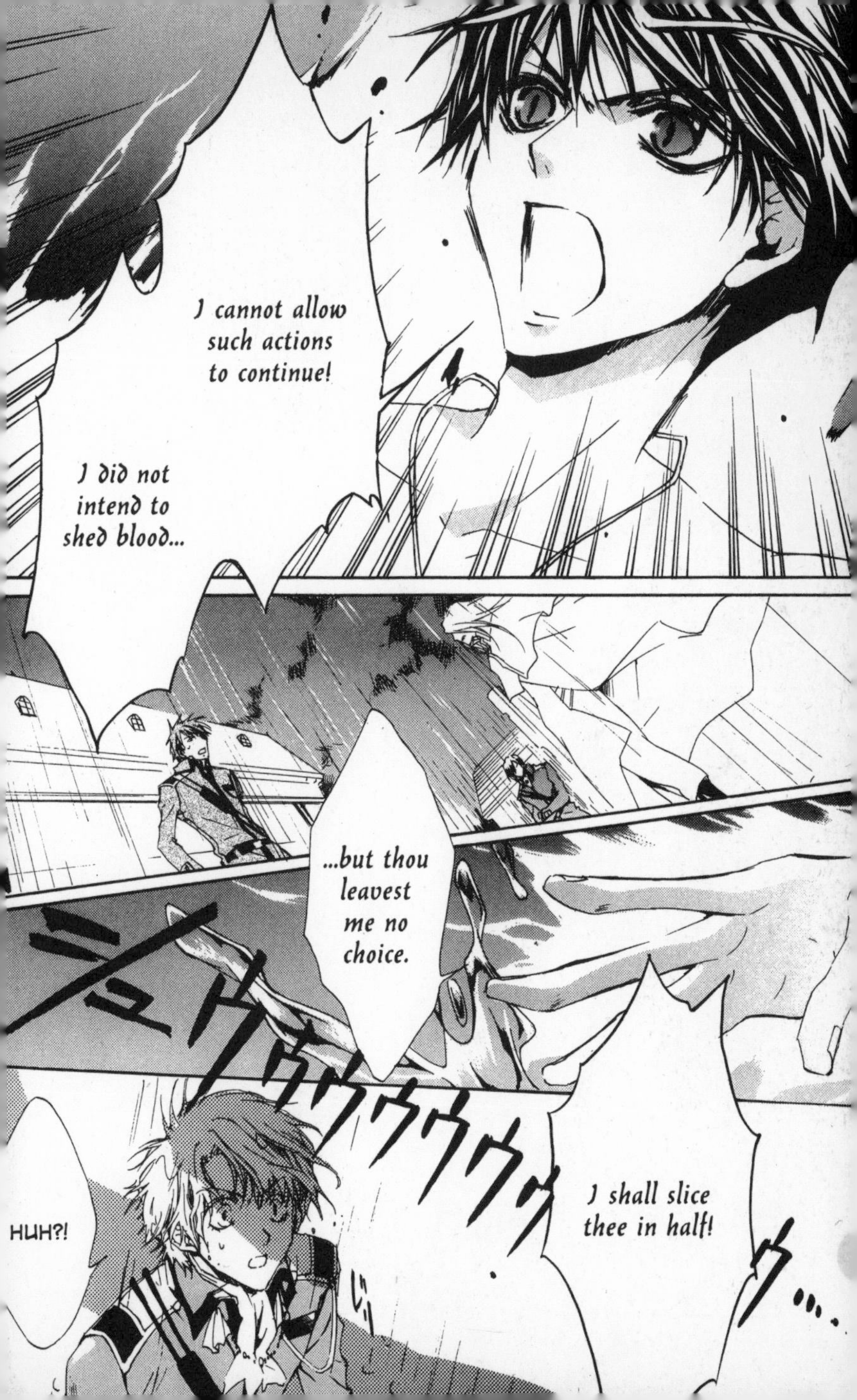
I cannot allow such actions to continue!
I did not intend to shed blood...
...but thou leavest me no choice.
I shall slice thee in half!
HUH?!

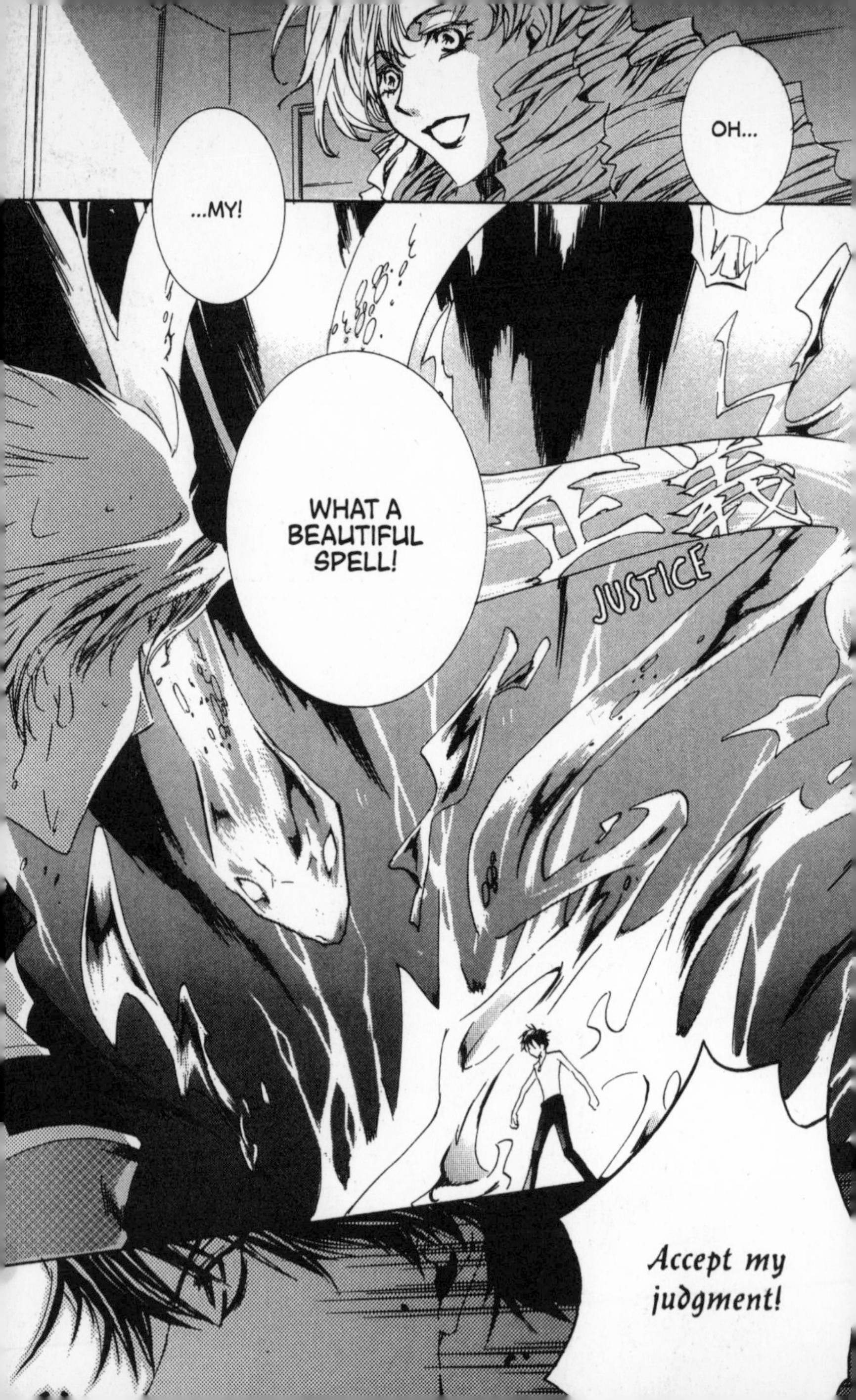
OH...
...MY!
WHAT A BEAUTIFUL SPELL!
正義
JUSTICE
Accept my judgment!

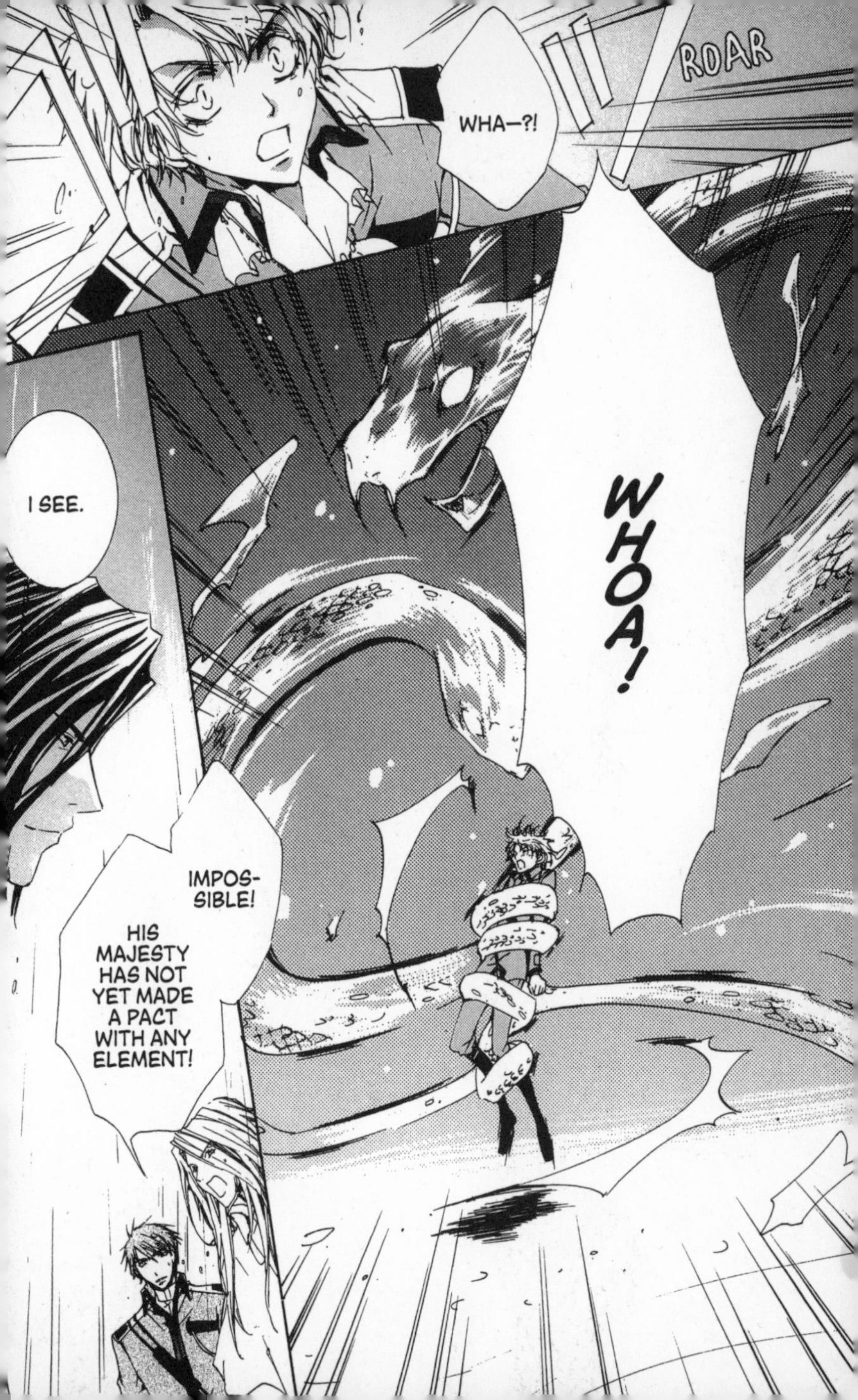
ROAR
WHA—?!
WHOA!
I SEE.
IMPOS-SIBLE!
HIS MAJESTY HAS NOT YET MADE A PACT WITH ANY ELEMENT!

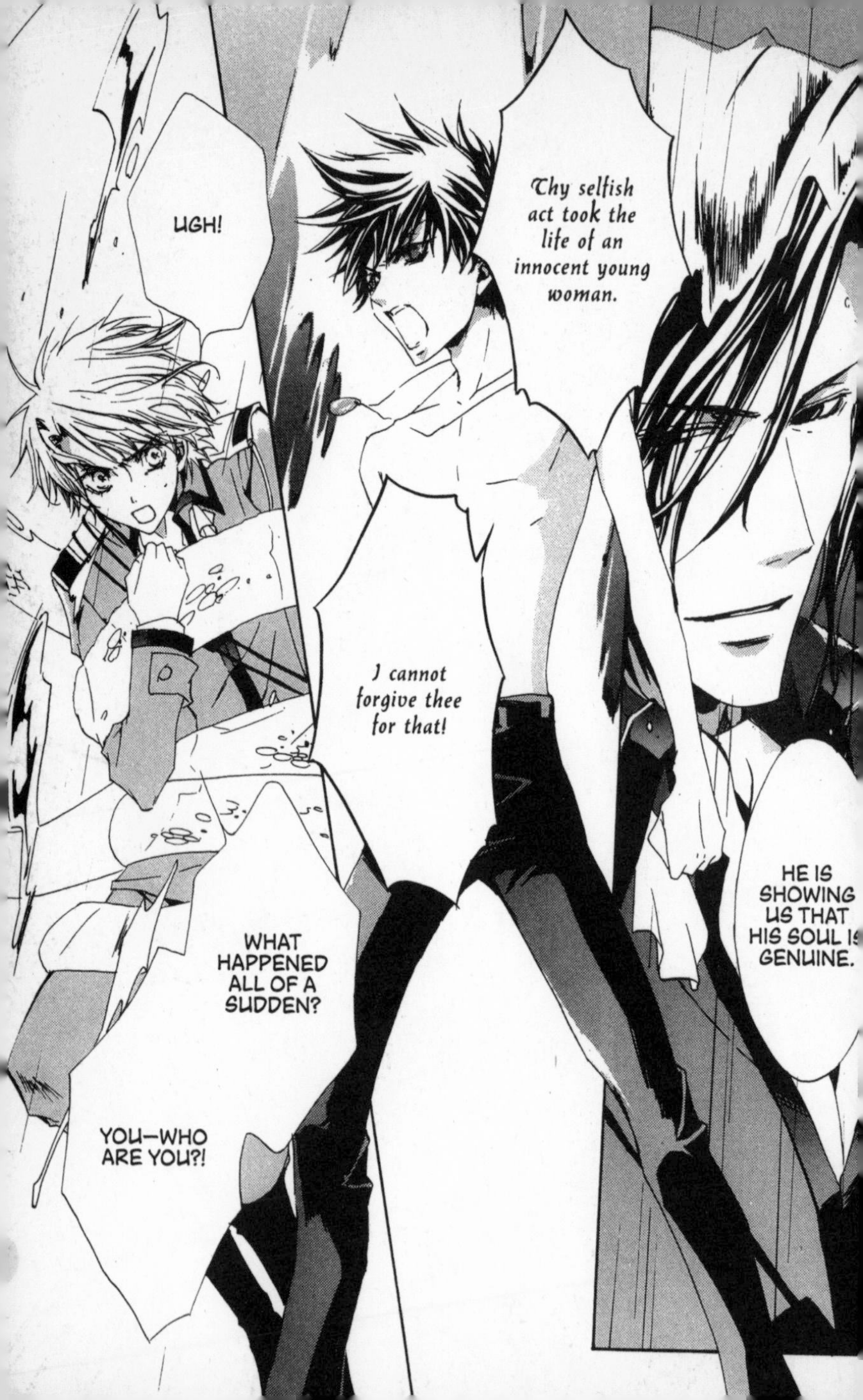

HE IS SHOWING US THAT HIS SOUL IS GENUINE.
Thy selfish act took the life of an innocent young woman.
I cannot forgive thee for that!
UGH!
WHAT HAPPENED ALL OF A SUDDEN?
YOU—WHO ARE YOU?!

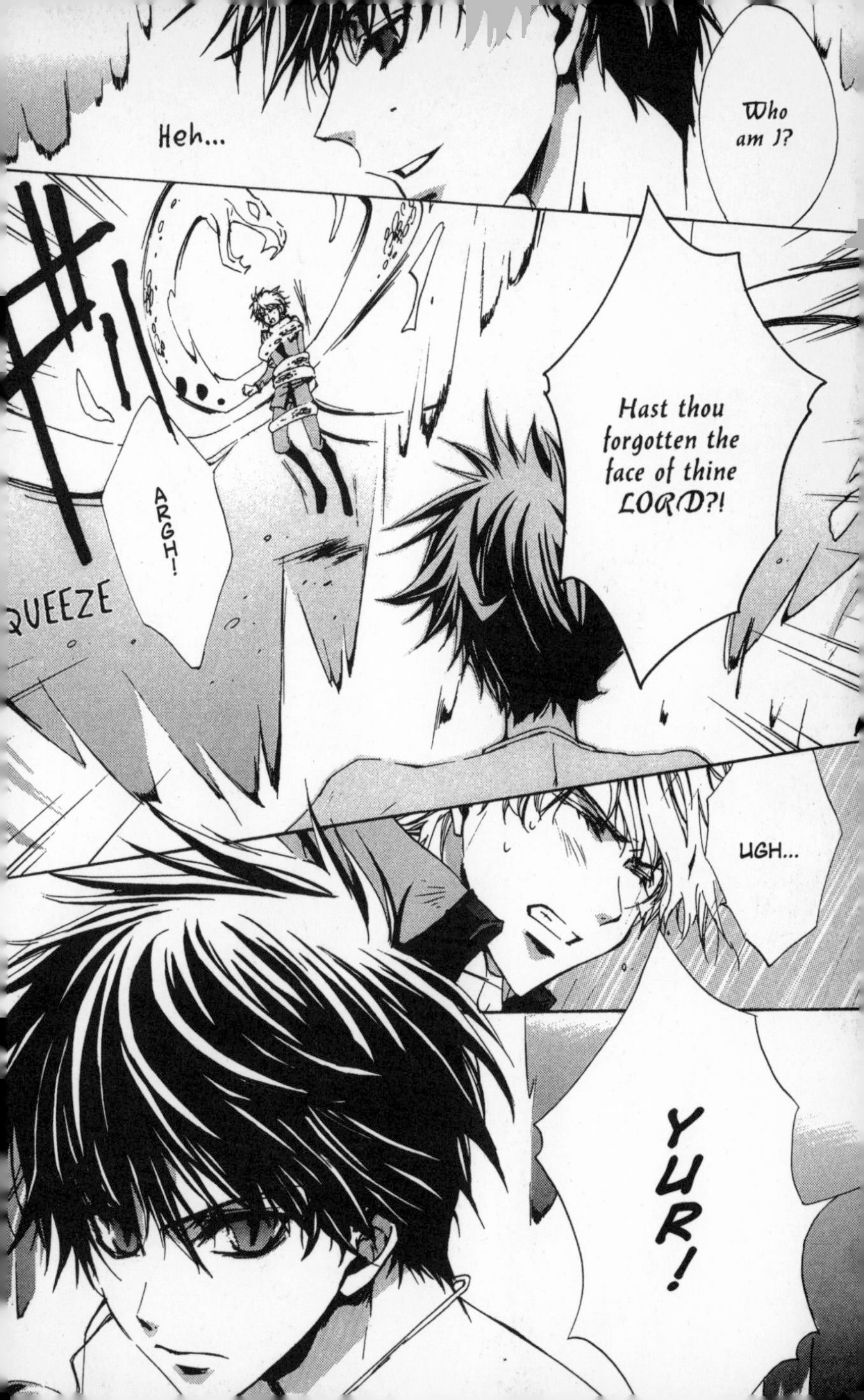
Who am I?
Heh...
Hast thou forgotten the face of thine LORD?!
ARGH!
QUEEZE
UGH...
YURI!

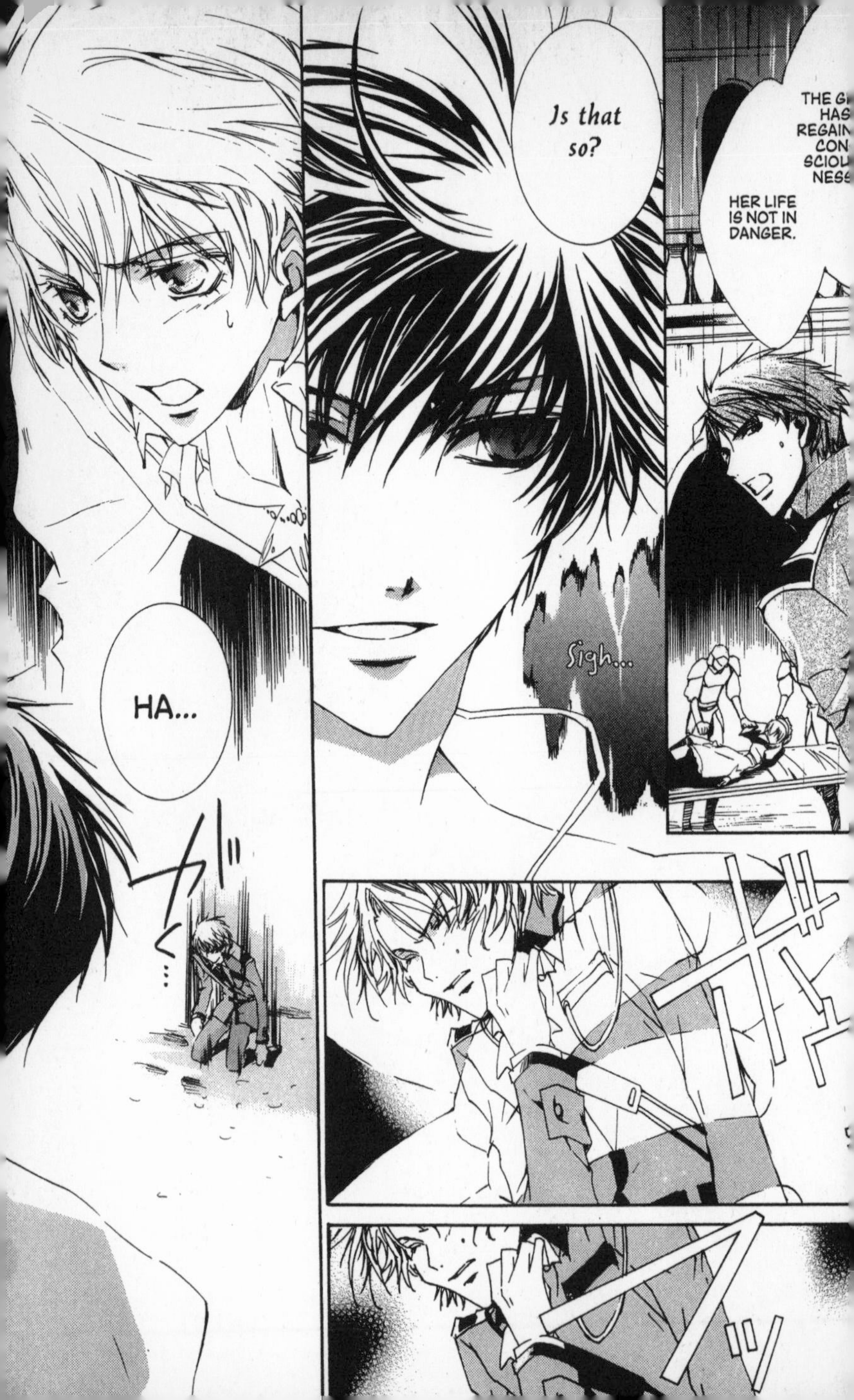
THE G HAS REGAIN CON- SCIOU NESS
HER LIFE IS NOT IN DANGER.
Is that so?
Sigh...
HA...

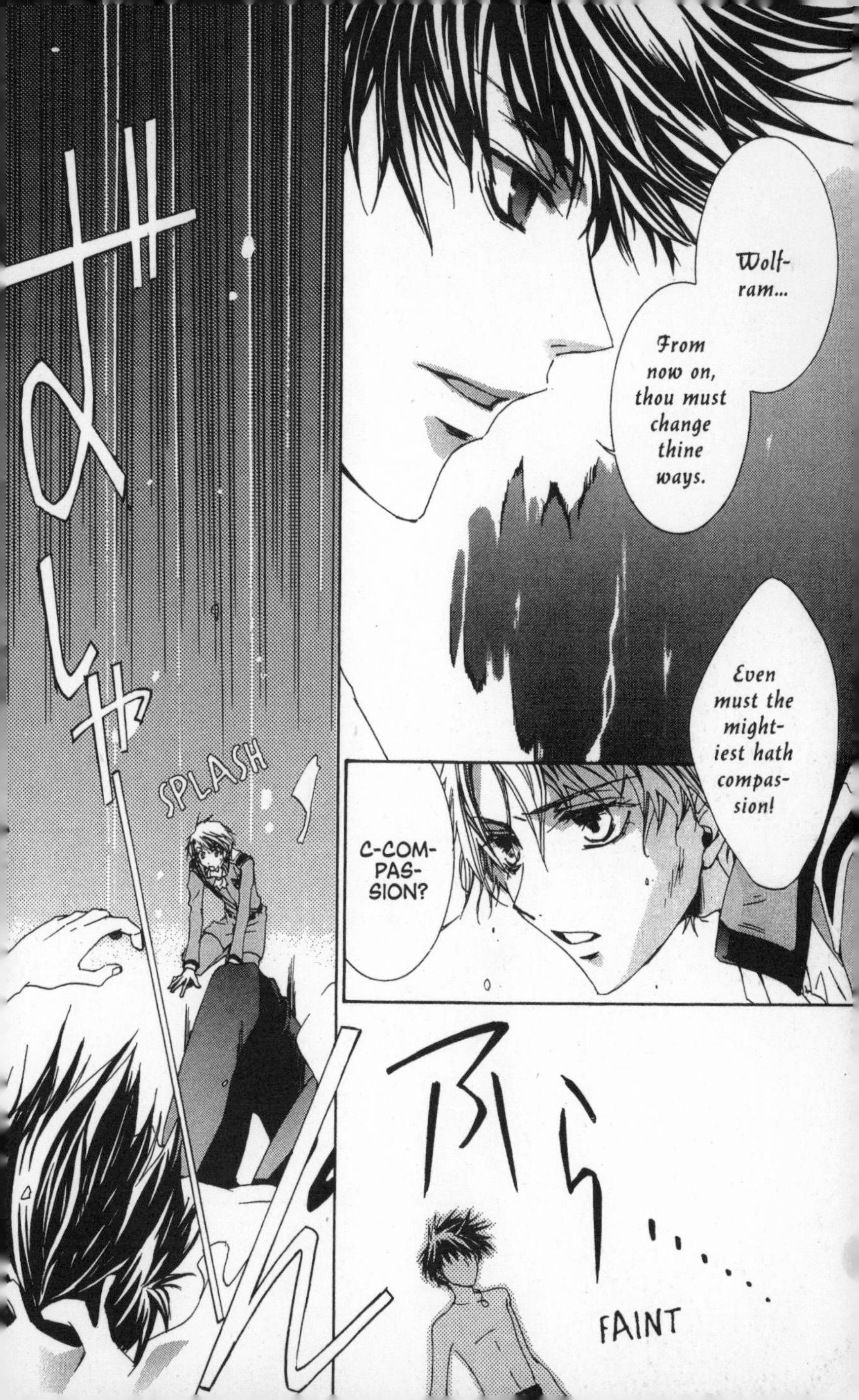
Wolf-ram...
From now on, thou must change thine ways.
Even must the mightiest hath compassion!
C-COM-PAS-SION?
FAINT
SPLASH

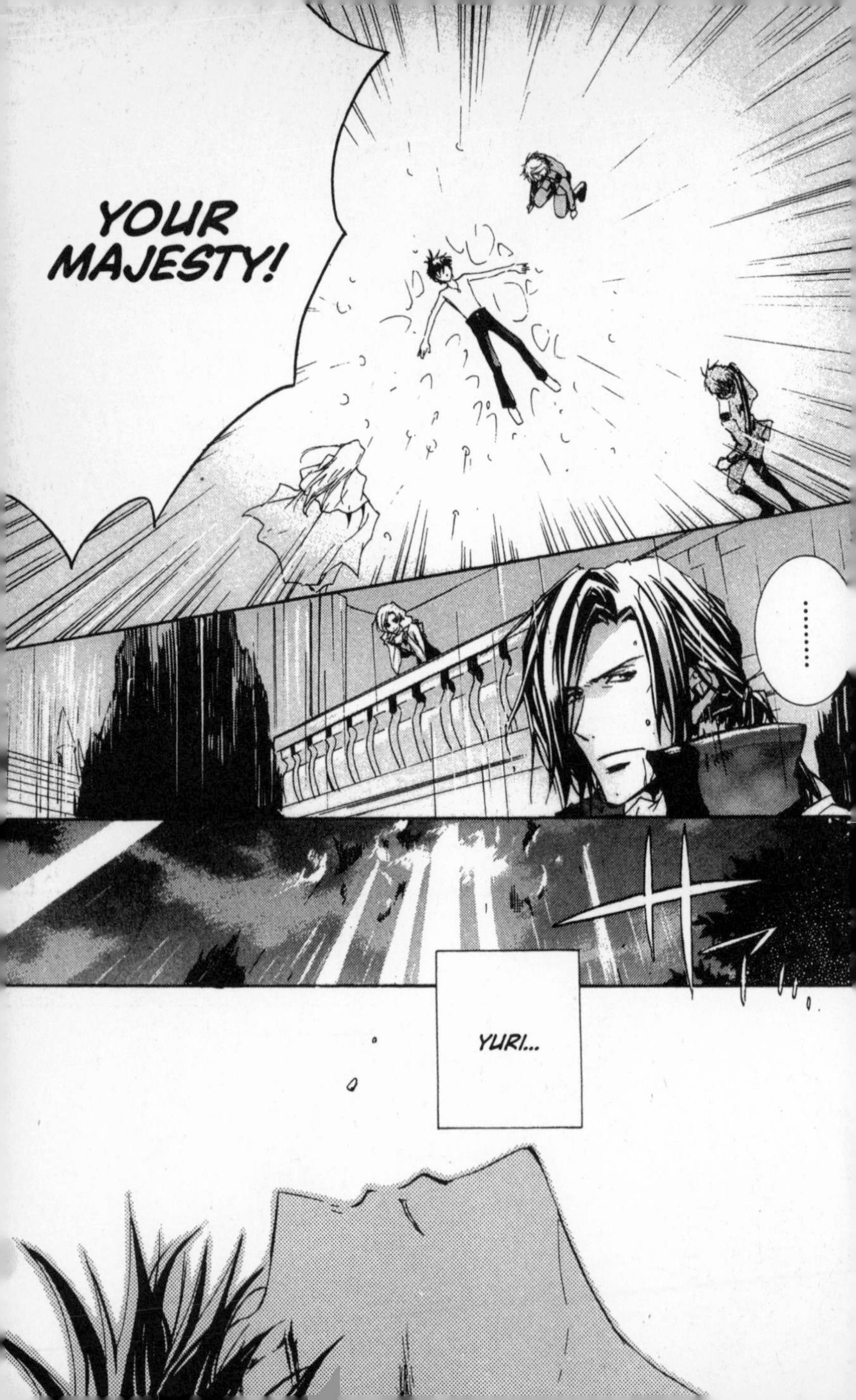
YOUR MAJESTY!
....
YURI...

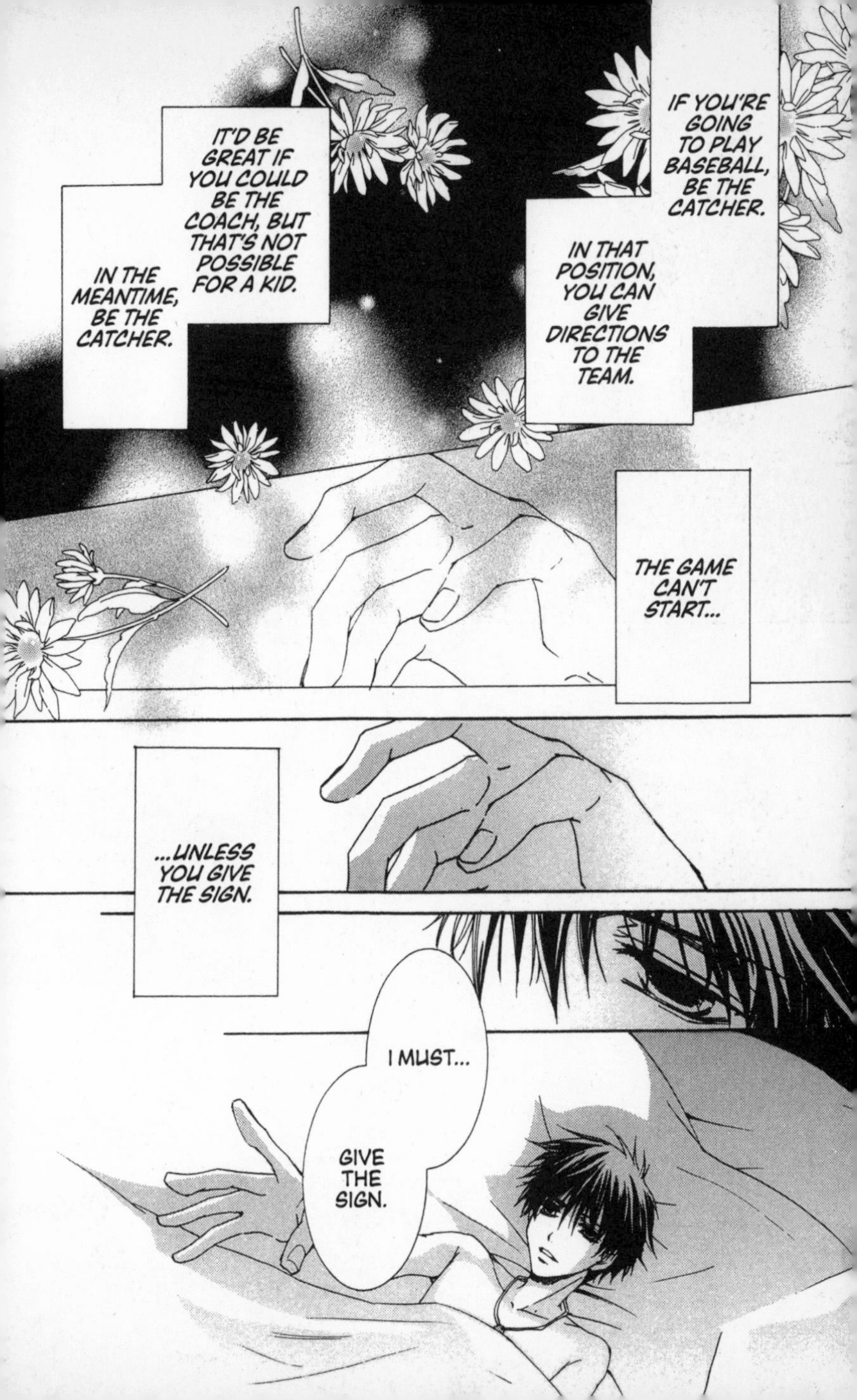
IF YOU'RE GOING TO PLAY BASEBALL, BE THE CATCHER.
IN THAT POSITION, YOU CAN GIVE DIRECTIONS TO THE TEAM.
IT'D BE GREAT IF YOU COULD BE THE COACH, BUT THAT'S NOT POSSIBLE FOR A KID.
IN THE MEANTIME, BE THE CATCHER.
THE GAME CAN'T START...
...UNLESS YOU GIVE THE SIGN.
I MUST...
GIVE THE SIGN.

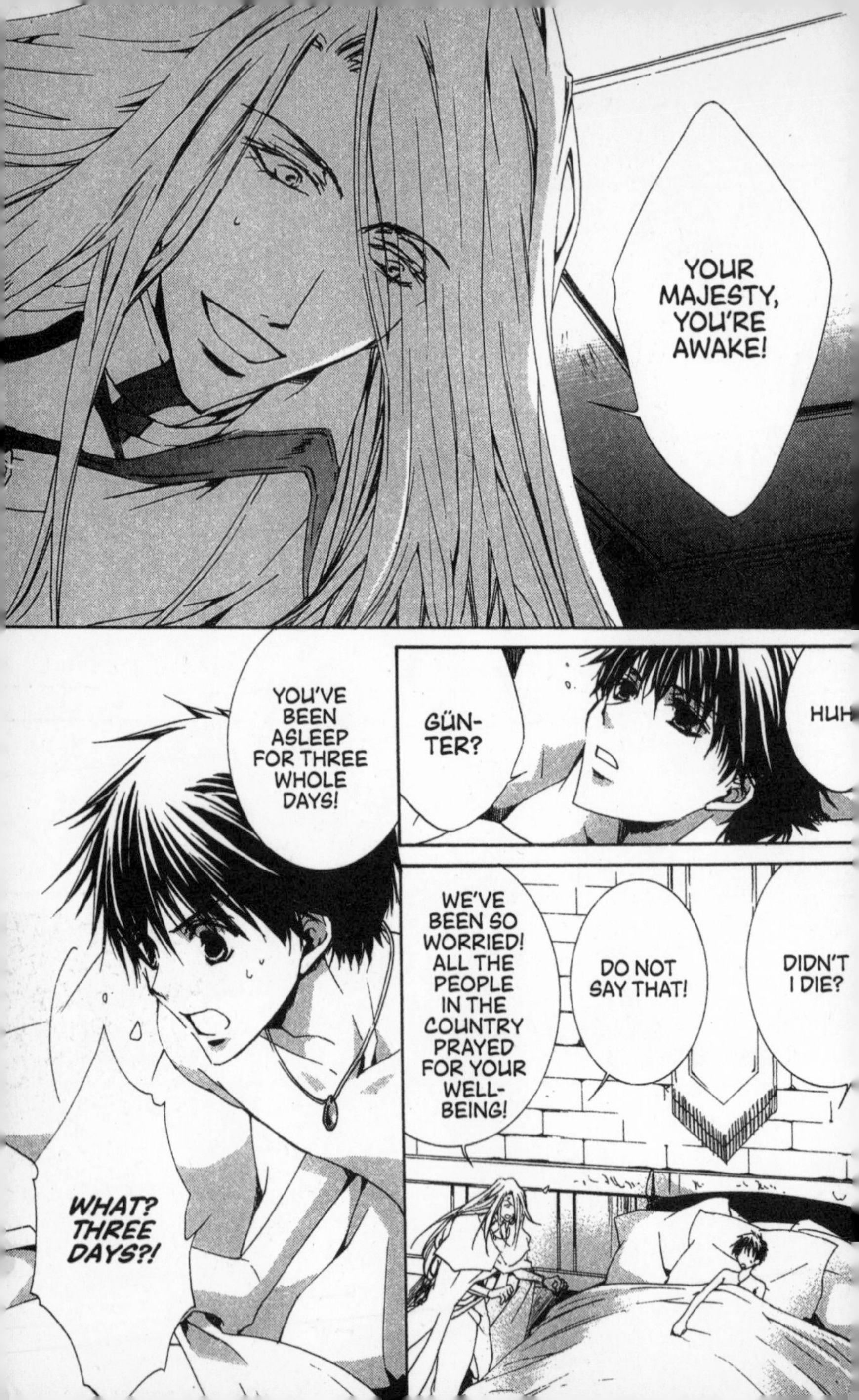

YOUR MAJESTY, YOU'RE AWAKE!
HUH
GÜN-TER?
DIDN'T I DIE?
DO NOT SAY THAT!
WE'VE BEEN SO WORRIED! ALL THE PEOPLE IN THE COUNTRY PRAYED FOR YOUR WELL-BEING!
YOU'VE BEEN ASLEEP FOR THREE WHOLE DAYS!
WHAT? THREE DAYS?!

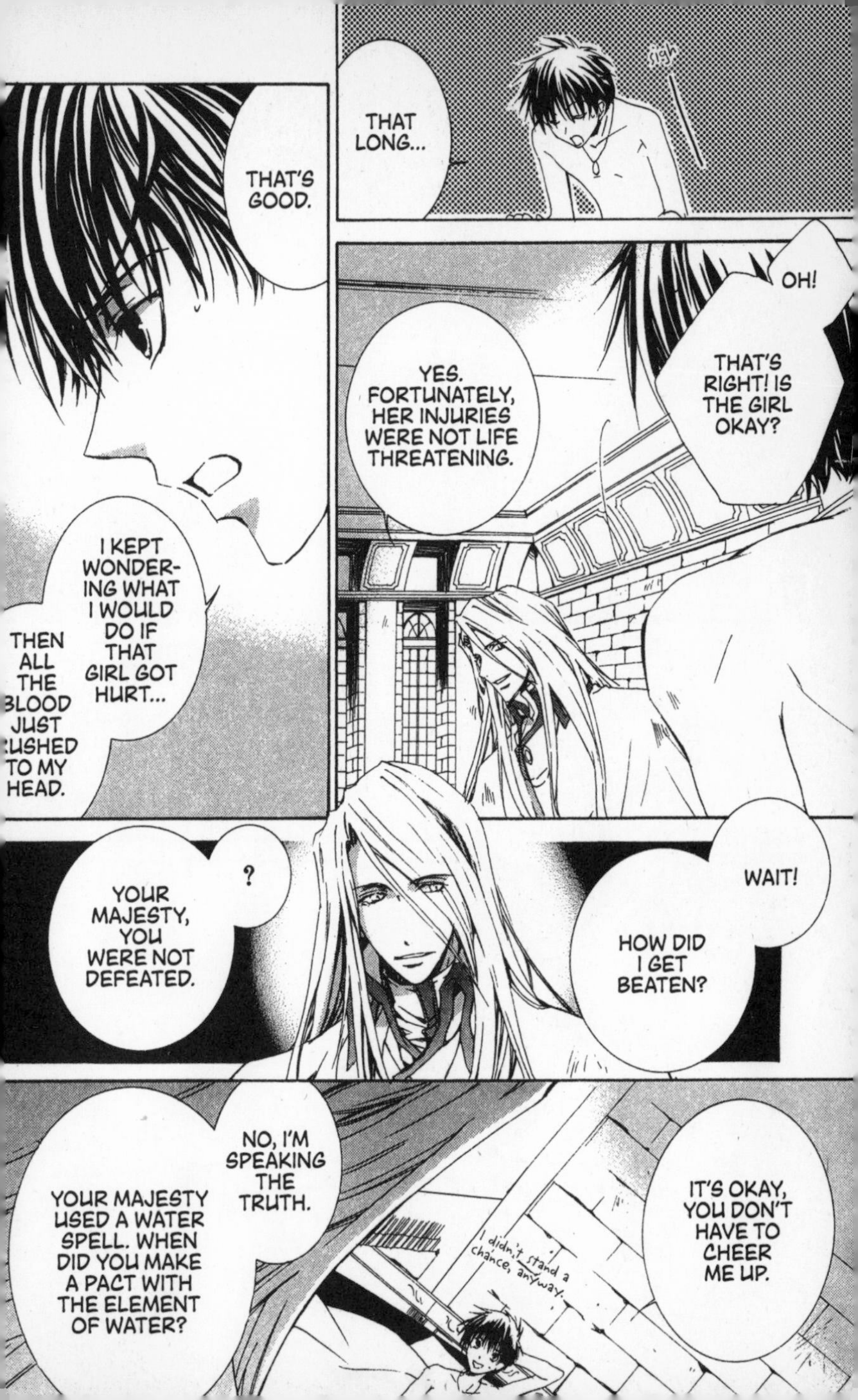
sigh
THAT LONG...
OH!
THAT'S RIGHT! IS THE GIRL OKAY?
YES. FORTUNATELY, HER INJURIES WERE NOT LIFE THREATENING.
THAT'S GOOD.
I KEPT WONDERING WHAT I WOULD DO IF THAT GIRL GOT HURT...
THEN ALL THE BLOOD JUST RUSHED TO MY HEAD.
WAIT!
HOW DID I GET BEATEN?
?
YOUR MAJESTY, YOU WERE NOT DEFEATED.
IT'S OKAY, YOU DON'T HAVE TO CHEER ME UP.
I didn't stand a chance, anyway.
NO, I'M SPEAKING THE TRUTH.
YOUR MAJESTY USED A WATER SPELL. WHEN DID YOU MAKE A PACT WITH THE ELEMENT OF WATER?

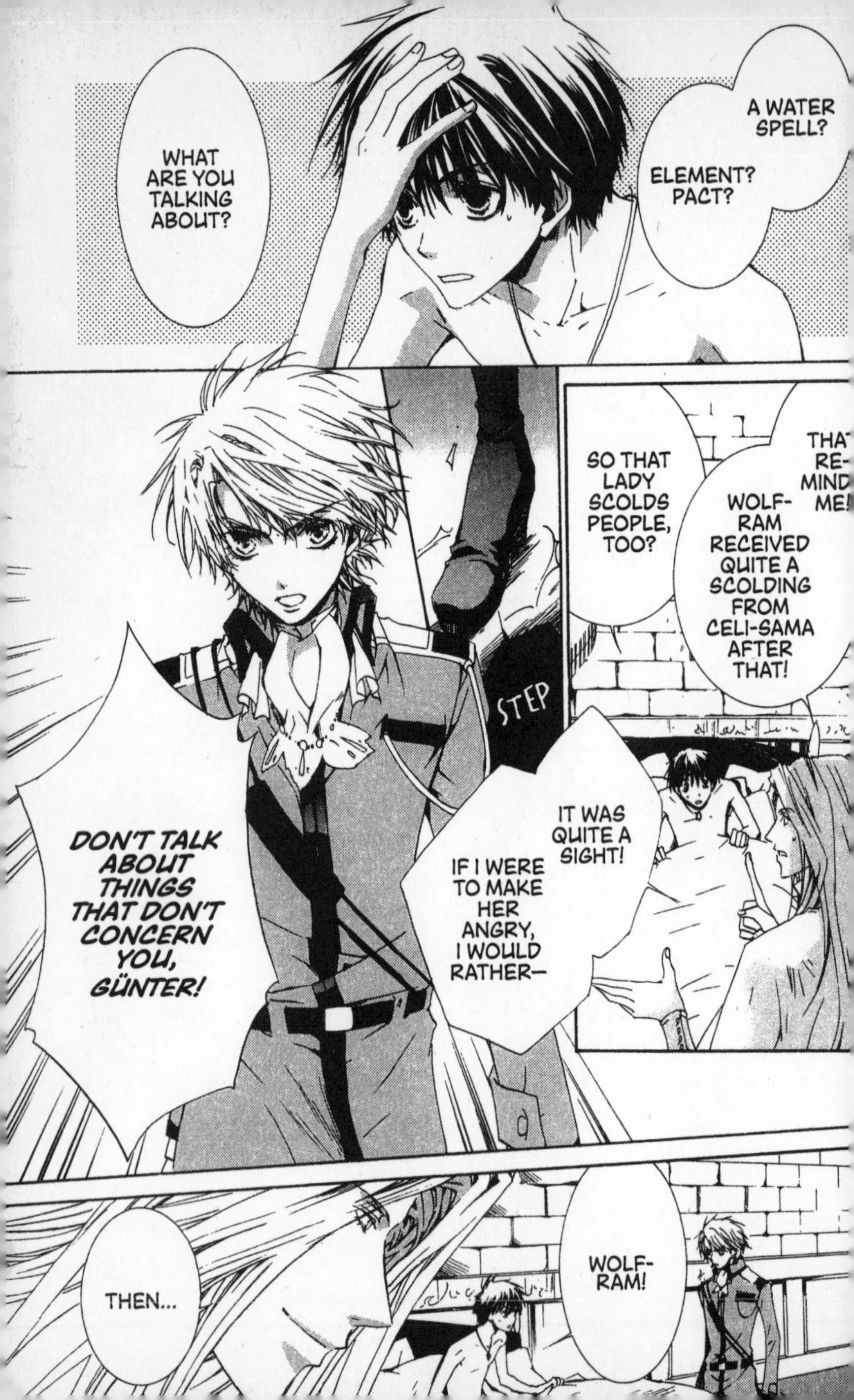
A WATER SPELL? ELEMENT? PACT?
WHAT ARE YOU TALKING ABOUT?
THAT RE-MIND ME!
WOLF-RAM RECEIVED QUITE A SCOLDING FROM CELI-SAMA AFTER THAT!
SO THAT LADY SCOLDS PEOPLE, TOO?
IT WAS QUITE A SIGHT!
IF I WERE TO MAKE HER ANGRY, I WOULD RATHER—
STEP
DON'T TALK ABOUT THINGS THAT DON'T CONCERN YOU, GÜNTER!
WOLF-RAM!
THEN...

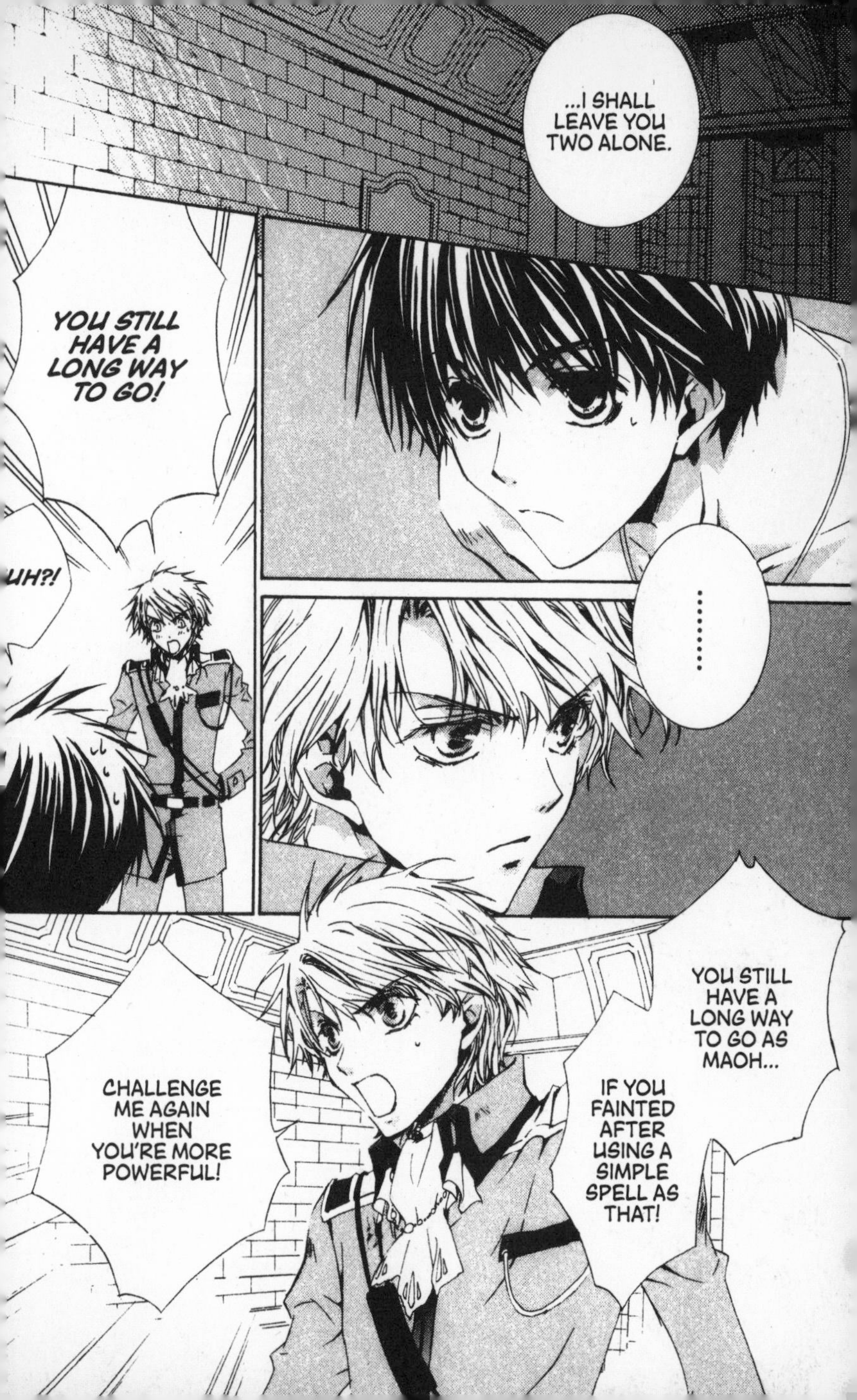
...I SHALL LEAVE YOU TWO ALONE.
......
YOU STILL HAVE A LONG WAY TO GO!
UH?!
YOU STILL HAVE A LONG WAY TO GO AS MAOH...
IF YOU FAINTED AFTER USING A SIMPLE SPELL AS THAT!
CHALLENGE ME AGAIN WHEN YOU'RE MORE POWERFUL!

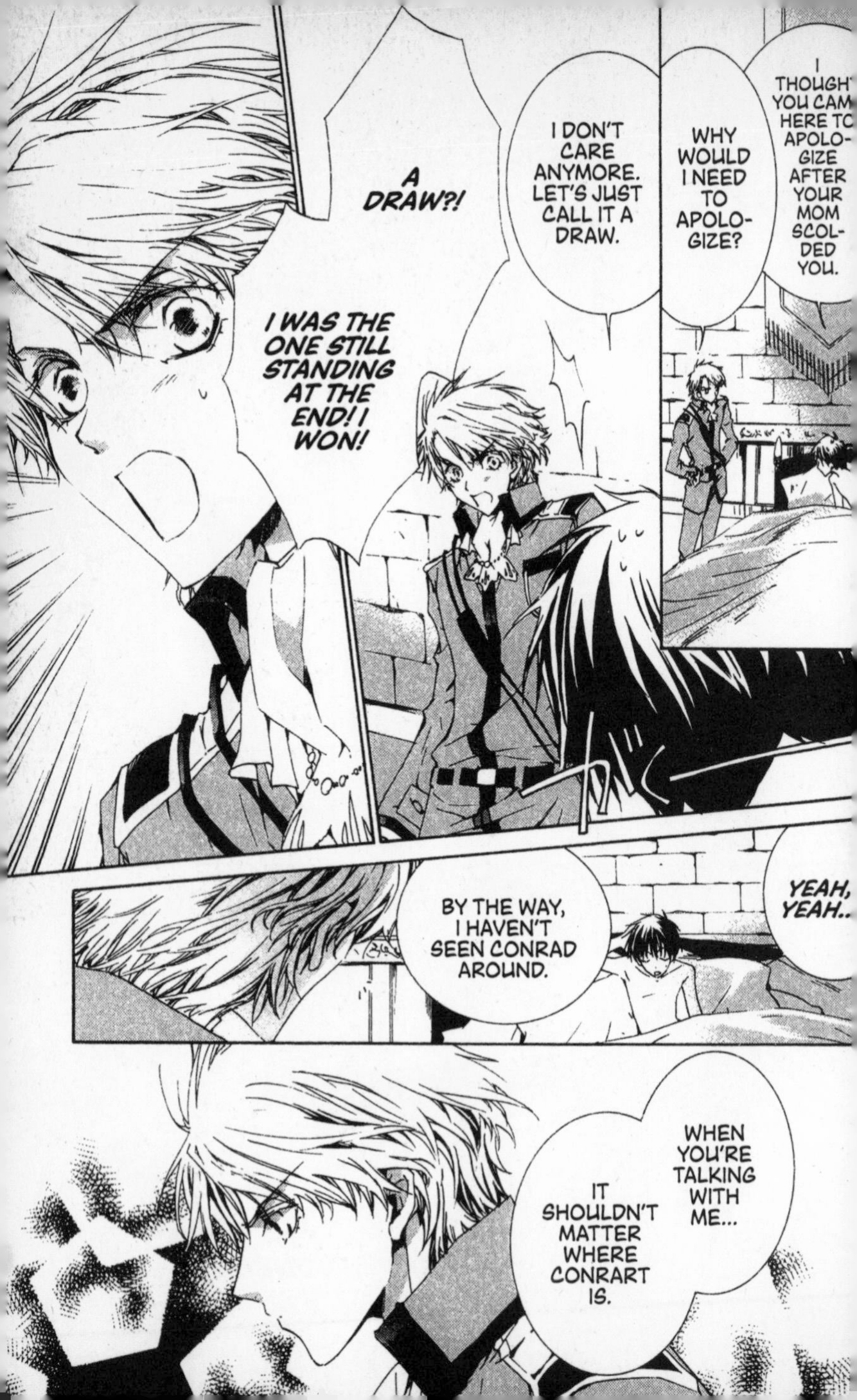
I THOUGHT YOU CAM HERE TO APOLO-GIZE AFTER YOUR MOM SCOL-DED YOU.
WHY WOULD I NEED TO APOLO-GIZE?
I DON'T CARE ANYMORE. LET'S JUST CALL IT A DRAW.
A DRAW?!
I WAS THE ONE STILL STANDING AT THE END! I WON!
YEAH, YEAH...
BY THE WAY, I HAVEN'T SEEN CONRAD AROUND.
WHEN YOU'RE TALKING WITH ME...
IT SHOULDN'T MATTER WHERE CONRART IS.

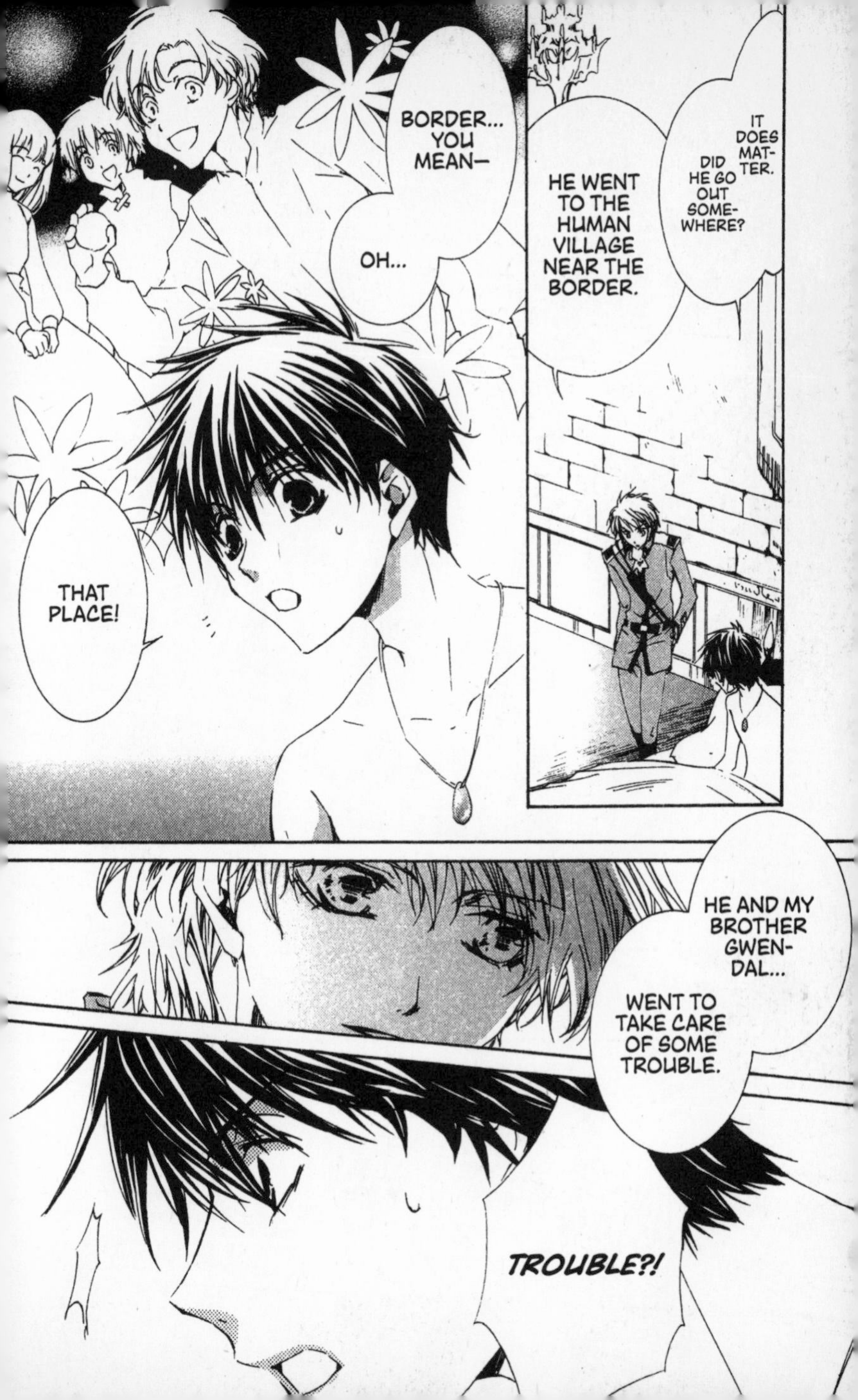
IT DOES MATTER.
DID HE GO OUT SOMEWHERE?
HE WENT TO THE HUMAN VILLAGE NEAR THE BORDER.
BORDER... YOU MEAN—
OH...
THAT PLACE!
HE AND MY BROTHER GWENDAL...
WENT TO TAKE CARE OF SOME TROUBLE.
TROUBLE?!

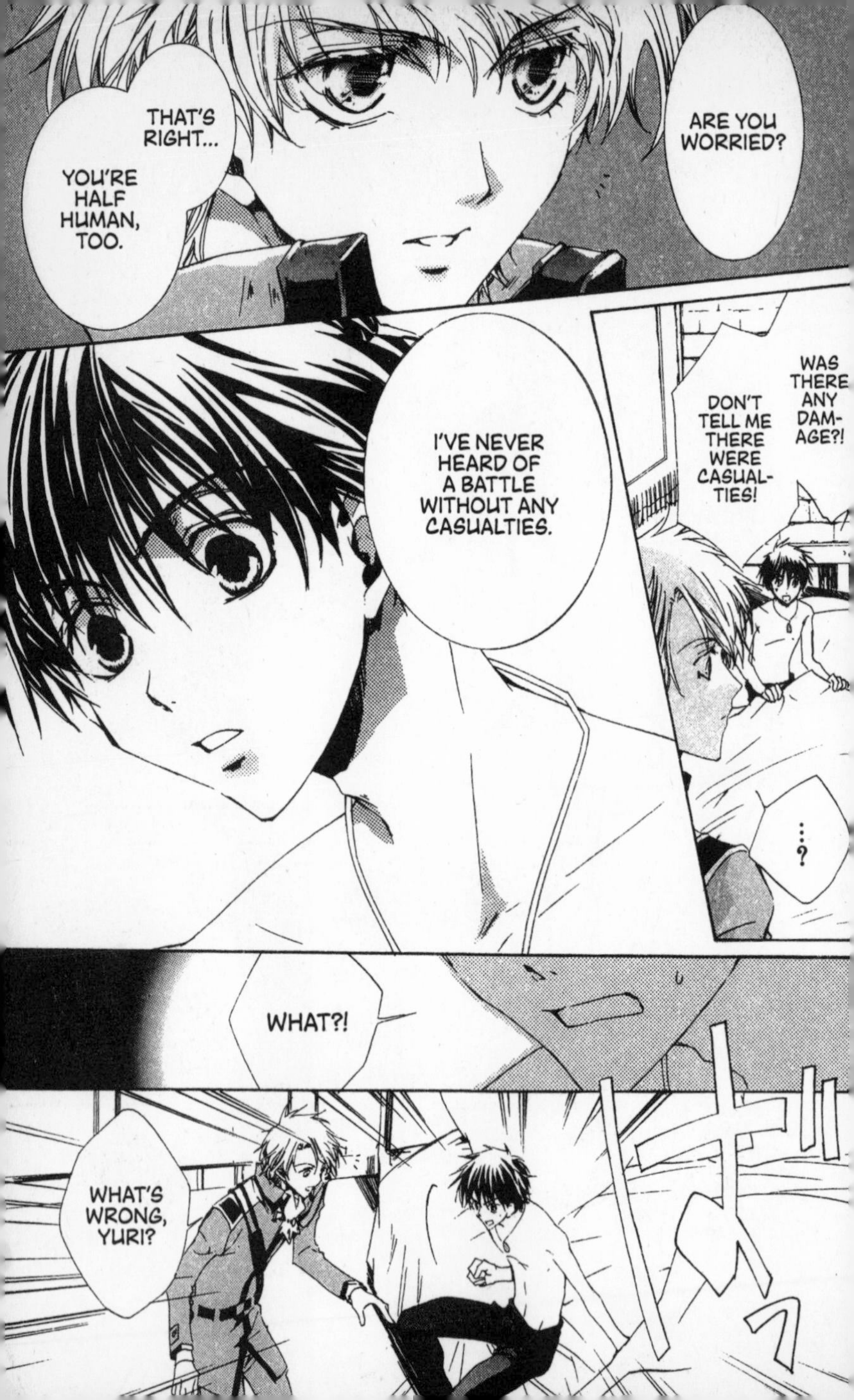
ARE YOU WORRIED?
THAT'S RIGHT... YOU'RE HALF HUMAN, TOO.
WAS THERE ANY DAM-AGE?!
DON'T TELL ME THERE WERE CASUAL-TIES!
...?
I'VE NEVER HEARD OF A BATTLE WITHOUT ANY CASUALTIES.
WHAT?!
WHAT'S WRONG, YURI?

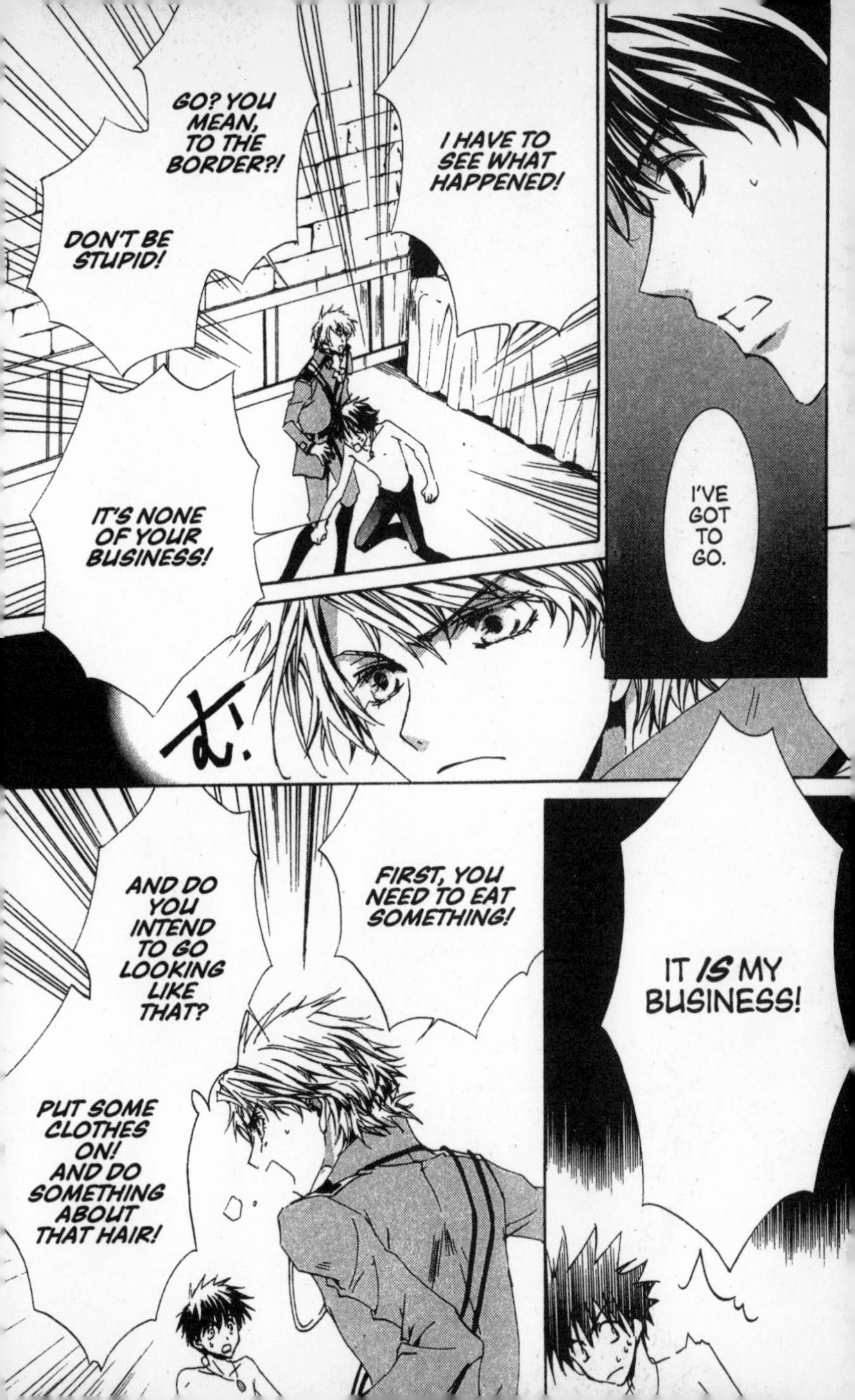
I'VE GOT TO GO.
I HAVE TO SEE WHAT HAPPENED!
GO? YOU MEAN, TO THE BORDER?!
DON'T BE STUPID!
IT'S NONE OF YOUR BUSINESS!
む
IT *IS* MY BUSINESS!
FIRST, YOU NEED TO EAT SOMETHING!
AND DO YOU INTEND TO GO LOOKING LIKE THAT?
PUT SOME CLOTHES ON! AND DO SOMETHING ABOUT THAT HAIR!

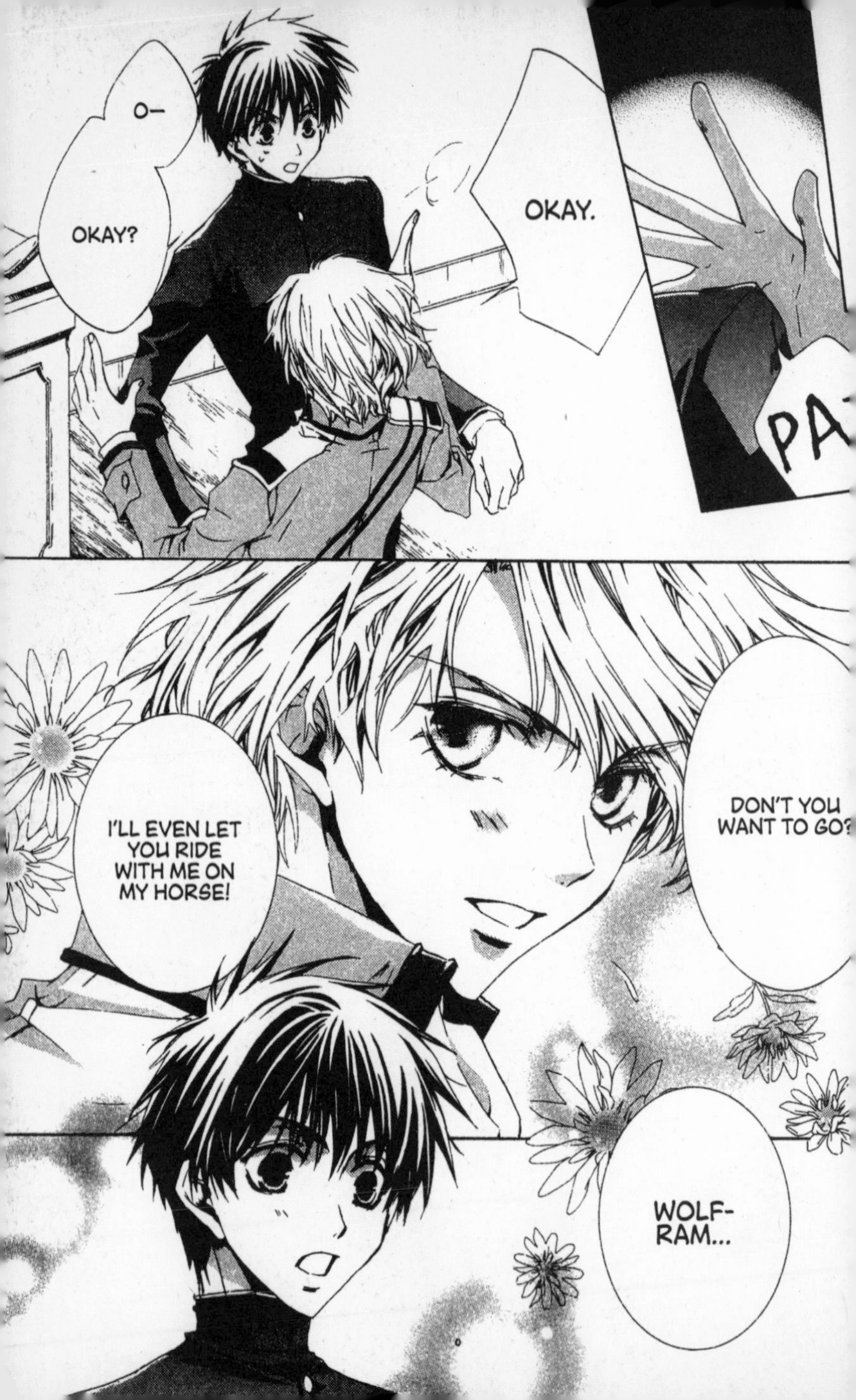
PA
OKAY.
O– OKAY?
DON'T YOU WANT TO GO?
I'LL EVEN LET YOU RIDE WITH ME ON MY HORSE!
WOLF-RAM...

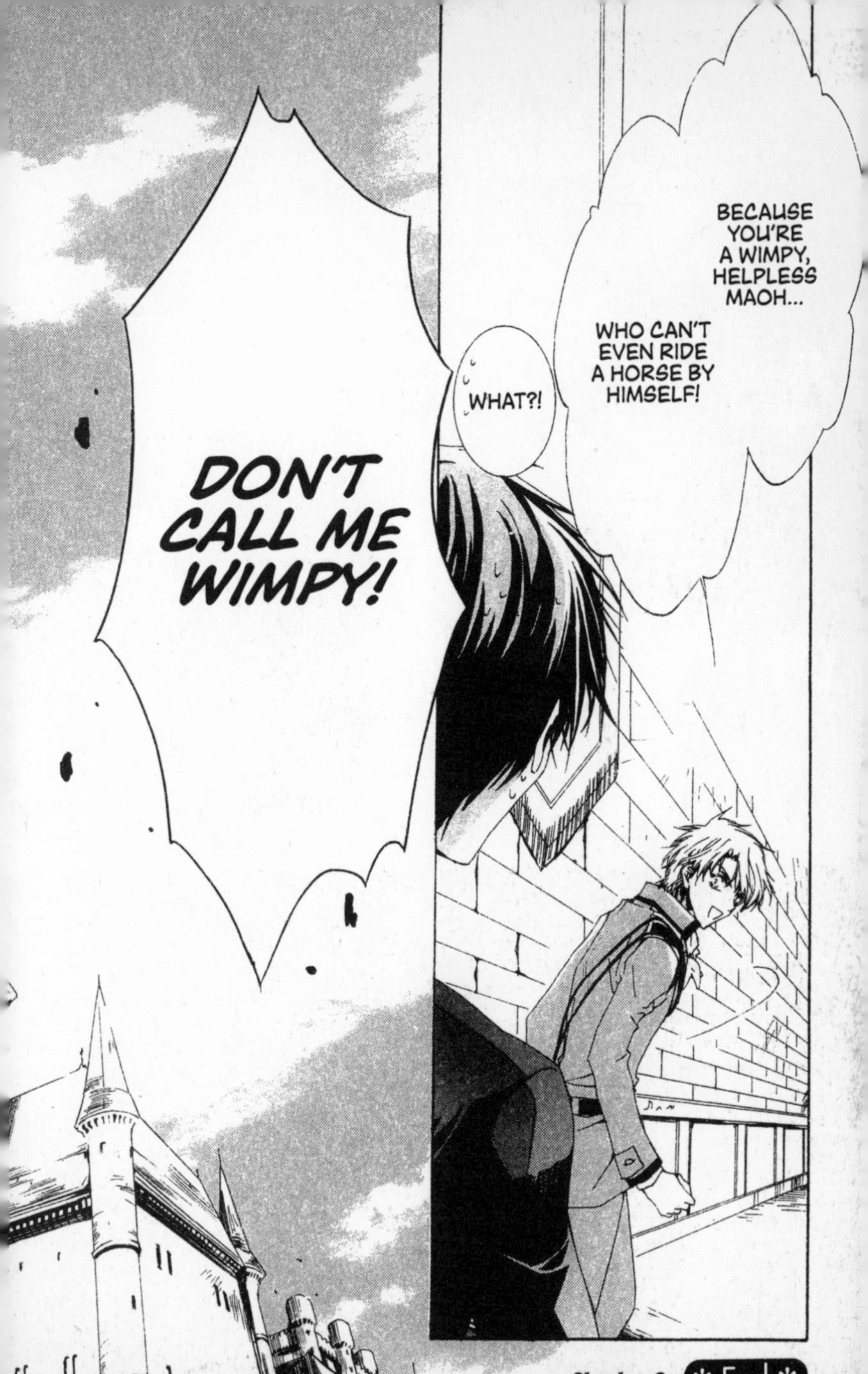
BECAUSE YOU'RE A WIMPY, HELPLESS MAOH...
WHO CAN'T EVEN RIDE A HORSE BY HIMSELF!
WHAT?!
DON'T CALL ME WIMPY!

Chapter 6 * End *

Afterword

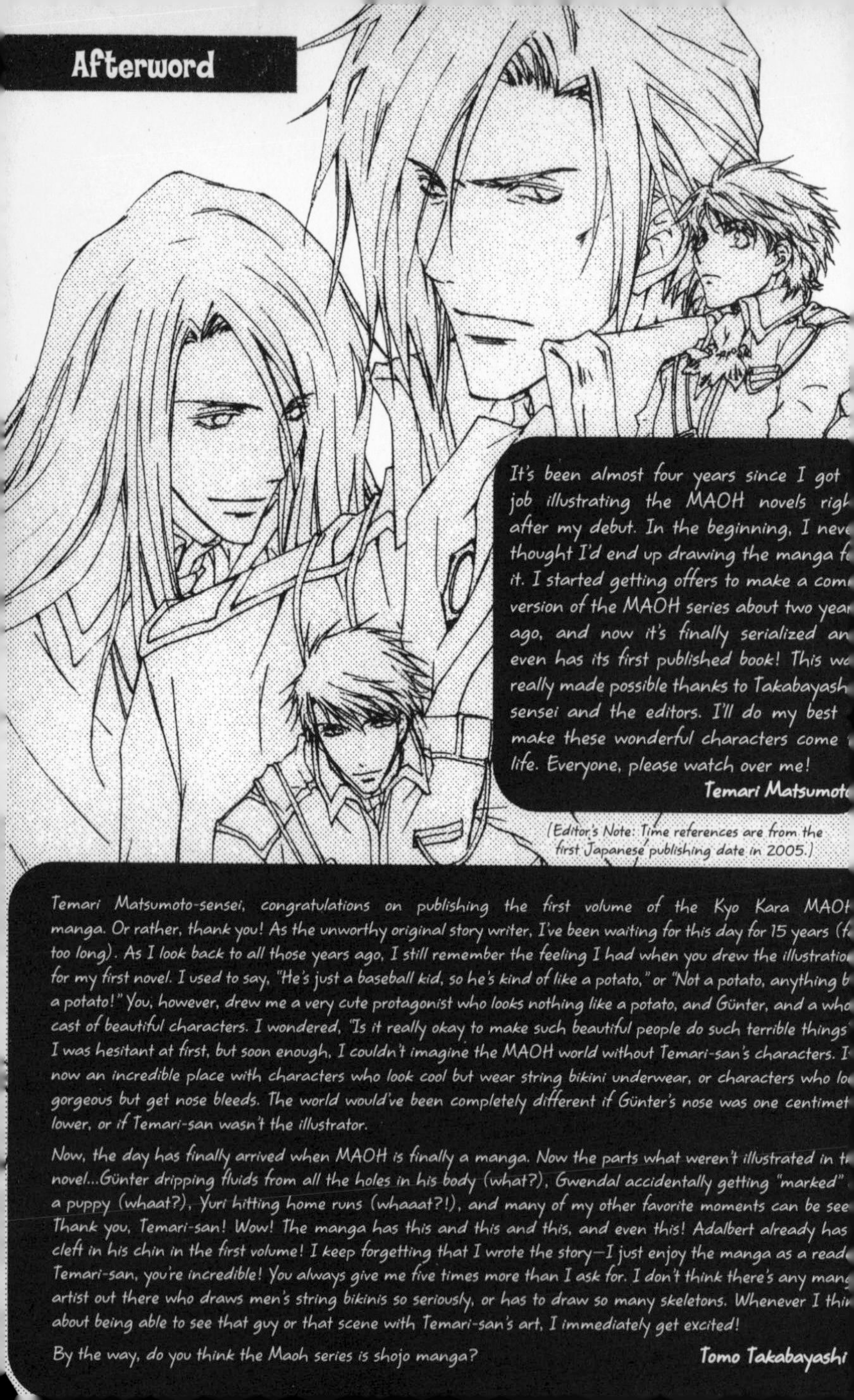

It's been almost four years since I got job illustrating the MAOH novels righ after my debut. In the beginning, I neve thought I'd end up drawing the manga fo it. I started getting offers to make a comi version of the MAOH series about two year ago, and now it's finally serialized an even has its first published book! This wa really made possible thanks to Takabayash sensei and the editors. I'll do my best make these wonderful characters come life. Everyone, please watch over me!

Temari Matsumoto

(Editor's Note: Time references are from the first Japanese publishing date in 2005.)

Temari Matsumoto-sensei, congratulations on publishing the first volume of the Kyo Kara MAOH manga. Or rather, thank you! As the unworthy original story writer, I've been waiting for this day for 15 years (fa too long). As I look back to all those years ago, I still remember the feeling I had when you drew the illustratio for my first novel. I used to say, "He's just a baseball kid, so he's kind of like a potato," or "Not a potato, anything b a potato!" You, however, drew me a very cute protagonist who looks nothing like a potato, and Günter, and a who cast of beautiful characters. I wondered, "Is it really okay to make such beautiful people do such terrible things I was hesitant at first, but soon enough, I couldn't imagine the MAOH world without Temari-san's characters. I now an incredible place with characters who look cool but wear string bikini underwear, or characters who lo gorgeous but get nose bleeds. The world would've been completely different if Günter's nose was one centimet lower, or if Temari-san wasn't the illustrator.

Now, the day has finally arrived when MAOH is finally a manga. Now the parts what weren't illustrated in th novel...Günter dripping fluids from all the holes in his body (what?), Gwendal accidentally getting "marked" a puppy (whaat?), Yuri hitting home runs (whaaat?!), and many of my other favorite moments can be see Thank you, Temari-san! Wow! The manga has this and this and this, and even this! Adalbert already has cleft in his chin in the first volume! I keep forgetting that I wrote the story—I just enjoy the manga as a read Temari-san, you're incredible! You always give me five times more than I ask for. I don't think there's any mang artist out there who draws men's string bikinis so seriously, or has to draw so many skeletons. Whenever I thi about being able to see that guy or that scene with Temari-san's art, I immediately get excited!

By the way, do you think the Maoh series is shojo manga?

Tomo Takabayashi

IN THE NEXT VOLUME OF

On the way to the border village with Wolfram, Yuri and the others run into Adalbert, who tries to convince Yuri to join the human side. This convinces Wolfram and Gwendal that it's necessary to start a war. Yuri must decide if it's worth it to become the Maoh if it means he could prevent future wars and change the way Mazoku think. Will Yuri embrace his Mazoku nature and his magical talents? Or will he return to Earth once more?

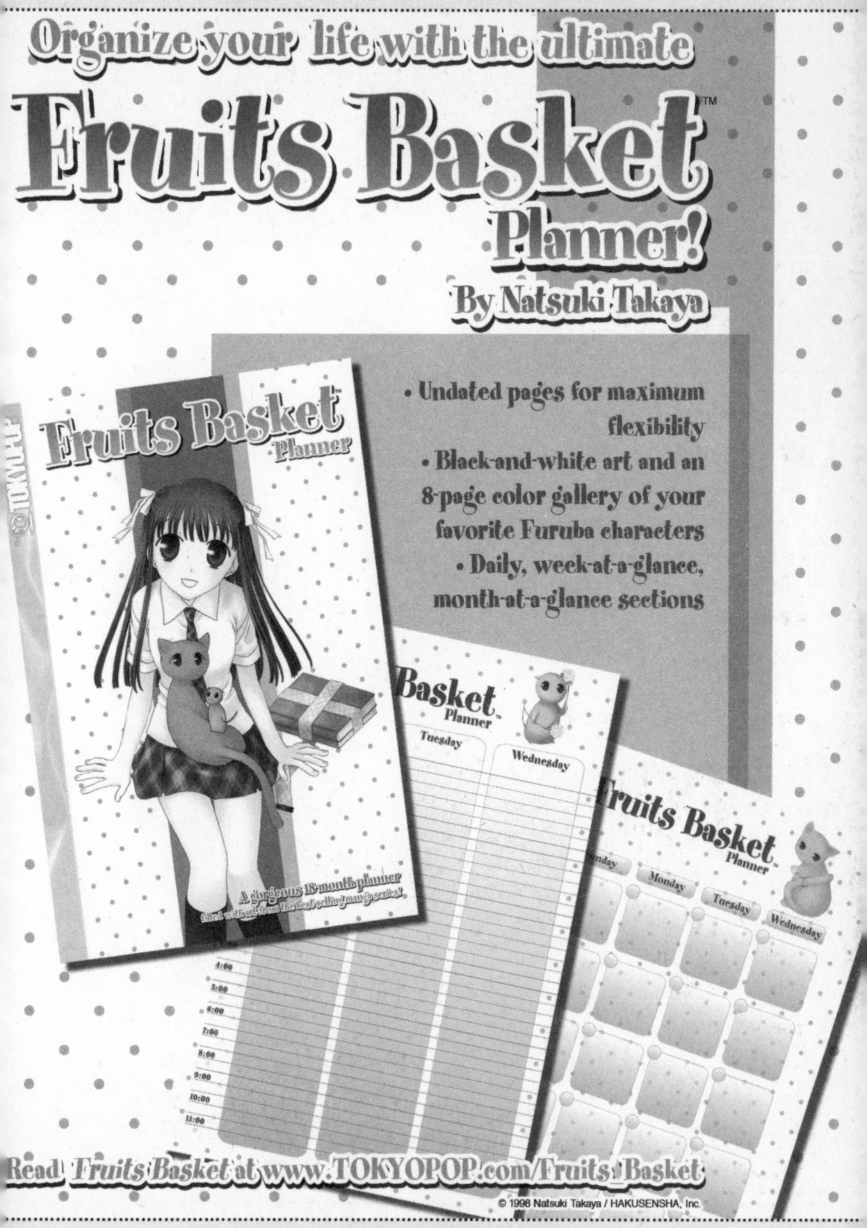
Organize your life with the ultimate
Fruits Basket™ Planner!
By Natsuki Takaya
• Undated pages for maximum flexibility
• Black-and-white art and an 8-page color gallery of your favorite Furuba characters
• Daily, week-at-a-glance, month-at-a-glance sections
Fruits Basket Planner
Read Fruits Basket at www.TOKYOPOP.com/Fruits_Basket
© 1998 Natsuki Takaya / HAKUSENSHA, Inc.

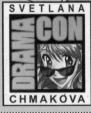

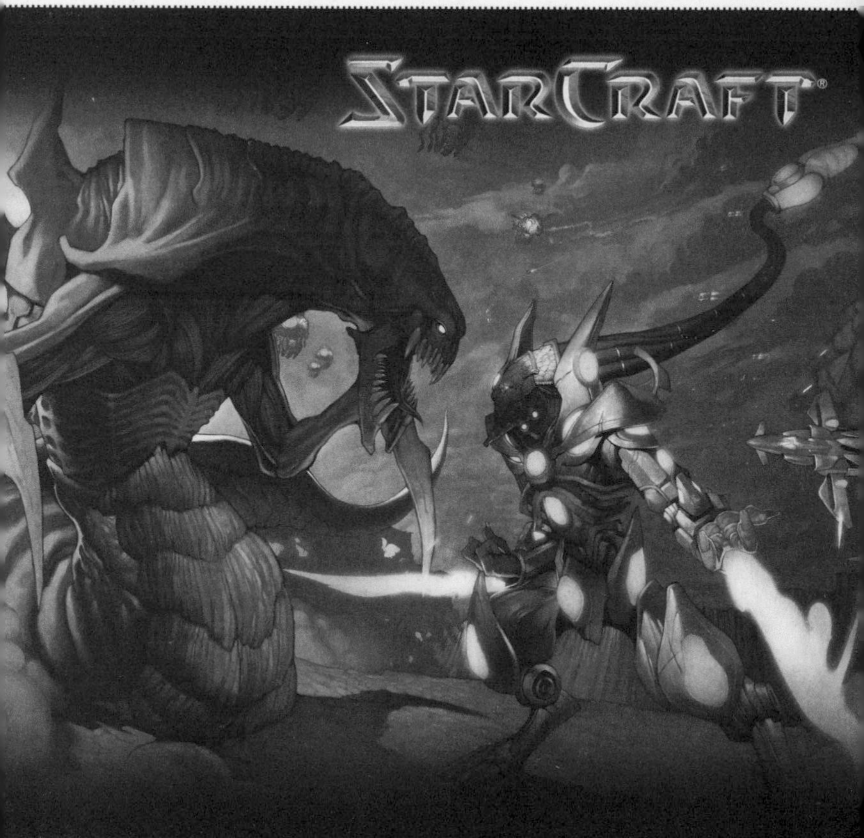
StarCraft®

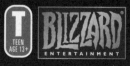

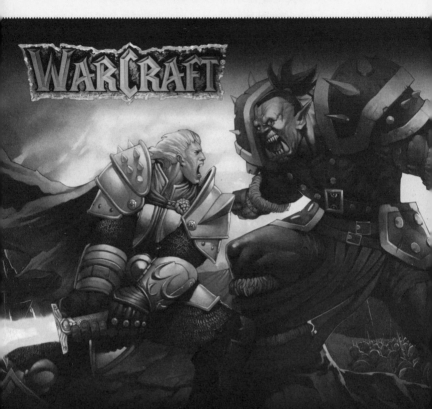

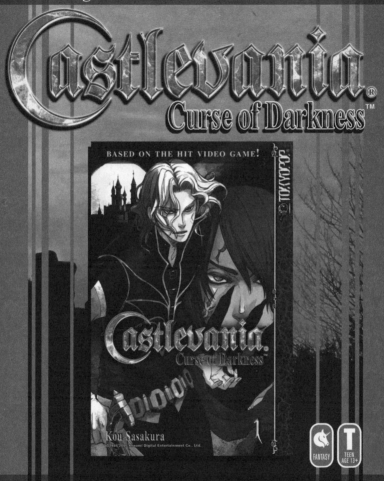

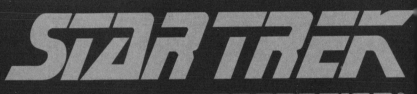
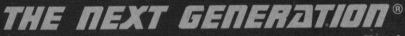

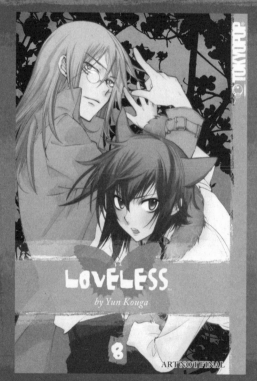

Fruits Basket

By Natsuki Takaya

Volume 20

Can Tohru deal with the truth?

After running away from his feelings and everyone he knows, Kyo is back with the truth about his role in the death of Tohru's mother. But how will he react when Tohru says that she still loves him?

Winner of the American Anime Award for Best Manga!

The #1 selling shojo manga in America!

FOR MORE INFORMATION VISIT: WWW.TOKYOPOP.COM

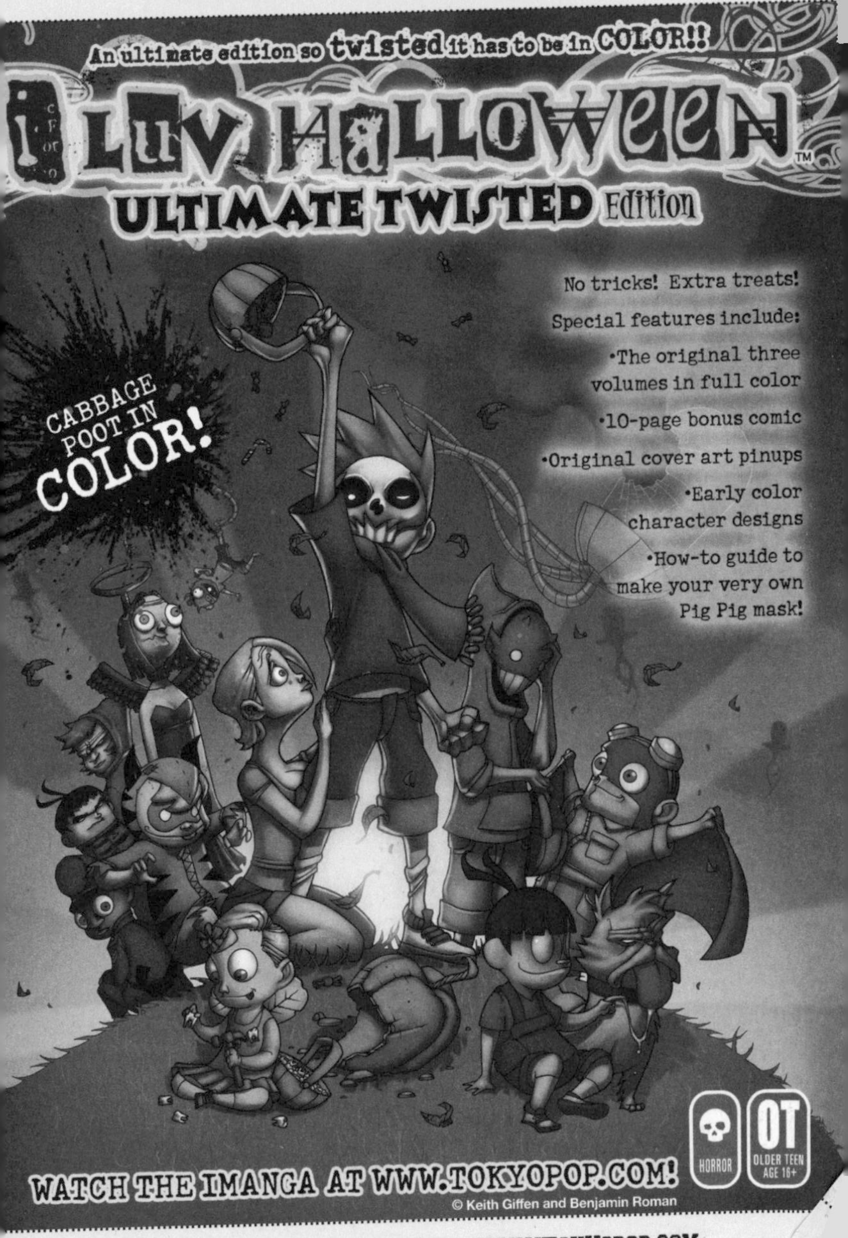
An ultimate edition so twisted it has to be in COLOR!!
I LUV HALLOWEEN™
ULTIMATE TWISTED Edition
CABBAGE POOT IN COLOR!
No tricks! Extra treats!
Special features include:
•The original three volumes in full color
•10-page bonus comic
•Original cover art pinups
•Early color character designs
•How-to guide to make your very own Pig Pig mask!
HORROR
OT
OLDER TEEN AGE 16+
WATCH THE IMANGA AT WWW.TOKYOPOP.COM!
© Keith Giffen and Benjamin Roman

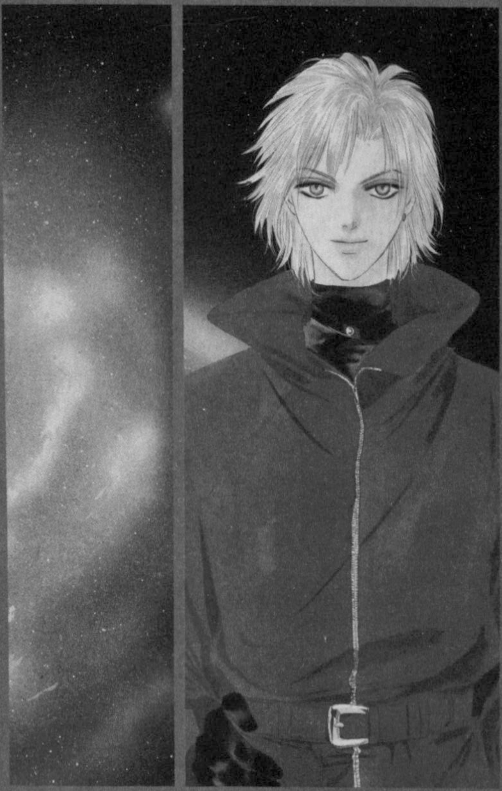

BIZENGHAST
BY M. ALICE LEGROW, NOVEL BY SHAWN THORGERSEN

Not every lost soul is a lost cause

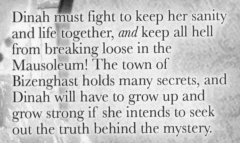

Dinah must fight to keep her sanity
and life together, *and* keep all hell
from breaking loose in the
Mausoleum! The town of
Bizenghast holds many secrets, and
Dinah will have to grow up and
grow strong if she intends to seek
out the truth behind the mystery.

FOR MORE INFORMATION VISIT:

STOP!

This is the back of the book.
You wouldn't want to spoil a great ending!

This book is printed "manga-style," in the authentic Japanese right-to-left format. Since none of the artwork has been flipped or altered, readers get to experience the story just as the creator intended. You've been asking for it, so TOKYOPOP® delivered: authentic, hot-off-the-press, and far more fun!

DIRECTIONS

If this is your first time reading manga-style, here's a quick guide to help you understand how it works.

It's easy... just start in the top right panel and follow the numbers. Have fun, and look for more 100% authentic manga from TOKYOPOP®!